RACE

. . . . .

OTHER BOOKS BY STUDS TERKEL

AMERICAN DREAMS:
Lost and Found

WORKING:
People Talk about What They Do All Day
and How They Feel about What They Do

HARD TIMES:
An Oral History of the Great Depression

DIVISION STREET:
America

GIANTS OF JAZZ

TALKING TO MYSELF:
A Memoir of My Times

"THE GOOD WAR":
An Oral History of World War II

THE GREAT DIVIDE:
Second Thoughts on the American Dream

RACE

······

STUDS TERKEL

······

SINCLAIR-STEVENSON

First published in Great Britain by
Sinclair-Stevenson Limited
7/8 Kendrick Mews
London SW7 3HG England

First published in the United States in 1992 by The New Press, New York

Some of the names in this book have been changed.

British Library Cataloguing in Publication Data
A CIP catalogue record for this book is available from the British Library.

ISBN: 1 85619 156 7

Book Design by Helen Barrow
Printed and bound in England by Clays Ltd, St Ives plc

A POLL

Fifty-three percent of nonblacks believe that African-Americans are less intelligent than whites; 51 percent believe they are less patriotic; 56 percent believe they are more violence-prone; 62 percent believe they are more likely to "prefer to live off welfare" and less likely to "prefer to be self-supporting."

> From a 1990 survey of the University of Chicago's
> National Opinion Research Center

A FINDING

Black males have the lowest life expectancy of any group in the United States. Their unemployment rate is more than twice that of white males; even black men with college degrees are three times more likely to be unemployed than their white counterparts. About one in four black men between the ages of twenty and twenty-nine is behind bars. Blacks receive longer prison sentences than whites who have committed the same crimes.

Suicide is the third leading cause of death for young black males. Since 1960, suicide rates for young black males have nearly tripled, and doubled for black females. While suicide among whites increases with age, it is a peculiarly youthful phenomenon among blacks.

Many black males die prematurely from twelve major preventable diseases.

Nearly one-third of all black families in America live below the poverty line. Half of all black children are born in poverty and will spend all their youth growing up in poor families.

> From a 1991 report of the 21st Century Commission
> on African-American Males

NOTE

You have to be careful not to think you're somebody else. I have to say to myself, "Look, Horton, get as close to people as you can, but don't get things mixed up: you're white." You've got to recognize that you can never fully walk in other people's shoes.

I think like a white person but try to understand how black people might think. Their way of doing things may be better than my way, can be worse than my way, but I can't take the position that my way is always right without being a racist. Racism involves believing that your own race is superior.

> Myles Horton

You see, there's such a thing as a feeling tone. One is friendly and one is hostile. And if you don't have this, baby, you've had it.

Lucy Jefferson

Goethe spoke of seeing with a feeling eye and feeling with a seeing hand. Henry Head, the British neurologist, always looked for something he called "the feeling tone." Color has a feeling tone. I got very excited when I came across Lucy Jefferson's phrase. Nothing is more wonderful or more to be celebrated than something that will unlock a person's capacities and allow him to grow and think.

Oliver Sacks

To be in someone else's power . . . induces doubts about the ordering of the universe, while those who have power can assume it is part of the natural order of things and invent or adopt ideas which justify their possession of it.

Albert Hourani

CONTENTS

ACKNOWLEDGMENTS   xi

INTRODUCTION   3

Prologue

MAMIE MOBLEY   19

PART I

Lucy Jefferson's Legacy

LUCY JEFFERSON   27   WILLIAM FREEMAN   29
CAROL FREEMAN   32   JULIAN JEFFERSON   37

Friends

DIANE ROMANO   41   ANITA HERBERT   48
PEGGY TERRY   51   LITTLE DOVIE THURMAN   57

Welfare

LYNDA WRIGHT   64   MARGARET WELCH   69

On the Job

JOSEPH ROBINSON   73   BEN HENSLEY   78
TASHA KNIGHT   81   JOE GUTIERREZ   84   FRANK LUMPKIN   88

Overview I

DOUGLAS MASSEY   92

The House I Live In

LEOLA SPANN   97   MARY FRAN SHEEHAN   102
PEGGY BYAS   107   BETTY RUNDLE   111   IANNA KNOX   114
JIM AND KATHY KISH   119

The Park

JIM CAPRARO   126

PART II

Yet and Still

JOSEPH LATTIMORE   133   DENNIS CARNEY   139
MAGGIE HOLMES   144   BILL AND YURIKO HOHRI   150
ROY MAYDON   153   NORMA STEVENSON   159
BOB MATTHIESON   163

Overview II

SALIM MUWAKKIL   166

Awakenings

CHARLISE LYLES   171

School Days

QUINN BRISBEN   179   CHESTER KASKO   183
PETER SODERSTROM   189   TIMUEL BLACK   196

Campus Life

DAWN KELLY   202   FRED WERNER   206
JENNIFER KASKO   209   CHARLES JOHNSON   213

Buddies

RICHIE DAVIS   218   JOSEPH BOONE   223

Passing the Corner

KEVIN ROBINSON   227   CHRIS DANIELS   232
ANDREA COLLINS   236   DAVID HILL   239

Lost and Found

ROBERT BROWN   242   TYRONE MITCHELL   245

911

SGT. DENNIS HINKSON   248   CLAIRE HELLSTERN   254
BILL WROBLESKI   258   ED REARDON   264

PART III

Occurrence in Durham

C. P. ELLIS 271   ANN ATWATER 280   HOWARD CLEMENT 283

Lawyer

GILBERT GORDON 288   ALEX BERTEAU 293

Reflections of a Bruised Tiger and An Ironic Cat

KID PHARAOH 302   FRANK CHIN 309

There Is a Tavern in Our Town

VAN GALLIOS 314

From the Far Side

MARK MATHABANE 319   RIAN MALAN 326

From the Near Side

MARIA TORRES 330

Overview III

DR. KENNETH B. CLARK 334

Rise Up, Shepherd, and Follow

REV. C. T. VIVIAN 338   WILL D. CAMPBELL 343
FATHER LEONARD DUBI 347

PART IV

Times Past, Time Present

EILEEN BARTH 351   JOSEPHINE CLEMENT 355

It's a Boy!

CLARENCE PAGE 358

The Birth Certificate

SYLVIA MATTHEWS 363   EMILY MATTHEWS 366

The Adoption

JUNE SCHROEDER   371   JIM SCHROEDER   377

Overview IV

LERONE BENNETT, JR.   380

Mixed

HANK AND PAMELA DE ZUTTER AND AMANDA   383
LEO AND VERA KING   392   LLOYD KING   397

ACKNOWLEDGMENTS

André Schiffrin has for the eighth time been more than my editor and publisher. He has planted the seed for each work. Diane Wachtell and Dawn Davis were his nimble associates on this one. David Frederickson took nothing for granted in editing copy, and his gimlet eye was of inestimable help. A salute to Sydney Lewis, Tammey Kikta, Lucy Bukowski, and Sheila von Wiese for their skills as transcribers.

High fives to my colleagues at WFMT, who were patient, forbearing, and cooperative far beyond the call of duty—especially, Lois Baum, Cheryle Rooney, Sandy Meyers, and Jim Unrath.

My special gratitude to my generous, though informal, scouts, who were always giving me hot tips: Quinn Brisben, Thom Clark, Father Len Dubi, Gilbert Gordon, Anne Guerrero, Claire Hellstern, Ben Joravsky, Carol Jouzeitis, Tony Judge, Kathy Kelly, Alex Kotlowitz, Roy Larson, Edna Pardo, Pat Reardon, Rose Rigsby, Ed Sadlowski, Florence Scala, Brenda Stevenson, and Mildred Wortham.

Cathy Zmuda died at the moment she had begun transcribing these conversations. It was to have been our eighth such adventure together. This one is for her.

Several people who appear in this book were visited before—some as far back as 1965. The works in which they first spoke their piece were Division Street: —America (*1967*), Hard Times (*1970*), Working (*1972*), American Dreams: Lost and Found (*1980*), *and* The Great Divide (*1988*). *When their earlier reflections are called upon, the year of the interview is mentioned.*

Aside from a few visits elsewhere, Chicago is the locus of this work. Of all our cities, it is America's metaphor. Here they came for a "job of work" : from Eastern Europe, from the Mediterranean, of all ethnic tribes; here, too, came the Appalachians from the border states; and here came the African-Americans from the Deep South, seeking, as the others, a better life. To the last group, it was the City Called Heaven.

RACE
#####

INTRODUCTION

Obsession, n. 1 (archaic) The state of beset or actuated by the devil or an evil spirit. 2. a. Compulsive preoccupation with a fixed idea or unwanted feeling or emotion, often with symptoms of anxiety. b. A compulsive, often unreasonable, idea or emotion causing such preoccupation.

American Heritage Dictionary of the English Language

Obsession, . . . The action of any influence, notion or fixed idea, so as to discompose the mind.

Oxford English Dictionary

"It obsesses everybody," declaimed my impassioned friend, "even those who think they are not obsessed. My wife was driving down the street in a black neighborhood. The people at the corners were all gesticulating at her. She was very frightened, turned up the windows, and drove determinedly. She discovered, after several blocks, she was going the wrong way on a one-way street and they were trying to help her. Her assumption was they were blacks and were out to get her. Mind you, she's a very enlightened person. You'd never associate her with racism, yet her first reaction was that they were dangerous."

It was a slow day. The waitress and I were engaged in idle talk: weather, arthritis, and a whisper of local scandal. She was large, genial, motherly. The neighborhood was an admixture of middle-class and blue-collar. On its periphery was an enclave of black families. As I was leaving, she said, "Of course, we're moving. You know why." It was an offhand remark, as casual as "See ya around."

You know why.

During the Boston school crisis, some twenty years ago, the leader of the fight against court-ordered busing proclaimed, "You know where I stand."

You know where I stand.

In Chicago, during the black mayor's first campaign, his white opponent's slogan was "Before It's Too Late."

Before it's too late.

Why were these people speaking in code? Why didn't the waitress tell me why? Where did the Boston mother stand? Why didn't the Chicago candidate tell us what it might be too late for? There was really no need. All of us, black and white, know what it's about. Yet, why the veiled language?

It is the speech of a beleaguered people, or those who see themselves as such. A tribe, besieged, has always been possessed of a *laager* mind-set. Every Afrikaner schoolchild has been taught the history of the Great Trek and the covered wagons drawn into a circle, holding off the half-naked Zulus. On late TV, we still see John Wayne and his gallant frontier-comrades holding off the half-naked Sioux. In neither of these instances was the language veiled. A savage was a savage was a savage. Yet, contemporary white America is somewhat diffident in language, if not in behavior. Therein is the exquisite irony.

Before Emancipation, black slaves, dreaming of escape and freedom, were forever talking and singing in code. Regard the spirituals. Jordan River, though heavenly in Biblical lore, was, in earthly truth, the swamp-land separating slave from free state. Pharaoh's army was not Egyptian; it was, in flesh and blood, the slaveowner. Daniel's deliverance was not from the lion's den but from pursuing bloodhounds. The Sweet Chariot was not driven by a Roman paladin but by underground-railway captains. There is no need to explain the veiled language in these instances. It was a matter of survival: life and death.

What is it, though, that impelled the waitress, the Boston woman, and the Chicago candidate to desist from direct reference to African-Americans? It certainly was not a matter of survival, though the *laager* fright was indubitably there. Had they been less euphemistic, they'd have suffered no public scorn. (Al Campanis and Jimmy the Greek faced the red eye of the TV camera; here, pretense must be maintained. Their punishment was manifestly unfair. After all, George Bush, in effect, employed Willie Horton as his campaign manager and was rewarded with the presidency.) It had to be something else that restrained the others; something that, perverse though it seems, offers a slender reed of hope.

Diane Romano, a mother of five, reflected on black depredations and her low opinion of most. "Maybe it's not really *me* saying this. I don't want to be that type of person. It makes me less a good human being. A good human being is rational, sensible, and kind. Maybe layers and layers of prejudice has finally got to me." She sighs. "I have such a mixed bag of feelings. I'm always fighting myself. One part of my brain sees all these things and is fighting the other part, which is my real deep, deep-down feeling."

A young schoolteacher, who had encounters with black schoolmates at college and black parents at her job, says, "Though I was brought up not to be prejudiced, I hate to admit that I am. I don't like my thoughts and feelings. It is not a Christian feeling."

A case *in extremis:* A small-time collector for the Syndicate casually refers to "shines," "spades," "jigs," "loads of coal." When asked whether he considers himself a racist, he is indignant: "Hell, no! Did you hear me say 'nigger'? Never!"

The young construction worker, after offering a litany of grievances, especially in the matter of affirmative action, assures me that the stereotypes of African-Americans are true. "I seen 'em. They live like low-lifes. Don't like to work. Let their homes run down." He quickly adds, "Oh, the black guys I work with are okay." He speaks of his black friend whom he'd defend against all comers. "Racism" is a word that disturbs him. Like Oscar Wilde's forbidden love, it dare not speak its name.

(A caveat: Since the election of Ronald Reagan in 1980, racial pejoratives have been more openly, more unashamedly expressed. His hostility toward civil-rights legislation was interpreted as something of a friendly wink toward those whose language may be more gamey than civil. John Hope Franklin, the American historian, is "astounded at the amount of rancor in some quarters. The feelings that once were covert because people were ashamed of them are now expressed overtly. This crude and barbaric outburst of racism that we've seen in the last several years has been encouraged somewhere." It has, in fact, become *à la mode* not only among tavern troopers, but in the most respected quarters.

(A visiting Afrikaner journalist was astonished. "Being from South Africa, I am obsessed with race. Any chance remark registers with me. Click. I just sense the whole *zeitgeist* has changed ever since Ronald Reagan was elected. In 1979, I ran into very few who expressed antagonism to black claims for restitution. Now you hear it at dinner parties, without any embarrassment. I met country-club patricians who were as outspoken in their racism as their blue-collar counterparts. You hear the litany, wholly uninvited."

(During a visit to South Africa in 1963, I was stunned by the preponderance of racial news in the *Rand Daily Mail*. In reading our local papers twenty-eight years later, I have come to accept the obsession here as a matter of course. Have I become an easy-going Afrikaner?)

"Our worst selves are being appealed to," says a black dowager in North Carolina. "The signals flashed by Mr. Bush are the same as those of Mr. Reagan."

A weary cabdriver at the end of a twelve-hour day squints as he sips his coffee: "When traffic's beginning to close in on me and I'm behind in my money, I'm really uptight. There's a black driver in front of me, the word "nigger" will come into my head. No matter how much education you may have had, the prejudices you were taught come out. These sinister forces are buried deep inside you."

Much more may be buried deep, interred within the bones of all of us. Including myself.

As I stepped onto the bus one early morning, the driver, a young black man, said I was a dime short. I was positive I had deposited the proper fare. I did a slight burn, though concealed. To avoid an unpleasant exchange, I fished out another dime and dropped it into the box. My annoyance, trivial though the matter was, stayed with me for the rest of the trip. Oh, I understood the man. Of course. I know the history of his people's bondage. It was his turn—a show of power, if only in a small way. If that's how it is, that's how it is. Oh, well.

As I was about to disembark, I saw a dime on the floor. My dime. I held it up to him. "You were right." He was too busy driving to respond. In alighting, I waved: "Take it easy." "You, too," he replied. I've a hunch he'd been through something like this before.

In this one man, I had seen the whole race. In his behavior (especially before my discovery of the dime), I saw all African-Americans. During the trips I had conducted a silent seminar on ontogeny recapitulating phylogeny.

A favorite modern-day parable of Martin Luther King concerned ten drunks. One was black, the other nine, white. "Look at that black drunk," says the indignant observer.

Several years ago, an old friend and I were in a car. He was regarded with great affection by his black colleagues. They knew his track record. He had been in the middle of civil-rights battles in the early days when very few whites participated. Anti–Jim Crow, that was the phrase. A black teen-ager rode by on a bike. "I wonder if he stole that," murmured my friend. To my stunned silence, he responded, "He's poorly dressed. I'd have said the same thing about a poorly dressed white kid." I wonder. About myself as well. As the cabbie said, it's deep, these sinister forces.

The paramedic, who has worked in the black ghetto, who understands cause and effect, was driving along with his nine-year-old son. "There's a black guy crossing the street. He breaks into a fast run to make the traffic. My kid says, 'Looks like he's running from the police.' I hit the ceiling. 'Where the hell did you get a racist comment like that?' "

Where? Everywhere, it seems. Consider our media.

A TV station chartered a plane to fly a black journalist and a crew to cover a routine speech by Louis Farrakhan. "We had to put it on the air that night. It was the usual stuff, nothing extraordinary. I know why they sent me down there. They were hoping he'd say something outrageous."

During the Continental Airlines strike several years ago, an unusual picket line had formed in Chicago's Loop. It was led by a handsome pilot and an attractive flight attendant. A sort of Mr. and Miss America. TV crews had assembled from all three major channels. I assumed this would be the lead story on the six-o'clock news. It was a natural. Seldom before had flight attendants hit the bricks. Suddenly all the crews took off. They had not yet begun shooting. They had received word from their respective news directors that a shooting (of another kind) had occurred at a black high school. One student had wounded another. That evening, all three channels featured the black high-school incident. The picket line didn't make it.

The petite, gentle mother of two, an accountant, softly offers her opinion of television and the press. "We usually see the young black men in a gang. They can't talk. They have leather coats and are trying to conquer the world by being *bad*. What do you see first? A black person killed another black person or killed a policeman or stabbed someone. Of course, you're going to be scared of black people. You can't help but think they're all that way. That's not really what black people are about."

"My father is the kindest, sweetest man you ever wanted to know," says another young black woman. She writes for a trade journal. "He's very dark-skinned. It infuriates me to think that some little white woman would get on the elevator with my father and assume, just by the color of his skin, that he's going to harm her, and clutch her purse tighter. To think that my father, who's worked hard all his life, put us through school, loves us, took care of us—to think that she would clutch her purse because he's there. The thought of it makes me so angry."

Visibility is high these days for African-Americans, especially in matters of street crime.

Mayor Daley, surrounded by bodyguards, aldermen, photographers, video cameramen, and print, radio, and television reporters, toured the gang-plagued Englewood neighborhood, site of the summer's worst violence.

The purpose of the visit: to motivate the community to help police fight gangbangers. . . . Residents peered through windows and watched from porch steps and viewed the mayor's visit with cynical eyes.

One thirty-nine-year-old man shared a cigarette with some streetcorner buddies. "His face ain't good enough. You got to have some action behind it. If they give us some jobs cleaning up and taking care of the neighborhood, maybe there wouldn't be so much crime. We're tired of being out here broke; we got family to take care of. We get up and have to look at each other every day. We got nowhere to go."*

Yet in our daily run of the course, the black is still the invisible man. Consider the case of the senior editor of *Ebony*. He, elegant in dress, manner, and speech, lives in an expensive high-rise. As he waited at the curb, a matronly white handed him her car keys. I would not trade places with him on a rainy night were we hailing the same cab. Nor would a shabbily dressed white.

When Mayor Richard J. Daley died, many Chicagoans were in a state of trauma: What will happen to our city? When the news of Mayor Harold Washington's death broke, the first question asked by a prominent elder citizen seated next to me was: "What will Eddie do?" He was referring to an alderman who was unremitting in his hostility to Washington's programs. In the minds of our makers and shakers, the five historic years of a black mayor's administration never happened. He was the invisible man. Or, at most, an aberration.

Is it any wonder that I came so close to being run down by a crazy black driver?

I am a professional pedestrian. I am also nearsighted. I have never driven a car. Often, as I cross the street, I hold up my hand in the manner of a traffic cop. One day, as the light was changing, a cab did not stop and came within inches of knocking me down. I shouted. The cab screeched to a stop. The driver, a black man, leaped out. His words sprang forth, feverishly, uncontrollably. "You did it because I was black." Though I was equally furious, my attempt to explain my raised arm was in vain.

---

* Frank Burgos, writing about Richard A. Daley, son of the more famous former Mayor Daley, in the *Chicago Sun-Times*, September 19, 1991.

Was my arm, raised in the manner of a policeman, the fuse that set off the explosive? In his stream of consciousness, was I, a white, giving him the official finger? Was he, once again, as I've a hunch he had so often been, 'buked and scorned?

The eleven-year-old black kid, with his comrade-in-mischief, a twelve-year-old white boy, cracked the window of an elderly neighbor. It was a small stone, sprung from a slingshot. When the woman confronted them, he was an indignant counsel for the defense. "You're accusing me just because I'm black." Why do I think he had heard this somewhere before?

"When I was young, I used to get a lot of grief from the cops." The musician remembers a bike ride through the park, somewhat roughly interrupted. "They thought I stole it. Cops still hassle me sometimes. I don't know one black person who has never had an encounter with cops."

The elderly ex–social-worker recalls a ride to Wisconsin with her black colleagues. "I was the only white in the car. Just as we were leaving the city, we were stopped by a cop. I don't know why. Our driver, the husband of my friend, was himself a cop. He got out, came back quickly, and said it was all right. I felt very uncomfortable. I remember saying, 'This is ridiculous.' Why were we stopped? I doubt this would have happened to white people. Nobody in the car said anything about it. We talked about something else. On reflection, I think this has happened to black people so often, they didn't think it was worth discussing."

Langston Hughes's dangling question is more pertinent today than ever: "Does it sag like a heavy load? Or does it explode?"

When I heard Big Bill Broonzy, the nonpareil of country-blues singers, moan the lyric, "Laughin' to keep from cryin'," I had to remember he died in 1958. He didn't live to experience the sixties, the civil-rights movement, and the Second Betrayal. Bill knew all about the First Betrayal in the 1870s. His mother, born a slave, had told him about the promise to every freed man: forty acres and a mule. It was in the nature of a check that bounced. A hundred and twenty years later, with a couple of winking presidents canceling one check after another, Bill's sons and daughters are "laughin' to keep from ragin'." The laughter is no longer that frequent.

"Is race always on a black person's mind from the time he wakes up to the time he goes asleep? Wouldn't that drive a person crazy?" The middle-aged insurance man is repeating the question I had asked on a black call-in radio program. "Remember my answer? We are already crazy.

"Being black in America is like being forced to wear ill-fitting shoes.

Some people adjust to it. It's always uncomfortable on your feet, but you've got to wear it because it's the only shoe you've got. Some people can bear the uncomfort more than others. Some people can block it from their minds, some can't. When you see some acting docile and some acting militant, they have one thing in common: the shoe is uncomfortable.

"Unless you go back to the roots and begin to tell the truth about the past, we'll get nowhere. If someone would rape my daughter in front of my eyes and sold my daughter and I'd never see her again, sure I'd go crazy. And if I didn't get any help to raise another child, with my insanity, I'd pass that along. The brutality that the next generations went through, it was enough to drive them mad. So our foreparents have been driven mad. It reflects itself in black hatred, too."

(In the late forties, *Destination Freedom* was a Peabody Award–winning radio series on NBC. Satchel Paige, the hero of one episode, asked Richard Durham, the writer, "Is colored folks in charge of this?" "Yes." "Ain't gonna be no good."

(Vernon Jarrett, a black Chicago columnist, says, "If I'm feeling good and want to have my morale lowered, all I have to do is drive out Madison Street and look at the throngs of unemployed youngsters in their weird dress, trying to hang on to some individuality. Can't read or write, looking mean at each other. You see kids hanging around, hating themselves as much as they hate others. This is one thing that contributes to the ease with which gangs kill each other. Another nigger ain't nothin'.")

The insurance man concludes: "I don't know where the story will end, but we are all kind of messed up."

It may be true, muses Lerone Bennett, Jr., a black historian. "But I still have hope. Know why? Given the way we were forced to live in this society, the miracle is not that so many families are broken, but that so many are still together. That so many black fathers are still at home. That so many black women are still raising good children. It is the incredible toughness and resilience in people that gives me hope."

"We live with hope. Otherwise we couldn't go on," says Professor Franklin. "But blind hope is not realistic. A strong sense of self had developed during the sixties, during the civil-rights movement. When there is no longer that kind of hope, the response is frustration, anger."

When I was seventy-five, I was mugged by a skinny young black man. Was his name Willie? My loss: a Timex watch, net worth $19.95. When I was twenty-three, I was jackrolled by a burly young white man. Was his name Bruno? My loss: $1.25. It was during the Great Depression.

It was Bruno whom Nelson Algren celebrated in his novel *Never Come Morning*. "This was the sleepless city where a street-corner nineteen-year-old replied to a judge, who sentenced him to the electric chair, 'I knew I'd never get to be twenty-one anyhow'—and snapped his bubble gum."

Was it Willie's little sister I ran into a few years ago, as she was skipping rope outside the Robert Taylor Homes? In response to my banal question, she sounded eminently sensible, considering the circumstances: "I might not live to be grown up. My life wasn't promised to me." She was ten.

The difference between Bruno and Willie lay in their legacies. Their forbears were hosses of a different color and their arrivals in the New World were of a different nature.

Maggie Holmes, a retired domestic, had little patience with the centennial celebration of the Statue of Liberty in 1984. She had followed its extensive TV coverage. "When you had your hundred years of that Statue of Liberty, I got damned mad. It was sickening to me. That wasn't made for me. We didn't come through Ellis Island. Do you understand what I'm sayin'? You came here in chains, in the bottom of ships and half-dead and beaten. What are you doin' to help them celebrate. A hundred years of what?"

Professor Franklin was interviewed during the centennial celebration. "I was reminded of Frederick Douglass's comment on the Fourth of July, 1852. 'This holiday is yours, not mine.' The same can be said of the Statue of Liberty celebration, 1984."

Dr. Kenneth B. Clark, with a sense of irony close to despair, reflects. "One thing white immigrant groups could do in America was to believe they were moving upward because the blacks were always there: down below.

"What I found fascinating is the tragically humorous condition of northern whites. The civil-rights movement made the white ethnic groups more democratic. The Poles, Jews, Italians, and Irish could all get together in their hostility to the blacks. It has become another aspect of the democratic creed.

"Being white in America made them feel equal to all other whites, as long as the black man was down below. They voted this way. Consider the blue-collar vote for Reagan. He may not have been their friend, but they felt equal to him."

The poor southern white had earlier teachings in this matter. Lillian Smith, in her short story "Two Men and a Bargain," writes of the rich white who persuaded the poor white to work for fifty cents an hour and, when the other complained, said, "I can get a nigger for two bits an hour. You're better than him, ain't you? We're the same color, ain't we?" Martin Luther King was more succinct in his 1965 Montgomery speech: The poor white was fed Jim Crow instead of bread.

Little Dovie Thurman had never met poor white people before her arrival in Chicago. "I thought all whites were rich. I began to understand there's somebody in control that I couldn't get to. It wasn't the person I could see. If white people hate black people so much, how come there's so many poor whites? Why are they doin' this to their own people, callin' them white trash?"

The maverick southern preacher, Will Campbell, dislikes the word "redneck." "Remember the Edwin Markham poem? 'Bowed by the weight of centuries/ He leans upon the hoe/ And gazes on the ground.' As he so leans and so gazes, this parching, searing midday sun turns his neck red. We've equated that with racism."

"I began to seek knowledge about power," says Little Dovie. "Who's got it? Who's benefiting from keeping people separated? If you keep us divided, we will continue to fight each other, while the one has all the pie for themselves and we will scuffle over the crumbs. He can't eat it all by himself.

"As long as you holler 'Black Power' or 'White Power,' that's fine with them because you're never coming together. Dr. King was knocking a dent because he was pointing a finger not at race, but at who was really in control. He was gettin' at *it*."

Peggy Terry, her "hillbilly" friend from Kentucky, quit school after fifth grade, but she and Kenneth Clark share the same thoughts. "When a wave of immigrants came here, there was always some just above them. There has to be a top crust and a bottom crust in our society. Somebody has to be on the bottom.

"I think you become an adult when you reach a point where you don't need anyone underneath you. When you can look at yourself and say, 'I'm okay the way I am.' One of the things that keeps my class of people from having any vision is race hatred. You're so busy hating somebody else, you're not gonna realize how beautiful you are and how much you destroy all that's good in the world."

Leona Brady is vice-principal of a black high school. She was seeing "good signs when things opened up a bit after the sixties. We had a smart group of students. They had IQs, good study habits, and marched for their inalienable rights. Then a more docile group of students came along. It was right after the rash of assassinations and the Vietnam War. We ran into the Reagan years. They stopped asking questions.

"The white American is not innately racist. I sense innate docility. He will follow the law if the leadership tells him to do that. He would not rebel if he thought he'd be punished. But if the laws are flouted and winked at, he'll wink, too. We should have a beautiful country by now. We have no business having to go back and remake this wheel."

During the sixties, the dream, so long deferred, was by way of becoming the awakening. Marches, gatherings, voices from below, and a stirring of national conscience led to the passage of civil-rights laws. It appeared that this nation, white and black, was on the threshold of over-coming. It seemed prepared, though stubbornly resisted in some quarters, to make the playing field more even. After all, the law was the law, and we prided ourselves on being a law-abiding society.

It was a difficult moment, a strange one, for many white working people, let alone the middle class, accustomed to old "comfortable" ways. It was a discomfort to make room for those whom they had been taught most of their lives to regard as invisible or, at best, below them. Some considered it an assault on their family-taught virtues.

"I went through a bad time," recalls a fireman's wife. "I felt like being white middle-class had a stigma to it. Everything was our fault. Every time I turned on the TV, it would be constant trying to send me on a guilt trip because I had a decent life. I was sick of people making the connotation that because I was raising a good family. I was responsible for the ills of the world. The white middle class was getting a bum rap. Even when I went to church. I was really getting angry."

She was ready for someone to calm her condition, to assuage her hurts: someone with simple answers. Along came Ronald Reagan in the fall of 1980, with anecdotes of welfare queens and Cadillacs. In winning the presidency, the Gipper reversed the field and made the eighties the decade unashamed. "I liked the things Reagan did," said the woman, absolved of sin and imbued with a newfound innocence.

Yet, a still, small voice disturbs the fireman's wife. "People's expecta-tions are too high. You can't expect us to like black people without knowing them. I'm very Christian, but not overly Christian. There's only a couple of people I dislike and they're white. I don't know black people well enough to hate them. Those I know, I like."

The embittered black man, sensing the dream once again deferred, responds in metaphors. "I'm not coming back to your house anymore, because you made it obvious you don't want me. I think we'd best be getting on, separating from these people. When Moses led the people out of Egypt, they didn't say, 'Let's integrate.' They said, 'Let's get the heck out of here.' " He sighs. "But I guess I still believe in integration. My daughter goes to the Eastman School of Music."

During the eighties, "the races have drifted apart in so many ways, have fallen out," observes Douglas Massey, Professor of Sociology, University of Chicago. "Even in language. Black English is farther than ever from standard American English. Increasingly, blacks isolated in ghetto poverty are speaking a different language with its own rules of grammar. It may not be inferior, but if speaking standard English is the minimum requirement for a good job, an increasingly large share of our population is frozen out.

"I don't think most whites understand what it is to be black in the United States today. They don't even have a clue."

"They don't like to work, the blacks," the young construction worker said. Yet why was that long line of job-seekers, mostly young blacks, snaking all the way around the block? In the building where I work, there's the hiring office of a large hotel chain. There were at least three hundred hopefuls, patiently waiting. I asked the personnel director how many jobs were available. "About thirty," she replied.

> Even though it was cold, even though only one in twenty could make it, even though the pay isn't so hot, about 5,000 people waited up to six hours outside the Cook County Building in the Loop Monday, hoping for a job.
>
> They were responding to an ad placed Sunday for 270 guard jobs that will open next year with the expansion of the Cook County Jail.
>
> "We had people waiting in line since three in the morning, and by nine, we had thousands of people out there," said William Cunningham, spokesman for Sheriff Michael F. Sheahan.
>
> The line, four abreast, circled the Cook County–City Hall Building at Clark and Randolph. About 4,600 single-page applications were distributed for the $21,000-a-year job of jail correctional officer.*

A ghetto schoolteacher tells of the new fast-food chain in the neighborhood. "They were gonna hire about twenty kids. Four hundred showed up for the interviews. This is common. They don't want to work in a job that pays below minimum wage and never get out of it. But they're as hardworking people as you'd find anywhere. I'm talking about full employment."

---

* Ray Hanania, *Chicago Sun-Times*, front page, October 29, 1991. The applicants were overwhelmingly black.

"Affirmative action" has become an explosive phrase as well as an idea. The president vetoes a civil-rights bill because he's against "quotas." Respected journals sound the righteous battle cry: "Reverse racism." Ben Hensley makes no public pronouncements on the subject. He's from Harlan County, Kentucky. He's driven buses and trucks, and is now a chauffeur for big-time executives.

"When I worked in Nashville as a helper on a delivery truck for Fred Harvey, a black fellow was working with me. He was older and had been there more years than me. They gave me the job driving and I became his boss. He knew the area better than I did, had to tell me where to go. I don't know how many guys he trained for that job. I always wondered about it, but never mentioned it. He didn't either. This was 1954.

"I never owned any slaves but I profited at that black fellow's expense. I think it's very fair to have affirmative action. For hundreds of years, the black people have had negative action. So they're not starting even."

Big Bill Broonzy laughs as he remembers his work-days at the foundry in the thirties. "I trained this white guy for three months. They kept him and fired me." Black laughter swells forth in the recounting of a hurting experience. It is both a survival mechanism and a saving grace. Else you go crazy. Or sing the blues:

> Me and a man was workin' side by side
> Here is what it meant:
> They were payin' him a dollar an hour
> They was payin' me fifty cents
> Sayin': If you're white, you're right
> If you're brown, stick aroun'
> But as you black, oh brother,
> Get back, get back, get back.

Frank Lumpkin, a retired steelworker, has seen it all, from the Great Depression to our current troubles. "This whole business of affirmative action was no problem at all till the jobs run out. It's no big thing when you're on the job. If the lion and the deer is both full, nobody attacks. It's only when the lion gets hungry, he really fights for the thing.

"At the mill, the Latinos said if the blacks gonna get up, we wanna get up. I says, 'Look, you got twenty white foremen and one black foreman and you arguing about the one black that come up!' It seems that we're just fighting against each other."

Howard Clement, a conservative black executive in North Carolina, favors affirmative action, "though there's a bit of unfairness to it. I see it as a way to level the playing field. There must be some other way, but what it is, I don't know. I do believe self-help is going to be the order of the day. We shouldn't go with our hands out, depending on white society to help us."

"When I found out I was an affirmative action case, I was devastated," remembers a black teacher of music. "I was not that hot spit I thought I was. I understood the historical reasons for it, but I found it tough to take."

Charles Johnson, winner of the 1990 National Book Award for fiction, teaches literature at a university in the Northwest. "On one hand affirmative action is justifiable. You need a structural solution to a problem that is centuries old. On the other hand, it's humiliating. A person, otherwise deserving, may be perceived as something special, having gotten a degree of help he didn't need. But without affirmative action, the first step toward hiring blacks would never have been taken.

"I suspect when I was hired at this university, it was an affirmative-action decision. It was in 1976 and there was only one other black in the English department. One out of fifty. Now there are two. So it's not that big a change."

What is to be made of Scholastic Aptitude Tests? The findings are, of course, devastating. As expected, black students fare poorly, in contrast to whites and Asiatics. Very poorly.

The irreverent Reverend Campbell has his own ideas. "What does it mean if the tests are written by white values? If the question has to do with pheasants under glass, white and black ghetto people will flunk. If you ask them about the breeding habits of cockroaches, they'll make a good score. You ask a black ghetto kid why his grandmother had iron beds, he'll know: to keep the rats from crawling up. A kid from Scarsdale will flunk. He'd say, 'I don't know. I guess she just liked iron beds.' "

A couple of years ago, I asked a black street boy about his grandmother. His "auntie," he called her. For the next forty-five minutes, there flowed forth tales, some apocryphal, some true, some hilarious, some poignant, all enthralling. He was Garrison Keillor, all five feet two of him. Others, freshmen members of a gang, danced around, eager to get in their two cents' worth. They had gran'ma stories, too. I was an hour late for dinner.

A week or so later, I asked a little white girl, attending a posh private school, about her grandmother, who was living in a retirement community in St. Petersburg, Florida. "Oh, she visits us every Christmas and brings me nice presents. She's very nice." That was it. She undoubtedly scored much higher in the IQ tests than the black storyteller. They were approximately the same age.

A high-school teacher, who has had trouble with black students, remembers an especially difficult one. "The girl can barely read, can barely comprehend what we're doing. Odd thing with this girl. We did *Romeo and Juliet*. We'd listen to a recording, chunks at a time. She was the first to go up and interpret what she had just heard. She just had that innate way. I can't understand it."

Hank de Zutter feels he understands it. He teaches at a black urban college. "There may be a literacy problem in terms of the written word. But there is no literacy problem when it comes to reading people.

"If I come into class not feeling good, my students will know it immediately. They'll say, 'What's wrong?' They'll want to know if I had a fight with my wife. They'll want to know my feelings first. Then they're ready for teaching.

"I think this amazing ability to read people must be able to translate itself into riches in the job world. How many jobs rely on the written word, anyway? They can wire computers to change every 'he don't' to 'he doesn't.' The highest-placed executives don't write their own letters. Why aren't my students, who have this unique ability to read people, working where this quality is so important? They're experts and could be marvelous at managing people."

In order to read other people, knowing them is the *sine qua non*. "We know more about you than you know about us," the invisible folk had been saying long before James Baldwin so informed white America. "Look at me!" cried Richard Wright's Bigger Thomas. We didn't, until he killed somebody. Somebody white. He was quite visible then, as the young gang member is when a white is his victim. Otherwise, the shades are drawn. And he's still invisible.

As I walk down the street, mumbling to myself, I see an elderly black woman, toting two heavy bags. She's finished a day's work at the white lady's house. She is weary, frowning. I say, as a matter of course, "How's it goin'?" She looks up. Her face brightens. "Fine. And you?"

Three young black kids are swaggering along. As they come toward me, I say, "How's it goin'?" The tall one in the middle is startled. "Fine. And you?"

A presence was acknowledged. That was all.

I am not suggesting a twilight stroll through the walkways of a public housing project. The danger is not so much black hostility as a stray bullet fired by one black kid at another. What I am suggesting is something else: Affirmative Civility.

Mamie Mobley serves as the Prologue to this book. She is the mother of Emmett Till, the fourteen-year-old boy murdered in Mississippi by two white men. They were acquitted. It was 1955, one year after the *Brown vs. Board* decision, desegregating public schools. The Till case was regarded, along with the Supreme Court resolve, as a turning-point in black-white America. "Let justice be done, though the heavens fall." Or so it seemed.

Those of a certain age, both black and white, remember the boy's name and the circumstances. Neither this knowledge nor its significance has been passed on to today's young. To an astonishing degree, when asked to identify Emmett Till, their usual response is in the form of a question: Who? It is not a commentary on them so much as on our sense of history. Or lack of it.

On remembering her son's battered face, Mrs. Mobley's grief is infused with awe. "I was reading in Scriptures where the Lord Jesus Christ was scarred. His face was marred beyond that of any other man, and I saw Emmett. Oh, my God! The spirit came to me and said: 'If Jesus Christ died for our sins, Emmett Till bore our prejudices,' so . . ."

The spirit that spoke to Mamie Mobley is the same one buried in Diane Romano. "One part of me is fighting the other part, which is my real deep, deep-down feeling." Have we the will as a nation to exorcise the one and evoke the other? In order for us, black and white, to disenthrall ourselves from the harshest slavemaster, racism, we must disinter our buried history. Only then can we cross the Slough of Despond. Though John Bunyan's stagnant bog was of the spirit, it is, in an earthly sense, the same patch of swamp that separates slave from free state. We are all the Pilgrim, setting out on this journey.

Lloyd King, who closes the book, envisions a somewhat more secular trip. "I have faith we can mature. Stranger things have happened. Maybe America, maybe the world is in its adolescence. Maybe we're driving home from the prom, drunk, and nobody knows whether we're going to survive or not.

"I am guardedly optimistic—definitely guardedly. If everything is going to hell, it would be hard for me to get up in the morning. But I can't honestly say, 'Sure, things will get better.' We might not make it home from the prom."

PROLOGUE

... But there was something about the matter of the Dark Villain.
He should have been older perhaps.
The hacking down of a villain was more fun to think about
When his menace possessed undisputed breadth, undisputed height,
And a harsh kind of vice.
And best of all, when his history was cluttered
with the bones of many eaten knights and princesses.

The fun was disturbed, then all but nullified
When the Dark Villain was a blackish child
Of fourteen, with eyes too young to be dirty,
And a mouth too young to have lost every reminder
Of its infant softness.

Gwendolyn Brooks*

MAMIE MOBLEY

In 1955, I was working for the United States Air Force. I was happy with my job. That was the year my son, Emmett Till, was killed. He was fourteen.

A salubrious air pervades this street of one-family dwellings; pine trees out front. A tall one overhangs the others. "My neighbor gave me that one when it was just a foot tall. We watched it grow. It was planted in 1960. Five years after Emmett."

It is a black community on Chicago's South Side.

"I'm pleasantly busy. My activities revolve around my house, my church, my family. My family consists of my husband. He has two daughters and quite a few grandchildren. Out of fourteen brothers and sisters that my mother had, only two boys are living. One of them is in Mississippi. He's Crosby, the one who accompanied my son's body back to Chicago in '55."

She overwhelms you with hospitality. You have a multiple choice: cakes, apple cobblers, pies, and of course freshly brewed coffee.

It is the morning after a light snowfall.

---

* *Blacks*, Third World Press, 1991.

Emmett and I were getting ready to go on our vacation. We were excited because we were driving to Omaha where some of my cousins lived. We'd set our date which was less than a week away.

But Emmett heard that Uncle Mose was in town and two of the boys that he grew up with, Uncle Mose's grandsons. They were going back to Mississippi. That's what he wanted to do. It messed up our plans completely. After a lot of pressure, my mother and I decided it would be all right to let Emmett go to Mississippi.

About three days into Mississippi, they went into a little country store. This was Money, Mississippi. They had games on the front porch and you could buy pop and candy, little junk. The boys were playing checkers and Emmett decided to go in the store and buy something. His young cousin went into the store with him. Emmett bought bubble gum and some candy.

As they came out of the store, according to the accounts I heard from some of the boys, someone asked Emmett, "How did you like the lady in the store?" They said Emmett whistled his approval. The word got back to the two men, the husband and the half-brother of that husband—oh, my goodness, Roy Bryant and Big Jim, W. J. Milam [She carefully spells out the name]: M-I-L-A-M.

When they heard about it, it just escalated into something all out of hand. When the younger man, Bryant, hesitated to follow up on it, his half-brother, Big Jim, said, "If you won't, I will." In order to make a man out of his younger brother, he pushed the issue.

It was about 2:30 the following Sunday morning that these two men stormed into my uncle's house and took my son out at gunpoint. And the rest, we don't know what really happened, but we do know how the body looked when it was finally discovered three days later. He had been shot, he had been beaten, they had wired a gin-mill fan around his neck. When the sheriff pulled Emmett from the water, the only way my uncle recognized him was by the ring on his finger.

I was successful in getting the body back to Chicago and it was then, when I looked at Emmett, I could not believe that it was even something human I was looking at. I was forced to do a bit-by-bit analysis on his entire body to make really sure that that was my son. If there was any way to disclaim that body, I would have sent that body back to Mississippi. But it was without a doubt Emmett.

Have you ever seen any pictures? Have you ever seen what he looked like? I will show you them before you go.

There was a trial. The men said they questioned Emmett and they decided he was not the boy, so they pointed him back to my uncle's house and let him go on foot. It doesn't take much to understand. You can look through certain things and see whether or not they're true.

They were acquitted within one hour and five minutes. The jury was all-male, all-white.

Mose Wright, my mother's brother-in-law, pointed out Bryant and Milam as the two men who came for Emmett: "Thar's them." It took unprecedented courage. Nothing like that had ever happened in the South before. That was an old black man, sixty-five years old. He stayed in the area until he was rescued by some civil-rights group and put under surveillance. One night he slept in the graveyard behind his church. He was a minister. He slept under the cotton house one night. He never spent another night in that house. No one did.

Emmett would have been forty-eight this year. I have no grandchildren. He was my only child. You can see coming up the walk, I could really use a grandkid to shovel snow. I often think about that. I like to have a garden and in the springtime, I'm trying to dig . . . So I have to depend on whoever passes by and finally get someone to help me in the spring and again in the winter. We just sort of have to hope somebody comes along when there's been a snow.

Don't you harbor any bitterness toward the two men—toward whites, for that matter? It would be unnatural not to—

It certainly would be unnatural not to, yet I'd have to say I'm unnatural. From the very beginning that's the question that has always been raised: "What would you do to Milam and Bryant if you had the opportunity?" I came to the realization that I would do nothing. What they had done was not for me to punish and it was not for me to go around hugging hate to myself, because hate would destroy me. It wouldn't hurt them.

The Lord gave me a shield, I don't know how to describe it myself. It was as if he put me in a neutral zone where I had no feeling whatsoever toward Milam and Bryant. I did not wish them dead. I did not wish them in jail. If I had to, I could take their four little children—they each had two—and I could raise those children as if they were my own and I could have loved them.

Now that is a strange thing to say, but I haven't spent one night hating those people. I have not looked at a white person and saw an enemy. I look at people and I see people.

I was brought up in the Church of God and Christ. A sanctified church. My great-grandfather was one of the first converts in Mississippi. It preached the gospel of Jesus Christ but with a different twist. I believe the Lord meant what he said, and try to live according to the way I've been taught. This has permeated our family from 1900, I guess.

Look back for a moment. Didn't you feel the Lord deserted you? You're a young mother, your only child brutally murdered, your life almost destroyed—wasn't there an instant when you wanted to hurt his two killers?

No, No. The only real change that came over me when Emmett was killed—I was a very private person. I could stay in my house one year and not go any farther than the front porch and be perfectly happy. My thoughts were centered around Emmett and myself and what we were going to do, and planning for our future. Then all of a sudden, in the midst of despair, it wasn't really important for me to live. Death at that time would have been welcome.

The phone rang one day and an editor from *Jet* magazine wanted to know, "What are you going to do?" I said, "I'm going to school and be a teacher." I was shocked. From the time I was seven, I wanted to be a teacher. I grew up in Argo, Illinois, and had never met a black teacher. There was no such animal. I didn't have a black teacher until I was in my second semester in college. That door was closed, so I gave up those dreams. Then all of a sudden—this was in the fall of 1956, about a year after Emmett had been . . . [*Sobs softly.*] . . . I'd buried Emmett.

I went to Chicago Teachers' College, where registration had been closed and they opened it up for me. Three and a half years later. I was working with kids.

My burning—the thing that has come out of Emmett's death is to push education to the limit: you must learn all you can. Learn until your head swells. This is what I was able to energize my children with, the desire for learning. And I must say I was blessed as a teacher. I taught twenty-four years, Chicago Board of Education.

I'd been out of school almost seventeen years and I graduated number five in my class. I burned a whole lot of midnight oil. Until then, I went to many cities and lectured for the NAACP. They say I was one of the best fundraisers they ever had.

There has been progress without a doubt. We cannot deny that. I see progress within myself and progress for those who will dare reach for it. Sometimes those steps are steep, they're not easy to climb, but as Langston Hughes said, "You have to keep on climbing."

What about the great many, say, those living in those projects? Is life any better for them?

You would be surprised how many great educators, lawyers, doctors, nurses have come out of the Robert Taylor Homes. Those people who are trapped, we even see them fighting right now. A lot are going to give up: they're going to succumb to dope, to prostitution, to robbery, to whatnot.

I remember when the job market folded, it was about '83. The loss of jobs is almost the key to the social ills we're having. That was the summer that the eighth-graders learned for the first time there was not a job for you to go into. I've seen the downward spiral beginning right there.

Everybody's entitled to that forty acres and that mule. You're going to do the work, but you have to have something to work with. If you don't have a job, where do you go from there? You hear people say Pull yourself up by your bootstraps, and you don't even have shoes. You're barefooted. What are you going to pull yourself up by? Our country owes every citizen of the United States of America a means of livelihood. Not a handout, but a way to make it.

This is what I had to do as a public-school teacher. I worried that Johnny was failing. I would go to Johnny's house. I would talk to Johnny's mother. I would offer to stay after school with Johnny. I couldn't give up and say: he'll never learn. I had to keep pushing.

Every morning I would tell the children: we're going to learn this and this and this. Some of those children that I thought were incorrigible ended up being the brightest. One of them—his mother told me he was now a manager of a transportation company. I almost fainted. I thought he'd be behind bars.

I first taught in a community that was considered nice and within three years was turned upside down. I was looking at a different group of people. I couldn't believe it. You know what happens when a neighborhood deteriorates, when the old-timers move out and the less affluent move in. I was there fifteen years.

During that time, I watched the Blackstone Rangers take over the neighborhood. I remember the first teachers' strike. I was always active in the union. I was the picket captain. We had heard that the Blackstone Rangers threatened to put us back in the classroom that day. They believed all the negative connotations about the strike. We didn't have any business striking for more money or whatever. They were going to make sure we went back immediately.

This young man strolled over. He recognized my car. I mean he was

walking *positively*. [*Laughs*.] My heart was going a little faster. He looked
in the car and said, "Mrs. Mobley?"

"Yes, James."

"How are you doin' today?"

"Just fine, how are you doing?"

I realized I knew this guy. He was in my third grade room when I was
doing my practice teaching, my very first class. He was not the brightest
student. I stepped out of the car and looked at the other youngsters, whom I
didn't know. They were his lieutenants.

He said, "What do you need?"

I said, "We need some coffee and doughnuts. We need it badly. We're
cold from head to feet."

He said, "I'll be right back."

They drove away and when they came back they had hamburgers,
they had coffee, they had doughnuts, they had sweet rolls. He put them in
my car. He said, "When do you think you need us back?"

I said, "Tomorrow morning."

Every day they came back and brought us just gobs of stuff. He said,
"You don't have to worry about a thing. We'll be looking out for you."

How do I explain it? James's regular teacher and I were almost like
mother and daughter in the classroom. She had the smart children in 3A.
She gave me the slower ones, 4B. James was in that one. They were going
over third-grade work again without being stigmatized as third-graders.
My group was the toughest to handle. She said, "If I give you these smart
children, you're not going to have any problems to solve. I can watch what
you do, I'll always be here."

These slower kids really tried my patience. I immediately handled the
situation the way she did. If it meant picking one up by the ear and letting
him know this was not the place for that, I did just that. "You're here for one
thing and I must do my job. I am entitled to good working conditions."
[*Laughs*.] I guess James remembered this. He knew I didn't play. I had a
reputation: "Don't mess with Mrs. Mobley."

I have done some things that I really should not have done. I've
slammed some into the wall. I shouldn't have done that. I would come
home and share with my mother the kind of no-nonsense approach I took.
Mama would sit me down and say, "Baby, that child might have left home
without any breakfast. That child might not have seen his mother since
yesterday."

When mother got through telling me these things, I did not see the
children as willful wrongdoers. I saw them as children who did not have the

tender loving care that I had, and along with that discipline, they needed a lot of love. I didn't withhold either one of them. Punitive measures alone will not do it, never.

It goes back to you and Milam and Bryant, doesn't it?

Doesn't it though! I knew that when I got through hating Milam and Bryant, they would be down in Mississippi laughing about what they got away with and they wouldn't be able to appreciate—or even laugh at—my sitting up here eating my heart out. So that wasn't for me to do. It was a job. Emmett had done his. Now there was a job for me to do.

The kids need an opportunity, not handouts. I believe that most people on welfare would get off it if they had jobs.

Since Reagan, it's going to be a little harder struggle. We all know that. We can see what's happened to the income tax, the health insurance, and a whole lot of other things. You wonder how these things were allowed to come about. Then when you think of dollars and cents, you can see that this is what it's all about: not the love of humanity, but the love of the dollar. It's just another river we're going to cross.

I was away from my classroom for two weeks on a special assignment. I was told that the whole floor had no classes because my kids tore it up. Substitutes went home sick and never came back. And I had the best class in school. I came back and my children became angels again. One teacher said, "I'm glad you're back. We haven't had school since you've been gone. I suspended everybody in the class." These are the things my mother said to think twice about doing.

Every child in that class was represented the next morning by a parent. It was my idea. Some came out of curiosity, but most were hostile. Some came with lunch buckets: "I'm supposed to be at work." I started talking at nine o'clock. At ten-thirty, I dismissed the parents. I spoke for an hour and a half.

I told them just how badly their children had behaved: what my role was, what their role was, what the children's role was. "If we don't get our act together, we're going to lose our children. They're falling through cracks every day." I picked out individuals. I did case histories. "Your son Michael over here. Your daughter Samantha over there . . ." I made it very plain.

Not once, during that hour and half, did anyone interrupt me. Instead of leaving, those parents started a line, to shake my hand and thank me. They promised me their wholehearted participation.

As a teacher, I developed this relationship, and any day, you could find two or three parents in my room. One lady came so faithfully until I said, "I don't mean that you have to come every day." She said, "I wouldn't miss this for anything. I'm sitting back there, learning more than the kids." It was a whole new world for some of them.

My friends cross every color line. I don't feel inferior to anyone. I don't feel superior to anyone. I think education is what gives us that surety, that foundation.

Toward the end of our conversation, the newspaper photograph of Emmett Till appears: the boy's mutilated face and body, unspeakably indescribable.

That was my darkest moment, when I realized that that huge box had the remains of my son. I sent a very lovable boy on a vacation—Emmett who knew everybody in the neighborhood. They'd call for him whenever they wanted something done. "Mom, I gotta go help Mrs. Bailey . . ." He was the block's messenger boy.

What might have been? He's never far from my mind. I was reading in Scriptures where the Lord Jesus Christ was scarred. His visage, his face was marred beyond that of any other man, and Emmett came to me. I said, "Oh my God, what a comparison." The spirit spoke to me as plainly as I'm talking to you now. And the spirit said, "Emmett was race hatred personified. That is how ugly race hatred is." I said, "Oh." I had to sit down. It struck me really hard. If Jesus Christ died for our sins, Emmett Till bore our prejudices, so . . .

PART I

Lucy Jefferson's Legacy

LUCY JEFFERSON

It is 1965, a few months after the Selma-Montgomery March.

When I first came from Mississippi, I was so young and ignorant. But I was freer, you know? I had a little more room to move around in than I have now. I think the white man wasn't so afraid then. There wasn't enough of us. There's too many of us now. I think that's what frightened him. Nobody noticed you then. You were there, but nobody bothered about seeing you.

She lives in a low-rise housing project, the Jane Addams Homes, the first in Chicago. Hers is a row house. The apartment is neatly furnished; some pies in the oven; books all over. "Books are my life. I read and read and read." She is self-educated.

She works as an aide in a fashionable hospital. "The clientele there are usually people that's got money. To me, they are fascinating."

Her two children, Carol, twenty-one, and Julian, seventeen, are seated on the couch nearby. Carol is pregnant; the child is due in a couple of months. "Her marriage turned out bad. Julian? Am I giving him a chance to be a man or not? I took that chance when I let him go to Selma. I was scared to death and I was very proud. He was only sixteen and I was afraid he was too young to know what was really happening. But I couldn't afford to tell him. I wouldn't have given him his chance to be a man. This was his chance and I didn't want to steal it."

I just don't like doles. I wouldn't accept one dime from anybody. I'm not gonna raise my children on Aid. Why should I? There's enough money in America for me to raise my children. Now one is seventeen, one is twenty-one. And I absolutely refuse to accept these handouts from anyone. How am I gonna teach these children of mine what a pleasure it is in accomplishment? Do you realize what it means if I'm gonna sit here and accept this check?

Everybody's screaming now, "Oh, these women on ADC." Why hasn't somebody told these people that they're on ADC because you gave all this money to keep from hirin' 'em? Years and years ago. This didn't just start, you know. You don't keep people in a certain category for hundreds of years and expect them to come out and do all these things. For generations and generations they've been just barely making it. Now what do you expect? Plums?

I happened to be the kind of Negro that became controversial, because I read such things as *The American Dilemma* and I walk around with the book in my hand, see? I defied them in so many ways, I almost terrified them. [*Laughs.*] You know, it got so every time I got on an elevator— "What are you reading, Lucy? What are you reading? What are you reading?" I'd begin to enjoy this thing, you know? I was having the best old time.

Here's this Negro woman, every time you see her she's reading a different book. You know what I'd do? I'd go to the library and read those books, and I'd just dash back home and read these. And truly it became a game with me. I don't think I ever had more fun in my life than I had working there.

I guess I was damn near fifty then. That's the reason I say I was havin' a ball. I'm carrying the book by Faulkner, paperback, in my pocket, you know. This particular time I didn't realize that the heading of the book was sticking out just a little above. The students, doctors, interns got on— "Faulkner!" [*Prolonged laughter.*]

You're just breaking down this stereo thing that all Negroes are ignorant, they won't read, they won't do this. They won't help themselves. Once they see you're trying to do it . . . You see what? They're not really worrying so much about the Negro, they're worried about themselves. When I really want to fight 'em, you know what I do? I glare at 'em. They cringe. [*Laughs.*]

Julian was doing very poorly in school and I was getting letters. You know, they send all these little items. Come to see me, come to school, because your child is not working up to his capacity. I don't know why they just don't tell you the truth about it, instead of using all these vague, false phrases. I thought he was just being lazy, but the child couldn't read. He couldn't spell. We was at Crane High, out there in the ghetto. I laid off from work the next day. I got up, cocked my hat Miss Johnny Aside—I wanted them to know I was plenty mad then. Oh yeah, I visited Crane.

Julian was having three study periods in a row. Gee, this is kind of crazy—studying what? I went to see this study hall. And this is the auditorium. It has a false ceiling, and there's very few lights, and there's children everywhere, male and female, and about the only thing they can do is make love. Most of the kids can't read anyway, but if they could, they wouldn't be able to see. So I went to the counselor and he said, "It costs $10,000 to put up this business of putting lights in, and the school system doesn't have money," and blah, blah, blah. I said, "But in the meantime, what are you going to do about all these children in there, these boys and girls, these young men and women?" I said, "Maybe they can't read but they can do other things in there, such as getting babies."

You're talking about teachers. I bet he never had the same teacher twice in two weeks in two years. It's a disgrace to call these places schools. Schools you learn in. They could take a storefront anywhere and clean it up, put some seats in there, and put some books in. But see, you can't learn anything where there is no books. Julian went a whole year in Crane, didn't have a book. If I woke up in a house that didn't have a book, I'd just burn it down. It wouldn't do any good. To me, they're my lifeblood. Types of caps, gowns, all that crap, it don't mean nothing.

Oh, what am I really looking for? My daughter to have her baby. I would like for her to finish her college education. She's gonna need it, to help her child, to rear her child. The only thrill left for me is to see my grandchild come and to see what I can do about him. Won't that be fun?

You know, I'll be able to afford things that would give him incentive to paint, music, literature, all these things that would free his little soul. Let's face it. What counts is knowledge. And feeling. You see, there's such a thing as a feeling tone. One is friendly, one is hostile. And if you don't have this, baby, you've had it. You're dead.

Lucy Jefferson died in 1984.

WILLIAM FREEMAN

The year is now 1990. This is Lucy Jefferson's grandson, now twenty-four. "You could say I was in the room when you visited my grandmother in 1965."

My grandmother put all her energy in trying to expose me to all that was possible, both good and bad, in music, art, and literature. I really wish my grandmother were here now to see the fruits of her labor. She died when I was a freshman in college. I was raised principally by her and my mother. We were not people with money by any means, but somehow, some way, they did do it.

I went to a small Catholic grade school and was fortunate to go to St. Ignatius College Prep. It was my first exposure to white society. I graduated with honors and went to Stanford University on a scholarship. I am now a second-year student at the UCLA Medical School.

I have a great many options open. I get to do things and see places that most black people never get to experience.

Most of my childhood years were influenced by my grandmother. She had only a grade-school education, but she had a book or a magazine or a newspaper in her hand constantly. She read more than any person I'd ever known. It's only after I got into college that I realized what a resource she was. Unfortunately she went when I needed her most.

I cannot imagine what my life would have been like if it hadn't been for my grandmother. There was only one way we could make up for four hundred years of slavery and another hundred years of exploitation: the efforts of my grandmother and mother. She had to carry history and she had to correct history, to release me from the burdens.

While he attended St. Ignatius, he and two white schoolmates appeared on my radio program as participants in a peace rally. It is 1983. I was unaware that I had "met" him at his grandmother's house in 1965.

I remember going to college with her when she was taking courses. I remember her telling stories of her arrest, protesting the Willis Wagons.* They had real problems with a fifty-year-old woman and a three-month-old baby.

I knew very little about my father. Many people say, "Oh, how horrible." I say to them, "You don't understand." I've had three wonderful people—my uncle, too—whose energy and lives were devoted to my success. There are a lot of differences and disputes in families, but they

---

* In the midsixties, Benjamin Willis, Chicago Superintendent of Schools, instituted mobile classrooms of limited facilities for black students, ostensibly to relieve overcrowding. It caused consternation in the city's black community. There were many demonstrations and marches.

faded away when it came to me. Everyone was committed to my going
where I needed to go. Escaping the evils of this society meant doing well in
school. It will mean being a good physician.

My grandmother wanted me to know what the real world was like.
She talked to me about politics a great deal. In history, there were instances
of people who attained success, but it came at a price. If you aren't the very
best, if you have doubts, there are all kinds of ways this society feeds on
those doubts, and that's the beginning of the end. I learned very early you
must first believe in what you're doing. You must say from the beginning: I
will be a very good biologist, a very good clinician.

I'm thinking about neurology. I'm thinking about a great many
things. I'm most concerned about the lack of primary health care for too
many people in Chicago, any large city. It's a growing problem every day.
Simple preventive things that could be done and they're not being done.
I'm talking about community simply because I was raised in a black community.

There is so much to overcome. I visited a white surgeon's home. This
is a man I met for the first time. I mentioned my interest in neurology. As I
was leaving, he bluntly said, in a very authoritative voice, "I don't think
this specialty is for you." He gave no reason. I thought of my grandmother.
She did not want to dictate the work I would choose. She wanted me to go
and find out for myself. Unfortunately, not everyone thinks as my grandmother did. It became clear to me that evening.

There's a struggle at a white school because you feel every day you're
in an environment not geared toward your success. It would not be uncom-
mon that I'd be the only black student in the class. You can tell among your
white colleagues that they don't really respect black students a great deal.
You can see it in their eyes.

During my freshman year in med school, I went to a party. There was
an individual who everyone knew had a drinking problem. He was doing
something we thought was dangerous. I grabbed him, told him to stop.
Next thing I know, he turned around and hit me. Many of the students came
to me and said he was a jerk. But later on, other white students came up to
me and said, "Why did you start that fight?" Black friends told me that a
year after that incident, I was still being blamed.

Many of the white students really know nothing about black people.
You feel you're treated as an affirmative-action case, not because you're
qualified, because you can do the work. Their attitude is one of looking
down on people. I sense less of it in medical school, but it's there. I have a
number of white friends and we talk about those things.

I don't feel threatened by it, but I recognize the potential dangers. You may not always know who's trustworthy, who may have your best interests at heart. It is an unwritten rule in much of black society: white friends may indeed be white friends, but how long will they be white friends? You're always on guard, even in the best of circumstances. You're always testing. It's a matter of protecting yourself. It's a necessary step. It's something that evolved out of the history of slavery, out of hundreds of years.

Sometimes you see it when you're called upon to give an answer in class. You feel as though you're constantly being tested as to how good you really are.

Racism on the campus is very much in the news these days. It may have to do with many of the white students in college knowing nothing of the struggles of the sixties. They grew up during Reagan and they see those few black people enjoying the fruits. They see it as being unfair in some ways.

I see things slipping into the gentrifying of education. You take black students from the better schools, not from the inner city. You don't send representatives to those areas to interview students. I found that most students on my campus didn't come from the same kind of household I did. They came from homes where their mothers and fathers were accomplished individuals, with a substantial amount of money. Every time someone sneers at the projects and says those people are not worthwhile, don't have the incentive, I think, "Are they talking about me? That's where I came from."

I see difficult times ahead, especially for the black people of this country. There is a growing anger among black people since this country has taken a turn to the right. The black man is now visible, but in many cases, he's just as invisible as he was before. It's easy for the white majority to ignore a black voice that tells them what is important. It's very foreign.

Education is the route by which everyone can liberate themselves. When people understand who they are and understand their history, they have more respect for themselves. Before integration can work, there has to be a mutual respect.

CAROL FREEMAN

William Freeman's mother; Lucy Jefferson's daughter. She is forty-six. She was the pregnant young woman seated on the living-room couch, alongside her brother, Julian, during my conversation with Lucy Jefferson in 1965.

She is executive secretary of the chancellor of the City Colleges of Chicago.

Hers is a one-family dwelling in a middle-class, working-class black neighborhood on Chicago's South Side. There are shelves of books and several Egyptian artifacts about. She lives by herself.

When my mother said "feeling tone," she meant that you get inside a person and feel what they feel. You can feel their troubles, you can feel their sorrows. A white can't feel what a black person feels because he hasn't gone through the experience we had. I think he is feeling, suffering in a different way. He is looking at a world that is totally changing and he is no longer dominant. It has changed before his eyes because he has allowed greed to take over.

When you visited my mother, I sat there, pregnant with my son. I was twenty-one. It's been a rough struggle, but my mother and I made a commitment. The reason I put William in a Catholic school was not because I love Catholics. It was for his protection. I didn't want him to go to school and fend for his life. I wanted him to learn.

I'll never forget the day I took him to take the St. Ignatius Prep test. It was a blizzard. When I came back to pick him up, he said, "Mom, I think I'm in. But what about tuition?" I said, "Don't worry about that. It will be paid."

When he won the four-year scholarship, we were so proud of him. He was accepted at Princeton, he was accepted at Yale, he was accepted at Harvard. But he wanted to go to Stanford. Princeton wined and dined and came to the house several times to try to get him to reconsider. My mother was alive during his first year at Stanford. Right here in this living room.

I think we've gone backwards. I'm looking at those children younger than my son. I'm looking at generations of people who don't have the hope we had. They don't have the kind of hope I instilled in my son. They don't have anything to hold onto, they don't have anybody to talk to, they don't have any place to go.

There's so much we have lost, it's hard to say where it began. Maybe it was just going on all along and we didn't know it and it just snowballed. Just like the drug situation. Our country always had a drug problem, but it was undercover. Now it's out of control. They might just as well forget it.

Along with that, we have illiteracy and no moral values. It's like Revelations in the Bible. We're actually seeing the glue come off the hinges. What will happen I don't know.

Maybe we'll have to have a Depression to get people to realize that we can't live in this world alone. We need each other. The people that do have the money will feel the pinch probably harder than they did in the thirties. People like us will say, "We just don't have the money."*

What I don't understand as a black woman is the white race not wanting to look at the issue. We wouldn't be here if we weren't brought here. I think I know why they hate us.

It takes ten generations to get rid of a slavery mentality. We're not that far from slavery. We're the only race of people that don't know who we are. We're such a mixture of people: different colors, different hues, different nationalities.

She holds forth an illustrated book and indicates a picture of an Egyptian king, Akhnaton.

See the long neck, the thick lips, the *keen* nose, and the eyes? He looks like my son. There is so much resemblance. Maybe my child is from that line. Who knows?

Whites have an advantage. They can say, "I came from Poland," "I came from Ireland." We can't say that. We can say, "I came from Detroit." Or Louisiana.

I know about a Jewish man in our family. On my grandmother's side.

There were four aunts. All of them were beautiful, light-skinned women. One of them, Aunt Maude, was the mistress of the mayor of this small southern town. The white women of this town took her out to lynch her. The mayor, this Jewish guy, made them turn her loose. He put her on a train that night and she came to Chicago. He followed her and was with her until she died.†

There has always been a white man somewhere in our family. A white

---

* "The Negro was born in depression. It don't mean too much to him, The Great American Depression, as you call it. There was no such thing. The best he could be is a janitor or a porter or shoeshine boy. It only became official when it hit the white man. If you can tell me the difference between the depression today and the Depression of 1932 for a black man, I'd like to know it. The American white man has been superior so long, he can't figure out why he should come down."

Clifford Burke, an old black pensioner, in *Hard Times* (1970)

† It is a variation on Lucy Jefferson's story as she told it to me in 1965. "My grandfather was half-Indian. He was the only real man I'd ever known. He feared no one. His life, in my later years, sustained me and gave me faith in the Negro man. One of my aunts lived with a white man. These women of the town—of course, this is kind of a legend—they dressed in men's clothes, they came and tied her to a tree. My granddaddy heard about it. He put his Winchester on him, went down to where they were, and told them, 'Cut her down or I'll kill every one of ya.' She died on Orleans Street here about two, three years ago."

man was in love with my mother for many years. A Greek. It's easier for a black woman to get a white man than it is for her to get a black man. The black man doesn't feel as though he's worthy. Take me, for instance. When I get involved with a black man, the first thing he finds out is that my son is in medical school. He notices that I'm living in this home. I have my own car. He analyzes: what do I need him for? With a white man, it's altogether different. He doesn't have to analyze. He commends me and wants to know how I was able to do it. I said, "Just like other parents do." I did without so he could go to school.

The black male appears to me to be the one who's having the roughest time. That's why I was so determined for my son not to get a job but get a profession. I told him, "By the time you're ready, there won't be any jobs." [*She points toward the south.*] Right over here, the steel mills are all closed.

You're looking at generations of black males that have been raised by women. We have not had the men to raise men.* We have been doing the best we can, but sometimes we've made a mess of it. The black men have so often been put down in this society; they just disappear.

When the few black men get up there, who do they communicate with? The white women are the ones who chase down the black men who are up there. When William was at Stanford, it wasn't the black girls who were chasing him. It was the white ones.

When you visited my mother in 1965, there was a lot of hope. I was exposed to a lot of things that many people weren't privy to. We never shopped at Michigan Avenue, didn't have the money, but mama always made it a habit to walk up and down the Magnificent Mile. That's when I realized exposure means a great deal to a child, and I knew how to conduct myself accordingly. I had also been to Selma and been arrested.

When we first moved here, a white family was next door. Italians. She would see mama working in her yard with the roses and said, "Your house looks better than mine."

It's this new generation that doesn't have any hope. They don't have anything to look forward to. I've heard little children say, "This day really went fast." Normally you hear other people say it, not children.

When William came up, McDonald's was a baby. Now it's full-grown and giving breakfast. We have a generation of children who have grown up living in McDonald's, because mama don't cook, because she's doing her

---

* Lucy Jefferson, 1965: "This is something that happened when we had this business of not allowing the Negro male to make a living. See? That's why I say that Negro women have not been able to raise men. The white man thought of that."

own thing. Grandmothers today are younger now than my mother was. They might be in their early forties, younger than I am. A lot of women don't want to get older and a lot of them will always have a boyfriend.

I don't know what's going to happen. I see lost souls. When I walk to the train in the morning, I see young ladies that are pregnant, that are drug addicts, trying to stop cars for a fix or to turn a trick. That time of morning.

So many of these young people take drugs, which are everywhere. Just to escape reality. And anger.

I see anger on my job. What they call attitudes. They don't know how to fight so they take an attitude: "You can't make me do something I don't want to do." "I dare you to fire me."

The reason I don't feel anger is because the white man's not keeping his foot on my mind. He can't do anything to my mind. I'm free to think whatever I want to think. He's afraid, but he doesn't know he's afraid.

The white woman is a lost poor thing. She's been put on a pedestal and she's had to come off it. Because of economic reasons.* She's searching for her identity, too. She has been able to see how her own man can not only treat her bad but other folks, too. He will not only use her, he'll use anybody to get where he wants to go.

There are white women on my job, have little children, a husband, work ten, twelve hours to make that overtime. They're servants to their boss and then come home to be servants to their husbands.

I'm not a church person. God is right here in what I do now. I burn a candle for William every day he's at school. I want spiritual protection for him. I do most of my praying and meditating right here.

There are some people that don't want to work. Who was that talking about black males in jail and putting them in boot camp? The Marines. That's something they should have started years ago. They need discipline, they need training. They come out of homes where there is no discipline, no ritual. Nobody really cares.

My son is over-average lucky. He had a mother, a grandmother, an uncle that truly loved him. The only thing missing was the father. A lot of black men don't have that kind of love. I made my son my life. How many parents do that? The black male in this country is a lost soul. My brother is one of them.

---

* "The white man has set his woman up on a pedestal. He's trying to prove to her how superior he is. Truly, he's not superior. He's just another little boy. She has to stay there if she wants to be anybody. But if she ever learns anything and she strays, she's an outcast. Me, I can do any cotton-pickin' thing I feel like doin'."

Lucy Jefferson in *Division Street: America* (1967)

I think the bottom's going to have to fall out and then there won't be any such thing as color. I think that in the 1990s and maybe all the way into the year 2000, the United States is going to go through a tremendous change. I think it has to. The wealth is too imbalanced. There's no such thing as a middle class anymore. We have to clear up a lot of things.

JULIAN JEFFERSON

Lucy Jefferson's son; Carol Freeman's brother; William Freeman's uncle.
    "You and mama sat on the couch and we were just there, listening. [Laughs softly.] *Hard to believe it was twenty-five years ago.* [Muses.] *Twenty-five years. She told us she was gonna be put in a book, so it was a big thing.*
    "When you came here that day, the neighbors thought you were either an insurance man or some kind of bill collector. They were the only white men they saw there. All eyes were on that walkway when you finally came. It was a big deal, a great whoopdeedoo.
    "My wife and I are divorced. I don't have a chance to see my son often."
    It is Martin Luther King's Birthday, 1989.

The trip to Selma was an experience that would last me a lifetime. Just today, I stopped at one of the lounges and they were playing Dr. King's drum-major theme, mixed with jazz. It reminded me of my day in Selma.

I was fifteen when we were sitting in at the Board of Eduction, trying to get rid of Ben Willis. I wanted to go to jail with the whole group. I put my age up in order to be locked up with the others.

Our schools were horrible. What really ticked my mother off was when she came to school and found our classes right next to the boiler room. I remember her really getting mad when she found out where my study period was. It was in the auditorium and dark. You couldn't hardly see to read anything. I remember what she said: "They can't study anything in the place but how to get a baby."

Everything is computers now. That's what I decided to do. Turn it all around and go in a new direction. I'm going to school now to be a computer engineer. It's been rough. I've been out of a job for four years, a meaningful job. I spent most of the time working whatever jobs I could work and going to somebody's school just to upgrade my education. I even finished a course in ultrasound.

I was able to get a job on the fire department during the strike.* I come to find out not only did they not want me because I was a damn scab, but also the racial factor. There was just too many black fellows that came in at one time. It was a very hostile environment, I just don't want to go through that again. I don't want to be the one to break ground as a scab. I stayed on the department for a year.

They nitpicked the slightest little thing you done. You got called on the carpet for it even though you hadn't been trained to know all the rules and regulations. One day I was on the job and that was it. The training we got was right there in the firehouse. You wondered if the very fellows you're working with are going to stand behind you when you're in one of these buildings. Was it because I was a scab or because I was black? It was both, I think.

At one time I thought things were getting better. I really did. I look back, the past years seems like we're backsliding, all the way backwards. It seems like everybody hates everybody. I don't mind your disliking me, but dislike me for what I do to you, not what I didn't do. Just don't categorize me and say, "Well, he's black; I can't like him." If there's something I do you don't like, let's discuss it. But to automatically categorize me when I walk through the door is a horse of another color.

I give my mother credit for everything, even if I may not be a doctor or a lawyer. She taught me manners, to stand up for myself and my rights. Those very things have gotten me as far as I've gotten today. I can converse with anyone on any level. I can be around people and not embarrass other people. All the little things that she said would help me go through life.

I get upset when I get on the el and a group of black fellows or girls, they act completely wild. Like they never had anyone to talk to them, "Hey, act like a lady, act like a man. Sit down, it's embarrassing." Then you look at yourself and say, "Well, I see white people think that, because what they normally see is the wrong image." But they don't think there's a flip side to every coin. If you would see my nephew, you would know that's entirely different. It's all about how you were raised, and they're not being raised today.

I give credit to Mom because she told me if you carry yourself right, you don't have to feel out of place anywhere. In certain areas, I know I'm being looked at. That's when I would look behind me and the feel would be

---

* During the administration of Mayor Jane Byrne, members of the Chicago Fire Department went on strike. To break the strike, she recruited men who had no previous experience as fire fighters; a good percentage of blacks, among them.

there. If you're in a store, you teach your kids not to be grabbing things off the shelf, running through the aisles, whooping and hollering. We go through, walk through, get what we need, then we go out.

My best friend and I came home from day camp and tried to steal some ice cream sandwiches from the store. The owner caught him and took his camp bag. Nothing in it but his swimsuit and towel. Nowadays it wouldn't even be noticed. But then his mother was gonna wash it and take care of the bag.

I look out the bathroom window and I see him and his mother coming back from the store, his head down and he's cryin'. I hear my mother's footsteps coming home from work. I lock the bathroom door. She says, "Open the door or I'll break it down." She has a clothesline in her hand, ties it around me and hangs me on the hook. I was there for a while and crying, of course. She said, "I work too hard to give you everything I could possibly give for you to be out there stealing." To this day, the fear of stealing was rushed through me so hard. She is why I am the man I am today.

Whites look at a group of them, automatically they assume—even though they can watch me sit, reading a book—that I'm the same way. It's like I don't even count. It's "them" they're afraid of. So if I come into their neighborhood to rent an apartment or buy a house, they still see "them." If people could accept us as individuals, we would get a hell of a lot farther. Until that day comes, we're going to be categorized.

You look at TV, as soon as you hear of some crime, the first question you ask: Was he black or white? Recently, the Boston story. The man killed his wife and baby. He said it was a black man and everybody was ready to boil over, pop. They never look at it and say it's just another man that killed another person. That's not important anymore. The only important part was: Was he a black man? We look like we're sitting ready for something to give us a reason to act completely crazy again. We're just a time bomb right now. You can't help feel the tension.

I've never had any run-ins with police. I credit that to my mother. I've known people that walk down the street and the police throw 'em against the wall and frisk them. I've never had that. Is it the way I live? The way I carry myself? It goes right back to my upbringing. How you carry yourself is what you'll get.

I got out of the movement. I'm from the ouside now.

As far as the movement, there are good memories and bad memories. It's a blessing to have once worked with Dr. King. I had a chance to meet personally with him in Selma. Those are golden moments in my life that I treasure. Now I'm just trying to live from day to day. Nothing spectacular. Just minding my own business.*

You have an Arab that might come here. They're here for six months and the next thing you know, they're opening up a business, whereas it would take you all these years to get a license to do that. I don't understand it. It's just like we can't get a foothold on anything in our own community. Before we turn around, it's somebody else is running it. We have qualified people that are able to run businesses. There are some brilliant black people and they all don't have to be Johnson and Johnson. Opportunity has always been denied. They give you just so much—you know the old saying: Just give them a little bit to keep them happy. I mean in the neighborhood where I live right now, I don't think you would find two black-owned businesses. Basically Middle-Eastern people and a few Asians.

Blacks got comfortable with the Jews, who used to be here. Now these new ones take all the money and send it away or whatever he does.

Some of the fellows I know, men who have taken care of their families, had a decent life—no great life, but a decent one—they're not looking for a revolution. There's more things to worry about than if one white person stepped on somebody's toe or made a statement which the media picked up and turned around and everybody makes a hullabaloo about it. It doesn't take much these days to start something that could hurt everyone in the process.

I know people who worked hard, and the steel mills folded out from under them and they had to get started all over again. Still trying to bring up their kids the way they were raised, strict. While we were still in the projects, there used to be a time that if I was caught doing something, if a neighbor saw me I might get a whupping by her first. Then she'd tell my mother and I'd get a second whupping.

Education is the key to solving our problem. Without that, no door will open to these kids. You wouldn't hire someone who couldn't read an exit sign. What makes you think someone else wants to? And to teach them respect for other people.

You have to admit that affirmative action is kind of unfair. I know why it came about. We had to have something that would give us a shot. At the rate things were going, we would never have gotten a chance at anything. We needed some law to give us a chance. But if I were working for some black company and they'd say, "We have to promote the white

---

* I spend six months mindin' my own business
and six months leavin' other peoples' business alone.
Before I know it, the whole year's up and gone.
     An old blues song by Big Bill Broonzy

because he's a minority here, even though he's scored lower than you," that would hurt me tremendously.

But I do believe in affirmative action for certain jobs, yes. City jobs like a fireman. You don't need a Ph.D. to pull a hose off a truck and spray water on a fire. But if it's someone else's computer company. I don't think he should have to hire someone who is not qualified for a particular job.

If my schools were anywhere up to par with what some of the white schools were at the time, maybe I would have been qualified for any job that came around.

I was out of work for four years and not once did I get on welfare. I'm ashamed of it. The stigma it carries. That stigma tells people that you're lazy and don't want to work. I don't believe it.

You're worried about what "they" believe?

Right. I want to show them that there's more like me, people who will not accept less. So you just keep looking around. Welfare's fine for other people. Get whatever help you need; there's nothing wrong with it. But I don't want it, not for me. If I could survive without it, I'm a *real* survivor. If things were even, nobody would need welfare.

I can't be bitter. I don't like a lot of things that go on. But what am I gonna achieve sitting back just day after day, just filling my heart with hate? I can't be bitter. I don't mean anyone any harm. I just don't want anyone to bother me. I would like to work in my field, just enjoy life and grow old gracefully.

■ ■ ■ ■ ■

Friends

DIANE ROMANO

1965
She is thirty-five. A mother of six children, she is separated from her husband. A devout Catholic, she is awaiting Vatican approval for a chance at remarriage, though it is out of the question for the immediate future. She

provides for her family with a county job as "baby-sitter" for jurors. She reads law books, listens to hearings in courtrooms, and hopes one day to go back to school and become a lawyer, "even if I'm sixty."

She has lived in the same neighborhood on Chicago's Near West Side all her life. It is predominantly Italian, with some Mexican families nearby. Much of the community has been "renewed out" to make way for the Chicago campus of the University of Illinois. The area has the feel of an island surrounded by cement.

I'm in sympathy with Negroes. I'll go march with them, if it's something big. I don't use the term "nigger" in the house, and I never allow it. I don't know if the oldest is testing my authority; I know he has to conform to the rest of his group. Their parents are not really anti-Negro. It's just fear of the unknown. People here are afraid of the new. I know changes are coming and it's not all bad. I feel just as sorry for the white people who are scared as I am for the poor colored people who don't have much of a chance in the city.

A Negro girl is a good friend of mine. I've invited her to the house four or five times. Definite dates. "I'll expect you Sunday, three o'clock, and you'll have dinner with me." She always said the same thing. You see she was concerned for my welfare. "Now what do you want me to do, come up your front stairs, and stay half an hour and have your windows busted before I leave?" I don't know what my neighbors will do. I believe I am well liked and respected by the majority of the community. Now she's married so I'll have to invite her husband, too. But I want my children to see these people are no different from any other people, that they talk and they have manners and they eat like we eat, and they think and they have feelings, and they're sensitive and they're artistic, and some of them are strange and some of them are dumb—they are just like we are. And I think I'll do that before the summer's out. So that everybody will be sitting outside and they're gonna see these people come in. This is the step that's gotta be taken. Somebody's gotta take it.

1990
She now lives in a high-rise condominium on Chicago's North Side.

"I went back to school and earned a college degree. I took a law-enforcement exam that lasted six to eight hours and I got a terribly high score." She works for a large federal agency, investigating violations of the law: "felonies, impersonations, extortion, embezzlement, thefts." Her job requires her to carry a gun.

Back in the sixties, I was very concerned with being a good mother and raising them in a proper way, not letting them have prejudices that I thought were unfounded.

Today I have mixed feelings. I don't know if it's because I'm getting older. I don't know if I've become a colder, harder person within myself. I still know all the things that the poor, that the black people have to go through. You notice the new term. I haven't yet got into the "African-American" thing. It was easier for me to go from "colored" to "black." But the new African-American thing, that's a little bit of a mouthful.

My feelings are really mixed today and I don't know why. Maybe it's because I've been out in the world now a heck of a lot more. I have seen things outside that don't please me. We're talking here about the race of black people. I have to be honest with you. Twenty-five years ago I was very sympathetic. Today I'm still sympathetic but I'm not a hundred percent sympathetic. That sounds terrible.

It probably has to do with the kind of work I do. I'm out looking for crooks and criminals. They're the people I deal with. It's a shame to say it, but quite a few of these are black people. They *seem* like they're all involved with the negative part of living: cheating, lying, stealing, dope, that type of thing.

Maybe it's not really *me* saying this. At least I hope it's not really me. I don't want to be that type of person. I've given up with the kids, *my* kids. I'm more concerned with myself and how *I* feel.

I think I'm a changed person. I realize one of the big reasons is that I see *only the bad*. I do have wonderful occasions to see the good. I've got friends. I hate to say black friends because they're just friends. They're wonderful people, artistic, thinking, profound, sensitive. Everything that I would hope I am, they are. But for the ten black people that I know who are very sweet and very good, a pleasure for anybody to know, I've got a hundred that are just the opposite. Maybe that's what's weighing on me so much. Because the majority of them are not the decent type of person that I would like to meet.

Yes, I know all the reasons that they are in the predicament they are today. I know they've been held back. I know they don't have friends who can push them into certain places. When Harold Washington was here, I think he was trying to do that. Here in the city most people look askance at that: "He's putting all black people in City Hall." Never thinking that when other mayors were in, they were putting all white people in. [*Laughs.*]

The office I deal with has mostly black clerical help. It angers me that a secretary won't proofread what she's supposed to proofread. If I write a misspelled word, she will put the misspelled word in there *knowing* that it's spelled a different way. She won't change it because she figures that's your job. She's extremely efficient, but she refuses to do anything that is not "her work." She's very snippy. I have to tone down my voice when I speak to her. I talk very soft and have to be very careful in my choice of words. Instead of saying, "Type this for me, I need it immediately," I have to say, "Do you have time to type this for me?" With other secretaries, I don't have to do that. She'll put all kinds of roadblocks up. I've called it a defensive mode. I think it's primarily antiwhite.

I'll go to City Hall, I'll see a bunch of people standing around, not doing their jobs. You ask for a little attention and they'll act like they're doing *you* a big favor by waiting on you. These things are magnified so much in my job.

Do you remember how it was when the whites were there?

[*Laughs.*] It was the same way. You give a little power to a clerk or someone behind a desk and they *immediately* grow with the power.

Do you feel guilty because you have less sympathy for the black than you once did?

Yes. It makes me less a good human being. A good human being is rational, sensible, kind . . . Maybe layers and layers, years and years of prejudice have finally got to me. Is it that I'm getting older and have less patience? I don't really want to be considerate of other people. I want people to be more considerate of *me*. Maybe that's it. All I know is I feel a sense of . . . loss.

I read that book again this morning.* I sat there and cried over the innocence of Diane Romano in 1965, how naïve she was. I sat and cried because I remembered how I felt at that time, in the hopes—oh my goodness, the hopes that I had for my own children, for the world, for the city. It has not come to pass.

All my children I'm proud of, but they all have their prejudices. What I attempted to do with their growing up was not a complete success. [*Laughs.*] I think the outside world and the neighborhood carried more weight with them than what I said. I brought them up to be honest, to classify people by what they really were, not by their color. Listening to them speak today—they're all adults, so I wouldn't *dare* tell them, "Why

---

* *Division Street: America* (1967).

are you saying that?"—They use derogatory terms for black people. I feel guilty because I laugh and go along with them. I would never have done it before. I would have said, "Listen, how can you say that? That's not so."

What I'm doing is the sin of most people. They classify them *all* as a lump. They're all on welfare. They're all selling dope, they're all selling their bodies. I know it's not true, but it takes me longer today to say, "I know it's not true."

I overcame prejudices in my own family. Now I'm reverting back to my parents' thinking. Blacks are poor, blacks are crooks, blacks are ADC, watch out for blacks. You're getting on the bus, there's two blacks on the corner, watch out because they're going to rob your purse, stick a knife in you.

If somebody makes a derogatory remark about blacks, I laugh with them, ha, ha, ha. Later I feel guilty. Why did I do that? Twenty-five years ago I'd tell them, "I'm sorry, but I don't appreciate that remark." I was a stronger person then. These years have taken a toll on me.

We have a new boss, a black man. Everybody's saying the only reason he got the job is because he's black. I feel bad because I agree with them. Not verbally, but with a smile, a laugh, body language. I come home and I think: why am I doing this? Why did I not say: "He's qualified, *extremely* qualified"? I'll say it to myself but not to the white people who are making the derogatory remarks. Years ago, I'd have said, "What the hell are you talking about?"

What is it with me? Is it fear? I want to be part of the group? I don't want to be an outsider. I *want* to be part of the group. I think that's what my children had to contend with.

You'll find people who are quite qualified to do their job, but they don't want to do any more than they have to. The blacks are defensive and content with doing the least amount of work possible.

Your friends—?

They're exceptions. Absolutely. And all the people from my church. It's ninety-five-percent black. Holy Name. I still go to the same church. It was once Italian. We're all Catholics and we all attend the same mass. I go to 8:30 mass on Sunday morning. I put the coffee pot on, I make the tea, I make the cool drinks for the children, etcetera. They know me and I know all of them. We're all different ages, from the very young to the very old.

We have two young women who have a shoehouse full of kids. Do you know how hard it is for these young women to get those kids up in the morning and get them to church by 8:30?

And some of your black colleagues at work—

—Are exceptions. Oh absolutely. [*Laughs.*] I know, I know. I feel the reason the civil-rights thing has slowed down is because of the black people, most of them. They've had time since the sixties to solidify a position in life. Most have had the opportunity to advance themselves and have made it bad for the next people coming in because they've been dogging on the job. There *are* exceptions but it's not enough to overcome all the negativism made by the others in the workforce today.

I'm ashamed sometimes of the way I feel. I went into a building to see a person who wanted to speak with me. It was an apartment building, three stories high. I didn't see any lights on anywhere. The door of her apartment was falling over, looked like someone had broken it. I tried to move the door and couldn't.

As I started to turn, the next door opened. Out came five black youths with bands around their heads. My imagination was going wild. They were between me and the exit. Now what happens? So I pulled a Clint Eastwood. I made sure my elbow moved my jacket so that my firearm was visible. And I talked to them in a very gruff, tough way. I walked past them with my back to the exit. So I could get out. And I did. *They didn't do anything except say, "Mama, what you doin' here?"* All they probably wanted to do was help me. But I couldn't take a chance. Why? Because it's a perception I have.

[*Sighs.*] Yeah, but if they hadn't seen my weapon, if they didn't know I was armed, might they not have done something? If I hadn't used my very official voice? I feel quite certain it was because I was armed, that I showed no fear, that I acted like I knew what I was doing.

You don't have the fear when they are white kids. You feel like you could talk to them or you could yell at them. You feel you could do that and nothing would happen to you. Even if they slapped you, you'd get real angry, but you wouldn't be terror-stricken. If these black kids did it to you, you'd be terror-stricken.

Most people have mixed feelings about the advance of blacks. Most have the impression that blacks are getting ahead because of the need for tokenism. You've got to fill a slot, we've got to have a black person. Nobody gives the black person credit for being a competent, intelligent worker.

Oh, I'm definitely for affirmative action. If affirmative action goes by the wayside, we're not going to have that opportunity for minorities. So it has to stay. [*Sighs.*] I have such a mixed bag of feelings.

I'm always fighting myself. One part of my brain sees all these things and is fighting the other part, which is my real deep-down feeling. I will come after an altercation and I'll think to myself, "That dirty, stupid, cheatin' black person." No, I don't use the N-word, not even in my head.

I want to be considered a high-class person. So I don't do the things that would typecast me as a low-class person. I wouldn't swear in general company. I wouldn't say dirty words nor would I talk about other people's race as being beneath mine. Because I know it's not true. I also know that low-class people think it's true.

It's all a contradiction. I want to be part of the accepted group. I just want to go along nicey-nice now. I don't want to confront people. I don't want to have arguments. I don't want to have bad feelings with anybody. Leave me alone.

I think it's going to take another hundred years, maybe two hundred, before the feeling of white superiority goes—this feeling against blacks, against Mexicans, against Orientals. Because they're different than us. Isn't that the whole thing? You look down on those people whose culture is different than yours. Naturally, you can't be as good as me.

That is human nature. How do we change human nature? I don't think we can. I think we can suppress it. Just like swearing. I'm the world's worst swearer, but in social activities, I hold it down. I don't use the F-word. I temper the way I speak. Maybe one day it will disappear, this racism. It's not going to happen in my lifetime.

Do you ever see your old friend, the one you invited to your old house twenty-five years ago?

I seldom see her, but we're still friends. We've gotten older. I'm a grand-mother, she's a grandmother. When we meet, we run and grab each other and hug each other. It's so good to see her again and talk to her.

[*Sighs deeply.*] What I see out in the field are *not* intelligent, hard-working, honest black people. The majority of hardworking good ones I don't see. What do I do now? Wait until I retire and only have things to do with the good people? And then I'll change again. [*Laughs.*] Come see me twenty-five years from now, if we're alive.

Postscript: "My closest friend at work, Anita Herbert, is black. I can talk to her without worrying how she's going to take it. She's one of the most intelligent people I know. I have an idea she's going to tell you the same things I did."

ANITA HERBERT

She is thirty-seven, single, light-skinned. She lives on Chicago's South Side in a six-flat building owned by her mother. One brother is a construction worker; the other, a hairdresser. Both are out of work.

She, like Diane Romano, is a criminal investigator for the IRS. "Although I had a college degree, I started out as a clerk-typist and worked myself through the system."

White-collar crime is committed by whites more than it is by blacks. If you're speaking of briberies, it would more likely be a white person. If you're speaking of assault, that's anyone.

Farmers are getting upset, desperate, by suddenly having the world turn against them because their loans are being called in. The IRS wants their money as they're losing property they've had for a hundred years. And you're dealing with black people who are just barely making it. They all get upset and take it out on us.

Each one is different. Extremely rich people feel like you need an appointment to tell them they violated the law. They feel their power and prestige should bring them more.

My brothers worry about me and my job. Though they're proud of me. They think it's dangerous. We have a problem with the Posse Commitatus, who are tax protesters. They are anti-Catholic, anti-Jewish, anti-government and, of course, antiblack. They cover much of the Midwest, my territory. I originally went up there by myself, but I was told this area might not be particularly healthy for a black female.

Law enforcement is still a male-oriented world. If you're male and aggressive, that's good. If you're female and aggressive, you're a bitch. If you're male and laid back, that's your nature. If you're female and laid back, you're not aggressive enough and they question your capabilities.

Being black and female puts you in the lowest tier. The pecking order is white male, black male, white female, black female. You're at the bottom.

A lot of times when they talk to you on the phone, they don't realize they're dealing with a black. So when you go to talk to them, they really want to question your right to the job. They question your mental capability. This is always amazing to me. They tend to overexplain very simple things. They want to tell you how to run the investigation. Some people show the initial shock on their faces. You ring the doorbell, you show your badge, and their eyes get big.

*In the late seventies, she attended a small college in southern Illinois:
"Forty blacks out of a thousand students. They made the* Six O'Clock News
this year because of racial problems."

I wasn't militant, I was just stand-offish. I felt the races were well defined
and I wanted to keep it that way. It was a big mistake. It was sad that I didn't
create better friendships. I created the line, that's the sad part. I wanted to
keep my image as a black person, so people knew I did not fraternize with
the white race. I think I could have done a better job if I had been a little
friendlier.

If I had to do it all over again, I would have gone to an all-black
college. It's easier to deal with, to gain an education when you're in a
comfortable environment. I think there was a lot of intimidation in college,
coming from an inner-city school. I think the teachers would have been
more compassionate. They know they're getting kids from the inner city,
who have been deprived of certain advanced classes, but still have the
capability if someone is willing to teach them.

I didn't feel any compassion from the majority of teachers in the
college. I remember one class. I wasn't studying and was getting a bad
grade. I made up my mind I was going to ace this test and ended up getting
an A. The teacher couldn't believe it. She wanted to know the source of my
information, refusing to believe *I* was the source. She implied I was
cheating.

I'll never forget the English teacher I had in high school. I wrote a
poem. She called me in and said, "Where did you plagiarize this poem
from?" I said I didn't. She said, "If I ever find that you plagiarized this
poem, I'll make sure that you get an F in this class and I'll have you kicked
out of school." If that had been a white student, she would have said, "This
is a commendable poem. Maybe you should pursue the field of writing."
She never gave me my poem back either. [*Laughs.*]

I marched with Martin Luther King, but I was too young to really
know what was going on, how bad it really was. When I was growing up, I
remember the National Guard patrolling the streets. It's really amazing to
realize what those people went through to enable us, within my lifetime, to
have what we should have had anyway. Now it's all changing.

When you get a professional job, where there were no blacks preced-
ing you, you really have to work twice as hard. You get white coworkers,
who honestly believe they're better. Instead of being happy that we're
getting what we should have always had, they become bitter. I see it
happening and I don't like it.

Affirmative action plays a big role in their thinking. Frankly, I hate to see someone advanced as a token black, as a token female. So when you get a qualified black female into a position, she has to catch hell because the first person was unqualified. I think race relations have gone sour. You see it everywhere. All these things mixed up have caused a lot of fear that's turned to anger. For Americans as a whole and for whites in particular. Nobody likes to have their boat rocked, and it's now being constantly rocked. It seems to be a little too much at one time.

Black anger? I don't know if I'd call it anger. Today people realize: I don't have to take that. It's not like it used to be. You have blacks who say, "I wouldn't let a black person slap me upside my head, so why should I let a white person?"

I used to date somebody who was white and a lot of my friends were really against it. I don't think it's any big deal, frankly. Today I find I'm more comfortable in an all-black relationship because I really don't want to fight with *exterior* things. I guess if you were madly in love, it would be different because you'd feel, "The two of us can make it."

As a professional black female, it's upsetting because there are not too many black men in your world—so many in jail, without jobs—you feel you're being deprived. I don't think the average black female wants to be married to a white man. You have to deal with your parents, with your siblings, with your peers, with your job. It's really no big deal until you realize how the total world is viewing you.

A lot of black men have double standards. In college, a friend of mine was dating a white guy. The black men approached her and felt they should have some say-so. She told them to go to hell. They never did anything physically, but they harassed her. It was okay of course for a black guy to go with a white woman.

A lot of people of other cultures fail to understand why people turn out certain ways. A lot of black families dissolved because it was easier for the black female to obtain a job.* So it put her in a stronger position. She not only had to appease her husband's pride that was damaged in being jobless, but she also wanted her kids to have pride, be educated, succeed in life. This was passed on to the black daughter.

The same old prejudices that existed years ago still exist, but they've taken on different ways. The feeling was always there, but it's more open today.

---

* In Richard Wright's short story "Man of All Work," written in the 1930s, a black man dresses as a woman in order to get a job.

I didn't realize how bad it really was until I got older because my parents never really told me. I was confused a lot of times. In traveling to visit our grandmother in the South, we stopped at a motel. My father would come out and lie to us: "They don't have any rooms." We knew the Vacancy sign was on, but when he got to the door, it went off. Today, it shows up in other ways.

PEGGY TERRY

She lives in Chicago with her daughter and grandson. "My dad worked in the oil fields of Oklahoma, where I was born. He was a coal miner in Kentucky. None of these jobs was too steady, so we went back and forth."

I knew black people were around, but I didn't know where they lived, in Oklahoma City. In Paducah, we lived on the edge. We could sit on the porch and hear the singing from the black church. That's where I really learned to love gospel singing. I never made friends with any of them because I was brought up in prejudice. How can you be raised in garbage and not stink from it? You pick it up. It's like the air you breathe. There wasn't anyone saying any different. Until I heard Reverend King, I never heard any black person say, "I'm as good as you are." Out in the open.

I picked it up from everyone in the family. My father never changed. In one of our trips from Kentucky to Oklahoma in 1929, we went there in a Model T Ford. Daddy slid the car off into a ditch. We were just laying sidewise. This old black man came by on a wagon and offered to pull Daddy out. Daddy says, "Nigger, you better get your black ass on down the road. I don't need any help from you!" Here was my mother, pregnant—she had the baby two weeks after we got there—and three other little children in the car. I was eight. I remember it was so cold. Here's this bigoted man, cutting off his nose to spite his face. That's what a lot of white people do.

Oh, sure, my father was sympathetic to the Klan. So was my grandfather. When they started lynching black people, my grandfather quit. One of my earliest memories is in Littleville, the poor section of Paducah. Blacks and poor whites lived out there together. My grandfather had a buggy with a fringe around the top. We all met at Fletcher's grocery and went to the Ku Kluck Klan meeting. I remember all those hoods. I was about three. My mother says I couldn't have remembered it, but I do. I lost my shoe at that meeting.

Funny thing, my father was a strong union man and always fought the bosses. He always spoke out and stuck up for the workingman. Walked off many jobs, without a penny in his pocket. But he had this blind spot when it came to color.

1970
She recalls her feelings of white superiority, her discoveries.

I didn't like black people. In fact, I hated 'em. If they just shipped 'em all out, I don't think it woulda bothered me. If I really knew what changed me . . . I've thought about it and thought about it.

You don't go anywhere because you always see yourself as something you're not. As long as you can say, "I'm better than they are," then there's somebody below you can kick. But once you get over that, you see that you're not any better off than they are. In fact, you're worse off because you're livin' a lie. And it was right there, in front of us. In the cotton field, choppin' cotton, and right over in the next field, there's these black people—Alabama, Texas, Kentucky. Never once did it occur to me that we had anything in common.

After I was up here for a while and I saw how poor white people were treated, poor white Southerners, they were treated just as badly as black people are. I think maybe that crystallized the whole thing.

I didn't feel any identification with the Mexicans either. My husband and me were migrant workers. We were just kids. I was fifteen and he was sixteen. We were on the road for three years in the thirties. I got pregnant along the way.

We went down in the valley of Texas, which is very beautiful. We picked oranges and grapefruits, lemons and limes in the Rio Grande Valley. We got a nickel a bushel for citrus fruits.

I remember this one little Mexican boy in particular. I felt all right toward him. The Mexican men and the women I worked with, they were just spics and they should be sent back to Mexico. I remember I was very irritated because there were very few gringos in this little Texas town where we lived. Hardly anybody spoke English. When you tried to talk to the Mexicans, they couldn't understand English. It never occurred to us that we should learn to speak Spanish. It's really hard to talk about a time like that, 'cause it seems like a different person. When I remember those times, it's like looking into a world where another person is doing those things.

1990

I was living in Montgomery, Alabama, during the bus boycott and that absolutely changed my life. It forced white people to take a new look at the situation. Not all of them changed the way I did. It didn't leave you in the same comfortable spot you were in. You had to be either for it or against it. I saw grown white men pick black women up and throw them into buses trying to force them to ride. I saw Reverend King beat up at the jail. He would be released on bond and they would pick him up again on some trifling thing. They just kept repeatedly doing these things.

I remember one time he came out of jail in all white clothes. About five or six white men jumped him. Suddenly something says to me, "Two on one is nigger fun." That's what they always said when they saw two white kids beatin' up on a black kid. When I saw 'em beatin' up on Reverend King, something clicked.

When I heard he was gonna get out of jail, me and some other white women wanted to see this smart-aleck nigger. I'm so thankful I went down there that day because I might have gone all my life just the way I was. When I saw all those people beating up on him and he didn't fight back, and didn't cuss like I would have done, and he didn't say anything, I was just turned upside down.

I'm sure it didn't happen in just that instant. I'm sure there must have been something within me before that. You know, poor white women don't see too much of the violence. The men, they *do* the violence. We women knew it went on but we never *saw* it. This was my first seeing it, actually.

While the boycott was still goin' on, I came to Chicago. Down South, they always said that black people run the cities up north. They'd say, "You don't want to go up there, niggers run the workplace." I really expected to see that. I was ready to cope with it as best I could. But I didn't see any black people, except early in the morning. They were going north on the buses and streetcars and el trains to work in kitchens and homes. In the evening, they'd all go south. That was the only time I saw any of them.

The nearest I came to making a black friend in the South was this lady who lived behind us in Littleville. This was during the Depression. My dad was working on the WPA, but we still didn't make enough money to eat properly. This black women used to call us kids over and feed us. Maybe that's one of the things that lodged in my heart and in my mind, this woman was so good to us. In Chicago, I met this black woman, she from Texas, me from Oklahoma. We'd say we're black and white hillbillies. I learned so much from her. My second husband knew her and invited her for supper. I

didn't want it, but I didn't make a fuss. It had never happened to me, eating at
the same table with a black. It was a cold winter. She had on galoshes and my
husband helped take them off. I'm sitting there just wide-eyed. A white
person helping a black person off with her coat and boots. I was so mixed up.

With all my feelings and what happened in Montgomery, I was ready
to take a step forward and try to undilute all the damage. When I believe in
something, I act on it. I went down and joined CORE.* I was in jail before
the night came. They were having sit-ins at the Board of Education.
Protesting the Willis Wagons. Instead of letting black children go to
integrated schools, they had all these mobile trailers parked around the
black schools on the South and West Side. I was in jail, oh, at least half a
dozen times and loved every minute of it. I felt I was doing something. I
don't belong to any church but I'm a deeply religious person. I believe that
you act on your beliefs.

I enjoy picketing, too. I don't remember who we were picketing, but
this really well-dressed white woman said, "Why are you out there doing
this?" I had about six kids with me, mine and my girlfriend's. I said,
"Well, where else could I go and be treated with this respect that I've been
treated with by Reverend King, the Nobel Prize Peace winner? No white
Nobel Prize winner would pay poor white trash like me the slightest
attention. Reverend King does."†

We reached a period in the movement when black people felt they
weren't given the respect they should have. White liberals ran everything.
They made the final decisions. Blacks said, "We want to do it under our
own power." There was a rift, but not in my mind. I felt black people were
doing what they should be doing.

I heard about these white Southerners in Uptown. I didn't want
anything to do with them, because, oh God, I just got out of that jackpot.
But this black guy told me about JOIN—Jobs or Income Now. Either give
us a job or give us money. I went to a couple of meetings and I realized
that's where I should be. White people, go organize your own. There were
two black women in the group. Big Dovie Coleman and Little Dovie
Thurman. The rest were southern whites.

My great discovery was that poor people, no matter what color they
are, have a hard time. They should stop fighting among themselves and get
together. We were having a meeting one night. Both Dovies were there. It
did deteriorate into nigger this and nigger that. I finally said, "I heard all I

---

* Congress of Racial Equality.

† As she recounted this incident at an Operation PUSH rally which I attended, the
overwhelmingly black audience rose to its feet, cheering, stamping, and singing.

want to hear. You don't want to talk about welfare rights and decent housing. All you want to do is sit around and talk about niggers. I'm going home."

I'm walking down the sidewalk and I hear three or four women behind me, these hillbilly women. I think, oh God, they're gonna beat the heck out of me. They came up to me and one of 'em—she was no bigger'n a bar of soap—was crying. She said, "Peggy, we never thought of things like that. You come back and we'll talk about something else."

Peggy Terry has suffered a series of illnesses during the past several years and has been, to some degree, housebound.

I'm not into much of anything these days, but I do watch all the black talk shows. From what I hear on these programs, it's better for some but worse for the majority. That goes for poor whites, too. The good thing is that it's out in the open. We're talking about it. Before the boycott in Montgomery, nobody talked about it. All this garbage existed but we ignored it. The black is now highly visible, thank goodness.

Sure there's an antiwhite feeling among blacks. Not in everyone, but in a lot. To me, that's understandable. It's unspeakable what black people have gone through since they were first brought to this country.

What about the young blue-collar white guy, who's out of a job, which he attributes to affirmative action? He says, "I had nothing to do with the past. Why should I be the fall guy?"

Oh, but he did. Just by existing. Whites had always been given better treatment. Even coal miners like my father, who had a terrible time, were treated better than blacks.* The white in many cases is better qualified because he had all these years a better chance at an education, a better chance at a job.

I don't think it's up to any white person to say what black people want or how they go about getting it. I'm not talking about open warfare in the streets. But the kindest, gentlest man that could have led us into great changes was shot and killed. Reverend King. How come there's no white Martin Luther King?

---

* Lord, I'm so lowdown, baby,
   I declare I'm lookin' up at down.
   The men in the mine, baby,
   They all lookin' down at me.
      A Big Bill Broonzy blues, 1930s

If there was enough work for everybody, there wouldn't be so much animosity. We wouldn't have this fear of a black person getting a job, who may not be qualified. I think most black people before they get a job have to be doubly qualified. It's changed a lot, but not that much. The media makes a big deal of it whenever a black goofs up on a job, whereas "A white would have handled it. There's affirmative action for you." But what percentage of the workforce is really affected by it? We have a long, long way to go.

We look at crooked black politicians and say, "See? Once they get in, see what happens?" Black men are American men just like white men are American men. They go into a corrupt system. Why expect them to be different? They're not.

What makes white people afraid of blacks in power is that they know deep in their heart black people have not been treated right. They're afraid with the shoe on the other foot, it will all come home. No matter how much they may deny it, my God, they've got to know.

To a certain extent, we're all racists. Maybe not to the point of burning crosses, but we have attitudes that we don't even recognize in ourselves. I know I'll never be free of it. I fight it all the time. It's things you've grown up with all your life. I will never reach the point where I can sit with black people and be unaware of their being black. I'm always afraid I'm going to say something wrong, even with those I love and trust.

There were all those years when I said and believed horrible things. I'm afraid that sometimes that will come out. Remember, I was forty years old before I went into the civil-rights movement. Being a Southerner makes it worse because Southerners say what they think. A lot of times they say it *before* they think.

I was raised to hate Jews, too. They killed Christ and all that. It went along with being antiblack. I heard black people say that Jewish people should be thankful every day that black people are here, because if they weren't, the Jews would be catching it. When each wave of immigrants came here, there was always someone just above them. The way I see it, Jewish people are just above black people. There has to be a top crust and a bottom crust in our society. Somebody has to be on the bottom.

I think you become an adult when you reach a point where you don't need anybody underneath you. When you can look at yourself and say I'm okay the way I am. I don't need anybody underneath me. One of the things that keeps my class of people from having any vision is race hatred. You're so busy hating somebody else, you're not gonna realize how beautiful you are and how much you destroy all that's good in the world.

LITTLE DOVIE THURMAN

At forty-four, she has become an evangelist. "I always believed in God and in the Bible because my grandmother taught me that. But I wasn't living it. I used to go say, 'I'm a Baptist.' I'm a child of God now. It doesn't take a name to make me something. God loves everyone. I don't go along with any separatism. I go along with what the Word says.

"I'm a black woman who grew up in poverty and on a welfare roll. I was raised in the Pruitt-Igoe Projects in St. Louis. They blew them up, they were so bad. I moved to Chicago when I was eighteen with three kids. My husband was in Vietnam at the time. I lived in Cabrini-Green for a year and then moved uptown and have been here ever since."

I got involved in the civil-rights movement with southern white organizers. It was 1965. I had never seen poor white people in my life. I thought all white people were rich because the only ones I seen were doctors, lawyers, nurses, people like that. In St. Louis, the only people who lived in our projects were black. We were isolated.

I was organized by Rennie Davis.* My aunt, Big Dovie, had gone to the welfare office to get supplementary aid for my children. Rennie was passing out leaflets for JOIN.

As a child growing up, I hated the welfare system. I didn't like white caseworkers. I thought they were all like the one who visited my grandmother when I lived with her. [*Indicates a photograph on the end-table.*] That's her. She looks white, don't she? Very light-skinned. She's mixed—Irish, black, and Indian. They would tell her she needed to give me back to my mother, me, this little black child. My grandmother chased her out of the house with a knife. [*Laughs.*] She said, "That's my black baby." She always hated welfare because she had to lick their behinds, and she couldn't tell them how she felt or else they would cut our check off. I said, "When I get grown, Mama, I'm gonna whup me some caseworkers." I didn't like what they did to my mama. [*Laughs.*]

I saw this leaflet Rennie was passing out: "Are you tired of late checks, no checks, midnight raids, caseworkers' harassment? Come to a meeting." I couldn't believe they were saying this openly. My aunt said, "Oh, we need to go there. I'm tired of all this."

---

* He is celebrated as one of the Chicago Seven at the trial—an aftermath of the riots during the Democratic National Convention in Chicago, 1968.

We went to the meeting that night. I walked in and saw this smoky room. I will never forget. A group of people was sitting around, but I didn't see nobody black there. We hesitated. It was me and my aunt. "Do you think it's all right to go in?" I wasn't used to being around all those white people.

They was carrying on a conversation about welfare and they asked me did I have anything to say. I stood up and made a couple of statements. "I'm sick and tired of this welfare system. I don't know what to do about it, but I want to fight, too. It's doing the same to all of us." It was my first encounter speaking to a group of people, and I got a big hand.

They were southern whites, who didn't like blacks at all. I was surprised when they applauded. They were surprised, too. They invited us to come back again.

Rennie walked us to the car and he said, "They never reacted like that to black people before. They really liked you." I said, "I have never seen so many white people before, and they are poor." He said, "Didn't you know there were poor white people?" I said, "No." At the next meeting I was nominated to be chairperson. Just that quick.

What was most exciting was somebody wanted me. I didn't even know what a chairperson was. I had a lot inside me that I always wanted to say, but I never knew how to get it out. I didn't use to be a person that would speak out a lot. 'Cause I was angry that night, it just came out real easy.

I think what made it easier is that we were women. If we had been men, they would never have accepted us. White men have never had a problem accepting a black woman. I guess it's that male instinct. They have been programmed to think about a black man. I found out in later years that's the way the system has programmed us all. We are taught to think a whole lot of different thoughts about people that you really don't know anything about. You just fix it in your mind that they are like that.

That's one of the things I liked about the group. I found out that poor white people ate like poor black people. They eat greens, they eat chitlins, they eat grits. We found out they were living in some worse apartments than we were. By this time, from the civil-rights movement of Dr. King, things had become more noticeable about how black people were treated. And poor whites. And about myths.

The white women have that fear of the black women, 'cause they have been taught that they steal their husbands. They have been taught that the black man is a stud. You see, we have myths about each other. They all look at it as a sexual object when it is not. The other threat is that black people work harder for less and will take their jobs. They have been programmed so much to look at the color, they are not hearing the contrary. They are not seeing any insight into what's happening here.

Even a light-skinned person in the black race could make a bother. Not now. I used to didn't like the light-skinned—except for my mama, I loved her—because I wanted to be light-skinned. I would say, "This black man, he could have had a black woman, why would he go and get these white-skinned women? We ain't good enough for him?"

I went through some stages. First, I went through the identification stage of accepting that I am black. I didn't like to be called black because black was dirty in those days, before the black-power movement. Kinky hair wasn't cool. You needed it long and straight and flowing in the wind, right? [*Laughs.*] When I seen a man step out of his race, I couldn't stand him.

I went all the way from not wanting to be black to being superblack. All the way militant. I went all the way into a black nationalist thing after King was killed, 'cause that was hurt and anger. I gradually started coming back out of it because God opened my mind. And knowledge.

Before King was killed, I was beginning to look at the system: "Who is the culprit?" I was excited because I was learning things I didn't think I could learn. I never learned in school these new things. I was using the word "system" instead of the word "you." I was beginning to understand that there's somebody in control that I couldn't get to. It wasn't the person I could see.

I began to see things. If white people hate black people so much, how come there are poor whites like this? Why are they doing this to their own people? Why do they call them "white trash" when they are as white as they are? The police beat their heads as badly as they beat ours. If they were so much better, why are they treated so much worse?

I had a lot of questions that couldn't be answered. The more we come in contact with each other, I got more and more used to white people. Peggy Terry and I lived in the same building. I didn't feel funny when I sat next to her. I forgot she was white. Virginia Hackney, I was the first black woman she took up with. Till then, she felt she was better than black folk. We went to Kentucky together. I had to take care of some business and she come along. We rented a room and we didn't think about whether we were white or black. We was wondering why the clerk was looking at us so strange. He didn't want to rent to us.

My husband was in Vietnam then, but he was messed up when he came back. He had a nervous breakdown over that. Here is my husband over there fighting for his country and they don't even allow me an apartment over here. He couldn't even feed his family. Like I had on that sign I was carrying for JOIN. I wasn't thinking on the race side. My thoughts were on the poor versus the rich. I began to learn about class.

I wasn't just interested in getting my welfare check. I wanted to know: How do we fight the main guy? The main guy isn't just one person. It's a group of whos. You just can't point the finger at one. It's a little group of people controlling a whole nation and putting all our thoughts and desires under their will. I moved on this. I moved a little too fast.

I wanted to work with Dr. King when he was coming to Chicago. Me and my aunt. I used to sit in on Saul Alinsky's classes.* We began to meet other people from across the city. I began to seek more education. Me and Big Dovie were really eating up this knowledge. And speaking and everything.

We wanted to be involved in the national welfare-rights program with George Wiley. When he came to Chicago, we split from JOIN and set up Welfare Recipients Demand Action. We initialed it WRDA. Lots of whites in it, oh yeah! [Laughs.] We began to integrate—whites, blacks, some Indians, too.

Dr. King asked Big Dovie and myself: How do we feel about organizing other locals in Chicago? We became citywide organizers. That's how we became involved with Dr. King and in the march in Cicero. He canceled out on that one because of Marquette Park.†

Here I am, still doing my black awareness. By then I had converted to my Afro and my dashiki and my wire-rimmed glasses. I was Right On, Sister, all the way there. [Laughs.] I am a little different now, but I had to get my black identification then.

I stood up and people followed me. I just didn't stand for black. It didn't matter. If you were poor, I fought for you and just took no stuff.

I also worked with SCLC‡ and went down to Birmingham. I led the first welfare-rights demonstration down there. They had them dogs out, and the fire trucks. I had never been exposed to that before, and let me tell .you, I was scared. But I called myself bad: "I'll die fighting; you can kill me, but you can't eat me." Right on! [Laughs.] We went to the church where the bombing had taken place, with the four little girls. We stayed there for six weeks.

Back in Chicago, they wanted to put me out of the apartment because

---

* One of the pioneers in educating and developing community organizers.

† Site of a violent racial confrontation in Chicago, described by Jim Capraro; see "The Park" later.

‡Southern Christian Leadership Conference.

we had too many "undesirables" coming to my house, all these hippies. I was organizing these white kids, too. And the hillbillies, as they called themselves. All these folks are not supposed to get along, right? They were all walking together, saying they couldn't put us out. They raised so much Cain, marching around the building, the news media came out, until they sent an apology letter.

When Dr. King was assassinated, that changed things. I had gone to the South Side for a meeting—me, my aunt, and a white lady. When it happened, we were in this church. They had just beat up this white priest down there and they was saying "Dr. King is dead." When we got back to the North Side, a car got stickers that quick that said, HAIL, HAIL, THE KING IS DEAD. And they had this Confederate flag flying outside the window. I got so angry. What was King saying? What was he talking about? Here he is nonviolent, always praying, and they beat him up and they put him in jail and now they killed him. I was saying, "Give me a gun, give me a gun, give me something."

This is when I went into my supermilitant thing. I'm sick of white people. You try to help them, yeah, *help* them too, and look what they do to Dr. King. I just broke loose from all my white friends. I didn't want to see them, I didn't want to talk to them. All I wanted to do was get the one who killed Dr. King.

It took me three, four months before I could get myself reorganized. Finally, one of my white friends called me on the phone and said, "Don't hang up." She started talking: "Do you realize how many white people got beat up and died in those demonstrations?" She kept talking and she was crying. I knew this person. We had been very good friends. Her children and my children played together, ate together, we partied together. We demonstrated, we went to jail, we had fun—I cared about her and I didn't like not being friends. I had never looked upon her as white before. I can't hold anything when a person comes to me in a humble way. I said, "Maybe you're right." [*Laughs.*]

Then I had to begin all over again, do some soul-searching of my own. I hated not talking to my friends, 'cause we went through a lot together. I had to cool it and take a little break.

I could see just how black folk who have not had this opportunity like me to see things—I could understand how they could have the hate, from what they had been through. Somebody needs to get the word over, that there is somebody else going through the same thing, that ain't even black. It's the *system*. There is somebody doing it to all of us, and you just don't see them.

At first I couldn't understand why they hated Dr. King so much. Then

I began to see he wasn't just working with poor black and white. He was talking at unionizing and against the war, all kinds of issues. That gave him a force of power that they didn't want him to have. They had to get him. He knew that black power, white power, that wasn't going to work. As long as he was saying, "Let the black eat at the counter, let them go to the washroom," that was fine. But that didn't get at *it*.

I began to seek knowledge about the power. Who's got it? Who's benefiting from keeping people separated? It began to weigh upon me now, that I'm getting in a little danger myself, because I am stepping out of my place. It's all right when I holler for the welfare, fighting for poor black and white folk, but when you start stepping into another political realm, you begin to get a little dangerous. I was beginning to talk a different language.

I had done so much marching and demonstrating, I wore my heart valve out. I ended up having open-heart surgery twice. Thank God, I'm okay now. I just don't get overexerted. I've slowed down completely.

Things has also cooled out. People got sort of bought out with OEO funds, sold out. That's another trick, they buy out the organizers. I am not into organizing any more. I had got involved in organizing tenants but that's when I had that second surgery. Plus I got called to the ministry.

I wasn't seeking to do it. That was my time, my calling. It was the spirit of God. I had marched and demonstrated and protested so long, taking thousands and thousands of people to Washington, D.C. and we don't get heard. They act like we ain't even there. And things is getting worse and worse. There's gotta be something else.

The funny thing is I think the gap between white and black is lessening because we are all beginning to see the bigger monster. It's out there trying to devour all people. I left the colored thing and went into class separation. Now it ain't hardly a class separation no more. It used to be the poor, the middle class, the upper-middle class and the rich. Now it's down to the poor and the rich. The middle class is nothing but putty. To be used.

If we got to be saved, we would form programs that would not hurt people, 'cause we would be constantly aware of needs. We would take monies and put them in the right place instead of thinking how to kill somebody. Instead of making more warheads, nuclear heads, and fast-flying planes that don't work, we need to be making houses, we need food. We have no reason not to. God made enough on earth for everybody to eat, for everybody to live. But somebody is grabbing it all up.

If a person like me was in charge—Crime in the street? If everybody had enough of what they needed, what could they steal? They wouldn't even want it. You always want what you don't have and can't get. Or when it's made valuable. If everyone had diamonds today, they wouldn't be valuable. They wouldn't be worth nothing. Society makes us struggle and try to reach goals that we were never meant to be there for. That's not life. Material things won't save you when you can't breathe. You can't take a diamond and get your breath back. Material things won't wipe away age. The Bible says money is the root of all evil, if you apply it in evil ways. Money can be used in an okay way, but not if you *love* it. If you love money, you will take it and use it the wrong way. You will fight to get it, you will kill for it.

If you don't let money be your God and love your neighbor instead, you will ask what they need. I think people need reprogramming. We have been programmed to think little and to look so narrowly at situations. People need to start talking. You should look at who's got the money and what they're doing with it. There's a certain group that's not going to let anybody else in. It's beyond color.

Dope and prostitution? If it wasn't making money, it wouldn't be going on. If we took the profit out of dope, if that stuff was free for everybody, they wouldn't even want it. If poor people went on strike against crime—that's if their real needs was satisfied—what would happen to the police and the jails and the lawyers and the judges? They would be broke. There would be nobody to defend or lock up, if we would stop being used.

I don't trust no man to change things, because I look back over the history of the times, I hear them talking about revolution. If they keep having revolutions, why haven't things changed? Every time the ones who fight for the revolution win, they become the oppressors. That is not the way it's supposed to be. So it's something else, something man can't control. I don't even look at race anymore. Color of skin doesn't make a person good or bad. Dr. King saw that. I'm looking for the inner, not the outer.

In the end we are all going to be together one way or the other. We will all be in heaven together or in hell. How are you going to get separated then? At the end, people won't win when they're separated here on earth or up there. Or down there.

■ ■ ■ ■ ■

Welfare

LYNDA WRIGHT

A single parent, mother of four, ages twenty-four, twenty-two, seventeen, and seven. She is light-skinned.
Hers was a middle-class family; her father, a real-estate dealer.

Until I was twelve, I thought the whole world was black. I had a friend who thought I was white and I thought she was black, but we never discussed it. Finally we discovered *she* was white and *I* was black. It was a hard thing to find out.

I was unaware of any racial issue until I was a teen-ager. When I was in high school, we moved into a changing neighborhood. There were only a few blacks in school and they would call us names. At first I thought they weren't talking to me. My friend and I cried, knowing we'd never be the same from that point on.

Some time before, her parents had told her my father was different because he was educated and knew the right things to say. But now it was over. We used to eat doughnuts in the back room of their Swedish bakery with that wonderful smell. When they told her not to come around us anymore because we were different, how we cried.

Another time I felt it was when two policemen came to the house. They were looking for someone. When my father answered the door, they pushed him out of the way and bumped him into things. He told me to leave the room and I don't know what else happened. It was the first time I had ever seen him break down and cry. He has always kept a certain stature and felt he had been invaded and humiliated.

My mother was a very active woman until she lost her sight in an automobile accident. My father took care of her and me. I was an only child and they gave me a very good life. There was lots of love. My father died when I was nineteen. I guess that's when I decided to get married, looking for the security I had as a child. It was '65.

I took a job as a busgirl in a downtown restaurant. Then I became a waitress. They employed a lot of young Irish girls. One who had just come from the old country said I was the first black person she had ever met. "Are you really black? Your voice is so soft." I said, "I talk like Andrew, who is busing this table." "Oh, no, you're different." That's when I saw the station you were in mattered more than your color.

In the office where I later worked, the women would say, "You don't act like other black people." They tried to separate me from the others. My father was darker-complected than I was. When we were on a bus, they'd say, "Who is that little girl?" To me, they'd say, "He can't be your father." It hurt me as a child because they were always trying to separate my father from me. I loved him very dearly.

My husband was raised in housing projects and had a different view of life. I wanted to understand the difference, so I started searching. We began at the bottom. Our income was $100 a month. We lived with his mother. We worked very hard together and made a life for ourselves. He took two jobs and I worked outside and at home. We had two kids then. He died of a heart attack. We had no insurance, no anything. I lost everything.

I always wanted more education, wanted to go back to college, but my father had died. So I didn't. I kept striving, reading, tried to understand what was happening in the world. Especially in my children's school. I had married again and had two more kids. We had an excellent school but they started moving principals around. We went down to the Board of Education with our children, marched around, and went inside.

At the same time, people from Cicero had come down and they were marching. They were fighting their own cause: antibusing. We just happened to meet. We had several kindergarteners sitting with their legs folded outside the board room. One lady accidentally touched one of the children, jumped back, and wiped herself. I had never seen that kind of hate before. She looked at me and it was instant hate. I didn't understand it.

After seventeen years of marriage, it ended up in divorce. Though we had built up an income and had bought our first town house and had two cars, I lost everything again. I was at the bottom once more. I tried to find a job, but they said I was a bit old. Over thirty-five was old.

I became a welfare recipient. I started beaten down by the divorce. In the welfare office, I was beaten down more. They told me I was dumb and stupid, I should have planned my life out better. It was mental abuse. I became a number. I was never given any hello. It was: sit down and wait. That constant making you wait for everything just tears down your self-esteem.

I decided to go back to school, a child-development program. I had studied for three years, with three part-time jobs: at a day-care center answering the telephone; a moms-and-tots program for English as a second language; and bookkeeping at an insurance company. I decided I had to go full-time or it would be forever.

While on welfare, I got all A's at school and was invited to join the Phi Beta Kappa society, but I couldn't afford the $5 fee. I was on the dean's list and needed some money for extra materials. The caseworker refused, saying I didn't need to be in college anyway. She referred me to a program called WIN. They told me they had a really great job for me, running a jackhammer. I said, "I want to be a teacher. I'm good at it." They said, "We want you to be a jackhammer operator to get you off the rolls." I had taken tests, moved blocks around, and they said, "You qualify—for jack-hammer." I refused, so they wrote me up.

I've had fights over the amount of food stamps. I've had fights at grocery stations, fighting for somebody else when I saw someone palm off food stamps because they were elderly or because they just didn't under-stand how to count. It does have something to do along a racial line, but I think if you're poor, you're poor. It doesn't matter what color. Poverty takes a toll.

People begin to feel this is another way to live, a lower way to live. I think that poor families stick together. They have a heck of a lot more problems, so they use each other for strength. It can be used in the opposite way, too. They can be pitted against one another.

I noticed in my times of need, being able to get close to my family is what held us together. When we didn't have enough to eat, making that one pot of stew last for all day made us close. I remember an instance when my son said he needed gym shoes. On welfare, there's no money for gym shoes. Or you don't have the books that you need because you hadn't received the check.

When you start using food stamps, when you start living under the stigma of welfare, you begin to feel less than a human being. Children feel it, too. They feel it because they can't have the clothes that their peers have or they can't do the things they want to do. It's the cost of being able to afford a tutu, if the child is interested in dancing, or a tennis racket or anything to let them dream. Welfare tears down dreams.

I recall my son dropping out of high school. He started hanging out at a game room on the corner. I panicked: "He's going to be like the street people here." I read an article in a magazine that advertised pilot lessons for $25. I saved up $25 and figured if I could get him as high in the air as I could, some dreams were going to come from somewhere. He's now working for American Airlines in the ramp service. He's been moving up.

Because we didn't have any money to do things outside, we did things inside. We did a lot of talking, we did a lot of reading together. Maybe if we had been affluent we would have lost that. I think there's an empathy among poor people that may not be in other places. There isn't that kind of racial cut. It's not based on a feeling of what a person's color is. There's an awareness that sharing has to be done more. Property isn't an issue here.

I have a rainbow coalition of friends. It took a lot of growth on my part, because in the sixties I became hostile to whites. I saw hate on people I didn't even know. They didn't try to know me; they just hated me instantly. I had a lot of anger. I did many sit-ins. As I've grown older, I've mellowed. It's all right if somebody else hates. I don't really have the time. I don't try to avoid hate; I just understand it better.

During the summer, I worked with some Asians. I had to come face to face with my own racism. I heard that they came from Vietnam to take jobs away from poor blacks. I believed it. Finally I got a chance one-on-one. It was a Vietnamese kid, a teen-ager, who decided to just be my friend and forced me to face my own racism. He started teaching me the language, and that's what broke the ice.

A black girlfriend got me to work on a project with whites. I had to work with them every day to realize that I had built up a whole thing in my head about White America trying to kill us, to do us all in.

The good thing about the civil-rights movement was the sense of pride it gave us—finding power to change laws and do things for ourselves. The bad part was we didn't accomplish enough; we didn't educate the young as much as we needed to. We all went off on our own, taking that $50,000-a-year job and leaving the others to rot away.

I remember all those things in the sixties that drew people together. There's a sense of history that is lost. A sense of isolation people feel that's just put them out of the running. So they turned to the underground economy: drugs, alcoholism, just everything comes up to play. The recruitment age for drugs is nine to ten. There's a disconnection in my neighborhood, no sense of community.

When I was a little girl, my aunt who was a hundred and one would relate stories of how she lived as a slave, how she ran off to the reservation, how she learned to read when she was ninety-nine. I was given a sense of history our children seem to have lost. My children say to me: "You're bringing up old-folks things. Who cares what went on in the past?" I think it's necessary.

There are all sorts of people in my neighborhood, and they get along because they have to survive. That's the common thread. I don't sense the kind of racism that I felt in the more affluent places I've been. I think it goes along with money. I don't have to pay attention to what's happening with you unless you get in my face and steal something I have. But there's another thread to poverty: divide and conquer. People fighting over jobs, misunderstandings. So I feel hopeful and sad at the same time.

I've lived with racism and had hoped that my children wouldn't have to. I don't think they're as racist as I was and probably won't go through the same fights. But I'm not sure they have a sense of pride and culture about their race. That bothers me a great deal. They feel that all of us have an equal chance and if they want to get somewhere, they'll get there. I'm afraid at some point they're going to be hurt.

The prejudice I have is toward people who take advantage of others. I associate racism with power. Power that can be used for good is bad in some people's hands. I still have quirks. I say to my kids, "You're going to go out with who? And they're what?" [*Laughs.*]

There was a time when I resented a white woman with a black man. I felt we should come together and stick together, and we'd be stronger. Now with such a diverse population, there's no way separation will work. I think we have to consider every culture in the world, if we're to be really strong.

When I walk into a room and there's a black male, I worry about where his ego is. He has a sense of being powerless. When a black woman says something that seems powerful, they feel threatened. Over the years, I've seen relationships between black males and white females. He's been able to take charge, have a sense of power. Black women are more matri-archal, heads of families. So when he comes into that setting, he has to deal with a powerful woman.

I have a problem with my sons. It's a constant battle for me not to step on their egos or come down on them. I am a very strong mother and will do things they feel I shouldn't be doing to them. I have to walk a very thin line. I had to decide where I'd allow him to think he had control over me. I'm always on guard.

If I had the power, the first thing I'd do is declare Cultural Days: people would have to live in the other person's shoes for a day. There would be projects to include all races. I'd be more creative in jobs. There are not enough places for kids to go to just to hang out and talk about their problems. There certainly are not enough treatment centers.

I wanted to stop the drugs in the neighborhood: a group of moms to walk around school and make sure the kids were home. One day the dealers came to my door and stood there. Didn't say anything. They just let me know they knew who I was. The cops had come up and shined the light on us like we were the criminals. Yeah, the cops. We think it was to point us out to the drug dealers. Common sense makes me careful now, but I don't worry.

I've lost a lot of kids in the neighborhood. Just a month ago, a friend of my son was killed. When I first came to this neighborhood, he was a child I was working with. I remember the time I took a bunch of them bowling. They got excited because it was a fabulous place. They started running to the elevator and the cops came from everywhere. Surrounded them real fast. All we did was bowl and have a good time.

I worry a great deal when I see a patrol car. Every child in this neighborhood has been harassed at one point or another. Some deserved it, some didn't. I pray for my sons every night.

MARGARET WELCH

"Everyone thinks that if you try hard enough, you can make it in America. I thought so too, but when I found myself a widow at age thirty-three, with two children to support, and forced to go on public aid, I discovered how the welfare system works.

"I have tried hard to make a better life for myself and my girls. I have studied hard to get an A average after being out of school for sixteen years, and it hurts to have to give up my dream, but the system won't let me out of the 'welfare class.' There are a great many of us who want out of the welfare class, but the system won't let us out."

Margaret Welch, Letters to the Editor,
Chicago Tribune, *March 26, 1987*

She had come to Chicago five years ago from Tennessee. Her second husband "walked out," leaving her with two girls, nine and five.

The image people have of public aid is black women with a lot of kids. Before I went on public aid, I had that impression: the more babies you have, the more money you get. I realized that you get three dollars a day if you have another baby. That's not going to raise a kid. I thought they were freeloaders, who like to live off other people. But when I was forced on public aid, my opinion changed. I was on an even keel with them. We all sat there in the office and waited five or six hours at a time. They weren't getting special treatment. They were having hard times, too.

What gets me is this:

I'm on public aid. I'm trying to stay in school and apply for all these scholarships. Blacks and Hispanics have hollered so much, they've got these scholarships. Even single white men can get scholarships if they have kids. But it's hard for a single white woman to get a scholarship, because you're not a minority.

If you're a woman, you're supposed to take care of your kids if you're left alone with them. If men are left with kids, it's "Oh, that poor guy." All the women in the neighborhood are cooking and bringing him food and finding hand-me-down clothes for the kids and babysit for free, so he's not stuck at home. Everybody's helping him. But if you're a white woman and your husband has walked out leaving her with kids—forget it.

I've just registered for my last year in nursing school. I won't be able to go back because the scholarship I got last year was just denied me. They said it was a Hispanic scholarship and enough Hispanics applied, so I lost out. It just hit me. This week. I can't afford the tuition, so I·don't know if I'm ever going back.

At this school, they have the American Indian club that gives scholarships. Even a Thai club. Of course there are black scholarships. But none for the single white woman. My dad was half-Cherokee. Maybe I can qualify as a half-Cherokee. [Laughs.]

I went on public aid when my job at the hot-dog stand ended and my house burned down. I lost everything. On public aid, they gave me $711. That was supposed to get me an apartment, replace all my furniture and all the kids' clothes. The cheapest apartment called for a $600 deposit. It doesn't leave anything.

I noticed a poster on the wall: public aid helps returning to school. I had a GED. I took the test and placed into the highest class. They were telling me about the scholarships and said I was a cinch. I got one last year and carried straight A's. But I found out last week I'm not a minority and out.

There goes my 86 average and my dream of becoming a registered nurse. It's something I've always wanted and never thought possible. I got so close. "I'm sorry, but this time we have enough Hispanics."

This is the first time in my life I'm really mad this way. It's a new feeling for me, and I don't know how to deal with it. My boyfriend is Mexican and my best girlfriend is Puerto Rican and very black. I've never been prejudiced, but why the hell are you doing this to me? I've been through enough. I was widowed at seventeen and married again and my husband took off, leaving me with two kids. Just because I'm white, I don't get something?

Always on TV, whenever you hear blacks making speeches, it's

"White people won't let us do this or that; we're put down." All of a sudden, they're giving me the short end.

Who is "they"?

The minorities. No, I don't mean that. I'm not saying they're doing bad. They band together and speak out when they're hurt and get something done. Right now, I'm just upset. I'm mad at people in general. Women in my position are being denied something because of the racial issue. It's crazy.

I *never, never* had any racist feelings. In that small country town, I never distinguished between people because of color. There's black people living in my building. We get along great. I've never looked at myself as better than they are. But with this scholarship thing, I *deserved* it. Just because their skin's darker than mine, why should they get it and I don't? It's the first time I've had feelings like this and it makes me very uncomfortable. All this happened last week and it's hard to deal with. I'm really torn apart. Last week, I was on the point of saying, "To hell with it. I'm going back to Tennessee with my girls to raise corn and beans."

I feel like I've been robbed of a chance to finish school. I had it counted down. I already had a job promised me in a hospital. I would be making $15 an hour for the first time in my life. I could feed my kids without begging, borrowing, or stealing. Selling food stamps is considered stealing. I get $308 a month to live on. My rent's $250. So that leaves me $58. You can't pay lights and gas and everything else. So you end up selling a few food stamps to buy laundry detergent.

For food, you buy a lot of rice and flour, make tortillas. That's all your kids have. They're the ones who are punished, whether you're white, black, or anything else. I was so sure that in a year, I'd have a job where I could feed my kids without feeling the way I do. I wouldn't have them laughed at in school because they get free meals. They wouldn't have to suffer that any more. Now . . .

My Puerto Rican black friend and I always applied for the same scholarships. We were always among the top in grades. She was straight A's all the way. We were promised jobs at the same hospital. We were in school together since the first day. This year, she got the scholarship, I didn't. She came to the house and said, "Don't be mad at me." I'm not. She's still my best friend. It's just—*why*?

We were sitting in my truck. I told her I got my letter. She ran out, checked her mail, and she's gotten hers. We didn't open them until we were together. She could tell by the look on my face. "What's the matter?" "I didn't get it. Did you?" She mumbled, "Yeah," and wouldn't let me see her letter. For a minute I was so mad at her. "I just want to kill you." [*Laughs.*] We're still great friends. I'm glad she's making it, she deserves it.

I think blacks are going ahead. They speak out, they fight for their rights, and they're getting them. We're almost afraid of them and let them push us back.

If you see one black guy walking by, it's okay. But if you see three or four standing on a corner, you cross to the other side of the street. I was mugged about two years ago by a couple of Hispanic guys. Now if I see several Hispanics standing together, I cross the street.

Suppose there were three or four tough-looking white guys?

I'd just walk through them. I'm a tough ol' hillbilly girl. I worked in taverns as soon as I got old enough. I wore my jeans and cowboy boots and I'd jump in the middle of the barroom with any of them, grab my pool stick. I've never been scared of a fight. I'm a big woman. I can handle myself.

Not far from my house is a motorcycle gang, Hell's Henchmen. They have their Harley-Davisons, tattoos, and beards. When I was tending bar, I'd walk past them at two, three in the morning by myself and not think anything of it. But there's no way I'd walk by a black club.

I myself really don't feel hostility, but I feel that a lot of whites are becoming more and more afraid of blacks. It's like "We're letting them learn to read and write and they're taking over." I don't feel that. My Mexican boyfriend says the neighborhood is running down. He gets mad because the blacks band together and push you around. I argue with him, we disagree. So we don't talk much about it.

Somehow, people have to talk about this. You shouldn't feel "I'm too dumb to get up and say something"; talk in your words, say whatever. If enough people talk, good ideas may come out of it. Nobody wants to give up whatever power they got. To me, that's the whole thing, power.

You see the old slave-day movies. They were scared of their masters, their owners. They did what they were told. It seems like they've almost turned the tables. It's like we're scared to stand up against them now.

In the small town where I was from, we had our part and there was nigger town. They stayed there and never came out. They'd just come in, get groceries, and leave. They just didn't mix. They didn't bother anybody and we didn't bother them. When I moved to the city, everybody was together all of a sudden.

Would you prefer it the old way?

No-o-o-o! When I went to City-Wide College, my supervisor was a black lady. She just knew when there was something wrong. I'd sit at my desk half-crying. I'd gotten my second five-day notice that month to move out of my apartment. One of my classmates told her. When I came back from my break, there was a check on my desk to cover my rent. I tried to pay her back, but she said, "No, that's my gift to you." I would never have dreamed there was a black person like that when I was in Tennessee.

I don't believe black people should be pushed back. But I don't feel because I'm white, I should be either. It goes both ways. I don't think the gap is that big on a street level, not in my neighborhood. But when you get into the bureaucracy, business, and school, it's those big people making the noise.

I myself am not intimidated. I would never have written that letter to the *Tribune*. I wouldn't have made it through three years of college. I got married when I was sixteen and dropped out of high school. I never dreamed I'd go to college. Here I am two semesters away from my graduation. It looks like I'm stopped for a while, but you can't sit back and never open your mouth.

■■■■■

On the Job

JOSEPH ROBINSON

He is president of the local union of the United Steel Workers of America. Its members are white, black, and Hispanic. "I came to Chicago from Memphis in '64 and went to work in the mills right away. I work in a small shop now. We've been on strike for five weeks."

He is divorced, "but my son (Kevin Robinson), who's nineteen, lives with me now. I got a thirty-year-old daughter by an early marriage."

As far as race goes, it depends on what neighborhood you're in. I live near South Chicago. There are whites that retired from the steel mill. When the blacks moved in, they didn't move. We get along just fine.

You go to Cicero Avenue, just across the river. I stop at a joint there to have a beer. I meet a different breed of white. I immediately know what they feel about me as a black man. Just my appearance in the place. Not that I'm a threat to them or anything. It's just my mere presence does something. It turns them into a different breed of person.

In this strike I'm going through now, there's a fellow, he subscribes to one of these racist magazines. *White Power* or something. A young fellow, most of them are. Yet we're on the same picket line.

A scab is a scab is a scab. You don't call an Italian scab a dago. You don't call a Polish scab a polack. You don't call a black scab a nigger. A scab is a scab is a scab, in my neighborhood.

I have a real gripe against the top hierarchy of the AFL-CIO in Chicago. They moved a trade school out of the city to keep from training young black men to be electricians. I see abuse and misuse of their power. They bring in a few blacks they can control. There's a white bastion, a good-old-boys' club. They're just as racist as anybody.

You got people teach this race hate. Skinheads, punks, they're a different breed. You got Louis Farrakhan. I think he's a bullshit artist, I really do. He's brainwashing a lot of young minds. Some of his principles are great, but he's warping people's minds. He's no better than that guy down there teaching Nazi stuff. The owner of our plant lays these magazines around where his white workers can get hold of them. He lets them take them home with them and read them.

Some of the young guys on the picket line have his concept, but I think they're growing up. They're learning who their enemy really is. It's not the black man, it's not the Hispanic. It's this guy, the owner. Some of these guys voted for me as president. They treat me with respect.

I can be standing there and they will forget that I'm a black man. A black man will walk down the street and they holler, "Hey, nigger." I'm standing right beside them. It's like I blend right in with them for a minute. [*Laughs.*] They forget I'm black. The other black guy, passing by, is a nigger.

When I hear these guys calling, "Nigger," my head roars up inside me but I can't let it defeat me. I've learned to live with it. Sure, it disturbs me when somebody calls a black man a nigger. It disturbs me when somebody calls an Italian a wop. Some of them will still be racists when this strike is over, but I feel good about a couple of them. They've been raised in that environment but they're growing out of it. If I can save one or two . . .

I got a son nineteen years old. He's gonna follow after all the winds. That's what you do when you're nineteen years old. So he joined Farrakhan and his group. I said, "Man, that's the biggest trick in town. That guy ain't about what he say he is." They wanted him to sell their newspapers and turn the money in. I told him I thought they were bullshit. You don't need this kind of thing in any neighborhood, whether it's Farrakhan or the guy who preaches Ku Klux Klan stuff. The boy switches back and forth. I followed the wind when I was nineteen, so I don't hold that against him.

The thing that's killing the neighborhood is drugs. The jobs aren't there for the black kids. For some reason we've never been able to build any base within our neighborhood. We'll go to a white shopping center and spend like hell, but if I build one here and sell the same product, I'd probably have to shut the doors in three weeks. I can't explain it. I'd say it's jealousy.

I was about fourteen years old, living in Memphis, when the civil-rights movement started. *Brown versus the Board of Education*. We were kids; we heard, Pretty soon you can go to any school you want to. Two, three years later, the sit-ins started. I got myself arrested in them. I wouldn't stand in the bus, even though the law hadn't been passed in Memphis. I got thrown off a couple of times.

I saw the first black busdriver hired in Memphis. I saw the first black policeman in Memphis. So I grew up with it. I was nineteen years old, the same age as my son, when the civil-rights movement was at the height. The Freedom Buses stopped in Memphis, going to Mississippi. I was right there.

I read extensively. I believe in what Gandhi taught. I believe in what Dr. King taught. My family was that way. I come from a Christian back-ground. I was raised in the church never to hate. All these things were instilled in me from the time I was little. I think the church played the greatest role. Baptist. I still go to church—not as often as I should. But I'm still a God-fearing Christian and a union man.

The first strike I was ever involved in was in that ice-cream factory in Memphis. I was eighteen, just got the job. I went right out with them. It was the funniest thing. We strike, whites and blacks, but we couldn't eat in the same cafeteria. It was crazy. But we got together and struck them. [*Laughs.*] We stayed on strike an hour and a half. Got a fifty-cent raise. It was June in Memphis, ninety degrees. That's the perfect time to strike. [*Laughs.*] Great-est thing that ever happened. I got involved in the union then.

Do you ever socialize with the white guys who walk the picket line with you today?

Yeah, I have a beer with 'em. But some of them, they still—if you got any kind of instinct you know when they don't want you, feel uncomfortable with you, even when you're together in this.

There's something I found out about young white guys. You can socialize with them if there are no women around. The minute that women come into play, it's a different setup. White women. That divides us deeper, even on the picket line. We've had one of the white guys, his girlfriend comes out there. She's a nice kid, helps out and everything, a friendly girl. But it tenses. You and the guy are this close, but if she comes, we divide. It happens at Christmas parties, golf outings, any event I've been to.

I've discussed it with black guys. If you're in a group with white guys, having a beer together, and a white woman comes around, the whole perception changes. If she sits down and shows more attention to me than to him, well, that's when the tension sets in.

My fear is that this guy's gonna do something to me when the ball's in his court. It's a different story when it's in my court. There are no fears.* It's a sexual fear, I guess. That's what you'd call it. A black woman around wouldn't have the same effect of divisionness. A black man's fears are different. Our feelings. It's, Why should I let them get away with something and I don't say nothing about it?

There's a strange feeling because of things some people would do if they catch you in a white neighborhood by yourself. But there's different kinds of white neighborhoods. Different kinds of people. I'm welcome at Eddie Sadlowski's house at three o'clock in the morning, but I'm not

---

* We are seated in a booth at Turner's Blue Lounge: my wife, Romila Thapar, and I. It is in the heart of Chicago's South Side ghetto. Dr. Thapar, a visiting Indian scholar, lovely in her sari, is eager to hear some of the city's blues artists. J. B. Hutto, with whom I'm acquainted, is performing this Sunday evening. It is but ten days after Martin Luther King's assassination, not the most propitious time for a visit to these precincts.

Two young men, feeling no pain, join us in the booth—Willie Hightower and Jimmy Johnson. I have no idea where they came from. I order a round of drinks for everyone. Eugene O'Neill's Hickey had nothing on me.

Mr. Turner comes over. He orders Willie and Jimmy to leave at once.

Two young cops appear, one white, one black. They are quite friendly. They invite Willie and Jimmy outside, to talk things over. No sweat. Willie suggests we keep the drinks fresh until they return. "Fine," I say. Romila and my wife don't think it's fine. They suggest we've heard enough blues for the night.

Outside, our sudden companions and the police officers are chatting amiably and laughing. The four wave at us. As we cross the street to the car, I call out, "See you around, Willie Hightower and Jimmy Johnson." "Can't you leave well anough alone?" my wife inquires. Does she know something I don't know?

Willie and Jimmy are in the back seat with Romila. How did that happen? My wife looks at me. I look back at them. "Where do you guys wanna be dropped off?" "We're goin' with you," says Willie. "We're heading for the other side of town," I say. "That's okay," says Willie. "You came to see our neighborhood, we'll go see yours." How do you answer that one?

As we approach the white section of the city, Willie's voice changes. It had a singing sound before; now it is strained. "You ain't gonna let 'em jump us, are you?" He and Jimmy have in that moment become *our* hostages.

Talking to Myself (1973)

welcome in the neighborhood. And it's only six blocks from where I live. The river divides.

When the mills were booming, they lived in my neighborhood, which is now mixed. They moved across the river, but their uncles stayed here. They weren't able to migrate because of financial problems. The retired steel worker couldn't buy that house because he's on fixed income. He couldn't run away, and finds himself locked up in a situation. So he adjusted to that. He accepted the neighborhood for what it was worth. Whites, blacks, and Mexicans all learned to mingle and live together.

If I go across the bridge and try to buy a house over there, I better have a fireman out there to guard it, even today.

Blacks, in their seventies and eighties now, were grown men when I was a kid. They felt they had to have a special respect for whites. A kind of fear. When my generation came along, we didn't feel we had to have that fear. 'Cause we were after World War II. I was six years old when the war ended. What I grew up to was Jackie Robinson getting into baseball. So I knew there was a chance. *Brown versus the Board of Education.* Soldiers in the door in Little Rock in '57, to get a kid in school. Oxford, Mississippi. Those are the things I grew up with.

I knew I didn't have to have that fear that my father had. My grandmother, God rest her soul, was seven years old when slavery was over. She used to tell me stories of horror, that men would catch men and beat them for no reason—grown men, like they were kids. I didn't grow up with these fears.

My son's outlook is even stronger than mine. What I didn't instill in him, he learned in the streets. I never taught him hate.*

Kid in a project—hell, he might not see a white man till he's nineteen years old, unless he's on TV. All he knows is that's your enemy. He's never met him. Why should I hate you if I don't know you? It's something screwed up in my head.

It's in the economic struggle that each person has learned they need each other to survive. The old ones, who've retired and have worked together, have learned over the years to intermingle. The fear of sex is not there, because it's an older neighborhood. I think that has a lot to do with it. You don't see nineteen-year-old kids in South Chicago.

On the West Side, all black, I got fears of being stuck up. They don't

---

* My sixteen-year-old son is not the person I was when I was sixteen. He has manly responsibilities. And he doesn't want any shit. When I was sixteen, I wasn't afraid to die. But the kid, sixteen now, is not afraid to kill.

Robin Langston, in *Hard Times* (1970)

care if you're white or black in that neighborhood. Poverty made it. The trickle-down that was supposed to trickle down didn't trickle down.

The wealth of this country has to be divided differently. They play off one race against the other. That white kid on the picket line got the same problems as that black kid who don't have a job. He's on strike because his wages aren't what they're supposed to be. All the while, the corporate heads take the money and invest it in foreign countries. America's not gonna last the way it's going. Unless there's a turnaround, we're going down the drain. Bush talks of a kinder, gentler America, but he don't want to give a $4.55-an-hour minimum wage. If people don't work, they'll steal—white, black—because you ain't gonna go hungry, especially a kid, eighteen, nineteen. I didn't do it when I was eighteen. I had a fear of going to jail. Kids today have no fear of going to jail. Kids don't have the fear of dying anymore, as they did when I was a kid. What's to lose?*

But what really makes me angry is when workingmen belittle themselves. They don't know how intelligent they are. I go back to this strike. We had scabs cross the line. I say to the guys, "You think they're gonna run the plant efficiently as you do? These greenhorns." The workingman underestimates himself. They're the smartest people in the world. Bosses don't invent the ways to make things better—working people do. If these people wouldn't put themselves down, they'd be the greatest force on earth.

BEN HENSLEY

He and his wife live in a bungalow on Chicago's Southwest Side, a predominantly white, blue-collar community. Their two grown daughters live elsewhere.

---

* If I'm feeling good and want to have my morale lowered, all I have to do is drive down Madison Street on a bright, beautiful day and look at the throngs of unemployed youngsters in their weird dress looking mean at each other. You see kids hanging around, hating themselves as much as they hate others. This is one thing that has contributed to the ease with which gangs kill each other. Another nigger ain't nothin'.

In Englewood, we had a little bay window. We weren't trying to leave the ghetto. We were going to stay there. We were sitting, watching TV. We had our windows open. There was a walkway alongside. I heard what appeared to be an explosion. I had one of these Mattel guns. Have you seen one of these toy guns? They're very realistic. It looked like a high-powered rifle. I grabbed this gun because I didn't know if somebody was trying to break in.

Here was an unarmed black kid sauntering in the gangway. He had evidently leaped up, hit a light bulb, and made it explode. I thought when he saw me coming down with the gun drawn—it looked like the real thing—he would have held up his hands and said, "Don't shoot, mister. I was just playing." He didn't do a thing but look at me out of the side of his head and say, "What are you excited about, motherfucker? Go ahead and shoot." He didn't give a damn. This kid went away into anonymity.

Vernon Jarrett, in *American Dreams: Lost and Found* (1980)

For the past twenty-three years, he has worked as a chauffeur for corporate executives. He is forty-five years old.

I consider myself a Southerner. My father and uncles were coal miners in Harlan County, Kentucky. There wasn't much of a racial problem. The few blacks worked the mines—same wages, same stores. But they lived in colored camps and were not always treated right.

My mother always corrected me when I'd say "nigger." I didn't know it was an insult, because the boys I played with always said it. She said I should say "Negroes." I realized they were different when we rode the bus to school. They had to ride another seven, eight miles to the colored school. Some of the black children were very small and they had to get up much earlier than I did.

I never had much of an attitude toward blacks, not as much as my friends. My father was a very fair man, not educated. He used to tell me they were mistreated in the mines, especially before the union. He said, "You wouldn't want to trade places with them. They have a hard time." They'd give 'em the worst places: where the top was loose, where the water was seeping through, was up to their ankles, where they had to pump, and take the slate down where it was dangerous. When it cleared up and the top was solid—good and dry—the superintendent would give it to the whites. My father noticed that.

I never went into Georgetown, the colored section. I was a little afraid. It dawned on me why I felt that way. I thought if I had been treated by them like a lot of them had been treated, and they came in my neighborhood, I might be violent. I thought they probably didn't like whites and they had reason not to. I must have been twelve, but I felt that even after I was a teen-ager.

I remember an incident in 1942 . . . '43? There was an election and this black man had supposedly taken money to vote a certain way. They killed him and threw him out of a car. Nobody was ever convicted. Something I remember. I could hate people for a long time after that.

Later, when I worked in Nashville as a helper on a delivery truck for Fred Harvey Department Stores, a black fellow was working with me. He was older and had been there more years than me. They gave me the job driving and I was his boss. He knew the area better than I did, had to tell me where to go. He'd been there when I was hired on.

I wondered about it, but never mentioned it. I wondered if he resented me, but he was always nice and pleasant. When we had lunch, I'd drop him off at a place where he could eat. I could eat anyplace I wanted to. He never complained, but I couldn't help thinkin' about it.

We were movin' something into an alley. It was hard. He just got in the truck and moved it back. The other helper said they don't trust him with the truck. It seemed to me he was trustworthy. This was 1954.

In '61, I came to Chicago. Times were tough. I was washing dishes, working on loading docks. Then I got a job driving a bus for the CTA. A couple of black drivers were my teachers, they gave me tips on the streets and neighborhoods.

I worked on a run where everybody getting on and off were black. I never had much trouble. They were pretty much like everybody else. On Friday nights, they might have celebrated more, but were too busy to pay any attention to me.

Only two incidents. There was a big accident at an intersection. Traffic was tied up. I thought if I could switch the trolley, I could get by. I took the changer, but left the little leather bag with the transfers. Two young black kids grabbed the bag and run off.

Once a whole bunch of teen-agers got on. They were drinkin'. Only three paid their fare. The rest went in the back and sat down. We had a buzzer. Police see the light and come on. Two white policemen came. Which three paid their fare? I couldn't tell. So they made them all get off. I felt bad for the guys who paid the fare.

People discriminate without knowing it, a lot of times. I'll never forget. I'd quit the CTA to get the job I got now. I still had the uniforms. I put on some weight and they were too small for me. Good clothes. The garbage truck was down the alley, two whites and a black guy. I offered the clothes to him, he got offended. "I don't take used clothes. I work and buy my own clothes." I told my wife about it. She said, "Of course, he was offended. He works hard, you pick him out and say, 'You need something given to you. You poor rotten man.' " I didn't mean to insult him, but I thought he's a black man, got more children, needs 'em worse. I made a judgment. I guess that's part of my racism, not realizing.

I think all of us have some racism in us. I don't get out on any protest line, but I know I profit from the system. I got that job at the expense of that black man in Nashville. I didn't refuse it even if it was unjust. I needed the money. I may have felt bad about it, but I took it. I guess life's that way.

I think it's very fair to have affirmative action. For hundreds of years the black people—parents, grandparents, back to slave days—have had negative action. So they're not starting even.

What about the guy who says, "I had nothing to do with slavery. I wasn't even here. Why should I pay for it?"

He's probably like me. He profited from the system. They been turned down for years and years, and he come up behind them and got it. I never owned any slaves, but I profited from that guy in Nashville. I don't know how many guys he trained for that job.

Affirmative action should take place for a hundred years. There's blacks who've never done anything but chop cotton and can barely read their name. You couldn't expect their son to catch on right away.

Of course if it's you who are gonna lose the job, you feel bad about it. When jobs are scarce and times are hard, there's a grievous feeling about affirmative action. It gets more static in hard times.

Racism will be around for a long, long time. The biggest reason is economic. If a man invested his life's work in his home and felt somebody was gonna move in and drag the value down, he'd be concerned. The blue-collar man is more worried than professional people. "I'm not makin' big money. If anything goes down, I wind up with nothing." If he had somebody like him next door, it would be all right. [*Laughs.*]

I think most white people realize, deep, deep down, that that other person is just as good as they are. But they don't want to be saddled with something so hard. They like to conform. It's easier. No matter how good a black man was, he was the bottom. He could be a hardworking man, take care of his family and treat everybody right, some people would look at him as just a nigger. No matter how tough it might be, you could always say, "At least I'm not a nigger." If you were an alcoholic, you could reform. If you went to prison, you could turn over a new leaf and people would soon forget about it. But if you're black, you're relegated to the bottom.

I feel hopeful, but it will take years and years and years. If we give it a chance. Otherwise, never.

TASHA KNIGHT

Three flights up. An apartment in a six-flat building. There are boxes of books, still unpacked; it is obviously newly rented.

The neighborhood is multicolored and multicultural: Hispanic, African, Asian, Appalachian, European, Native American; a United Nations enclave. Its economic strata: poor to lower-middle-class.

"I find it exciting and cosmopolitan. I like being around different cultures. I learn so much."

She had lived in Cleveland before moving to Chicago. It was an integrated community. "There were synagogues and kosher stores every-where. You know the typical prejudice against Jews. I heard it from other black children: 'I don't like Jews because they killed Jesus.' I would go to the kosher bakery and they were very friendly. Nobody ever treated me badly. I think black anti-Semitism has been greatly exaggerated. It's not so much anti-Jewish as antiwhite.

"I've gone to predominantly white schools all my life. I was at Case–Western Reserve for four years and graduated with a degree in English, though I had two years engineering and one year math.

"In tenth grade, I was approached by this group that provides help for minority students who are interested in business engineering. I had very good test scores in everything. They said, 'Oh, wow, a black woman engineer. You could write your own ticket.' I was what, fifteen? I didn't know what I wanted to be. I switched to English.

"I worked as a technical writer in Cleveland for a while. Then I decided to see the world. On my way, I stopped off in Chicago and have been here ever since. I write software documentation for a trade magazine. I'm the only black person in my department."

I get along with my coworkers very well. They're a lot of fun. Sometimes I feel uncomfortable because I don't see anybody black. I've made it a point not to get involved in politics, because I notice how racial it is. I can feel it every day. It's difficult for me to talk politics with my coworkers because they usually take one side. I really try to see every side, but sometimes I feel these people don't understand what it's like to *be* the only black person somewhere.

Most people I work with are about my age. I've seen them in college. They've never had any reason to associate with black people and they really don't know them. They've never had any real desire to know them. Sometimes they'll say, "We were at this party last night and we got lost. We ended up in Cabrini-Green* and I thought we were going to die." Or on the South Side. They say it in front of me.

It infuriates me when I hear stuff like that, because they seem to think that's all black people have to do is sit around waiting for white people to jump on. They don't seem to realize that the majority of people in the ghetto are decent people. They're just victims of a handful of thugs, the gangs, the drug dealers. They are people who love their children, they work hard, trying to overcome all the difficulties that beset them. I hear this stuff

_____
* A public housing project.

and it makes me mad. Sometimes I'll get sarcastic and say, "Black people are just waiting for white blood. We crave that stuff." They look at me, like, Excuse me, and they walk away. They don't realize I'm being ironic.

This one woman passed up a job to sell books in the inner city. Even though she had a company car, she said she was afraid for her life. "I'm a young white woman, you never know what would happen." I got really angry. I said, "Those kids need books. You could have been out there helping them!" She came back at me, "How do you know? You'd never work in the ghetto." She forgot I was black. I must not be quite like *those*.

I can feel their discomfort because they don't hear that kind of stuff. The great many of them are really quite decent. They *say* they aren't racist, aren't prejudiced. But it's just in the little things they say, ignorant things.

When people lose jobs, they blame the Japanese. We can't assume because this man has yellow skin, he's caused you to lose your job at the auto plant. In college, I belonged to an Afro-American Society. There were about fifty of us blacks listening to a lecture. The door opens and this Chinese guy walks in. We thought he'd made a mistake and was about to leave. He sat down very quietly and listened to the speech with the rest of us. We were curious: What's this Chinese guy doing here?

Afterwards, a couple of us came up to him, friendly: "How you doin?" It came out, he was from China, an extremely poor family. The other villagers laughed at him, called him dirty names because he was so poor. When he came to Cleveland, he was told that he couldn't have black people in his apartment because they were niggers and they were dirty and no good. He remembered hearing the same thing about himself in China. He said, "I never met any black people and I wanted to find out for myself about all these bad things. It can't all be true." So he came to this meeting. Well, we were like, "Wow!" We were just knocked out. I mean, if white people would do that, I think we would have . . . It happened some years ago and it *still* amazes me.

I get mad because they don't see *me*. They see black. I'm not trying to act like I'm better than anyone else, but they don't see that I'm fairly intelligent. That I have opinions on different things. All they see is that I'm black and all that goes with it: "She must be good in the kitchen. She must be a good dancer." Definitely not true. "She must be good at basketball." Not true. "She must like watermelon." I've actually had people say to me, "We're going to have watermelon, you'll like that." I don't like watermelon. I don't like *any* melon.

The hurts? I don't have the hurts of the people who came before me.

I'm post–Jim Crow, post–Martin Luther King, post–civil-rights movement. I didn't grow up with all those other hurts. Yet it shouldn't be the way it is. We're supposed to have gotten over all this. To see this silly stuff still around, these stupid little prejudices that people have about other people— it just amazes me. It really does.

I'm not militant in the old sense, though I probably would have joined the demonstrations. I am in corporate America. There aren't too many of us around. Sometimes I have the feeling I can go either way. I can be the pseudo-white male and do what they tell me to do, or I'm just going to be myself. If they can't deal with it, that's their problem.

I don't feel I've compromised myself. I'm paying the bills. That's all I care about. I do the best I can at my job, at anything I do. They love my work, they tell me. I hope. Shoot. But I'm not corporate-minded. I'm never going to be corporate vice-president. I really don't have any desire to. I'm a writer at heart. I wouldn't feel comfortable, much to the dismay of my mom, who keeps asking me when I'm going to get my MBA. She would love to see me up there making sixty, a hundred thousand dollars a year. My little sister is getting her MBA. The corporate world does not appeal to me. It's not because I'm a black woman, it's just the whole idea of corporate America. It's just so very closed. There are some things in my company that are *so* old-guard white male. *Oohh.*

If I had the chance to talk to a white audience, I'd say, "There aren't that many differences between us." They'd have to really overcome what they've been taught most of their lives. I'd say to black people, "You cannot blame all your woes on the white man." Granted, I'd read Malcolm X's autobiography and he's shown how the collective white man, throughout history, has messed up every nonwhite race on the planet. But you cannot lump all white people together as racists. There are decent whites, too. It's assumptions and stereotypes on both sides we have to deal with.

We're on this merry-go-round just once. The least we can do is get to know the people we're riding with.

JOE GUTIERREZ

He is fifty. He has worked in the steel mills for thirty-two years, ever since he was eighteen. He is now "union full-time for Local 1010.

"I was going to be a priest, had four years in seminary with the Carmelites. We went to school seven days a week, had ancient Greek, Latin, physics, chemistry—a fantastic education. I just got mentally ex-

hausted and had to get away. I went right to the steel mill. Jesus Christ, what a transition!

"*My father worked at the Ford plant in Detroit when he first came from Mexico. Then he came to Chicago and the steel mill and worked there as far back as I can remember. During the Depression, he paid a guy fifty cents a week to teach him how to weld.*

"*My mother was a hillbilly from Georgia. She married at fourteen. We're fifteen children. She didn't speak Spanish and he didn't speak English. I didn't know two words of Spanish until I got out into the steel mill.*"

I didn't identify with Mexicans until people started throwing racism around. My name is José but I've always been called Little Joe. The whites didn't know my last name and thought I was Italian or Greek. So they let out their true feelings.

I was not accepted by the Mexicans because I couldn't speak the language: "You look white, so you don't want to be a Mexican." I forced myself to learn the language so at least I could get by.

We were the only Mexican family in the neighborhood. The Mexicans, Puerto Ricans, and blacks lived on the East Chicago side by the mills. Now it's all changed. You've got a neighbor that's black, another Puerto Rican, another something else. All on our street.

We were about eight years old, my brother, Vince, and I when we went to a public swimming pool in a park in East Chicago. We took a black kid with us. This was 1948. As soon as we dove in the pool, everybody got out. The lifeguard got out, too, a female. They shut down the pool. I was never raised to be a racist, so I didn't know what it was all about.

There's a certain amount of racism among Mexicans against blacks, and Mexicans against Puerto Ricans. But I see more racism with the blacks than with the white or Latin.

We went through a union election. We're about thirty percent black. Every time I ran for office, there was a solid black vote for the black, regardless of the person. It made no difference. Over the years, I felt it would change because people would look at the person's qualifications. For the most part, it hasn't changed. That's true among Latins also. They'll vote Latin just because he's Latin. Whites? Yeah, pretty much the same.

A good friend of mine, a white from Kentucky, just got elected griever in the metal-plate department. I said, "The black griever we have is simply unqualified; he's done a terrible job. I don't expect the blacks to vote for him. He won't get over twenty votes." He said, "The guy's gonna get a hundred votes." He was right. For three years, the guy did an awful job.

They still came out and backed him. I understand the past injustices, but . . .

The guys who are honest say, "Look, we've been down so long, the first time we get somebody to represent the black community, he projects an image of leadership and we overlook the bad. We just want a black there."

It baffles my mind because I've had an ongoing fight in the mills: I don't care if you're black, brown, or white, we're all workers. I sometimes get chastised by the so-called leaders of the Latin community because I don't stand up and say we should all go for la raza. There are some Latins who always vote that way. I voted that way before I got involved with the union. I didn't know people. If I saw a Sánchez or Gonzalez or Rodríguez, I voted for him. I met a Cisneros who couldn't write his own name and didn't give a damn about the union, was a company guy. I said nah, nah, nah. He may be Latin but he doesn't represent the interests of working people. I don't care about image.

With whites, what comes first is my pocketbook. I can work with a black, with a Latin, but as soon as I leave that steel mill, I get on South 41 and go back to my world. Here it's a temporary world for eight hours a day, five days a week. When you park your car and walk into that plant, you walk into another world. All your prejudices, all your hates, you leave in the parking lot.

At the workplace, there's not much tension. You still have people who feel they're treated unfairly because they're black or Latin. When some whites get disciplined, they say, "I'm white, you didn't discipline the black guy." It's a crutch. But in general, it's not there. You're working around heavy equipment and you've got to look out for your buddy. It's very easy to get hurt in a steel mill.

As for whites, there's still a lot of prejudice out there. I know how to erase it. If you give other people a chance—if you give me the opportunity to present my views, maybe you'll get to know me and like me. Look, there's some people you just don't like. It's got nothing to do with color; it's got a lot to do with personality.

Latins are right in the middle. For the longest time, they were classified as blacks. You go to Texas, and Latinos are treated like blacks.

With people losing jobs, there's always got to be somebody to blame. We had nineteen thousand people at Inland Steel. Now we're below ten thousand. For years, whites had all the better jobs. In 1977, the government came in and said you've got to do something about discrimination in the workplace or we'll do it for you. They signed a Memorandum of

Understanding that implemented plantwide seniority. It was good for everybody. Now a black or Latino as well as a white could transfer in any department and utilize seniority.

At the time, whites ran the trains, Latins worked on the tracks, and blacks worked in the coke plants. When the changes took place, there was a lot of hatred among whites against minorities in general. "I've worked in this mill for twenty-five years, and here's one of them coming over and bumping me out of a job." It didn't happen that way for the most part, because you still had contract language to go by. You couldn't leapfrog over somebody.

We had an election the other day and won by a landslide. I acted as a watcher. Some voted only for Latins, others only for blacks, and some whites only for whites. Our slate had a president who's white, a Latin who's vicepresident, and two black trustees. It was a mix all around. We voted for the person. We represented the rank-and-file against the old guys. For the most part, we're forty, forty-one years old. You don't have a younger crop because there are no jobs for them.

What's ahead doesn't look good. With a new power plant, a lot of departments will shut down. The coke plants will go. You'll see some of the old hatred coming back. Blacks will say, "You gave us the rotten jobs whites wouldn't take, working on batteries, causing cancer and so forth, and when things get bad, we're the first to go." We're hearing it now. With fewer and fewer jobs, it'll get worse.

I don't like racists—white, black, Latin, anybody. Life's too short for meanness. There was a lot in the army when I was in it. Sometimes it comes out of people you don't expect it from. There's a guy who's decent, a hard worker, a good family man, and he'll say, "That fuckin' nigger." It's like getting hit in the gut. I stop him: "Why do you say that?" He just shrugs. He's Mexican, a deacon in the church. I'm a lector there. I tell this guy, "If a white guy says nigger, the word you use, I bet he calls you spic, taco-bender. Cut out this bullshit."

What's happened is that people were getting tired of the sixties. There was a legitimate grievance among the blacks in this country and a lot of us took part in the marches. But about twelve, fifteen years ago, younger blacks started coming into the steel mills. The older guys found allies among the Latins on the shop floor. But the younger guys came in with one thought in mind: We've been screwed and if we don't keep on their backs, they're gonna screw us again. To them, we're no different than the whites. It started backfiring.

Those of us who were sympathetic are less that way today. I had won over a lot of blacks because I did a good job. But there are some blacks, I swear to God, I don't care what you did, it made no difference. All they saw was black. It's damaging to themselves. What more can a boss wish for?— divide and conquer!

When the government came down with a consent decree, Inland Steel ignored it. Every other company—LTV, Bethlehem, USX—paid minorities monies—two, three thousand dollars apiece—on the basis of years of discrimination at work. Inland Steel paid not a penny. They had a sharp lawyer who said, "Look, people are tired of civil rights, of marches, of busing, of affirmative action. The mood of the country is changing. Let's fight it." The government didn't follow through, and they didn't pay a penny. It's the Reagan years, and Bush is going even further.

I don't think the company is racist. That's too simple. It's the bottom line, the dollar. They don't care about you, no matter what your color is. You're nothing to them. If you're black or Latin or white, if they can set you up against the other workers, they're going to use you. They don't give a damn what color you are. It's the profit.

We have to keep on working together, and when we hear the word nigger or spic—or cracker—stand up and say, "I don't appreciate that. Enough of this bullshit!"

FRANK LUMPKIN

He had worked at Wisconsin Steel "for thirty years and one week," until the gates were shut on March 28, 1980. Long before, he had worked the mills in Buffalo and had sailed merchant ships during World War II.

After the shutdown, "I started this Save Our Jobs Committee. I'm still puttin' in six days a week, sometimes more. [Laughs.] We started in with this surplus food. We'd pass it out once or twice to workers and their families. We give out five pounds of cheese and some butter. We get some rice and honey and make them a bag and these steelworkers come around and pick it up for their families. Five hundred bags run out, just like that."

He and his wife live in a one-family dwelling on the South Side of Chicago. It is a street not much different from one in any solid working-class community in the city. "It's a neighborhood where peoples care about their property." Though predominantly black, there are white neighbors. "Next door is white, and two doors is white, and across the street is a Chinese lady. They're old-timers. They just didn't go when they had the flight."

When things is good, it's not so critical. But when things get bad, like now, like the depression startin' in, the advantage of color really amounts to something. They got white, black, both hungry. If both of them is full, everything seem to be working all right.

This whole business of affirmative action was no problem at all till the jobs run out. It's no big thing when you're on the job. But when it comes to the point where giving you your equal rights would be a real hardship for me, it's why should I do this? I saw this affirmative action coming at the beginning of the cutback on jobs.

If the lion and the deer is both full, nobody attacks. It's only when the lion gets hungry he really fights for the thing. This is the way that life is.

It ain't easy for a man to give in if it hurts his family, for equality or for what's right.

When I come north to Buffalo, I come from where you pick oranges. In the South, a black boy could run the tractors, the heavy work, and the plows. When I got north, it was all white running the big things. Because of the union scale, the pay was higher. It wasn't according to how much work you done, it was according to how much pay it was on the job. So blacks was eliminated from truckdrivers, crane operators, because they were big-paying jobs.

Race is only used when it's to somebody's advantage, and I don't mean the workingman's advantage. It's never to our advantage. It's always an advantage to the man that's making the money, who's using these guys, to use this thing to divide them. It's not an advantage to the white *or* the black in the final analysis. During the war, when we had to do it, we did it together. The sea and everything else. Critical times, man forgets color.

I remember Trumbull Park, near our steel plant. Roughly, '53. This black family movin' in. Gangs come by and break windows. Black and white protected the family. They would break glasses of black workers' cars when they was comin' in. The gang boys told the white guys to put white handkerchiefs on their car and they wouldn't hit it. But whenever a black worker seen the white worker car with a hanky on it, he'd say, "What the hell are you doing?" They stopped doing this kind of thing because they seen that it was self-serving.

There was a black guy got off the bus with his lunch bucket in his hand, he started comin' to the mill, and a mob got in behind him. They start running him. And the white guys in the plant saw this and they says, "Son-of-a-bitch, do you see them runnin' that guy? We gotta stop this." And we did, never mind the politicians and the police. The guys who work together know each other and that's what it's all about. It's no problem walking through Trumbull Park now. It's integrated to a great degree. They got a project in there now that's white and black.

My observation is that racism is dying. But as things die, sometimes they intensify. It's like clinging on to whatever it can grab. It don't mean it's not dangerous, it's intensified. You do everything you can to try to stop the changes with everything you got. But it don't mean, like in Trumbull Park, peoples is automatically opposed to anybody that comes there. While all this racism was going on, they never attacked the mailman and he was black. They never attacked the black crossing guard. They just didn't attack black per se.

If you worked at a steel mill at one time or another, you may have saved your fellow worker's life, leg, or arm. We had to support each other in that mill, otherwise—I remember one white guy arguing with another white guy when he called another guy "black bastard." He said, "You-son-of-a-bitch, if he hadn't of pulled you out from in that hole, you'd have been dead, gassed to death." One looked out for the other, had to.

Another struggle I was in was in Buffalo when they had racism on a boat that goes from Buffalo to Canada. They wouldn't let black guys on, only white. I organized a protest. They got mad and the police grabbed this guy and they was twistin' his arms. I grabbed the cop to try to tell him not to hurt this young guy. And he cracked me across and busted my hat. They got me for interfering with an arrest by an officer.

They had a trial and the jury was stacked with white tavern owners. They got a black prosecutor. You could look at the jury and you said: Son-of-a-gun, you's a dead duck. I expected a write-up in the papers, convicted by an all-white jury. The jury come back: Not guilty. Everybody in the courtroom jumped up and started clapping. Unbelievable.

It tells me simply that racism is not an automatic thing. It's an organized prejudice against people. Racism, you just don't come out and be this way. It's got to be some motivation behind it, by telling peoples they're gonna lose the value of their house or this or that. I'm saying racism is unnatural.

In the South where I come up, I used to play with two guys, Paul and Frank Harvey, white boys. We made boats, we made everything together. Only when it was time to go to school, we had to part company. Slowly but surely, this thing grew out of the system in the South.

When I come up from Georgia and got off the bus in Washington, D.C., they said you're going into God's country now. I thought I was going to be equal. I'm still looking for that equality. Actually, it isn't a simple thing that equality will come automatically. It's a system. In some countries, it's religion. It's anything that causes one man to feel superior to another.

Racism is a business. When they was organizing the packinghouses, they brought in these black guys in from the South on boats to break the strikes. What happens? Some of these black guys become the main organizers of the union. The backbone. It's black and white.

I can see the light even though it's still dark around you. I don't think nothing can stop it. I'm talkin' about integration.

I see black nationalism as a dangerous thing. My son is a doctor and he was investigating these homes where they keep peoples at state expense. Nursing homes. This home was really bad and it was black-owned. When he talked about improvement, they gets a lawyer and he says, "How come you bother about a black home?" He says, "This home is not suitable for poor black peoples and I'm gonna fight it, lock 'em up." He says, "I'm not doing this because it's black, I'm doing it because of what you're doing to black people. They're not being served. I don't care if it's run by black or white, it's wrong and I'm going to fight it."

He lost the case because the big town people said: You ain't gonna shut down a black home. This is part of the whole segregation that's got to be analyzed.

I am open-minded about a lot of this thing. We had one of the peoples come to see me, and he's a good friend. I had a picture of Christ. He had a cup of coffee and he looked at the wall and say, "You mean to tell me you got a blond-head, blue-eyed Christ on your wall?" By ding, I thought, You so-and-so. Honest to goodness, I said, "I very seldom do this, but it's a good idea if you get out of my house. I don't mind you being critical, but don't come in and tell me what I got to put over my walls."

There is a gap between the Latinos and the blacks. It's what happened in our shop in the seventies when the affirmative-action program started. They had to make some changes for the blacks in all departments. They had to have black foremen, black superintendants—everything but owners. [*Laughs.*] This went right down the mill. They got a black and a white.

The Latinos said, look, if you're gonna get a black, you gotta get a Latino. So they *centered* not on the white, but on the weakest link in the chain: "If the blacks gonna get up, We wanna get up." I says, "Look, they got twenty white foremen and only one black foreman, and you arguing about the one black that come up." It's not that they're fighting the black, they're fighting for the *just end*, but it seems that we're fighting against each other. I'm watching the schools and it could easily turn out that the Latino principal is going to fight the black principal.

When I set up our Save Our Jobs Committee, I put two white, two blacks, and two Latinos in leadership. I did it purposely because I know working people. They want representation. When we go into the room to discuss anything, all the nationalities discuss it. The only strength we got is integrated strength.

I know one thing, there is good peoples behind all colors of skin. If I don't find it in this white guy, I'll find it in that white guy. It's there. I'm one hundred percent sure of that. It's good guys in the white group, it's good guys in the black group, it's good guys in the Latino group. What we have to do is search and find them. When you're in a struggle, you can't leave a part of society out. Nobody wants to be *told* the story. They want to see it, they want to feel it, they want to be there.

There's something inside a man that can make him become extra. When you read John Brown, when you read the lives of great mens, who went beyond the norm, it was something that was behind them. Something that propelled them into these things. I don't know where it comes from, but it's just something that won't let you run away from a fight. If you walk away, you walk right back and say, "Wait a minute, I'll never be right if I walk away from this fight." You walk back and get involved, and when it's over, you're glad you did it. You hope that you'll be able to do it again.

But you have to generate this kind of *better living*. When you walk in a picket line or walk by the police and then look back and see the multitudes, the people behind you, you begin to feel high. No drug comes close to it.

■ ■ ■ ■ ■

Overview I

DOUGLAS MASSEY

Professor of Sociology, University of Chicago.

I don't think black neighborhoods deteriorated because of the departure of middle-class blacks. Middle-class blacks aren't different from the middle class of other groups. Doctors and lawyers don't like to live like poor people. The only difference is that black doctors and lawyers are stuck within a segregated housing market.

It happened because stable working-class blacks became poor blacks over the past fifteen years. The mobility wasn't so much geographic as it was social and economic. They moved down the income hierarchy from working class—or lower middle class—to poverty status.

Jobs were once abundant for blue-collar people, who did manual labor that did not require a lot of education—in steel mills, in the auto industry, in factories. They were fairly well-paying. With the economy restructured, these jobs disappeared. It hit blacks particularly hard. The factories that closed down had provided most of the jobs in black neighborhoods. Blacks are less free to move where new jobs are being created because of their difficulty in entering the housing market.

The few professionals who left the old neighborhood did provide role models. But role models don't provide the income to keep a neighborhood alive and vibrant. They don't provide the money that supports stores and small businesses and churches that keep families, neighborhoods, together. As the income disappears, these institutions go with them. These tremendous economic changes overwhelmed inner-city neighborhoods.

Where jobs are lost, families are disrupted. Since income is not coming in, nobody has the incentive to keep up their homes anymore. It sets off a vicious cycle of abandonment. Lots of housing disappears. There is more homelessness and living on the streets.

The jobs aren't there for the sons. They have very little they can aspire to. The kinds of jobs in the service economy that provide a good living are at the upper end. For a poor person, living in a neighborhood of poor housing and poor schools, to leap to the upper end is impossible. People working full time, earning a minimum wage, say at McDonald's, can't stay above the poverty line.

You have young black men coming up now who would have worked in factories. But there are far less such places today. Aside from working at McDonald's for the rest of their lives, what can they aspire to, without an education? They're not in a position to support a family.

There used to be a well-developed path, where fathers would introduce their sons into the world of work, into the factory. You'd talk to the foreman: "My son graduated, or dropped out of high school. Can you put him into something?" Maybe he'd start pushing the broom around, but if he was diligent enough, he might rise through the ranks and wind up with a relatively fair-paying job. That whole tier of employment has gone now.

In the old days, before unions, whenever blacks entered a factory, there was tremendous resistance. They were kept out of certain classes of jobs. There was a time when blacks couldn't rise above the rank of janitor. The sad irony is that just when blacks gained something approaching full access to the jobs, the factories began to disappear.*

Male identity in this culture is heavily bound up with work. If you ask a man who he is, he'll tell you what he does for a living. If you don't do something for a living, you're nobody. You're pitching pennies on the streetcorner, dealing in drugs, engaging in criminal activities. If you resist temptations, you're working at a minimum wage at the low end of the service sector. A busboy.

In these past years, we've become a more unequal society. It started in 1973 with the recessions. In 1980, when Reagan came to power, the tax cuts benefited the better-off. Incomes for the top ones just shot way upwards.† By the end of the eighties, the income inequality was the greatest it's been in fifty, sixty years. There's been this tremendous transfer of wealth from the poor and the middle class to the rich.

The quality of our public life has deteriorated so much, we need something like a new WPA program. Look at our bridges, look at our highways, look at our buildings. By rebuilding these facilities, we can create jobs for people without a lot of education. It will benefit everyone, not only blacks. Private affluence and public squalor, something John Kenneth Galbraith pointed out thirty years ago, is the accepted order of the day. It's gotten worse.

Now you have three classes of people. There are those who own capital. They've done extremely well these past twenty years. There are those who own human capital—their education, their skills: the upper middle class. They've done pretty well. And you've got those who have

---

* Milwaukee, March 16—It has an unemployment rate well below the national average, a booming downtown, a generous budget surplus, and more jobs than skilled people to fill them. . . . But it has had a devastating effect on the city's poor black neighborhoods, whose residents thrived in the high-wage union jobs of the city's manufacturing heyday and are now adrift on a rising tide of unemployment, crime, and despair.

"Milwaukee is a classic case of how a restructured economy has diminished the employment opportunities for blacks and for black males in particular," said Dr. James H. Johnson, Jr., director of the Center for the Study of Urban Poverty. . . .

The result is a city of 628,000 people where black men stand idle on street corners just blocks from the breweries and factories that used to employ them, while well-dressed white-collar workers sell insurance or computers out of some of those same factories, now converted into office parks.

New York Times, March 19, 1991

† "Just before the stock market crashed, *Forbes* magazine announced that the number of billionaires in America had doubled in the past year."

Lead editorial, *Los Angeles Times*, October 25, 1987

only their labor to sell. They've done badly. The only way out of this bind is making sure everyone has a chance at education. Until then, we need governmental WPA projects to jump-start this whole process.

Our recent administrations have been hypocritical in their talk of nonintervention. Markets don't exist in a vacuum. Markets are created by human acts. The only question is: Whom does it benefit? During the 1980s, the markets were structured for private gain at public risk. In the savings-and-loan fiasco, some few gained a lot of money as the risk was assumed by the public, which picked up the tab.

Everything is filtered through a system that is not racially neutral. All these things make it much worse for the blacks. Reagan came to power because of race. The welfare programs begun under Roosevelt were seen as handouts to blacks. In the white mind, "welfare" means "blacks." More than any single factor, race is responsible for the demise of the Democratic coalition. It's divide-and-conquer in its purest form.

I don't think most whites understand what it is to be black in the United States today. They don't even have a clue. They blame the blacks to a large degree for their own problems. I think black citizens have a job to do: they have to organize themselves as a community. As a white, I can tell you that whites have a lot to do to make it a fair game.

The races have drifted apart in so many ways. In the last ten years, Black English has drifted farther than ever from standard American English. Increasingly, blacks isolated in ghetto poverty are speaking a different language, with its own rules of grammar, its own structure, its own choice of words, its own pronunciations. It's not inferior, but if speaking standard English is the minimum requirement for a good job in this country, an increasingly large share of our population is frozen out completely.

It's common in a black community to find a thirty-seven-year-old grandmother. More and more white women are trying to have their *first* child at that age. They live in different social and economic worlds. White women are exposed to a world very different from the one black women face.

Since the Kerner Report of 1968, finding two societies, separate and unequal, it's worsened. There is more toleration of it. In 1968, as bad as the riots were, there was hope, among whites as well as blacks, that things would get better. Despite the assassination of King, the Great Society was still in full swing. But since the midseventies, public investments have disappeared and the commitment to civil rights has completely gone.

Among black people, there is frustration, anger, hatred. Among whites, there is fear, hatred, denial. People deny an obvious truth just to get on with their lives. When you create two societies, so separate, so unequal, people at the bottom half are ultimately going to lash out at the people at the top half. There will be violence.

The violence takes two forms. There were the civil disturbances of the sixties, the riots. Now, it's taken a different form: normal, everyday violence, perpetrated on people that can least afford it. Street crime, property crime, illegal economies like drugs. Crime has a way of begetting more crime, and it may become self-perpetuating. Legitimate activities are driven out. Families in the neighborhood are afraid. The people that pay the most are the poor themselves. Ultimately we all pay. Insurance rates increase. We pay for more police enforcement. We pay directly when we are its victims. Eventually, it spills out and comes home.

Increasingly, white America has adopted private solutions to public problems. As public citizens, we do nothing about it. As public institutions refuse to deal with it, individuals are forced to cope. They try to put more distance between themselves and the others. They demand more repressive police-state tactics to control these others.

As people invest in private solutions—home-security systems, moving to the suburbs, private security companies, setting up a police force, as this university has done—it further undermines support of public solutions. "I'm already paying for this, so why should I pay for better education?" "I've moved to the suburbs. My kid goes to a nice private academy. Why should my taxes go up to pay for these other people who are just criminals anyway?" The less support for public solutions, the worse the crimes get. It's a vicious cycle.

I think whites have a difficult time separating race from class. They look at a black person and the color of his skin triggers a number of assumptions about his behavior. Black skin means crime, drugs, welfare dependency, lack of work values. These perceptions make it more likely that those conditions will in fact occur. I know a black professional—who's moved to the suburbs, who's attended college—who went to the country club and someone handed him a bag of golf clubs. They thought he was a caddy.

Neither group is very good at separating race from class. Black kids, especially in the ghetto, will often ridicule other black kids, who are doing well in school and learning to speak standard English, because they're "acting white." What is white English anyway? Is it Appalachian English? No. We're talking about what ghetto kids consider a middle-class accent and middle-class behavior. To them, this is "white." Both black and white are trapped by race.

■ ■ ■ ■ ■

The House I Live In

LEOLA SPANN

We are in the basement of St. Angela's rectory on Chicago's Far West Side. It is adjacent to the suburb Oak Park. There is all sorts of activity here: interviews, casual conversations, newsletters being mimeographed, phones ringing . . .

It is the office of the Northwest Austin Council. She is the director. Though her staff is paid, she is a volunteer. "We offer prepurchase counselling to first-time homeowners."

She has three daughters; one is a nurse, another a secretary, and the third a social worker.

My husband and I came here from Natchez, Mississippi, in 19 and 54. I love the South but the jobs were up here. We first moved to the West Side. It was predominantly white. It was really a nice neighborhood. My children went to Precious Blood, a parochial school. I saw it become a ghetto. As the area began to depreciate, we moved. I was guilty of what we're all guilty of, fleeing.

I moved out here in '69. We were one of the first black families. My daughter attended a predominantly white school that was becoming integrated. My neighbors were fighting it. I'd never seen a mob of whites until that time. Never in my whole life. It was so bad that the teachers let the children out the back door. There were maybe four hundred, five hundred whites protesting the black children.

The next morning, I went to school with my daughter, and the people were all lined up on the other side of the street. We walked through the crowd of whites, and it was scary.

Laura was fourteen, her first year of high school. She began to get really nervous and didn't want to go to school. It got so bad that I thought maybe it was drugs. So I had taken her to a psychiatrist. We come to find out it was just the fear of going to school there. I didn't know she was a borderline epileptic. The pressure brought it out.

I guess they were trying to frighten us as we walked past that line.

I was frightened but I wouldn't let them know it. [*Slight laugh.*] I thought to myself, "I've gone as far as I'm going to go. No more moving." I said, "I'm going to fight for this community." It eventually worked out that way.

I think the main thing—and this is sad to say in the nineties—is not knowing one another. That's the key. I think if we ever know each other, we could iron out all our problems.

My daughter joined the choir. We did fund-raisers together. There were a lot of whites stayed on that year because they didn't want to pull their children out. My daughter's yearbook is much different from the yearbook of today. Now it's predominantly black.

It is a very nice neighborhood, basically single-family dwellings. The housing stock is excellent. There had been so much redlining and scare tactics by the realtors. With their panic-peddling, they were scaring whites out of the community. That's the way they do neighborhoods. The whites do get upset because they think the property values are going down. It's the same with everybody, black and white, If you've invested your money in your home—we all have the same dreams and goals. It's just that most blacks don't have the jobs, the salaries of the others.

Even if your husband is working, he's not making a salary capable to taking care of a family. It's just to have our children decent is sometimes a sacrifice. Blacks have learned to do without.

You look back in the sixties, you didn't have as much dropout as you have today. Men were staying with their families. Today we've gotten into the computer and high tech, and black men aren't prepared for that. To see their families where they can't give their child a pair of gym shoes, it's embarrassing to them a lot of times. So they leave.

That's why we're here counseling people on foreclosures and pre-purchasing. These are people owning homes for the first time. They don't know how to own a home unless they're educated to it.

When you have little money in the first place, if you got a bad roof, you're in trouble. You've got these contractors who say "I can get you this roof for $10,000." You're burdened down with a second mortgage, facing foreclosure. We're trying to educate people that if you buy your first home, you're eligible for a city program if need be. There are other avenues beside this contractor.

You hear people say: Why does this neighborhood go down as soon as blacks move in? You know why it goes down? When a black person buys a home, most of the time he has just enough money to put a down payment. If he has any type of repair, he has a problem. So he goes out and gets a second mortgage. Now he stands to lose the house, so you've got another boarded-up house in the community. It's simply economics. That's why properties go down when blacks go in.

If you got a single mother with three children, she can't go out there and pay seventeen dollars for that turf-builder to make the lawn beautiful. It's simple little things like this that add up, that cause deterioration when blacks move in. It's not that they don't want a beautiful place; they can't afford it. So we try to educate them in these little things.

We were property owners when we came to Chicago. We were paying off a home in Natchez and we rented here. Before we had left Mississippi, we bought a little brick bungalow. It was my first home and I was so excited. My husband wanted to come up here because he could get a better-paying job.

So we came here to this little kitchenette. This little bitty thing with a sink as small as a face bowl. I had never seen such a little one in my life and I cried for a month. I wondered why people chose to live like this.

I grew up in Natchez around white neighbors. A lot of antebellum homes there. There was prejudice, but it was a different type of prejudice. My children played with white children. I'd walk in a store, the clerk she would know me. "The dresses just came in, Leola." I go into Carson's here, I'm standing there, nobody's concerned whether they serve me or not, very cool. White and black clerks, the same. After a while, you get adjusted to where you're living and don't expect certain things.

When the realtors came into this neighborhood with their scare tactics, we fought back. The area has kind of stabilized now. It's black and white. People are finding a lot of pride in the community. You've got a lot of young whites moving back into the neighborhood. They begin to know that you are people, and not all these myths are true. That's the key to race, knowing.

When I was a young girl in Mississippi, I seen what they called substandard housing. They're not much, but better than no houses at all, being homeless. I have never in all the years up here seen as many people on the streets like I see today. People lived in shacks in the South, but they didn't live on the street.

I always said what I wanted most was to own my own home. That had been with me all my life. So I worked very hard at that. By the time I was twenty, when I came up here, I had purchased my own home. I think we must have paid $500 down, and our notes were like $43 a month. House didn't cost but $5000, a little brick bungalow, two bedrooms.

How I got involved with all this? It must have been in the early seventies. I didn't work because my husband made a pretty good living as a sanitation man. I said to him one day, "I just can't sit here. I'll go crazy." I saw an ad in the paper. They were looking for a manager of an apartment building. Bill says, "You don't know anything about managing." I said I'd learn.

It was two lawyers owned a building. When I was interviewed, they said it was a plush building, fabulous, nice and predominant white and da-da-da-da. I said okay. But God blessed me with inner sight. I said to my husband, "Let's ride over and look at this place." I see this huge building, screens all torn, dirt in the vestibule, garbage everywhere. Everything looked awful. I said to these lawyers, "I wouldn't pay you rent to live there and I certainly wouldn't manage anything like this and expect people to pay me. It's cold and I'd never ask people to pay rent where they're not getting any heat." So we said good-day and I never expected to hear from them again.

About a week later, I got a call. "If you'd just come in and collect the rent for us, we'd pay you by the day." So I said, "You go around locking people out. Don't you know that people work hard and live from week to week, and you think I'm going to lock them out of their apartment? You have to be out of your mind." They had quite a few welfare tenants they didn't tell me about. I said, "I don't like your attitude."

They said, "You're the best thing that's been here in seven years." [*Laughs.*] "If you'll take this job, we won't come out here unless we're invited." I took the job. It was a fantastic building I kept. It was about 60 percent white and 40 percent black when I left.

Oh, the tenants! [*Laughs.*] One of them, a white nurse, wouldn't even hand me the rent. She would ease to the desk and lay down the check. One old woman refused to give my husband the rent. He was about two shades darker than I was.

One day I went upstairs and told her she'd have to give it to my husband when I'm not around. She locked me in the room and was telling me all about black folks. [*Laughs.*] I found out she was really afraid of black people. If a black was coming down the hall, she'd scurry over the side. She'd get sick, she was always getting sick. I'd take care of her. We became very good friends. She believed all the myths about black people. When she came to know me, she realized I was the same as her.

When I left and went back to Natchez to take care of my grandmother, she called me up long-distance. "Do you have an apartment building down there? If you do, I want to move in." It all comes back to knowing the other person, doesn't it?

This community would be one of the best if we didn't have the drug traffic. That's the one thorn in my side. What a lot of people don't realize is that welfare doesn't pay enough for a person to live. So drugs supplements the income of some of these young men. Where are the jobs for them? Wouldn't that be the answer? You've got a lot of white kids that comes right here to buy drugs. It touches all phases of life.

I'm a Christian and I ask, "Is God trying to get our attention with this plague?" I was raised by a grandmother, and God was practiced in our home. I knew God was watching me if I did wrong. I knew He knew everything I did. I attend Keystone Baptist Church and I'll tell you something. I'm not going to just sit and think God will come down here and drop everything in my lap.

As a young woman I had a lot of prejudice. I did not understand why this white young woman was able to go here and do this and look pretty. In the South, I had this example. Here was this beautiful house and here was this shack. I had a good focus on how divided we were. It was a resentment, I'll put it that way. Not of the persons themselves but at the difference of the quality of life.

I'm sure there's a lot of black people that felt the same way. I couldn't figure it out at the time. Now I'm beginning to see it wasn't prejudice geared toward the person. It was society itself.

Twenty-five years after the death of Dr. King, we still have the same problems. The years of Reagan set us back in many ways. People like myself are still trying to and praying to fulfill Dr. King's dreams. The way we're going to do this is with educating and preparing our people in jobs and programs that will help them become independent.

I don't feel pessimistic at all. I think this is a period of adjustment. We have to reassess these years and find out what we have been doing wrong.

You know how we come together in time of crisis. Earthquakes. You see blacks and whites together. Look at the little girl when she fell in the well. I was just as upset about that baby as if it was a black baby. The Lord is saying something to us. We're just not listening.

We have difficulty when it comes to change. We don't like changes. A lot of people don't even want to move. We've got to, because this new generation is wise. They're born with their eyes open now, they're ready. They say, "World, here I am. I'm ready to go." Schools are not giving the children what they want, what they need. Some of these young people here [*She indicates the quiet activity around her.*]—some white, some black— things they are teaching me about, I'll never encounter in my whole lifetime.

MARY FRAN SHEEHAN

She's a mother of thirteen—"The oldest is twenty-five, the baby is seven."
They all still live with her. She was born and raised on Chicago's Southwest
Side. Her husband is a firefighter, as her father was.

Things haven't changed that much in the neighborhood. My growing-up
friends don't live near me. Most of them live in the suburbs. The turnover
of people has changed but the atmosphere hasn't. We have many more
Hispanics now, living around us, some gang problems. But they're a couple
of blocks away and don't involve my family, so it's okay. My children go to
Catholic school and no gang symbol, sign, hat, is allowed inside.

There's not that many blacks. The kids across the street look very
black, but they're really South American. Otherwise, there aren't blacks
right around me. I'm a little overprotective. [*Laughs.*] Since grammar
school, my children are not off the block that much. They play with the
children across the street and the Hispanics. To kids, people are people.

I don't have any problem with the Hispanics if they speak English. If
they don't speak English, I have a problem. I work with them at church on
different projects, no problem.

I went through a very bad time. I felt like being white middle-class
had a real stigma to it. Everything was our fault. In the last few years,
everything in the paper, it seemed like it was my fault. It was my fault there
were homeless people. It was my fault there was trouble in government.
Everywhere I went, it seemed like it was my fault. Even when I went to
church. I was really getting angry.

It was my fault people moved out. How could it be my fault? I'm still
here. I've calmed that down now, my anger. I used to sit sometimes
in church and just glare. I would think it can't all be my fault. I have enough
to do in my own home, I can't take care of the whole world. I live my
life caring about other people and I don't know what more they want me
to do.

Maybe I overreacted, but it just seemed to me that I would turn on the
TV or the radio and it would be constant trying to send me on a guilt trip,
because I had a decent life. I had a good husband and we weren't having
marital problems and we had a nice home and a car. How dare I have that
when there are homeless people?

Well, nobody gave that to us either. We worked very hard for that. I
was sick of people making the connotation that because I had all that

somehow I was responsible for many of the ills in the world. The white middle class was getting a real bum rap. By the media, by our own churches many times.

White middle-class people work very hard for what they get. Nobody hands them anything. At the end of the month, we give to church and we give to charities, but I certainly can't be magnanimous because by the end of the month, I don't have anything to be magnanimous with. [*Laughs.*] Maybe I'm easily led on guilt trips, maybe it's just me. But I had friends that felt the same way also. Every time I turned on the news, it was slanted as my fault. Frankly, I don't know what more we're supposed to do about the neighborhoods and the homeless and the unemployment.

I certainly thought we needed affirmative action when it first came in. Now I think it's to the point of being ridiculous. Now we have to take people who score lower on tests because of the color of their skin. What an insult to their race! They have people smart enough to pass these tests, just like the white people do, if they choose to take these tests. I think we've gone past the need for affirmative action.

I really did think we needed something, because it was real difficult years ago for a black man or woman to get a job. I don't think that's the case today. We've come a long way with that, and I think it's outlived its usefulness. People now resent it so bad that it creates more problems than it solves.

My friends pretty much feel like I do. Many of them have jobs with the city and have to live in the city, so we're worried about the tide of things in the city. If every neighborhood's gonna overturn to completely black or completely Hispanic, I don't think that's good for any city. Diversity can make a city run so much better.

We raise our sons and daughters the best way we know how and resent it when they go to take an entrance exam for a college or a job for the city and are told, "We can't use you because you're white, we have to fill our black quota." That doesn't make a heck of a lot of sense to me if the white boy is there to get the job and there are no blacks around applying.

I don't feel any differently about them than I do about anybody else. They're just people to me. But you know the history of neighborhood change in Chicago. It's frightening. It went block by block by block. Crime rates went up. You were afraid for your children, afraid to go out of the house at night. It gets to the point when you have to move. That happened to me a couple of times.

There's a black family on the corner. I hardly run into them because I work every day now. I know the parents where my kids go to school. I know the couple of black people at church. I just say hello and goodbye. Their children don't attend our school. My kids go to parochial school.

There's a public school just north of me. It was interesting to me as I was coming to work. They had a fire drill, the entire school. It was peaceful and organized and I was impressed. There's blacks and whites and Hispanics. There's busing in and out of the neighborhood.

The black people around here, the few, are just like—there are so many good people. I don't know why it all can't finally come together and get over all this nonsense. We have to get to know them, not just look at their color.

I never knew any black people when I was little. I was terrified of blacks. In a white middle-class Catholic family, murder was about the worst thing you ever heard of. There wasn't all this terrible stuff that goes on today. I don't know the statistics, but most of the murder and crime seemed to be happening out there. So I was always terrified of black people until I got older and went to high school with some black girls and realized they weren't any different from me.

I would be scared to get on the bus if they were on the bus. I'm talking about a little girl now. I thought they might take it out on me because I was white. I wouldn't walk into a poor black neighborhood today. I'm not that naïve. But I wouldn't be afraid to go into Chatham, perhaps.* Their values seem to be the same as mine. Whereas I'd be afraid to walk through the streets of the West Side.

When you're talking about race, TV blows that out of proportion. And the press, too. If something happens between two people, it should be between those two people only. They try to turn anything that happens to involve a black person and a white into a totally racial issue. They can disagree and not have anything to do with race. But they blow it up into a racial incident. It's usually the headline or on ten-o'clock news. Of course it sells more newspapers than if it was just individuals having a disagreement. I don't think the media gives the regular person any credit for intelligence.

Most of the time, the news is slanted in favor of the minorities, because that's the popular way to go.

My husband feels pretty much the same way I do. Our children have black friends but they seldom come to the house. I don't know if it's planned or where they live isn't convenient. Now that I'm older, it isn't that big a deal anymore. If people are nice to me, I'm nice to them. If they're not . . .

---

* A black middle-class neighborhood.

I think people are far more intelligent today. Both white and black were manipulated in the fifties as far as selling and buying property. Black families were sold a bill of goods that they couldn't afford. That created all those board-ups, which enabled the realtors to move to the next neighborhood and say to the whites, "Look what happened. You better move." It happened overnight. People are too sophisticated now for that to happen again here. I think there's less flight today.

About that newspaper thing. A black family moved in on the corner in a nearby neighborhood. There was a fire and wow!—it was automatically white people set it and it must have been this big racial thing. It was in the papers and it died out. It was in fact not anybody who set the fire. The guy mistakenly left a candle and something happened with the cleaning materials he was using. The press never bothered to come back the next morning, when the people from my parish were sweeping up the sidewalk and helping this guy clean up the mess. It was a simple cleaning-solution accident.

Our pastor, Father Jim, asked people if they could come and help, but by the time he got there, they were already at it. They didn't even need him to ask. The TV cameras were all gone. It was such a one-sided thing.

I've gotten to know some very fine black people and I don't have that every-one-of-them-is-a-criminal attitude. You have to get to know people in order to accept them. I think it's the same with white people. You look at a long-haired hippie type, but sometimes you get to talking with him and he turns out interesting and very kind. We've come a long way.

I see much less tension. There are people out there creating tension where it doesn't exist. For some people it's more profitable to have this tension. Politicians. If you can split votes racially, it may work to your benefit. News media. Unscrupulous realtors and mortgage brokers.

Even though it's improved, there's still bigots out there. Sometimes I doubt myself. Sometimes I think, Am I a bigot? If you say, "I don't understand why he got that job just because he's black," automatically you're a bigot, because she should understand. Well, I don't understand. I don't understand if my son and a black's son goes for a job, he gets thirty points for being black and my son gets thirty points away from him because he's white. That's sixty points before my son puts an answer on a paper. How's he ever going to get the job? [A slight laugh.] They'll say that's a bigoted remark. I'll start to think, Well, maybe I am. [Laughs.] I don't think I am.

I'm essentially a Democrat but I've been voting Republican more and more lately. I liked some of the things Reagan did. I believe we should help the poor but we have to be very careful about people who take advantage of the programs. We're real good about giving money away, but people paying for the programs get aggravated when they see all the abuses. No one would be upset about helping feed a little infant, no matter what color, but if you see people getting away with things and laughing at you because you're paying taxes for it, that's where the trouble comes in.

The working stiff is paying the majority of taxes in the county. He wants to help the guy that is down and out, but he doesn't want to help everybody. [*Laughs.*]

There are all kinds of abuses. I was in the hospital emergency room one Sunday. They were going in there with sniffles that I would have let go and gone to a regular doctor. Because they had the green card, they were going to the emergency room. It had nothing to do with race. They were of all colors. They did not need to be there. These were not babies. These were thirty-, thirty-five-year-old men and women, who could have taken an aspirin. But they've got that card which is government funded. It doesn't cost them anything. Sometimes when you're the guy sitting there for four and a half hours, you want to kill for the nonsense going on around you. I certainly wouldn't have been there if I didn't have to. The guy who is paying $150 to use that emergency room for half an hour is going to be irritated. I think that's where some of the racist feelings come into it.

My children feel the same way we do. It's not something we discuss a lot. I think the problem is people's expectations are too high. People who are always harping about racial bias expect us to like all black people without knowing them. Well, there are a lot of white people I don't like either. I never *hated* anyone just because he was black. I'm very Christian, not *overly* Christian. [*Laughs.*] There's only a couple of people I really dislike, and they're white. I don't know any black people well enough to hate 'em. [*General laughter.*] Those I know, I like.

It's hard for people. They have a fear for their neighborhood and a fear of the crime that goes along with it. We didn't create it, but if you say that, people look at you and call you racist. Look at the police blotters, I didn't create it.

I don't want my children going out and coming in saying every filthy word in the book. They don't hear it in their home. As far as this neighborhood, I'm not a coffee-klatcher. I say hello if anybody's out on the street, whether I know them or not, black, white, or Irish. My life is going along very well. My kids are wonderful. My husband is great. I don't have too many complaints at all. I'm a very lucky lady.

PEGGY BYAS

We are in the community room of a fourteen-story high-rise. Eighty-seven families live in this one—"lots of children." It is part of a public housing complex, Ida B. Wells Homes. There are three locks on its iron door, which is partly open. Occasionally, a young face appears, a fleeting glance: Am I a cop? What's this old white man, with turned-up topcoat and battered hat, doing here? The look is not at all hostile, merely curious. A little girl, wide-eyed, peeks in. I cross my eyes, Ben Turpin fashion. She scurries off, giggling.

A few moments ago, Mrs. Byas had greeted me at the streetcorner. As we passed through one of the dank, cellarlike, sunless walkways, a half-dozen young men were busy not doing much of anything. In response to my casual greeting, they, after momentary hesitation, nodded. It was patently a mark of respect for my companion: "If they see you with one of us, it must be a positive thing that's going on. You're not doing anything that would harm them. They're just wondering. Since we've gotten the building orga-nized, you could have come in by yourself and no one would have bothered you."

She has a husband and three children: a son, twenty-eight; a daugh-ter, twenty-three, a cosmetologist, living in Arkansas; and "my baby, he's thirteen." Her husband, who has just completed his courses at a trade school, "loves working with automobiles. He's looking forward to get him a garage where he can work on cars."

I've lived here since May 5, 1967. When I first got married we were living in a furnished hotel. We had went everywhere, looking for an apartment. The places that we could afford, they weren't decent to live in. The places that were decent, we couldn't afford.

I always looked at the projects—I can't stand that word—as a place I would never want to live. Just from hearing people talk. But we had no other choice. When we moved in, it was nice. You didn't see all this graffiti, we had telephones in front, we had grass, we had fences. At that time, I had to be screened before I moved in.

We had janitors that lived in the building. If he saw a child doing something, like walking on the grass, which was not allowed, throwing garbage, which was not allowed, he didn't come and tell you. It was turned in to the management office, and when you got your rent statement, you were fined. I'm blessed that I never had to be fined.

Somewhere along the line, CHA stopped living up to their agreement according to the lease. When the residents saw that, they stopped. The residents knew that if they did certain things that broke the lease, they had to suffer the consequences. But once they saw where you could do it and get away with it, it just got out of hand. When you stop having to be accountable to someone, it just gives you a free hand to say, "Well, I can do as I please because nothin's gonna happen." It's hard to explain. It maybe had something to do with King being killed. A lot of people was hurt because King was doing things not only for black people, for people in general. It had a big effect on them.

Now, things is getting beautiful again. There are three people as reps out of each building. We had been picked by the LAC, the Local Advisory Council. But we have elections. Just had one two weeks ago. You get a petition signed that you want to run for your building and people come down to vote.

We had went through a lot of training. Now it was time to decide if the residents wanted to go into management themselves. But what we did have to do was go around and make sure everyone come down to vote. We meet downtown and strategize things we want done in the buildings. Then we had to bring it back here to the whole building council. Everybody is invited.

We had twenty-eight residents last week. Out of eighty-seven, that's a big showing. Before, we had something like thirteen. That's because a lot of people had dropped off because CHA never did do what they said they'd do, so they got disgusted. Now they're getting a little confidence that maybe things are going to change.

This building were without lights in a lot of places. The excuse was: "We don't have lightbulbs, or fixtures are broken." Now we got lights on every porch, in the hallways. For three years or more, the handrails going up and down the stairs had rotted. Some floors, from the fourteenth down to the eighth, didn't have any railings at all. Now both sides have brand-new handrails.

The tenants have to be involved, because they are here twenty-four hours a day. Who know better what they need than the tenant? Everybody had to help. Our new office here was just painted by women and one man. We did a survey of tenants. What could we do to improve the building with no money? We decided to have a big clean-up.

We went to the manager and requested mops, buckets, SOS pads, whatever was needed. We got volunteer residents, we had something like sixty or seventy. We took one Saturday and we washed down the halls on the fourteenth floor. We mopped all the hallways, all the galleries, and

Miss Emma Price had all the little kids outside raking and cleaning up. We had a little young man, three years old, cleaning the grounds. They were doing it all. They were so proud, so afterwards we gave them a little party, hot dogs and potato chips.

The next week, about twenty-eight young men come out with paint. The supervisors were nothing but young men. They were trying to see who was going to finish first. It was like a little contest. You know it only takes for the young men and the children to see that someone cares about them. When they clean up or fix something, they're gonna protect that 'cause they did it.

We have a lot of young men that the paper talks about, TV talks about, but those young men give us respect. Because we respect them.

It was beautiful. There was one young man they used to say, he was really bad. He didn't even live in the building. He was over visiting. He saw what we were doing. He came up to me and said, "My mother used to live in 730. I grew up around here. I admire what you're tryin' to do." He went and brought hamburgers, hot dogs, and just barbecued for everybody when they finished.

Know what the trouble is? The way we're classified. By HUD, by the papers, TV. Our development is, say, Project 156. A number. When you say this person lives in a project, right off the bat he's no good. You don't want to deal with these types of people. They're low-class. "Project" is nothing but a slang word. People are so used to using it till it automatically means something bad. You can't blame anyone for saying it 'cause for years and years that's what they've said. Why can't you say "low-income housing" or "CHA development"? But the news media all the time says "project." If something happens, where? A shooting? In a project. A robbery? In a project. A raid? In a project.

I hear people say: they don't want to do anything, they're lazy, they sit back and wait for the state to care for them. Some, because they have no other choice. You just don't put everybody in the same class. We found out that among some of our residents is a cosmetologist, there's a seamstress, they've worked in day-care, catering, clerks, typists. The point is no one has given them the opportunity to show this talent. This is untapped potential.

They say there's gangbanging all the time. That's not true. We can be a community, too. We had a party. All four buildings. We had a cake table, candy, we had a barbecue. Young children, older ones, a lot of dancing, and no fighting. No one kept out. Like it was a community party on Lake Shore Drive. Only we didn't make the social pages. It was beautiful.

You know a big danger? The design of the high-rise. Whoever did it did not think of the safety of the people that were in it. All they were thinking about was stacking something up real fast to put people in. They did not sit down and think: There's a danger. Someone can just bust your window and step in. Or if we leave elevators out in the open, anyone can just walk in, there's no questions asked. Or if we got stairwells and the door is not secure, anyone can walk in, and stick you up in the hallway or do whatever they want to do.

We're hoping in the near future, it will be different. Some architects donated their time for free, came out one night and we had what we called a wish list; what we wished for the outside of the building and what we wished for the inside. I met with the architects, part of a rehab-and-design team. I make suggestions: the residents don't want it like this, they want it like that.

When you come up, you see the red fence. To keep you from falling off or throwing anything off. The fence only went half way up on that floor. So they put it all the way up, but it look like you're behind bars. So the residents said: What can you do to make it safe, but make it look like an apartment building, instead of behind bars? That's an association to people, a prison. They wanted safety from a fence, but look like something people live in.

The residents were thinking about, not plexiglass, but something you can see out of, which you can't go through or throw out of. I wouldn't know exactly what it is until I see the plans again. It's to have pride where you live and when people drive up, let them look and see your pride. It should be when somebody pass by, even though it's a CHA development, they be saying: "Boy, look how they did that!" Pride.

You know, people have been taught from babies that blacks are, what's the word?—inferior. A lot of white children are taught that, 'cause I was raised up with them in Arkansas. I see it in Chicago, too. They say we don't work, everything we get is a handout. I was taught by my daddy early in life to work for everything I get. It hurts to have this stigma put on people in developments. I'm one of them.

If I was president of the United States, my first priority would be education. The best. For all races, not just some. Instead of sending people to the moon, buying arms, guns, the money should go for positive things, to make life better for people, not worse. As it is, young people have nothing to look forward to.

Years ago, you could get a job being a dishwasher, a maid in some-one's house. Nobody wants that anymore, but they have not been prepared how to go into the workforce today. If I'm on drugs, the only way I know to get my money is to stick someone up. Why do so many take these drugs? They might be crying out for help. They're not getting it, especially in black neighborhoods.

All this waste of young people, right here in this building. The last newsletter we did, Emma Price's son drew pictures of spring flowers coming up. It was beautiful. Another young man, his mother lives on the fourteenth floor, for Christmas, he drew Jesus in a manger. Had the holly trees. I mean it was lovely. When we had that Black Power, he could just sit up and draw that fist, just like a real artist. We got the potentials, all we gotta do is pull it out of you. Give you something that's inspiring to you. We need space to breathe.

BETTY RUNDLE

It is a neighborhood of modest one-family dwellings, mostly frame. There are trees, offering an arborlike appearance; the lawns are, of course, well-kept. The car, another year's model, is in the driveway; the bicycle is slanted against the front porch. It is a quiet street on the South Side of Chicago. An occasional police siren is heard some way off—"out there."

Once upon a time, it was an affluent community, predominantly WASP and Irish Catholic on the rise. Her people have been in these parts for several generations. It is now black. Hers is the only white family on the block.

She has seen better times. "My father was a very wealthy man. My mother had servants and a personal maid. She never soiled her hands, she was la grande dame. *He lost all his money during the Depression. But we held onto our house. Beautiful neighborhood.*

"We are Irish Catholics. The WASPS resented us moving in. The children in the neighborhood wouldn't play with me because I was this—this Irish Catholic. You know the song, 'No Irish Need Apply'? It was almost the way Northern Ireland is today.

"I am educated quote unquote, but that doesn't mean a damn thing. I have a master's degree in chemistry. It impresses other people. That's what I think degrees are for. You don't really learn from them, but they're necessary sometimes to get jobs."

She is a retired parochial-high-school teacher. Her husband, also retired, is in the backyard, "painting screens and stuff." Her older son, Rick, thirty-three, works for the city. Johnny, twenty-nine, retarded, is reclining, as he watches us. Her married older daughter lives in the suburbs—"a marketing analyst, whatever the hell that means" [Laughs.] Her younger daughter was killed in a car crash in 1974—"a drunken driver. He was killed, too, poor devil."

The twenty-year mortgage was finally paid up in 1982.

The black neighbors that we have are nicer and more loving than the white neighbors we had. They were all social climbers, scrambling. They moved either to the southwest suburbs or up to the Northwest Side. To get away from "them." We stayed, as the neighborhood was changing. My father-in-law had his countdown every day. He used to sit out there with his cane and just stare mean [*Assumes low, gravelly voice*]: "I saw six colored walking down the street today." [*Laughs.*]

My daughter's friends that live out in the suburbs are paranoid about the black situation. I never had any problems. I did when the neighborhood was mixed, white and black. When it became all black, nobody could accuse me of prejudice.

They're high-class black people. The man who lives next door retired from the post office. He was an engineer or something. The neighbor on the other side is a salesman. We've been invited to their weddings and graduations. You go down the street, teen-agers, anyone, you smile at them, act decent toward them, they give you back what you give them. It's an exchange between two equals.

My old friends say, "How can you stay there? Aren't you afraid?" They rationalize, have to defend what they did. They can't say, "I moved because I'm a white racist." They have to say, "I moved because the neighborhood is so terrible." There are incidents here. We've had our car stolen. We got it back. The garage has been broken into. But it happened when it was a white neighborhood. But if you're a racist, you use that as an excuse to hang your fears on.

(Johnny calls out from the couch. For the moment, he leaves his private world and the pages of the TV Guide. *His mother and he have an easy exchange about a television program.)*

When our daughter was killed in that crash, our white neighbors said: Too bad it wasn't him. [*She indicates Johnny.*] Is he any less worthy than any other human being just because he is retarded? They thought it was surprising that we didn't get rid of him right away, which the doctors all told us to do. Our black neighbors like him. They think he's darling.

Remember what J. M. Barrie said, I forget the play: "In love's army, only the wounded can serve."

When he was a little guy, I'd take him to the grocery store. He'd pat women on the butt, just friendly. The white women would be furious and make remarks to me [*Assumes a low, mean voice*]: "Why don't you have that child put away?" If it was a black woman, she'd turn around and say, "Oh, hi, honey." I don't know what it is. Do white people, white women, have some kind of sex hangup? Right away they'd put some kind of sexual connotation on his loving act. Could it be a legacy of the puritan revolution?

A lot of black children are misclassified. They're put in with the mentally retarded when actually they have been socially deprived. A black kid who was put in Johnny's class would come over here and play with him. To Johnny, there are no enemies, only friends. We came home from church one day and he had a load of Jehovah's Witnesses booklets. He bought them. He asked how much, opened up his wallet, and they just took it all. [*Laughs.*] I was really angry about it, but I didn't say anything 'cause he was so proud he made this purchase on his own.

Teen-aged black boys, that is something to worry about. Once when I was driving, coming up the light, one of them superfly boys pulled up his car alongside of me. He had a hot young gal in the car with him. I started forward and he said, "White bitch! You stay right where you are. Don't you dare try to get ahead of me!" This white bitch stayed where she was, I wasn't going to argue with him. I think he was showing his manhood to his girlfriend. I don't feel that's indicative of everybody.

When I was younger, I used to go in Jackson Park all the time. In high school, me and my boyfriends, we'd go in there and neck. Today, if I were a young person, I wouldn't. I think you're asking for trouble.

Think of that boy who stabbed the poor devil on the CTA the other night. Who is he? Where does he come from? He has no home, he lives on the CTA. Home is where they have to take you in. I think, There but for the grace of God go I. My father's family came here to get away from the potato famine, 1840. They worked on the Erie Canal. So much Irish history suppressed. We were the niggers of the time. I can't understand that people who were victims of prejudice can turn around and do it to somebody else.

I think the only change can take place if there's a mingling, but I don't see how it's ever gonna be. Any more than, say, the Palestinians and the Israelis. The Palestinians are like the Irish Catholics up in Belfast. Or like the blacks here.

In order to justify prejudice against another group, the superior group has to regard them as subhuman. The same as the Irish were regarded by the Protestants. The APA, the American Protective Association. They were saving America for Americans. Get rid of all these damn Irish who were the cause of all the trouble, of the crime. The Irish were the ghetto people in those days. There probably was a lot of crime because they were denied jobs.

When my daughter was killed, I went to the inquest. The other driver, who was drunk, swerved over and hit her. He was killed instantly, neck broken. At the inquest, his wife and children were there. Did I tell you he was black? I felt so sorry for her. I didn't have any guilt that my child caused this. But she knew her husband caused it. When I went up to her, she flinched. She didn't know the girl who was killed was white. She thought I was going to hit her. I said, "I want you to know that I don't blame you or your husband for what happened. I'm going to pray for you." She started to cry. She didn't expect this. She thought I was gonna scream at her and holler: "Your husband and you, damn you black people." But I think she had a much worse thing to bear than I did. I just walked away.

IANNA KNOX

"My father worked in a steel mill for thirty years. My mother worked at Carson, Pirie, Scott in the domestic area for thirty years. When I was little, I worked as a popcorn girl in a movie theater."

She has four children. Her oldest daughter, twenty-six, has a family of her own; her son is twenty-two. Her two youngest girls are nine and seven. She is twice divorced.

For the past three years, she has been an outreach worker at a public housing project. "I also worked with drug-abuse women, who needed their self-esteem lifted. I took young mothers to the clinic to get better health care, to reduce infant mortality. Most unmarried, all black. My youngest client was thirteen."

Less than three feet from the door, there was a dope drop-off. You would see wads of money in their hand and you'd see the transference of drugs. They just became very disrespectful of us. Within earshot, you would sometimes hear them talking about a shoot-out or a gang war. This was about to happen any minute.

Recently, I was robbed within the area by one of my so-called brothers. I had picked up my children from school. As I opened the door of my car, here was this guy with a revolver, putting it into my side. "Get in before I blow your blank-blank off." I was naturally terrified because my children were standing right there. So I got in. He reached over and took my bag. The one right here. [*She indicates a leather purse, embossed with complex African designs.*] I was just really devastated. He ran down the street.

I sat there for a moment and I said, "No, you won't." I told my kids to hit the floor. I made a U-turn in the middle of the street and followed him. I had a moment to contemplate whether I wanted to run over him, but that's not really my nature to do. [*Laughs.*] I'm not a person just to hurt somebody. He continued to run.

I saw these brothers on the street and I called them to stop him because he had my bag and I wanted it back. They chased him, he turned around and fell. He got up with a gun, okay? The brothers jumped back. One guy said to him, "Hey, man, give the lady back her bag. It could be your mama or your sister. Don't do your people like that." He threw the bag down.

I followed him straight back to the building that I worked out of, okay? I flagged down the police that was coming down the street. In the meantime, here come the brothers running up: "Lady, lady, here's your bag!" Okay. It was a good feeling to know they were really my brothers. These little girls was standing there and they said, "The man just got in the elevator with the gun stuck down in his pants. He lives up there in 1406." So the police went up there and brought him down. I had all these witnesses along with my children. The guy is still in jail.

I have been counseling his wife. She asked was I going to continue to press charges against him. I told her, "Yes, because he violated me. You just don't disrespect people like that." So she said, "Okay. I hope you don't change your mind. He steals all my food, he steals everything in the house and sells it for drugs. Maybe I'll have the opportunity to get my life in some better order." Okay?

I was a little suspicious of her. "Did you not know that your man was going out to do something like this?" From what I understand this was not his first time. She says, "I didn't know just what to do." About two weeks ago, she came down to the office crying. Housing had promised her a refrigerator and all her food was spoiled. I said, "Sister, dry your eyes. We can work it out." I sat there and did a budget with her. She had enough money coming in to buy her own refrigerator. I gave her the phone number of a company where she could get a pretty good one for sixty dollars.

She said she didn't have any food. Her babies need milk. We had a food pantry with powdered milk. I had it taken up. She went to hug me: "I love you." I stood back: "Sister, I love you, too, but that's my job." A hug I could do without because I just don't trust this lady. You just don't hug everybody. She coulda had something under her bag. Since then, I've taken a self-defense course.

This guy recently sent me a letter. He's been in jail about eight months. He was very sorry for what he did and they're trying to give him ten years and to please forgive him and help him. I sent the letter back. He's had many offenses.

The self-defense course is one of the best moves I ever made. A lot of times you cannot have a man with you, and some things you have to do go beyond sundown. Now I have the Lord with me and God is my protector. I'm vice-president of my church choir. But God has also given me intelligence. Now if someone comes up to me, I have a way to protect myself. I like that.

I'm not worried but I've become very stressful. I'm in the middle. There's a lot of people in the community that want something out of life. You have some private homes that people take time with and care for their property. They pick up all around. And you hear the natural English language being spoken. It sounds good to me. But then you also have another language, commonly known as cussing. I become very tired of that. You wake up in the morning and a lot of times it comes along with the chirping of the birds. [*Laughs.*]

The neighborhood is a combination: working people, trying to do something positive with their lives, and a class of people around that don't want to do nothing. Drugs is very high in this community, and I refuse to believe that the police don't know nothing about it. One of them would go to jail and be out within a couple of days. When the police was called, with which you didn't have anything to do, the implication was on you. It was very stressful to me and scary.

To relieve the stress, I used to smoke marijuana as a form of self-medication. But I got to the point where I didn't need it. The God that's within me is my comforter. I wanted to be in control of my life and my brain is important.

What happened is: I fell in love with me. Your first love should be yourself. I began to have a purpose in life. You have to set an example for the young. I cannot be on drugs. I cannot be out of control. How can my children find themselves if I don't know myself?

I've been looking through magazines, seeing another part of the world and saying, "Oh, I would like to go there. I'm going to Africa. That's my motherland. My foreparents were kings and queens. I'm a queen." You can't work toward that when your mind is all cloudy.

My first husband did nothing for my self-esteem. I was constantly put down. I needed more than just cooking, cleaning, taking care of the kids. To let him tell it, I didn't do that very well. I wanted to be able to do something for somebody else. I went into the hospital field.

I was an EKG technician, electrocardiogram. I started cleaning out toilets and emptying beds. When you're in a hospital, you can give a person a drink of water or someone has to use the bathroom real bad and is too weak to get up and the nurse's aide is busy. Can you imagine just the good feeling you feel if you just slip a little bed pan under them? It makes you feel like you really did something.

I stayed at the hospital for thirteen years. When I got pregnant and my first husband had left, I experienced public aid for the first time in my life. I hated it because I was used to taking care of myself, and public aid is such a put-down. You're looked on as lower than low.

I hated to go sit there with all the people asking you, "Where's the father?" You don't know and look like a whore. If he does come around with a little bitty money to help, you're cut off.

I got to the point where I couldn't pay my bills and was fixin' to be put in the street. My phone, my lights, and my gas were fixin' to be cut off. It was difficult for me to feed my children and I was at the end of my rope. The father of my two small children, my second husband, was piecing some of the rent together but he hardly had nothing.

I saw this faith lady. She told me about this old man, eighty-two, eighty-three years old. He was looking for a room. He laid down in the bedroom and gave me $400. He said, "I'm old and I'm sick and need the phone. Get it." He said, "I need lights and stuff. Get it." I got it. He started giving me $300 a month.

A lady friend said she wanted somebody to take her phone calls. Since I was home during the day, I answered it. So I started an answering service business and had six clients. I bought me a massager and started doing massages on the side. [*Laughs.*] Then I had a whirlpool at home because I had trouble with my knees. Some older people wanted whirlpool baths, so I started giving them whirlpools and massages. Then I took a course in reflexology to do feet. So I started that, massaging nerve endings. I also studied with a naprapath and nutritionalist. And helped women with weight management. It was just perseverance. I was getting over. I had to survive.

I heard of this agency that taught self-esteem as well as nutrition and exercise. I excelled to such a point that they asked me to work with them. I also studied at home and got my GED in nine months. It was all very stressful to me and I gained a lot of weight.

Friday's my last day here as an outreach worker. Now I'll be working for another agency as a housemother for six teen-age girls who have behavioral problems. I'll be working on their self-esteem as well as nutrition. Giving them food for the mind as well as body, just uplifting them.

I've been exposed to a few race incidents. Being overweight and black with nappy hair has its drawbacks in the white society. [*Laughs.*] When they see this excess weight, the reception is not the same as a big old white woman. It's a little different if you're small and black with straight hair. She has a better chance. It's no mistake about who *I* am. [*Laughs.*]

When someone looks at me, they know I'm an African queen. I come from kings and queens in Africa and there's nothing I can't do and nothing I can't have. All I have to do is claim it and work toward it.

You're studying my bracelet, aren't you? That's a Susan B. Anthony dollar. On the other side is a calming stone from Africa. It gives off a certain vibration, has healing power. It's turquoise and was a gift from a white man. He was the man in my life, Jewish. Twenty-five years older than me. We'd see each other a couple of times a week. I was about thirty then, not the heavy woman you see.

It was my first close encounter with a person of another race. I felt very strange when we'd meet and people would look at us. We'd walk down the street and he'd want to hold my hand and I wouldn't. He was nice.

My exposure to white people has been very limited. I go to white folks to buy my clothes, my shoes, things like that. The principal of the school my children went to was white and she was beautiful. The pastor of the school was white and he was beautiful. I was raised around white nuns and white priests. I went to Catholic school from kindergarten and almost finished high school. I was treated fairly. A lot of white people are warm and lovable.

Louis Farrakhan's got a strong following and he's got some value. But I don't go to his lectures because I don't like the frisking. You go into the tent and they feel you all over to make sure you don't have any type of weapons. They go through your bags, feel all over your body. I don't need that.

In some ways, race relations has gotten better, and in some cases, worse. You're in some white area of the city, a little turned around, trying to get to some point. You see in their eyes: "I hope you're lost and not looking for some house over here." They will gladly tell you where you want to go, so you can just get away from there. My feeling was, "Lord, I hope nothing happens to my car. Don't let me have a blow-out, don't let my gas get low, because you never know."

I remember I got turned around a little and all I saw was white faces. I was looking for a black face to ask, but there wasn't any. I asked this white couple and they were so happy to give me directions. [*Laughs.*] They were like, "Hurry up and get on away from here." [*Laughs.*]

I wrote a poem that says it all. Would you like to hear just a few lines?

> There are many spirits in this land
> It is the land of good and plenty,
> Plenty of bad, plenty, too.
> You must be strong or you won't last long,
> It's all up to you.

JIM AND KATHY KISH

He is plant manager of what was a small ma-and-pa shop "that's growing and getting people of different ethnic groups and philosophies." She works for a travel agency. They have a seventeen year old daughter.

JIM: I was born and raised on the South Side of Chicago. Both my parents emigrated from Hungary. I played with black children. I used to go to their house, back and forth. I consider myself a person grown up with the principles of the old country, a hardworking individual with responsibilities.

I live right now in an integrated suburb, south of Chicago. Middle-class, blue-collar. They worked in the steel mills and International Harvester. It's a good place because of its caring people.

KATHY: I'm Chicago-born. My mother, first-generation Italian. My father is many-generations-removed Irish. Our neighbors are friendly. It's been integrated for a long time. We're again seeing some panic and stuff going on, but it's stable.

My dad's mom was from Kentucky, so he thinks of himself as a Southerner. He tells a story that when he was a child, he had a black mammy that he ran away from home to be with. In reality, he's very prejudiced. I'm sure as soon as two black people move on his block, he's gone. He's not afraid to talk about it. He thinks that absolutely this is the right thing. He believes that there's actually intellectual differences between the two races. My mom also feels the same way, pretty much. She's more condescending about it. It's like if you work with them, it's okay. But she too would move as soon as two families came on the block.

I grew up thinking when black people crossed 95th Street, we better all start to worry and move. I was scheduled to go to a high school that was seventy-percent black, so my mom pulled me out and I enrolled in a nice Catholic all-white girls' school. So I grew up that way.

About ten years ago, when my husband and I started going back to church, it certainly changed that perspective. It was about the time I began to realize that all policemen weren't real good and that all black people weren't real bad. I've never had any real bad experiences with black people any more than I would with white people.

JIM: We moved to Rosemoor, and I married the girl next door. Race started to become an issue. They had what you call the Rosemoor Association. Businessmen: "If you have to move on us, we'll buy up your house for X amount of dollars to keep the blacks out." My dad adamantly refused to take part. He didn't believe in it. He might dislike a person because of who they are, not because of color.

KATHY: My folks didn't take part either, but it wasn't because of all these noble reasons. They just thought it wouldn't work. [*Laughs.*] White flight started and people just started running.

I was taught from early on that you went to an all-white school. If the school had too many blacks, we'd sell the house, we'd move. You just didn't associate with blacks. I remember coming home and telling mom that I thought this little boy was so nice. I was maybe fourth-grade. "What do you mean he's nice? He's black! What's the matter with you?" The black people, you just stayed away from them and that's it. You never questioned things.

When Jimmy and I got married, our wedding ceremony was to begin at four. Previous to ours was a three-o'clock for a black couple. My mother was so furious because the girl stayed over to take some pictures. It just wrecked the wedding for her, this black person and all her relatives all over the church steps. It was twenty-two years ago, but my mother tells it with the same enthusiasm that she had then.

JIM: I'm the baby of the family, two brothers and a sister. Their feelings are comparable to mine. My sister had a house in Harvey, which is mostly black. It's integrated but a lot of whites have left. Harvey has a terrible reputation. I don't think it's that bad. It's got a bad rap. Her husband has a lot of prejudice in him. He makes derogatory remarks.

Where we live now, it's changing. I hold a lot of responsibility toward the real-estate people. They don't advertise that people live here to keep it integrated. And it works. We all live here and we live differently. There's a lot of appealing features and it's a stable community, although the realtors don't put anything in it to make it more appealing. I think it will always be that way. The black people that live here are *really* outstanding, good people.

KATHY: We have maybe four or five black families on our block. They're all working people. Single-family dwellings. They're either real young families or older, retired.

What happened that led you to change your attitude?

KATHY: Jimmy happened. We were married about five years, we had our daughter, and he wanted to go back to the church. I was baptized, had my confirmation, otherwise I couldn't go to the Catholic school, but I had no religious values at all. We thought it would be good for the kid. It was a real conversion for me.

I had to begin to have my own ideas, my own opinions. I just really couldn't get enough of learning. I began working on a peace-and-justice committee, about the nuclear-arms issue. I saw myself changing and realizing that it was okay. You don't have to say, America, love it or leave it. You could still critique some of these things and it didn't mean you were less of a citizen or less loyal to the United States or your parents. And when Len* went over to St. Anne's, we went along with him. The parish he left, the one we were in, the social-justice end of it was flying out the window.

JIM: Len's a real activist. It's hard to be Len's friend and not be involved. He can certainly energize people so it's real exciting. Many of the pastors are afraid to say what he says. They're afraid to go to their parishioners and say, "Why don't we work together to integrate?"

The issue of race is *the* issue, especially in the workplace. I get a big charge when I bring it up. I see how defensive people are. I'm in charge of this one plant that has a hundred employees. There's four blacks. I'm the

* Father Leonard Dubi.

one that brought them in. I learned just a couple of weeks ago that a person's big secrets are his own fears. The biggest fear is the black issue.

The one fellow kept saying This dumb nigger this, this dumb nigger that. I called the black guy over and said, "Why does this guy keep on calling you a dumb nigger?" He says, "That's how he is because he's from the South." He understands it. But, you see, I want accountability from these people. If you're going to make derogatory remarks, say it to the person. So I bring the black guy over. "He's right here. Say it to him." The guy stutters and says, "Well, I didn't mean to say it." Now his back's against the wall. So now he's quieted down on it.

Funny thing, when I worked at Harvester, this black committeeman would always holler when there was a confrontation. I said, "Why are you screaming at me?" He said, "You know I like you and I know you like me. But when I'm in front of the black people out there, I got to put up the image."

The Mexicans that work for us? The next guy says, "Boy, that taco-beaner." So I say to the Mexican right there, who didn't hear him, "Why are you a taco-beaner?" The guy that said it becomes real nervous and fidgety on me: "That's not what I meant." "Well, that's what you're telling me." He never called him that again.

KATHY: I'm a travel agent. I had an experience a couple of months ago. A rep from one of the touring-bus companies came to me. I'm looking at her new brochure. "If you look on page fourteen, you'll see our Natchez, Mississippi, tour. You don't want to put any black people on it." I said, "Who do I want to put in it?" "You want to put on WASP." I said, "I do?" She said, "That's who the tour is intended for. We take them through these antebellum homes. It's going to be strictly a WASP group." I said, "Aren't there a lot of black people who might be from Mississippi that might be interested in going home? Out here, we're integrated and you're going to get yourself in a world of trouble, lady, running around like this."

JIM: When Len first went to St. Anne's, we did over a hundred interviews with residents. We went to the homes to find out their needs. The absolute number one thing was the racial issue: "Is my neighborhood going to turn all-black? Am I going to lose my services? Are the schools going to get bad?" Every interview started out differently, but it always turned into that.

We had house meetings. We'd invite a hundred neighbors together. It was real enlightening for me. I started out where black people lived on the same planet I did. What I came to find out was that black people had those same fears white people had. They don't want to lose their services. They don't want to have bad schools. They don't want the same things that white people don't want. Where you can bring these people together, it stops all panic. I don't know if they'll ever work on a worldwide scale, but it does in these smaller situations.

When I was at Harvester, I used to have lunch every day with a woman who was a Black Muslim. We used to sit outside in the summertime and she was having her white garment on. Everybody used to jazz me about it. It was an education for me. She said one thing that stuck in my mind after all these years. What would happen if we took all these babies on an island? How would they grow up? We plant a seed in the baby's mind, that's how they grow up.

Want to know my personal fear? I don't want to live in an all-black neighborhood. My next-door neighbor wants to move in an area that would be seventy percent white and thirty percent black. That way he knows his kids will get a proper education. I feel to live in an all-black area is unhealthy because of crime. There's crime in the white area, too. I'm not naïve. But there's more poverty in the black area.

I'm strongly against interracial marriage. I have a daughter and I'm not against the marrying, it's where are you going to live? If he moves to a white neighborhood, how do the poor kids grow up? I don't want babies to grow up where they hate each other.

KATHY: I'm right in line with Jimmy on this. We all have our level of prejudice. Here's two of mine. I don't want my kid to go to a school that's ninety-five percent black, where there's armed guards in the hallway. An integrated school would be fine, even if it's more black than white, say even seventy percent to thirty percent. So since we've been districted into Harvey, where the school is almost all black, we've sent her to a parochial school, even though it's much further for her to go. Busing is okay, if it kept the school on an equal level.

With interracial marriage, it's the practical problem. The kids are really behind the eight-ball as they're growing up. The adults I'm not so concerned about. When I see an interracial couple, I wonder how the kids are doing. It's society in general that bothers me on it.

Another feeling I have is towards an element of black people that do think we owe them something. I don't think we do. There was this one black pastor who would always come from that kind of an attitude. I finally said to him, "I'm sorry but I don't owe you anything. Right now you and I are working together and that's it."

I worked in a totally black neighborhood for a long time. My dad! We had to pass a black neighborhood to find out about his stolen car. Jimmy was driving. We're just sitting normally in the car and he says, "Get down on the floor! There's a bus there and we're comin' to a stoplight. You never know. One of them may have a gun and shoot you just for the fun of it." I said, "It's okay." "This is a terrible ride," he says. "At least put your head down in the lap like this." When we'd come up to the stoplight, he'd say to Jimmy, "Don't stop. Slow down so you won't have to stop at one of those lights."

I go to my parents' house and tell them how wonderful it is to work in these integrated neighborhoods. "That's real wonderful, yeah. Uh-huh. We know you love them. Uh-huh." I've had to deal with all this.

Has he changed?

KATHY: No.

JIM: When we had those riots in 1968, I was visiting her. He came home from work and took off his guns. He put them on the table next to his chair. He starts going on, "When the niggers start breakin' in on the neighborhood, I'm gonna start shootin'." Fear, fear, fear.

KATHY: The night we were writing out my wedding invitations, we were sitting at the dining-room table. My dad's working the three-to-eleven shift at the steel mill. All us girls are sitting there. He smiles real nice, says, "Hi, kids." Goes to his bedroom, takes a handgun, goes to the back door. When he comes back, I said, "What are you doing?" He said, "When I was coming down from the bus, I thought I saw a black person in the backyard." What he did seemed normal to me then.

JIM: Her father is a nice, easy-going guy, but he has all these fears.

KATHY: He was liked by the black people he worked with in the mills. I remember him talking about some guy in trouble financially and the guys taking up a collection for him. It didn't matter if he was white or black. But put him on the block, no. It was fine at work but not where he lived.

JIM: He swings like the Dr. Jekyll–Mr. Hyde pendulum. It's okay as you're over there but don't come over here. I see a lot of that in the workplace. They'll associate with the guy but don't come in my neighborhood. I asked a guy the other day, "How would you feel if Ernie Banks moved next door to you?" "Oh, that would be great." "What's the difference between him and some other black person moving in?" "Ernie Banks has money."

At one of our meetings, a black fellow made a profound statement that stuck in my mind. "You sell me the house for $95,000. The day after I buy the house, you people run away and my house is only worth $75,000. What you fail to realize, next place you run to, I'm going to run there, too." What a lot of people don't realize is that black people move to where they are because they just want better for their families, same as the white person does.

KATHY: My cousins, my whole family think Jimmy and I are whacked out, nuts because we live in an integrated area. I tell them that their $200,000 house in Palos, they can get here for $100,000. But they don't care. *We're* the crazy ones. When they come over for the holidays, I say, "Be sure to bring your guns."

JIM: This black friend comes to my house now and then and he always locks his car doors. He said, "You have a lot of crime here." I said, "What? You live on the West Side, where there is real crime." He said, "The only difference is I know about my crime. I don't know about your crime." So he comes into a mostly white neighborhood with fear.

I have another black friend who comes over, and I tease him: "You walk in the house now and all the neighbors will start talking out there." He starts laughing, gets a big kick out of it, and he'd walk around the house and start shouting, "I don't know about that stuff over there, it belongs over here!" Just to have fun, to infuriate the neighbors. Every once in a while, the neighbors say, "Who was that black person?" I say, "Don't worry, I'm selling the house." They know I'm joking, but that's what fear does.

KATHY: I think we're ahead of where other people are.

JIM: Suburbs like ours are the best-kept secret. I think it's an awareness and a growing thing. We're the thing of the future.

KATHY: These churches coming together has played a big role. It has allowed us to organize grass roots, so we can know each other and then go to some of the problem-causers. Go where the money is: to the realtors and banks who are putting tons of money in commercial stuff, building in Colorado, and no money in the community. We've been devastated with unemployment. We've had Harvester move out, steel mills close. We're now able to take people and go to these banks and big places and say, "You're here, put money here and put people to work."

For me personally, race relations has improved. There was only one way to go and that was up. My mom and pop think it's a way of turmoil. They're uptight. I don't have that in my lifetime anymore. I feel more peaceful about the way I think.

JIM: I was driving through Robbins, one of the poorest suburbs in the nation. All black. I saw some little kid playing in the street with his toys. He has his little car and he's going mmm-mmm, making a car noise. I thought to myself, "We're no different. He thinks like I thought when I was his age."

■ ■ ■ ■ ■

The Park

JIM CAPRARO

It is an easy, sunny autumn afternoon, 1990. He is driving me along the streets of Marquette Park, Chicago.

The name immediately calls forth a troubled memory of this neighborhood on the city's Southwest Side, 1966. It was here that Martin Luther King, while leading a march, suffered what he described as his most traumatic experience; never had he encountered so much hate, not even in the South. He had been struck by several hurled rocks. Cars were overturned and burned.

Jim is the executive director of the Greater Southwest Development Corporation, a not-for-profit neighborhood group. "We set out to revitalize this area.

"I lived here all my life and married a girl who grew up in this neighborhood. I live three blocks away from my wife's parents and seven blocks from mine. I have two kids. My son is a sophomore at St. Rita's, a high school I attended. When he was in sixth grade, he was in the same room my wife had been in."

In 1966, this was pretty much an all-white neighborhood. There were some Hispanics, not many. No blacks. It was more fear than hate. They thought that if black people moved in, stores would be abandoned, factories close down. Because of race. There was something about blackness. They feared the neighborhood would deteriorate.

(*Throughout our ride-around, he is continuously pointing things out.*)

Sears we're in front of is very profitable. When I started working here in 1976, it was surrounded by vacant, burned-out buildings. It was just a desolate, threatening area. You should have seen the charred bricks and rubble, the boarded-up buildings. People were afraid to walk here. It didn't make any difference what color you were, you were just fearful of being here.

We set out to put together an economic-development program. Our feeling was if people could do normal things together, like shop in a grocery store—See those two women walking into Sears?

(*A young white woman with a child in her arms is accompanied by an older woman, probably the grandmother. Immediately behind them is a young black couple. They enter the store together. The avenue is busy. People of all colors are strolling, window-shopping.*)

See that church in the background? I went to grade school behind that church. St. Rita. We're building a senior-citizen apartment complex right next to it. On the waiting list, we have black people, whites, and Hispanics.

There's Marquette Video, right across from the church. It was a real-estate office. I was sixteen, stood across the street, and I watched Martin Luther King and a number of other people picket this office, surrounded by jeering crowds.

We still have a problem we're working on. This is a burned-out building that was an insurance fire.

(*We're passing* the *park.*)

If this were summertime, you would see loads of children in the play lot: black, white, Spanish kids playing together. See those three girls? Walking out of Maria High School, run by the Sisters of St. Catherine. One's white, the other two black and Hispanic. 1966? Oh, God! Never in a million years.

I was sixteen, when Martin Luther King marched through the park. That corner we just passed, I grew up on that block. One day I walked out of my house. I had just gotten my driver's license and was really excited. Dad said I could borrow the Chevy and I had a date. I was flying high. There's the house! I couldn't pull the Chevy away from the curb because, in front of my house, bumper to bumper, up my whole block and the three blocks around, there were buses. They were the size of the yellow school buses. But these were blue. I didn't know what was going on until I watched all those police officers get off in riot gear. It was the first time I had ever seen the riot helmets that became famous during the Democratic Convention in '68. They were forming up on my block in little platoons and double-timing down to Marquette Park.

My world changed that day. All of a sudden things I didn't understand happened. I grew up believing that this was part of America, with equal opportunity for all. That's what the Adrian Dominican nuns taught me at St. Rita, what my parents taught me. Here I was watching police going down to protect people who were trying to exercise free speech. I went down to the park to see what was going on. This was troubling, unsettling, and confusing.

I watched a car with two black people, who were unfortunate to be stopped by a red light. They were surrounded by a crowd of angry people. I watched a teen-age girl, who under other circumstances I might have thought was pretty, a girl I'd have liked to ask out on a date. I watched her jump on the hood of the car and start to kick at the windshield, yelling and screaming. Her face was twisted in rage and fury. I watched as cars burned and other things were set on fire. I remember the helicopters overhead. I had never seen them before, close up. The people standing around screaming and yelling.

At that moment, I went through a transformation. I wasn't really aware of much. I had made it through geometry and was interested in girls and had learned how to make good grades on tests without doing homework, and I was learning I would never be the world's next best shortstop for the White Sox. It had been one of my aspirations, the new Louie Aparacio.

My friends felt the same way I did, troubled. But a lot of the kids I grew up with were out there throwing rocks and bottles. They acted as if the stereotype was true, as though it was programmed to happen. Like there was a sickness here. What the nuns taught us about Jesus and the law of love, I didn't see that day. It sounds corny, but in the 1950s, you believed in your heart of hearts all those phrases about America and opportunity.

All this happened in August. In September that year, there were announcements on the school p.a. that anyone who took part in the rock-throwing would be immediately expelled. The violent reactions had somehow become part of their being.

How come you weren't one of the rock-throwers?

I don't know. I just knew it wasn't right. I didn't have a clue in those days what was the side of good, but I knew throwing rocks was the side of evil.

My mother and father were hardworking people with good values. They were always upset when I was a kid and people talked all the time about the Mafia and stereotyped all Italians. Al Capone and all that. I think about that today when people talk about the El Rukns or the drug-traders and stereotype all black people. I think they could relate to these things.

My maternal grandparents came from Italy, and as soon as they landed, my grandfather went to work in a large Italian printing shop. My mother and her two sisters and her brother all went to work. They pooled their resources and bought a two-flat right here. It was the ethnic American dream, to move up a little bit in the world.

I grew up living in the first floor of that two-flat. I was one of those Southwest Side Catholics who believed there were two kinds of people in the neighborhood, the Catholics and the Publics. There were eastern Europeans. Mostly Lithuanian. Some Polish. Irish and Italians, too. All lily white.

It was in the fifties, when the economy was pumping. TV had just come into its own. I was one of the first TV children, I guess. There was something strange about that. We all grew up wanting to live like Donna Reed. We all wanted to be out in the suburbs someday. Later, we wanted to be like Dick Van Dyke. He had this nice, placid suburban setting with his beautiful wife, Mary Tyler Moore. They had one beautiful child, Robbie. And that's the way it was supposed to be: successful, affluent, upper-middle-class. The suburbs, that's where the good life was.

Although we had a great neighborhood in a lot of ways—pick-up baseball, Little Leagues, the YMCA swimming pool—we always expected that we wouldn't live here someday. We expected it to racially change and the neighborhood wouldn't be quote good anymore. That it would be a bad neighborhood. There was some sort of fixed time period when all of a sudden things would change and get bad. In their minds, it was linked to racial change.

There was fear. There were some who felt actual hate. But the majority, I think, simply felt fear that the cohesive neighborhoodness wouldn't be here any longer.

The Adrian Dominican Sisters instilled in us a number of values. I'll never forget fifth grade and a class on Jesus and what it meant to love your neighbor. It may sound silly, but it sticks with me to this day.

My mom and dad worked in a factory and they had a lot of black and Hispanic friends. They come to our house. It never dawned on me that they didn't really live in the neighborhood, that they had to come from somewhere else. We'd go on company picnics and I would play with their kids. It seemed quite natural, though in retrospect it was actually unnatural when you think of my neighborhood.

After the King march, the neighborhood went back to being what it was. Nothing changed immediately. In the interim, there had been other incidents. Marquette Park became the symbolic battleground in the war of the racists. It became to that war what Vietnam was to the fight against communism. It was the place where people of strange ideologies would come to do battle. The American Nazi Party, with twenty-four members, opened up an office, just down this street. It was stuff of high visibility.

Meanwhile, the people who lived in bungalows and two-flats continued to lead their routine lives. Working-class people. They were never rich people out here. They were the people who worked for rich people. They worked on the production line or on the shipping-receiving docks. With blacks and Hispanics.

When people talked about neighborhoods deteriorating, they attributed it to race. That was the first thing our group challenged. Deterioration is not due to race; it's due to economics. You don't have a bakery that stays in business if the people don't have enough money to buy jelly rolls. People looked at the old neighborhoods, where once there were bakeries, and they'd say, "See what happens when 'they' come." So we put together an economic-development plan.

We started on this corner, the racial dividing line. There were no stores here, because the whites didn't come here and neither did the blacks. You had vacancies, broken windows, and fires. We said there's enough of a market here, in this middle ground, if people could do routine things: going to the store together, standing at the butcher counter of the supermarket, stocking shelves, doing brake jobs in the Sears automotive section, going to McDonald's together. Living life as most people see it. Being normal. We chuckle around here, thinking about it. We got about $45 million in investment along this main street. People drive down here now and they'll come in, sit down, and say, "This looks pretty normal."

In 1982, when the first black families moved in, we had some rocky times. Nothing happened with the very first black family. As more and more moved in, there were fire-bombings by young thugs. Through the diligence of community groups and church groups, those people were prosecuted and sent to prison. It's been a long time since something like that happened. Five years ago was the last incident.

We've been very active with banks and savings-and-loans to make sure the area is not redlined or disinvested. No more withdrawal of credit offerings in a neighborhood so it's hard to get a loan. Conventional mortgages as well as FHA are still available here.

We also act as a developer. The building we're sitting in right now, our group's headquarters, was our first project. When we took over, it was seventy-five percent vacant. One of our two tenants was a pornography shop. We rehabilitated the building and started to rent it out. Where the adult book store was is now a black-owned business. It was the first one at this intersection. Now we have Spanish-owned and Palestinian-owned firms here as well as black and white.

In '68, I was in Grant Park during the Democratic Convention. In college, I got involved in organizing the antiwar movement. That's when I realized I wanted to be a community organizer. These were the years in my life when I felt really alive. Things were changing and I was learning so fast, it was incredible.

I was in a church meeting a few months ago. Right here at St. Rita, a multiracial parish now. A little old white lady spoke: "I've spent all my life being scared to death of what would happen when the coloreds moved in. Some of my neighbors moved out when the first black family moved in. My black neighbors are a lot better than a lot of my white neighbors ever were. They care about their kids, they care about their property, and they care about me, as their neighbor." So you have this fear that comes from stereotyping and generalities. And you have the individual, personal experience.

I'll never forget the meeting at one of the church basements here. It was the first time we got together in a public setting to talk about race. This was taboo in Marquette Park. We had maybe a hundred and sixty people in the crowd. At the end of the meeting, a woman from St. Claire's parish got up and said, "I went and talked to my black neighbors as soon as they moved in. I found out their name was thus-and-such and that they had two children. It was the first black family on the block. One child was learning-disabled and the other was an honor student. The kids are mischievous, just like anybody else's kids. They stopped being the blacks who moved in and started being Mr. and Mrs. Whatever-their-name-is." It's so crazy in that it's so simple.

Property is the big thing here because it's the only investment these people have. The fear goes beyond property. It's fear of speaking out.

Unfortunately the word "gradualism" had had bad meanings in the past. But in the seventies, where you had sudden, immediate changes, things went downhill. It involved block-busting by real-estate guys. People were scared out.

I have a black brother-in-law. Who would have thought, in 1966, when I stepped out my door and saw all those police in riot gear, that twenty-four years later, I'd still be living in Marquette Park and have nephews of a mixed race whom I love very much. My brother-in-law, my sister-in-law, and their children sleep over on occasion, as people in families do. We have a happy life as an extended family. Would that sixteen-year-old kid, a Marquette Park regular, ever dream it would come to this?

I'm beginning to feel that the greatest changes come from people who may hold an extreme position to begin with. It may be the ultimate irony is what has happened here in Marquette Park. A change occurs in people when they feel a deep need. When the troubles are visible. It was easy to see here.

Where it's invisible is where the real trouble is. In the corporate board room, in the suburban setting, on the management level, where pretense is everything. It's not as visible as people throwing rocks, but may be potentially more damaging because it has a nice face on it.

Working-class people know in their guts what our Judeo-Christian ethic tells us. It calls on us to try our damnedest to work at it. If we fall short, that's okay, because we're trying.

Sometimes I get up in the morning and pinch myself. We've made it to this place. It isn't that the challenge isn't still with us. If I could call on a baseball analogy, it's believing you could make it to the pennant and wanting to stay alive in the struggle long enough to make it. I have to remind myself when we have a down day that we never expected to still be here to have this down day. That in itself is a victory.

PART II

Yet and Still

JOSEPH LATTIMORE

"I am a typical African-American."

He is fifty, an insurance broker with another small business. During my appearance as a guest on a black radio station, he, a listener, responded. We subsequently met.

"I was born and raised in Mississippi and after a stint in the army, I came to Chicago to make my fame and fortune.

"I grew up in a small community. Piney Woods. My mother was a music and math teacher; my father was blue-collar, a plasterer.

"Piney Woods was founded by a black man at the turn of the century for underprivileged black boys and girls. We had a lot of northern white people who would donate their time. They were not your typical Southern whites. I played with their small children as equals. It had an integrated staff.

"I didn't have any real southern experience, but I was well aware. If I went to Jackson, which was twenty-two miles away, I had to sit in the back of the bus, and there were the 'Colored Only' fountains and bathrooms."

Some things are better today and some things are worse. In 1954, when the Supreme Court outlawed school segregation, it felt like Christmas was coming. I was fourteen. A year later, Emmett Till was killed. It made me realize that going into Jackson, I could have gotten the same treatment. I was a pretty spirited kid. If I saw a pretty white girl, I might say something, go beyond the borderline of what a black kid could say. It was all in innocence, but it could get you killed.

When I was about five, I was making noise in the classroom. The principal, a white woman from the North, said, "Little Joe, will you be quiet?" I used some profanity that the big boys had put into my vocabulary. I think I call her "a white s.o.b." She was going to tell my mother, I said, "I don't care, 'cause mama don't like white folk anyhow." When I would hear my mother and father talking about the dirty things that had happened, not by someone like this woman, I didn't know one white from another. It was real embarrassing to my mother, and I couldn't sit down for a week. [*Laughs.*] In another environment, I might have been lynched.

We used to go to the black drugstore in Jackson. They were just ordinary people, but someone we could look up to. We didn't think about it as anything glorious. It was just a fact of life. The neighborhood I live in now, all black, still has no black businesses. You've got a few in the city, but not nearly enough where kids in the summertime could work at somebody's drugstore or cleaners.

We encouraged our children to go to college and become computer experts. We didn't encourage them to come back to the family business, help it grow, and become owners. We told them to go to IBM where, even if they were geniuses, they'd never be president. After they finished college, they bought houses in the suburbs or a middle-class community.

We have left the hard-core underprivileged poor, have moved away from them and, as a result, they don't see us, the professionals.

My idea of Chicago, pre-1962, was almost like going to heaven. It was coming to integration, where you could sit anywhere you wanted on the bus, anywhere you wanted in the theater. Utopia. After I got here, I began to realize there was not the integration I had envisioned.

I had just gotten out of the army. I used to hitchhike home across Highway 80, and go through Montgomery and Selma. I could hardly count the number of state police cars. I didn't know what the heck was going on. It was some Freedom Riders or somebody.

I never had any trouble with southern whites. They would give a person a ride if he knew "his place." I wasn't threatening them in any way. My soldier's uniform. Yet I began to realize the dangerous situation I was in.

Vietnam was heating up. We were talking about going over there to fight for freedom, and all these buses were getting bombed and people were getting their heads cracked. I began to wonder, "Why should I go and fight for something that I don't have on my own?" I began to take a closer look on the America that I love. Until that time, although I was aware of things, I would have jumped on a hand grenade. I loved the United States. I had seen all the John Wayne movies. [*Laughs.*]

Mama, who is going on eighty-nine, was in academia and living in a world few blacks knew. She just closed her eyes to everything. My father was pretty close to militant. Mama used to get scared that somebody would overhear him talking about this country. He would be talking about Russia in a favorable way. He wasn't political, but he just knew that we were the one meddling rather than them meddling us. And he'd talk about injustice in this country. I'd get a little ticked off, though I never said anything to him. Oh yeah, I was patriotic.

In Chicago I started out as a bus driver for the CTA. That ended in 1968, with me getting fired and put in jail. I was a so-called leader of the strike. We had a great number of black CTA employees, but nobody in the hierarchy. It was during the Martin Luther King years. We were going to a union meeting one night. We had the numbers and were going to make changes. The president gaveled the meeting to a close as soon as it was opened. One of us jumped up and said, "If you don't bring your ass back here, ain't a bus that's going to move tomorrow morning."

It wasn't really planned. We went back to somebody's house and to our separate bus garages and didn't know what was happening at the other ones. The radio picked up the news. Other drivers on the way to work heard this. It helped us.

Finally it happened.* We were babes in the wood up against the sharks in the water. We weren't going to budge until they gave us our demands. It's difficult to take a working person past payday and keep him loyal. [*Laughs.*] We had a negotiated settlement that was really in a forked tongue. We were outmaneuvered.

They fired us in the leadership positions. Some of us got five days for violating an injunction. We didn't spend but a couple of hours in jail.

During the turbulent sixties, I remember driving the Archer Avenue bus. I'd look back and see a bunch of white folks just reading their papers and feeling very comfortable. I was up there bored over whatever the hot issue of the day was and I said to myself, "Boy, I ought to run this bus right into Lake Michigan, fly it, and jump off." [*Laughs.*]

I'd driven a charter bus of policemen over to Marquette Park during one of Dr. King's marches. That was the first time I had seen him with my own eyes.

I saw the mob. I remember down South we used to say as soon as the

_____

* Larry Heinemann, a returning Vietnam War veteran, remembers the moment, in the midst of the riots surrounding the 1968 Democratic Convention: "Halfway through that Chicago summer in '68, the streets were just crazy. I was driving a bus. The drivers were all tense. There were still reverberations of the King assassination. A week before the convention, the black drivers called a wildcat strike. Anywhere you went, there was this undercurrent."

The Great Divide (1988)

old heads die out, things will be better. I didn't challenge it. But now I saw women with two- and three-year-old children hollering, "Niggers, get out of here!" I knew that a parent was as close to God as a child would encounter. If mama was doing this, it had to be the right thing to do. Now these kids are on their own and I'm sure they have these same attitudes. I know that just living will never end bigotry. There's a lot of things that got to be changed before these attitudes will be changed.

I was thinking about how we celebrate George Washington. If we do anything to knock him off his pedestal, we're really gonna run into opposition. But we got to start telling the truth. He owned other people. If they were good slaves, somebody made them good by beating them half to death or whatever you have to do to a person. It's kind of like the Jews being made to celebrate Hitler. That's the way black people have to celebrate slaveowners of our past.

Remember what you asked on the radio? Is race always on a black person's mind from the time he wakes up to the time he goes asleep? Wouldn't that drive a person crazy? Remember my answer? We are already crazy.

Being black in America is like being forced to wear ill-fitting shoes. Some people adjust to it. It's always uncomfortable on your foot, but you've got to wear it because it's the only shoe you've got. You don't necessarily like it. Some people can bear the uncomfort more than others. Some people can block it from their mind, some can't. When you see some acting docile and some acting militant, they have one thing in common: the shoe is uncomfortable. It always has been and always will be.

Unless you go back to the roots and begin to tell the truth: everybody who participated in slavery was dead wrong. Sure, black folk are probably a little insane. If a soldier back from Vietnam was captured when the war began and had been in a bamboo cage and beat half to death, first thing we'd do is rush him to a psychiatrist.

Same thing with black people in America. Some children were sold from their mothers. A mother seeing her teen-age daughter raped by the slavemaster—I could talk forever about that. If someone would rape my daughter in front of my eyes or sold my daughter and I'd never see her again, sure I'd go crazy.

And if I didn't get any help, for me to raise another child with my insanity, I'd have to pass some of that along. The segregation and discrimination that the next generations went through, it was enough to drive them mad. So our foreparents have been driven mad.

When you see a black like myself proud to call myself Joseph

Lattimore, I don't even attempt to find out who my folks were: the African name that I would truly have. It doesn't cross my mind. Nor does it cross many blacks'. Some, like Malcolm X, yeah. But the vast majority of blacks, none of us are trying to find our way back after we have gotten out from under slavery. I don't know where the story will end, but we are all kind of messed up.

In the black community, we saw the same TV shows as everyone in America. So it is natural for me to want Liz Taylor more than I want Aunt Jemima. And it's normal for my sister to want Tony Curtis over Stepin Fetchit. How would you define madness? [*Laughs.*]

To get out from under this yoke, black people will try to be lighter if that's what it takes. It's like a mouse in a cage with a boa constrictor. The mouse will do everything he knows how to please the boa constrictor, but when the boa is ready to eat, the mouse is gone. [*Laughs.*] Same thing with us. I don't care what we do, if they want to rub out King, they rub out King.

A lot of us are still praying and trusting in God and hoping for a better day. I don't have a lot of faith in a better day coming. I think we'd best be getting on, separating from these people. When Moses led the people out of Egypt, they didn't say, "Let's integrate." They got the heck out of there.

When World War II was over, the Jews didn't break bread with the Germans and be brothers and all integrate. They said, "These people was trying to wipe us off the face of the map. Let's get the heck out of here."

The Indians, as meager as their reservations are, are not in the civil-rights marches saying, "Let's integrate." They say, "Hey, I've still got this little piece of dust, but I will stay here because this man will annihilate you." I just don't have the faith in integration I used to.

I feel like I'm going over to someone's house and they mistreat me. They make me sleep on the floor, they just do me all ways. I say, "Hey, I'll go back home and anybody that visits me, I'll treat you fair. Anybody can come visit me and I will make them feel just as welcome as the flowers in spring. But I'm not coming back to your house anymore, because you made it obvious you don't want me."

You once believed in integration . . . ?

I guess I still do. My daughter is going to the Eastman School of Music. [*Laughs.*] She got pissed off at me the other day. She said, "Dad, I was talking to someone and I sounded just like you." She had protested a tiny bit because Eastman was not respecting Martin Luther King's birthday.

I don't want to build up any hatred in my children, but I want them to know the truth. And the truth is not gonna be found in an American history book. We grew up with these false notions, with these rip-off things. Somebody cheated some Indians out of some land and today history books tell us what a great thing it was to get Manhattan. Taking advantage of another man . . .

As far as integrating with you—we have sang "We Shall Overcome," we have prayed at the courthouse steps, we have made all these gestures, and the door is not open. I'm just tired. Pretty soon I'll have grandkids and they will want to sing "We Shall Overcome." I will say, "No, we have sang that long enough." We should not make a lifetime of singing that song. I refuse to sing it anymore.

I respect Farrakhan. He's an honorable man. I don't go along one hundred percent with anything anybody says. I would question anyone who went along one hundred percent with me, as smart as I am. [*Laughs.*] But I thinks he's got a lot on the ball and he is scratching where it itches—on me and whole lot of other folk.

I don't think he wakes up in the morning and says, "Let me tell off Whitey." I think he tells the truth as he sees it. Whitey interprets that as being told off.

He's advocating starting black businesses and whatnot. I agree with him. Booker T. Washington hit the nail on the head with "Cast down your bucket where you are." It was shortly after slavery and he said, "Hey, let's build up a community."

I don't think college is a total solution. If a kid is gifted and intelligent, he should be encouraged to go. If after about ninth grade, you give him a bite of the apple and show him the way to the library, he will go and get it. And let him do something the neighborhood needs. But in the black community, we're all saying, "Let them be computer analysts." I don't think that will do it.

As for Farrakhan and anti-Semitism—In Mississippi, I didn't distinguish between Jew and white. They were all white people as far as I was concerned. Even today I feel that. Jews might be the step-children of the white race, but they are still white. Tomorrow, if he decided he was no longer religious, he is still white.

There was this thing about Jews having bad meat and inferior merchandise. I'm sure there is some truth in that. I think Jews got caught with their fingers on the scale, but I don't think they were born to do this. Anybody in this capitalistic society will try to get over.

I think Farrakhan is having a bigger and bigger influence. I don't think it's his religious doctrine. I don't think there is any shortage in the

Baptist churches of black people. His social ideas are what is scratching where the people itch.

It's like the black community has been hit in the jaw in a prizefight and they have been stung. If there are two fighters in the ring and one doesn't know he's in a boxing match, this other guy is going to hit him mercilessly. Black folk are still courting white folk, and white folk don't have it anywhere on their mind.

We went out for integration and it hasn't happened. We put our eggs in that basket and they're cracked. You can march, you can shout, you can do anything you want to, but I think we have to cast down the buckets where we are.

I did really believe there would be a harmonious getting along. I was all for Dr. King's March on Washington in '63. But I wouldn't take part in that now. I understand a little more now than I did then. I thought all we had to do was march and let them know we weren't going to bomb them. And put on nice clothes and let them know we bathed and everything. And they would accept this . . . [Laughs.]

I never really thought much whether I would be living next door to whites; that wasn't a burning desire. When I'm in an elevator with all whites, I have said, "Hey, they feel uncomfortable." I have always felt it. But I am not going to let their problem be my problem. I know the problem is there for them. I'm trying to get over mine: wearing an ill-fitting shoe every day of your life. I'm a practical joker. Sometimes I want to say, "Boo!" [Laughs.]

I have no desire to make anyone uncomfortable. I pity misinformed white people. Here we are, a nice, gentle race that has a great desire to be friends. I imagine if I had raped your sister and cut your mother's neck off and castrated your father and you came and told me you wanted to be buddies with me and live next door to me, I would feel awfully uncomfortable. I think white folk, deep down inside, do have that uncomfortable feeling. He feels that if he, the white, was treated the way he treated the black, he'd want to get even. That isn't the case, but he thinks it is.

DENNIS CARNEY

"I'm twenty-five, single, a carpenter. I go out with a girl I might marry. I play softball four nights a week. I like to golf and that's about it. Kind of taking it easy now."

Where I live, they're all alike. Working people, middle-class, white. There
was no blacks in any of the schools I went to. Everyone was pretty similar.
Now there are some other people moving in. Some Arabians and stuff. But
there are still no blacks. Marquette Park was changing when I got out of
there. A lot of Mexicans moving in and Arabians taking over. That's why I
got out.

Where I am now, there's a big stink about the shopping area right next
to us. It's bringing in a ton of blacks. Some people get all uptight about this.
There's blacks I wouldn't mind moving in, working-class blacks with
families. It might cause an uproar. If it did, I'd go with the people in the
neighborhood. They have their reasons why they don't want them there,
and if they want to stick with their own people, they have every right and
I'd back them. It shouldn't be forced on them, like busing. If it happens, it
should happen on its own.

I see what they did to a lot of neighborhoods they have moved into,
and they ruin them. It's not the few that are okay, it's the majority that aren't
that people are afraid of. They lost money on houses. Where I grew up, a
working-people's suburb, everyone moved there from the city. They took
baths on their houses because property values went down. Right now, my
main concern is finding a neighborhood that's not going to change, so I
don't lose money.

About three years ago, I didn't feel that strong. I didn't go through
having to move. I'm not as bad as the people I grew up with. They hate no
matter what they see. You're a nigger and they don't like you. I'm not that
way. I take everybody as I see them. But no one can tell me that the
stereotypes they have about blacks ain't true. They do act like people say
they do. There's a lot of them don't act like that, good people, but there's
more bad than good right now.

What's the stereotype?

They don't take care of their homes, let them run down. Don't like to work.
They get married ten times. I'm not saying a large majority, but a majority.
Just from the neighborhoods I drive through every day on the way home.
They look like shit. They live like low-lifes. I work with black guys that are
okay and all that. They're hardworking, they have families. I've met lots of
them. They don't think anybody owes them anything.

That's another thing. They have attitudes. Just because what happened fifty years ago, everybody owes them something. The guys I know
don't do that. Seems that the ones that have come here from the South are
better than the ones that have grown up in the city their whole life. Just like

my daddy came here from Ireland to work. I don't think any of them have anything against me and I don't have anything against them. They're just good guys.

The ones that left the South were the go-getters and left poor farms to come up here and make something of themselves. But the ones living in these housing projects, they're like third-generation welfare and all that. When I was working hard for a few bucks for a few beers, these guys had everything paid for them, a hundred dollars' worth of clothes, going to a party at night. They had attitudes and they're as big racists as the people in my neighborhoods. My white friends run around the same way, but these black guys are cockier.

A guy walks around with a plastic bag on his head, worried about his curly hair lookin' good. He's got the walk and talks weird. I have a hard time understanding him speaking English. Those people are the stereotype and there's a lot.

I don't think Martin Luther King would be too proud of the way half the people in Chicago act. The first thing they should do is maybe try to speak the language halfway decently. How do you expect to go anywhere in the workplace when you can't even barely speak English? When you see five of them hanging around the corner, yapping, with the music going real loud, it bugs me.

The older blacks are more the working guys. They live in other neighborhoods that I don't see too much. We all eat lunch together every day. We'll go out, have a beer. We're good friends. So I don't think it's the color thing. Once in a while, someone might joke here and there. A black guy might say, "Oh, you gray boys, this cold doesn't bother you." Just joking around. But not too much. If I'm sitting around with a white guy, somebody would say how much they dislike Jesse Jackson. But if a black guy came up, the conversation would halt. Maybe they say things about whites that they wouldn't say when we're around.

There was things that had to be changed in this country. They were definitely getting a bad deal in a lot of ways. But I don't see them taking advantage of the new situation as much as they should. They're just as American as anyone else.

I was in a tavern with two of 'em in their neighborhood. I was treated all right. Everyone in there was okay. If I brought them into my neighborhood tavern, they'd be all friendly to them too. A lot of guys might not like them, but they'd be okay. If they came in alone, some people might say ignorant things to them. It depends.

I live in a border neighborhood. There's a lot of people in and out of buses, and none of them ever get hassled. They're walking up and down the blocks, some deliver papers, no one messes with them. I never hear of any of them getting jumped or beat on. But I wouldn't walk around 63rd and Stony Island.* The only place I go around there is the Checkerboard Lounge, where it's mainly white inside.

They're safer in my neighborhood than I am in theirs. I wouldn't feel safe on the El with money in my pocket, no way.

They might be driving in my neighborhood and they might jump off to go into a liquor store or grocery to pick something up. But I wouldn't jump off in some of their neighborhoods and show I had money in my pocket. Maybe it's me. Nine times out of ten maybe nothing would happen to me. But you're taking a risk in those neighborhoods. Anyone who doesn't think that isn't too smart.

There's just as many white low-lifes. There's a lot of these hillbillies. There are stereotypes about everybody. About me, about Irish people, about Italians. But when you run into the stereotype, you say "that hillbilly," "that dago." I know there's exceptions to every rule. There's some good hillbillies and there's some who let their house run down.

I hate to admit it, but I wouldn't write off a white guy, who gets away with things, as quick as I'd write off a black guy. If I saw some drunk in a tavern and he was white, I might just think, oh, he had a bad day. Maybe he's not always an asshole. But if I saw a black guy bouncing around drunk, I'd think all he does is sit with his bottle of port and drink all day. You find yourself doing that.

I realize some of the bigotries I have. But no one can tell me there aren't people who act like niggers. You can't tell me there's not people that act like hillbillies and there's not drunken Irishmen either. There's good and bad in every walk of life. But I can't be completely open-minded about certain things. I think blacks have done more harm to the city than they've done good. I think this city would be a much better place if there wasn't a majority of black people living here. Things were cleaner in the old days. Oh, I'm sure there was a lot that did their part here when we needed manpower.

Why do you and the other white guys go to the Checkerboard Lounge? It's right up against those housing projects.

Listening to the music. I like the blues. [*Quickly.*] Hey, wait a minute. I never said that if they weren't around, things would be better. They give some good things to this country. If there weren't so many of them, if they

---

* A black community on the South Side.

didn't take up as much space. The country would be better if we didn't have a lot of people on welfare, a lot of people unemployed. I don't think it has to do with the color. If it wasn't for them, we wouldn't have half the good music we have.

My mother is a lot more open-minded. She'd never use the word "nigger." She doesn't have them feelings. But even if she wouldn't admit it, she wouldn't like to see her white neighborhood change. But she'd never scream and yell about blacks. My oldest sister, the one that's a lawyer—she has black friends. She's not a bigot, she's not like me. She's around a different class of people.

If I'd already bought a house and a black guy moved next door, a nice guy, I'd have him be my neighbor and get along with him. I'd invite him to my house.

What if the rest of the neighborhood threatens him and wants to drive him out?

I wouldn't help anybody harm the guy. I wouldn't be out in front of the house throwing bricks or burning a cross on his front lawn.

If I was walking down the street with a black guy that's a friend of mine, a guy I work with, and somebody walked up and called him a name or spit on him, I'd defend him in a minute. But I'm not gonna defend a guy just because he's getting a raw deal, if I don't know him. He has to be a friend. Oh, if I saw a couple of young punks hassling someone, white or black, I'd help him out. On the other hand, I'm not gonna go in and get myself hurt.

If I see a black guy arm-in-arm with a white woman, it doesn't bother me. I don't know if I'd want my daughter comin' home with one, if I had a daughter. But this woman has a right to do what she wants to do. I see a lot of black women that are very nice-looking that I wouldn't mind taking out. [*Laughs.*]

If I'm dealing with them one on one, I'm not a bigot in the least. But if I thought that, as a whole, they're comin' into my neighborhood, I would have my feelings.

I think tensions have diminished a little. Things are a lot more accepted than they were twenty years ago. I remember there was always big riots in the school lunchrooms. Now those kids all go together and they have their little quarrels just like any other kids. You go to a shopping center in my neighborhood, where ten years ago there was no blacks. Now they're around and people just take it for granted.

But there's another thing people complain about where I live. There were places where high-school kids could work, like fast-food restaurants. Now it's all black people working there. They're coming into our neighborhood and taking away the summer jobs that our kids used to have. It's still there. People who were strong about it are just as strong as they ever were.

I've worked with some Hispanic people and my only quirk with them is that they speak English when they're together, but they wouldn't speak English around you. They talk a different language in front of you. I don't think they get the knock on being lazy as much as black people do, because they're working in every restaurant. They work for cheap money. They're bad about that, as far as I'm concerned as a union carpenter. I know they need the money, but it's not good for me.

The only people I really dislike are the Middle Eastern. Arabians. They're dirty, they're loud, they're ignorant. They were all over the neighborhood that I moved out of. The ones I knew from high school were okay.

It irks me that those people can come over here in droves, but there's a bunch of Irish people that want to come here and work, they can't get papers. And the unemployment in that country is terrible. Here's English-speaking, hardworking people that can't get in, and we let these people in. That really bugs me.

What would it be like if this country was all white? Would it be better or worse? I don't know. We wouldn't have jazz, would we? [*Laughs.*] Oh, it would still be pretty diverse, all those different nationalities. [*Muses.*] If this country was all white, it would be different. Better or worse, who knows?

All I know is I hope the neighborhood I live in doesn't change. I hope it doesn't happen to me what happened to other people, going back to a neighborhood they grew up in and cared about and had a lot of memories. Then go back and see the place trashed. I hope that never happens to me.

MAGGIE HOLMES

She worked as a domestic most of her life. I last visited her seventeen years ago.

1973
"What bugs me now, since I'm on welfare, is people saying they give you the money for nothin'. When I think back what we had to come through, up from the South, comin' here. The hard work we had to do. It really gets me when I hear people . . . It do somethin' to me. I think violence."

1990

About race? It's worse. What really bothers me is these whites calling in on the radio and they get uptight, very angry when you get to speaking about the way you was treated here.

What I got angry about, when you had your hundred years of that Statue of Liberty and I got damned mad because it was sickening to me.* That was not made for me. We didn't come through Ellis Island. Do you understand what I'm saying?

What are you celebrating? You came here in chains in the bottom of ships and half-dead and beaten. Why are you going to help them celebrate? A hundred years of what? You was not free. They was in chains, and sold off like cattle. When you think of what you done give up for this country and you got so little. Do you understand what I'm saying?

When I looked at the Statue of Liberty and looked at all them black people up there, I was so mad I wanted to strangle every damn last one of them. Excuse my expression. What are you up there singing and shouting for? You see how them Jews got upset when Reagan went over there to see about the Holocaust in Germany.† They had a fit on Reagan. He had no business to go there. I feel the same damned way about the Statue of Liberty.

Also the flag don't mean nothin' to me. It is just another rag flying through the air. It ain't got nothing in the world to do with me. 'Cause when Dr. King was marching, they were burning things and wrapping themselves around that flag. What is it saying to me? I have no respect.

Now when they put that bra on Mayor Washington and had made him up to look like a lady, the whites wanted to know why we was getting so upset. But the minute you put this rag on the floor and go walking on it, *they* got so upset and angry. But when it comes to a human being, somebody who really tried to do something for this city, they don't see what everybody's so upset about.‡

You look at all the pictures being made in Hollywood and, by the way, Jews made them. They made black people look dumb. Blacks had to act like they're scared, eyeballs bulging and dancing in their head. And, "Yassuh." You wasn't even able to speak. They made money off making

---

* She was referring to the celebration of the Centennial of the Statue of Liberty in 1984. She had followed the extensive television coverage.

† His visit to Bitburg and the graves of German SS men, among others.

‡ A reference to two incidents at the Chicago Art Insitute: the first, a painting of the late Mayor Harold Washington in bra and panties; the second, the American flag on the floor, with an implied invitation to walk on it.

fun of people. They wouldn't give them no decent roles. Why do you think that I shouldn't get upset?

I get so mad at black people, you don't have to stoop like that. Or they want you to be a prostitute or pimp or selling dope. You can get them roles any time. I looked at Ella Fitzgerald and, God knows, I was so mad at her. She was a dope addict in a picture. Ella don't need to be puttin' herself down like that. I was so sick at her. I wouldn't even look at it. Same thing with *Pinky*.* Remember when they had this white woman playing Pinky?

I sits and looks at it. Now I let my kids know what black people have come through, so they don't forget. I teach them about our history. "You having it good besides what your foreparents had it." Even when I come along, in the South, it was horrible. Do you know what I'm talking about?

That's another thing that bothers me when I see this Statue of Liberty. I was thinking about the time they was hanging black people, dragging them, burning them. That's when I get upset when these white people tell me how good it is here. Don't tell me how good it is here. I live here. It's good to you, it ain't good to me. We've got this tradition that anything you do, it may be a long time, but it will come back to you. When they had that storm in Mississippi, they had killed this black preacher, made him curse and sing and dance. That's when they had that terrible storm that flooded them all out. My friend from Mississippi said it came right down their sides.

They say, "Why do you always bring up the past?" Why do whites always bring up their past? They always telling you when they came over here and what kind of a time they had. They never let you forget their history, but they want you to forget yours. Is it so painful for you to think what you have done to us? Do that bother you? They don't have us in their history books. They don't tell you what you contributed to this country. When our kids read a book, you would think that nobody did nothing in this country except the white man.

Take it to the Bible. They are always painting Christ with blond hair and blue eyes. Anybody know that if his mother was from Egypt, how would he have come out with blond hair and blue eyes? Keen features like the English. [*Laughs.*] How could he be like that? How?

1973
When I was in Texas, when I was fifteen, wartime, I was working at this army post. Coffee shop, like. I would see these white guys sit all day long. Black boys standin' an' waitin'. I said to myself, "I will fix them." All

---

* An early film on race relations.

the rest of them black people were scared of their jobs. I didn't care. I've always been like that. When they get through eating, I watched them get their last crumb off the table and I get up and tell them they have to go. If they didn't move fast, I would go there and rake all those crumbs off the table in their laps. They had them khaki pants on, when you put all that grease on it, it spreads. They are neat and clean and don't want all these crumbs and crap in their laps. I'm brushing like hell. "Soldier, no loafing." Just *whop, whop.* I could hear guys whispering, "Don't go on that side, that girl is mean." I said another thing I'm gonna do is sit these blacks in front.

The manager, he calls me in the office. He wants to know why I would sit the soldiers in the front. I said, "I'm glad you asked. I get a letter from my husband and he told me that gun's shooting over his head, and he's on the front line over there. Now would you please tell me why I would seat them in the back and he's up front?"

They called the OD, the MP, the captain, all of them. 'Cause I had some three thousand blacks and the lieutenant said, "Take her out of here—she's a hell-raiser." [*Laughs.*] Do you know what the captain told me?—that I wasn't born here. I said, "What do you mean? I was born in Texas, one hundred miles from here." He couldn't see a young southern black woman talkin' the way she talks. 'Cause I was tellin' the soldiers not to shoot in front, to shoot behind. [*Laughs.*]

1990

When you come up as a kid, you see all this and you know it is not right. You think about when you going to school and the bus pass you. We was walkin' through the woods and the snow and the ice and be frozen. You was payin' for the bus but it wasn't pickin' you up. It passed right by you with all the white kids on it.

I got grandkids, but what is it that as blacks we have to really teach? If you sit and look at that TV, what are their values? Everything on that thing is really artificial. My grandmother and aunts and uncles, they had a certain time for you to be home and you was home. There was no law in the South and the only law you had was your parents. We run away from that. We got a white value and it destroying us good. Kids didn't even smoke, that was a no-no.

We don't have black families no more like we used to have. One thing that makes me sick about public aid, you got this social worker and she tells you right away how you should structure your family. Most of the time, if the mother is on aid, the husband has to leave. Why couldn't they fix it so he could stay at home? I don't mean for him to stay on aid. Just find him a job. So the family can stay together.

Why do you think Cabrini is the way it is? You got all young peoples over there. Years ago, when it first opened, you had families over there. The mother, the father, the families. Now they got nothin' in there but kids. You don't have no structure in the family. Whites made this problem in the projects. And the grandmother was always there, the backbone of the black people's family. I got two of my own grandkids with me and I'm gonna keep 'em.

Let's face it, the whites don't want us to be equal with them. I don't care how much schooling you have. And you've got all this dope in public housing that is destroying young blacks. America can go all over the world and conquer the world, but they can't get rid of the dope. That dope is got to come here on a boat, in a plane. Now how in the world are poor people gonna get that dope on them planes? Who are those millionaires that have made all that money from dope? They sure ain't those blacks in the projects.

It's always a struggle. That's how we got to live in this building here. And where my mother lives across the street. We went downtown with them ropes and police, poking our heads around City Hall. We started around 1966. It was all whites here. You could not live here. They had this "White Way" sign. The first family that moved in here in the fifties, they were set afire. The police station was right on the corner. The lady had to call, but they would not come.

Me and my mother was at that other place. They didn't have no blacks before then. They was putting out the whites 'cause they wouldn't pay the rents 'cause the place was goin' down, they wouldn't fix it up. They would always send you to a place that was goin' down. Do you know what we was doin'? As fast as they was sendin' them out, puttin' out their furniture, we would put them back in. Black an' white together. A lot of whites was chained. Dr. King's people was doin' it. We did it so fast that they would beg to give them a break. [*Laughs.*] Anything that is worthwhile, you have gotta work for it. It's not going to just come to you.

The black people and the Jewish people used to be okay. But the Jews challenged the quota system because of that Bakke thing. In the early seventies or so? He was sayin' he couldn't go to school on account of so many blacks they had put in school. If they had done the right thing in the first place, you wouldn't need no quota. How else you gonna catch up in the fire department, in the police department? It will never even up anyway.

I'm hoping our kids can go to school and get a good education. Kids coming out now can't fill out an application, can't hold a decent job. I am hoping we can get by this racist stuff and look at a person as he is. Like when you go for a job.

Half everything you get now is being made out of this country. We got
people making things for years—airplanes, ships. I'm looking at that ship
with them kids that got killed the other day. The way that ship was made!
They can't make it no more. If you got people who made ships like that,
why can't you let people make refrigerators and stoves and TVs? We was
doing that at first. Why not now? They didn't have no job training. When
wartime comes, they put you on the assembly line, showed how to put this
screw in there and you did it. Why can't they do it all over again? And we
wouldn't have to get mad at the Japanese people all the time. 'Cause we'd
have all these old people who made the good planes. Why can't we take
them to teach the kids? You won't have to pay all this money.

There wouldn't be all these kids selling dope. I'm listening to what
these kids are saying and it's terrible. He can make more money selling
dope. If there is no job for him, he sees this dope and that's what takes over.
You see these guys riding around in these big cars and he's not working,
you know he's selling dope. What is that saying to the young child coming
up? The American dream.

The American dream for the white child is to go to school, go to
college, get a good job. Then you get this home in the suburb, you get this
white picket fence, and your car. Have your two kids or two and a half,
whatever. This is the white man's idea. Well, this black child is looking at
this dope and he's looking at it the same way that all of you are looking for a
home.

Money—we was all brainwashed with that. That's what you was
supposed to do, get it any way you can. The house, the car. The black kid is
thinking the same way, with the dope. If you get that, you have it made.

The first thing I would do if I was president is stop sending our money,
our kids to other countries, helping people kill people. Another thing, take
those companies out of those countries that is helping them. I think all
those places that America is at, those people would be getting along better
if America wasn't there.

Let America keep their hands off. Everywhere he goes, he starts
something up. The white man, the minute he get there, he starts some
fight. They think if you ain't living like them, you ain't right. The American white man knows nothing but to fight. Have you ever noticed they
always go to a colored country to fight?

I hate to see people lose their lives. But people are going to be free. I
don't care how they do it. Because, you know, freedom is a yearning inside
of you. You can't stop it, it won't let you stop. It is something that was born
inside of you. I don't care how much you want it to be still, it will not let
you. It may take awhile, but they are going to be free. It is the same thing

with the peoples here. You don't feel like a whole person until you are free. You can't express yourself, it is just like breathing. If you don't have it, it's like you are starving for something.

BILL AND YURIKO HOHRI

They are both Nisei, first-generation Japanese-Americans. During World War II, they were interned at "relocation centers" : he, at Manzanar, she at the Santa Anita race track. Her home was a horse stable.

He is fifty-three, she is fifty-one. They have lived in Chicago for more than forty years. He works as a computer programmer; she keeps house.

BILL: For me, race is something between whites and Japanese. That's what I grew up with. I lived in one of the few areas of Los Angeles where Japanese could live. In those days of restrictive covenants, it was perfectly legal to discriminate against persons of color. Westwood was off-limits, though I went to junior high school there. There were few blacks, so the conflict was between whites and Japanese. And Mexicans, too.

YURIKO: At school, I was conscious of prejudice against poor people. The children were stigmatized, outsiders. It was more class than color.

BILL: I think racism today has gone underground. It's more covert. We don't have restrictive covenants and things like that today. But it's still there, harder to detect.

The problem of racism has something to do with our self-image. I can't speak for white people, though I think their image of themselves is one of being superior to yellow or black or what have you. Better than anyone who is not their color.

There was racism in the Japanese community, too. Not toward white people. They were viewed as being dominant, someone you learned to cope with. That was the way I grew up.

YURIKO: Just last week, at the checkout counter of the supermarket, there were very loud remarks for my benefit. The elderly couple immediately in front of me were having a conversation with the clerk. "I'm glad I'm not *that* color." They were aware of me, of course. It doesn't happen every single day, but it happens. Racism is very deep-seated. With the world economic situation and competition with the Japanese, we're visible persons to attack.

BILL: I've been on a lot of radio call-in programs, and many comments, especially from older people, indicate there is still a tremendous amount of hostility to the Japanese.*

Racism is universal. I can never understand why the Japanese are so anti-Chinese, when they're the source of much of our culture. I think there's a natural tendency when you go to war to denigrate the other side.

The Japanese have gone through a process of adaptation in this country. Acculturation. Part of it is to pick up all the mannerisms, the language, and the prejudice of the majority culture. If the white culture is antiblack, so are the Japanese-Americans.

YURIKO: I'm afraid I don't really represent the Japanese-American people. The older I get, the more I see that I'm not with the rest of the folks that look like me.

BILL: I think I know why we're considered the model community. When we were being put in camps, during the war, a substantial number of us said, "We're opposed to discrimination, *but* if the government orders us to be put away, we're going to support it and cooperate." This is an attitude the white majority *loves*. What could be a better, more American, attitude to say, "Please don't discriminate against us, but if you do, it's okay?" That makes you the model minority.

I get a strong whiff of racism directed toward other people, because they recognize me as not being black. They feel free to express their opinions. They also know I'm not Jewish, so I get a good sense of the level of anti-Semitism. I had an assignment with a big client, a former president of a downtown bank. He says, "You got to be careful with this prospect. It's a Jewish bank. Those Jews, they're very crafty."

YURIKO: The neighborhood we live in now is multicolored. We have everybody: Koreans, Middle Eastern, Indians, and quite a few blacks moving in. And some whites who've lived here for generations. It has problems of course, but so much vitality. I like it. To my mind, it is what America should be in the future, this mixture. It's the ideal.

---

* He has been one of the leading spokesmen for the Movement for Japanese-American Redress.

BILL: It's a lot healthier. In the old days, if a black moved into the neighborhood, there would have been panic. With nonwhite people, they just don't seem to have that panic. It's beginning to reflect more of the world, the rest of the world.

YURIKO: In the sixties, in our old neighborhood, when I saw a black person waiting on the corner for a bus, I'd put myself right there, too. There were such tensions between whites and blacks that I really did fear for the life of the lone black person. I didn't see why a person might be harried if he happened to be of another color. It's just not proper. I would stand there hoping to neutralize it. In our neighborhood, I feel no need to do it.

BILL: I never would have done that. I don't have the courage—

YURIKO: I don't think that's courage.

BILL: —Because the hostility was very, very thick. I think there's been an improvement. Right after the first Civil Rights Act was passed, they had to integrate the place where I worked. It had been all-white, except for me. Whites and blacks seemed to get along pretty well. The underlying feelings didn't go away, but at least people could work together.

I don't expect feelings to change, because that's something you grow up with. But if you can learn to accommodate, to discover . . . One of the things I don't understand is racial fear. I remember driving to Washington with some colleagues. We were going through the black neighborhood of the city and some guy says, "Gosh, we're in the wrong neighborhood." I said, "What's the problem?" He was afraid we were going to be attacked. I think so much of this fear is born of ignorance.

A year ago, I was in New York and took the wrong train. I wound up in the middle of Harlem. So I started walking through the streets. The fear I might have felt was in not quite knowing what was going to happen. Nothing happened. The only thing I noticed was that the area seemed so depressed. They had their own troubles without bothering me.

YURIKO: You get hundreds of thousands of people to greet Mr. Mandela and there is no violence. We are an unusual country, so full of contradictions. During the civil-rights days and the peace days, a few of us were just standing in a row, vigiling. Six feet away, a crowd of young white men were shaking their fists at us and calling out names. My goodness!

I am more fearful of whites than blacks. Blacks seem to express to me exactly how they feel or think. They are very upfront. I don't know about white persons. Being interned at Santa Anita may have had something to do with it.

BILL: I'll be quite honest with you. If I were alone on the street and three blacks were approaching me, I'd be more fearful than if it were three whites. That's because of my own racism and the way our culture works. Am I a racist? I think so. I'm probably racist toward whites, too. [*Laughs.*] I don't have a real high opinion of white people. Racism is a hard thing. We've got to learn somehow to respect ourselves without having to put someone else down.

The one thing that's lacking in my life is a sense of peerness with other people. A feeling that we're equal. It's just the way people act, the vibrations they give off, the looks they give you. I go through my life feeling not quite like the invisible man, but pretty close. Very marginal. Someone that really doesn't count or matter, who can be ignored.

It's something we have to get over, this business of our self-respect depending upon putting someone else down.

I don't think the problem is insoluble. I'm not an optimist, but I have a lot of hope. People change. Maybe it won't happen in our lifetime. That's why we shouldn't live forever. The fact that we have only a limited life is a sign of hope. A new generation may not have the experiences and prejudices of the older.

YURIKO: How do I feel? It depends on the mood you catch me in. It's very ambiguous to me. I do whatever I can do. The change may take another century. Yet I do see hopeful signs. There are pockets of communities like this one that we may not know of, that doesn't appear on the six-o'clock news.

RON MAYDON

"I'm a forty-two-year-old Mexican-American, born and raised on the Southeast side of Chicago. I have worked since I was sixteen. I lied about my age, so I could make some money. While going to college, I worked summers in the steel mill, side by side with my late father."

His father's flight from Mexico, across the border, is a walking, hitchhiking saga; town to town; odd jobs picking cotton in Texas, peeling potatoes at the Rice Hotel; gandy-dancing for the railroads; water boy in a Chicago steel mill.

"We are a Godfearing, religious family. Every Sunday we're in church, my mother, my sister and me. 'You take a few knocks coming up,' my mother used to say. 'That's why God gave you more padding in the butt, so it could be spanked.' She and my father both worked hard."

He is fair-complexioned and could easily pass for an Anglo, if he wished. He does not. "Throughout my life, I've been a proud nationalistic Mexican-American."

Hispanics are used as a buffer, and also a wedge, between white and black communities. Show me a white community and a black community and I'll show you an adjoining community between both. We're kind of a geographic Ping-Pong ball. Whites may let us move into their neighborhood because they've got a choice. "We'll take the lesser of the two evils," they say. They make it seem like they're doing us a big favor.

I call him a dumb Hispanic, the one who moves into a white community and is not even greeted as a neighbor. He thinks it's a miracle from God that he was let in. Or he did it on his own. "Oh wonderful! I've been accepted." He thinks he's moved up the ladder socially. I tell him, "Look, dummy, the only reason you're here is because right behind you are the blacks about to move in. They'll use you to hold off the blacks, and when they move, you'll stay here as the buffer." They're under the illusion that they're accepted. Of course they're not.

Because I could pass for Anglo, I got a bird's-eye view, an inside view of a racist country. I kind of snuck behind enemy lines. A kamikaze. When I was playing football in high school, they thought I was Italian or Greek. I got to hear comments about Mexicans. I'd immediately stand up, and the next thing I'm in a fistfight. "Oh, Ron, I'm sorry, I didn't mean you." "Who the fuck did you mean?" I've heard it all and it has gotten me angry and inspired and determined to keep fighting. I know how they really feel.

When my name confused the other kids, they'd ask me what I was. I said, "I'm an American." Today I'd say, "I'm an American of Mexican descent."

I don't like the word Hispanic. It sounds nice and says nothing. Which Hispanic? Mexican? Cuban? Puerto Rican? Every ten years, the United States government census gives us a new label. Spanish-Americans. Latinos. Chicanos. It's a lot like black labels.

Economically, the Puerto Rican is the lowest-income, least educated of the Hispanic community. They are our blacks. We look on the Mexican-Americans as the Polacks, the Polish-Americans. Family-oriented, hardworking, Catholic. The white Cubans are our Jews: the professionals, pharmacists, doctors, lawyers. Know why? After Batista lost, Castro sent them here. They were the elite, the landlords, the robber barons, the well-to-do. They were the ones with the money. They didn't like to identify with the Indians or the racially mixed Cubans. They came here with skills, education, and money they had socked away. They took over Florida. They're successful up and down the coast. They don't like black Cubans. There's racism in the Spanish community as anywhere else.

I would get into some arguments with dark-complected Latinos. They'd make racist remarks about blacks: "Niggers are getting everything." I'd say, "Look, you so-and-so, black as you are, you got a lot of nerve talking about blacks. You've been a victim of discrimination as much as blacks. You're the new niggers, you dummies."

I guess you'd call me a community activist, working for a black-Latino coalition. Our own people were calling us nigger-lovers. We had to let them know the police were beating the shit out of us, too. We organized the first Mexican-American march on police brutality in 1971.

I'm a strong believer in minority coalitions. Whatever gains the Hispanic community has made, we have piggy-backed on the black movement. I say every time the blacks make political, economic, and social gains, hooray for them, because we get some of the fallout. They sneeze, we catch cold. They make inroads, we get hired. There are also problems in the black-Hispanic coalition. It's really a mixed bag.

The black community says they haven't made any progress. But the Hispanic sees the blacks as moving up and taking over. It's piggy-move-up. We're on the bottom of the totem pole. We're the busboys, the new ditchdiggers, the new laborers. We see Hispanics on the assembly line with a black supervisor, a black boss.

Historically, it's always been so. The Irish dumped on the Italians. The last one in gets the shit. So we're the latest. The Asians are behind us, but they're intellectually making the greatest gains. The Japanese may be getting lazy and the Koreans, the Jews of the Asian community, are working hard round the clock.

There are two kinds of Hispanics: the ethnic and the racial. The first identify with the whites and act, think, and try to be like them. But there are those who say: "We don't have a low self-esteem. We know where we stand. We know we're not black or white. We're in the middle and not trying to be either."

The Hispanics who believe they are white often try interracial marriages. Personally, I'm against that. When I get married, it will be to a Mexican woman. My kids will be one-hundred-percent Mexican. I'll be frank with you, I don't want to see halfbreeds. It's a personal preference. When I wake up Sunday morning, I want *menudo* or *carnitas* or *chorizo* and eggs. I don't want to have to go through a historical explanation to my Anglo wife of what I want. We're going to dance to the same tune. I'm not nationalistic to the point of being blind to the cultures of others. But what I want you to know we're definitely Mexican-American and proud.

This is not a melting pot. It's more of a layer cake. I believe we're a pluralistic society. This city is divided by viaducts, railroad crossings, thoroughfares. We say: This is Polish, this is Italian, this is Jewish, this is a Mexican community. Live and let live, but we must maintain our identity.

Once you lose your identity, your whole psyche is twisted. You're at the whim of anything that occurs in a society. I don't want to be a Mexican Fritz Mondale, who wanted to be everything to everybody and wound up being nothin' to no one.

In our country at this time, there is latent and blatant racism. You meet these closet racists who are condescending and patronizing, but deep inside they don't really want us.

This is part of the racism between Hispanics and blacks. I know some nationalistic black activists. I understand where they're coming from. I have no problems with them. I ask myself, Are blacks capable of racism? Of course. Are Hispanics capable of racism? Of course. I think these two extremes are going to have some kind of come-together. There has to be some serious coalition-building if we're going to live side by side.

We'll have to work on the Hispanic Uncle Toms, who do everything they can to ingratiate themselves, to please their white racist neighbors. Tio Tacos we call them. A Tio Taco is worse than an Uncle Tom.

You don't find many Hispanics living in black areas, period. If they do, they're residual, the last ones left. I know this city like the back of my hand. I was a paramedic for three years and a building inspector for three.

We have Hispanic huppies, urban professionals. The huppies, the buppies, and the yuppies are living alongside one another on the lake-front. Junior execs. It's a real paradox they find themselves in, the Hispanics and the blacks. On the one hand, we say: Get an education, get that degree, make a better life. But when they leave the old neighborhood, they're sell-outs. Uncle Toms, Tio Tacos. The rest of the people say, "You're too good, you don't come around anymore. You've made it now and you can't talk to us."

This is the crisis of the black and Hispanic professional. They're in two worlds. Some talk of depression and suicide. Should we say: "Don't make any progress and stay put?"

As for role models, we have very few. Up until recently, we haven't had a Martin Luther King or a Harold Washington. We don't have people breaking the ice. We have a few unrecognized, unsung heroes anonymously chipping away. Mostly in the neighborhoods.

The only time you see Hispanics on TV, it's a street gang, an immigration raid, a drug bust. If I landed here from Mars and turned on the TV, I'd say, "All these people named Sánchez, Gómez, Rodríguez and García are troublemakers. You better get them out of this country. Every time I turn around, they're taking away a job and they're illegal."

On the lowest rung of the Mexican society is the illegal. He, she cannot surface. He had come here to earn a living, to send money back home to mom. They're terrified of exposure. They will go to the supermercado to buy their Mexican food products. They will listen to Mexican radio and watch Mexican TV and stay in hiding.

To Hispanics, the word "minorities" is a code word for blacks. I fault both communities. The blacks were too exclusive and didn't try to recruit us, get us involved. The Hispanics were not aggressive enough, didn't say, "Cut us in or cut it out." I blame the Church for our fault. It's always been, "Whatever your plight is, accept it. God will take care of you later." Look at its history in Mexico.

The Mexican loves the authoritarian personality. He loves to be told what to do. The strong church, the strong father figure. But there's a contradiction here, too. It's still the mother who holds the family together. The father gives the appearance: "I wear the pants. I'm the *chingón*, the bad so-and-so." His perception is that he must be assertive. Yet the little Anglo supervisor calls him every dirty name in the book: wetback, illegal, spic, greaser. He chews him out. And he meekly says, "Yes, sir, no, sir, I'm sorry." He comes home and asserts himself as the main man.

His kids and wife are thinking, "You could have beat the shit out of the little Anglo, but you didn't say nothin'. You come home and take it out on us." That's what's happening right now in Hispanic families. But the father is just finding out you can't talk tough at night and be a sissy during the day. If you're going to be a man, be a man twenty-four hours a day, not part-time. Now the mother and kids are saying: To hell with the damn job. Your self-respect is worth more than that four-dollar-an-hour job. You should have grabbed him and kicked the shit out of him.

It's a new sign. It's one of the first indications that we're going to make serious attempts to break down the barriers of racism. We're seeing this at college and high-school levels.

But we're also seeing Hispanic street gangs fight black street gangs.

This may go on for years. The guy will say, "I fought with this black kid twenty years ago. He came into our neighborhood. I just don't like niggers now." He'll remember, "It was a black kid shot at me." The black kid will remember, "It was a Mexican cracked me over the head. I just don't like grease balls."

The fights are over drugs and turf and money and gang signs. We're having trouble in four high schools right now. That is what's happening in this country now. We're turning on each other. Whites will blame the blacks. Blacks will blame the Hispanics and vice-versa. Hispanics will say of affirmative action, "They hired seventeen blacks and one Hispanic." They're using us against them.

In the sixties, everyone was more aware. We always lived next door and worked with blacks. We were car-pooling because we didn't have any money. We shared lunches together. We went to school together. We worked in the stockyards together. We worked in the steel mills together. We worked in the fields together, migrant workers, side by side. We were in the same boat and it was sinking.

Now because of racial consciousness, groups are trying to assert their identity and get their share of the American pie. The economic pie is not big enough for anybody, not the way it's divided. Now we're competitors. We're not allies, we're adversaries. We're on a collision course.

I don't know if many Hispanics view affirmative action as a program to benefit them. They don't really identify with it. Many Hispanics believe affirmative action is a black program. We don't aggressively apply, seek out. I've heard that from every college recruiter: "Send me Hispanics." How many get their degree and do something about it? Few. I see signs of change. The kids are becoming more aggressive and are not going to take the bullshit their mom and dad did.

Our women have never been recognized. Mexican-American women have never received their just due. They've held our family together, period. Our women have taken the abuse, kept their mouths shut: "Don't tell anybody." Dad comes home drunk. He's a real man now. The boss has told him off and he's taking it out on his wife. We have a saying: "When Anglos drink, they drink to forget. When Mexicans drink, they drink to remember."

I see a duality in the Mexican community. The wedding, the Christmas ceremony, the stores, the music, the food, the art, the culture. We must never lose our identity. But I also want assimilation. We can't carry it off alone, separately.

We're at a crucial period in black-Hispanic relations. Do we want to be identified with whites or blacks? I think we're schizophrenic now. We really don't have a sense of where we fit. We're the buffer.

NORMA STEVENSON

She is an accountant who works for a radio station in Chicago.

    She has two children, a daughter, fifteen, and a son, eleven. She is in the process of a divorce; her husband has moved back to New York. "I have no other family here." She is the sole breadwinner. She speaks very softly. Even with my hearing-aid, I occasionally miss some of her reflections.

It's very funny sometimes. A woman I know told our mutual friend, "I don't think of Norma as black. She's so neat and intelligent and so quiet." The stereotype of black people is being hard and boisterous and dangerous. I think it's ridiculous.

    There's a fear of black people because of economics. Black people are more prone to being in poverty, and because of their status, they sometimes steal from other people. To live. They don't have jobs. Or they just start hitting you out of frustration. There's a great fear that black people are going to mug them or do bodily harm. Most black people are not like that. White people are out there doing the same thing, but we always think black.

    TV and the newspapers don't help the situation any. We usually see them in a gang. They can't talk. They have black leather coats and are trying to conquer the world by being *bad*. What do you see first on the news? A black person killed another black person or killed a policeman or stabbed someone. Of course you're going to be scared of black people. You can't help but think they're all that way. That's really not what black people are about.

    I live in Evanston, where the majority are white. A black CTA busdriver said to me that it was so good to see a black person getting on the bus who lives here and isn't just coming to work. Some of my friends say, "Oh, you live in a rich neighborhood." Why do you have to be rich to live in this area? They would tell my daughter, "You're going the wrong way home!" They would be so shocked. We're not rich; far from it. [*A soft laugh.*] We just happen to live there.

    Things *are* in the open. When I was moving in, I asked the realtor, "How are people in the building? Are they racist?" He said, "Oh, no, we don't put up with that here." I haven't had any trouble.

    I don't know my neighbors. My son does. He's more at home than I am. They're very nice to him. But there's one gentleman in the building who told me he doesn't like black people. When my son was eight, he happened to be standing in front of this man's car. The man wouldn't get out. Every time my son would walk away, he acted like he was about to get out. My son told me he wanted to see what the man would do. So he walked back to the car and the man got back in. My son was playing with him to see how he would react. Now this was a grown man and an eight-year-old child. He finally got tired of sitting there, got out, and grunted furiously. My son thought it was so silly. A child should not be noticing things like this. But he does.

Why do people put themselves through these things? They're not putting *us* through things we haven't already contended with as we've grown up.

I think black children see more of what's going on than white kids the same age. They see their parents struggle a little more. White people hide a lot from their kids. Black people do not hide their feelings. When they're hurting it's no crime to show it. They let you know exactly where they're coming from. White people don't. Blacks also know when to put on the act, if necessary. So black children at an early age become more hip to what life's about.

I like to watch other people and the changes they go through. In the elevator, they keep staring at you but try to make it seem as if they're not looking at you. Some people get really uptight, frozen, as if they can't move until the elevator reaches their floor. It's really hilarious.

You know the Evanston Express hasn't come yet, because white people are standing on the platform. I know it's going to the South Side because the majority of people on it are black. That's the way I notice what train it is. I notice that white people will sit with another white before he'll sit with a black. They look around and if there are no more seats, they'll sit down next to me. Blacks sit anywhere. They don't have the fear white people do. It's quite obvious how people feel. You read your book but you notice them out of the corner of your eye. They're standing there looking silly because they really don't want to sit next to you, but they have no choice. Then they'll sit down so far away from you that they're almost falling off the seat. [*Laughs.*] I just want to laugh and say, "Why don't you move over? There's enough room. I'm not a big person." You just know they're afraid of touching you. It's hysterical to watch what people put themselves through. When they approach black people, they just don't know what to do.

Aren't you, deep down, a little hurt?

[*Laughs lightly.*] No, not at all. It's their problem if they don't want to sit next to me. There's nothing wrong with me. I do have more room.

I don't think the gap between the races is any wider than it's been. There are more black and white people who have become friends. When I was growing up, we didn't have black and white people spending the night over at one another's houses. My daughter and son have a lot of white friends and often spend the night with them. Things are more liberal, but we have a long way to go.

Here's how the media has messed things up. I get more afraid of three black people looking really hard than I would of three whites. Isn't that terrible? It's because of what you hear they're capable of doing. They frighten you more than whites. Yet when I was in junior high—this was Flushing, New York—and bused to a white school, the driver let some grown white men get on and beat up one of the black boys. This was 'sixty-seven. They caught the guys. We had to go to court at that young age. Nothing happened; they were let go. The driver didn't even move to help these seventh-grade kids being battered. Have we advanced since then? It depends on who's driving the bus. [*Laughs.*]

Of course I get sore at white people sometimes. But I also get sore at blacks. I think I get more sore at them when they don't try hard enough. Because of the society we live in, and welfare, a lot of them have become handicapped. They know they can rely on welfare and that makes them lazy. It's easier to cop out and say I can't do it.

I grew up in the projects of New York. I used to hear people say that white people have put chains on us. There were children my age, thirteen, fourteen, fifteen, talking how we can't do this or that, because of the white man. It used to make me so angry, because you can, despite that.

Children shouldn't be afraid of going to school. People shouldn't be afraid of going home. There must be a way they can clean up the areas. Out here, when the gangs would come in, we had families, white and black, patrolling the streets. We still have problems but not as much. My daughter, who's in touch with the goings-on in the neighborhood, keeps me informed.

When I lived in the projects and was growing up, it was really nice. It wasn't until I was fourteen that drugs started coming in. People really cared a lot. We had rules. We couldn't play in the hallways. There was a park in every area. That's where we played. We stayed off the grass, there were flowers there. Parents used to patrol the projects to make sure the kids weren't messing up. Now they don't care as much. The tallest building was seven floors. The mother could call down to the child.

We had a lot of racial fights at the projects. A lot of white high-school kids would chase us down the hill and scare us to death. Then the tables turned. Black people started beating up on whites. Revenge, I guess. The police were up there almost every day.

The projects here are like prisons. The windows are so small, with bars in front. My feeling is if kids grow up here, going to jail is nothing. It's the same kind of environment. Jail is built into them.

"My mother was a big factor because she believed in education." She attended a vocational high school. "Passing the test and getting in was an accomplishment. I started meeting other people and expanding my horizons." She graduated from Wilberforce University in Ohio, one of the first-established black colleges. She had jobs in Cleveland and Pittsburgh. She's been in Chicago eleven years.

It's so hard for a black man these days. It was hard for my husband. He's a person who speaks his mind and who always was head-to-head with white people. He was fired from a lot of jobs. I was the one who kept the jobs. The stress drove him to cocaine and things like that. It's bad that the black woman has always been the head of the family because the black man hasn't been able to get a job. So he would feel little and leave. It's belittling not to be able to take care of your family. It was easier to leave and feel like a man than to stay and not feel like a man. It was the image thing.

I still think the black man is beautiful. A lot of black men who've had such a hard way in life don't trust black women. Some of them go to a white woman because they feel she might make him feel more like a man. I've heard men say that. You have black men who feel, because they weren't able to touch the white woman, they had to have one. I think it's the same with some white women, because black men were taboo.

In some ways, there's a lot less tension than before. My son came to me one day and asked how I'd feel if he married a white woman. I told him that love doesn't have a color. It's fine with me as long as she makes him happy. I think there are going to be more interracial couples. I don't know if it's part of the solution. I think we lose something when whites and blacks intermarry. We lose our identities. It may really be confusing for the children: Should they be white? Should they be black?

I'm into my religion a lot. I really love the Lord and praise him wherever I am. It doesn't have to be in church. It can be anywhere. I grew up a Baptist, I've been a Methodist, and now I attend the Church of God in Christ. I go anywhere they worship God.

I don't hate white people, but I get very angry when I think about slavery. I always say the Lord knew what he was doing when he didn't put me in that era, because I don't back down to any man, white or black. I don't believe I should call you Lord or God. Oh, no, I'm not servant-minded. No one has to tell me what to do. In a work setting, give me my instructions, but don't stand over me. I don't need a boss. I feel I have common sense and I know what I should do in this life.

POSTSCRIPT: *"When I sent out my résumés for jobs, I was called on the phone by a headhunter. I'm sure he thought I was white. He sounded very enthusiastic. 'Come down as soon as possible.' As soon as I walked in, I could see on his face deep disappointment. His enthusiasm vanished. His voice wasn't what it was on the phone. I didn't hear from him again."*

BOB MATTHIESON

He publishes a monthly journal that frequently publishes articles on race. He is a former Catholic priest.

It's fashionable these days to say that there have not been changes for the better. There have been a lot of them. You see them all around you, But basically they are changes that affect individuals. There are blacks who are making it. It's gotten worse, too.

I just spent time in Palm Springs with a friend. It was great for a week. But the obsession with security there was just bizarre. You have to put a card to get in here and a card to get out there. You go from one security village to another. It's no wonder, because the wealth concentrated in that one place is scandalous. It feels like South Africa, where you have to keep the other people at a distance. The Mexicans come in six o'clock in the morning and do the lawns. You can get by an entire day without seeing anybody that's going to disturb you or interfere with your life-style. So you go in the pool and talk about where you're going to have dinner that night.

We received a wedding invitation a year ago to a place in suburban Chicago. Enclosed with the invitation was a pass that gets you into the grounds where the wedding reception will take place. It's one of those pristine villages. Security has become a growth industry.

Do you associate this obsession with fear of blacks?

Of course. Today, a black man walking down the streets of many of our suburbs at an odd hour will usually get a response from the police. The squad car will cruise by and keep an eye on him. Even if he's carrying a briefcase. The denial that race is a factor is absurd. I think every black male will tell you how it feels to go into a parking garage at night. Just by his presence, he evokes fear. Imagine how it feels to walk down the street and by your very presence, you evoke fear.

When you visit the jail, it's just unimaginable to go past cell after cell and see nothing but black faces. It's heartrending to the blacks who go there. We had a story a month ago about the wildly disproportionate number of blacks who have records.

We're talking about fear. It's pervasive. Yesterday, coming to work on the El, I was seated right behind a very large black man, well-dressed, who was sitting on the edge of his seat. When I got up to get off, the train swayed and I began to fall, partly because his foot was out in the aisle. As I was getting off, he was glaring at me. I couldn't figure out what was going on. He got off then, too, and came up to me. "You stepped on my foot." I said I did stumble and fall but I was not aware I'd stepped on his foot. He said, "Isn't there something you should say?" There's a supersensitivity here that reflects the degree to which things are right now. On the edge all the time.

I was playing tennis at a neighborhood park one Sunday. I'm a lousy tennis player. I hit a ball that went over into the next court where a black man was playing. He came over incensed, accusing me of hitting the ball that struck him in the testicles. He made a big thing about protocol and the courtesies of tennis. It was all kind of silly, but again, it's a reflection of the degree of tension right on the surface.

There's a feeling now among many black leaders that some of the rhetoric of the recent past is not serving the interests of the blacks themselves—it's simply self-defeating—and that spokesmen who play upon that are not really leaders. Farrakhan has done quite a bit of good within the black community that he is not given credit for. Getting people off drugs, for example. But then he complicates his own life by saying things that are absolutely outrageous.

Since Reagan, the gap between the races has widened. White rage has become chic in some cases. Hatred for black people has been made socially acceptable in a surprising number of places. We see what's been cropping up on college campuses. Racism has been legitimized.

Some of the worst offenders are the ex-liberals, who differ from the old-time racists only in the academic language they use. The played-out white liberals who overcompensate, as they did thirty years ago, are just as bad.

Not long ago, one of our reporters visited a South Side housing project. She was part of an entourage of observers. She was accidentally left behind as the others headed for the north side of town. Later, a member of the party explained: "We sent someone out to look for you and they couldn't find you. So we assumed you had left." She asked, "How did you describe me?" "Well, short and dark." "You didn't mention that I'm white?" "No." She was the only white woman in that space. That kind of crazy, overcompensating white liberal isn't doing any good. It's nuts to play color-blind in this manner. It's funny and phony.

As for race relations, the economic factor is still the key. It may not determine what people feel, but it certainly plays a role in what people do. You have to be sensitive to market a product these days. I don't think the Gannett papers are the most enlightened sector of the American public, yet *USA Today* goes out of its way to make sure that pictures in the paper reflect the diversity of American life. All kinds of people have come around for marketing reasons, but they're coming around. They have become more sensitive because they have to. I don't care why they do it as long as they do it.

David Lawrence of the Knight-Ridder newspaper chain describes what industry has to do. You need to practice a kind of inconveniencing commitment to affirmative action. You have to be imaginative, creative. Once you set your mind to the idea of affirmative action, you'll find a way to do it. And your paper will be better as a result.

You don't do anyone any good by hiring them simply because they're a minority and let it go at that. We not only recruit them, we tie them in with a mentor who can help them over the rough spots. We build things into the program that assure their success.

Our paper has an editorial board of eighteen people. They're not just names on a masthead. They are critical to our life. At one time, it was pretty much a white, downtown sort of board. Right now, the majority are minorities. Eleven out of eighteen. There's been no compromise in the quality of these members. We are now plugged into the life of this city in ways we could never be if we had just been downtown, good white guys. If there's a moral commitment, with imagination, you can do it.

We did a story on the cultural institutions of Chicago: the Art Institute, the Chicago Symphony Orchestra, the Lyric Opera Company, the Museum of Contemporary Art. We listened to them describe how difficult it was to find minority board members. Baloney. If you really want to do it, you can do it.

■ ■ ■ ■ ■

Overview II

SALIM MUWAKKIL

He is 44, a journalist on the staff of In These Times, *an alternative newspaper published in Chicago.*

"*I got radicalized while in the service, during the sixties. It was the Vietnam era. I had been in Germany, but during my four months in Thailand, I found out what we were doing wasn't kosher. When we did incursions into Cambodia, I was a radio operator.*

"*I didn't see any action there, but when I got back to the States, I was shot. It was at a Georgia motel, near the Robbins Air Base. This was in '68. I was speaking a kind of radical jargon. The clerk said I threatened him, so he shot me in the abdomen with a .38. I was hospitalized for quite a while. He was exonerated.*

"*It was the same year King was shot. I came out of the hospital very bitter and joined the Black Panther Party. At Rutgers, I started the Black Student Union.*"

I think the Panther Party was a noble, grass-roots effort, but something was missing. Although I was hearing about the Nation of Islam, it represented something alien, sinister. However, they possessed qualities the Panthers didn't. They were really serious, changing their life-styles, their behavior patterns. We had been socialized in this culture to be self-destructive. I saw the Nation of Islam as counteracting this impulse. Not the doctrine. It was alienating. I never accepted it. But it leveled the community in terms of class. There were none of these distinctions that we emphasized in the black community. It was serious about family at a time when many of ours were fractured.

I worked for the Newark bureau of the Associated Press. On the side, I started to do some writing for *Mohammed Speaks.*

It then had a circulation of 800,000. I began to see the difference in the way black people regarded the news and the way the mainstream society saw the same events.

In Newark, the blacks were for a mixed housing complex. I hate the word project because of its negative implications. It was to be in the North

Ward, traditionally Italian. It was provocative, to be frank. The residents demonstrated against it. They chained themselves to gates while playing Kate Smith's "God Bless America."

I would write a regular AP kind of story for the milkman in Nebraska. For *Mohammed Speaks*, I wrote of Kate Smith's steel-hard voice crooning about America's promise. Sure, I took a position. In some ways, it was emblematic of how black journalism developed as opposed to mainstream. It has always been a protest medium.*

In '74, I came to Chicago as news editor for *Mohammed Speaks*. After Elijah Mohammed died, his son, Wallace, really opened things up. I began to see how closed we had been. I did a lot of reading on the phenomenon of nationalism and how it tied in with fascism. I started to have a lot of questions.

I understood that black people needed some serious therapy to get us out of the situation we were in. It was historically unique, the legacy of slavery. The Nation of Islam tries to take a shortcut to cultural development through a totalitarian method, coercing people toward a certain kind of behavior.

In many ways, they were disrespectful of the black people's ingenious adaptations to the situation. There's some genius to the way we've adapted to this oppression. The Nation of Islam simply glossed over this, rejected it as being a slave response. The nuances of the black experience were lost to them.

I repressed my skepticism because I knew that black people needed some kind of transformation. I figured, whatever way we could do it, let's do it. But I became very skeptical of what I call its genetic theology, of black supremacy, of all that mysticism.

If you're serious about human equality, freedom, you must reject any doctrine that condemns people because of their genetic makeup. Black people especially should be wary of any such doctrine.

In many ways, Farrakhan, to whom I was quite close, is the mirror image of apartheid. There's a serious strand of anti-Semitism in this black nationalism, and it's real. I don't think black people are anti-Semitic. I think you'd find less in the black community, by and large, than among whites. It comes from the pseudo-Islamic approach to black nationalism.

---

* "I get so distressed at the way mainstream media treats racial matters. There's so little sensitivity to certain issues. A good example is police brutality. Amnesty International made the point that Chicago police deserved to be investigated because of charges of torture. The media played it up as a publicity stunt, as something to embarrass Mayor Daley. A serious problem in the black community was given short shrift."

You try to point out to brothers, who are otherwise very humane and have good intentions, that it is essentially the same thing white people have said of us: we're shiftless, lazy, blah, blah, blah. "Don't you see that's the same thing as calling Jews this and that?" They'd reply: "What they say is propaganda; what we say is true."

The Ku Klux Klan and the Aryan-movement people like Farrakhan because he's saying the same thing, essentially. They liked Marcus Garvey, too. He had a meeting with the Klan back in those days. It's a historical trap for people's grievances.

Farrakhan is an intelligent man. He's very eloquent in couching his criticism. He doesn't have to resort to demonology to make his point, but that still underlies the doctrine. He does point out that what black people lack is any connection to our home. Every other group is connected by mythology, by folkways, by cultural habits, to their homeland, to the land of their origin. Black people have been totally severed from their history. What Farrakhan represents is a kind of bridge, and many people see that. The clamor for Afrocentrism in schools is based on a serious need. Especially for young black men who are falling by the wayside.

We have a hole in our psyche and Farrakhan fills it up with ersatz culture. Islam is not really an authentic African religion, but still it's a counterbalance to Christianity, which a lot of people think of as oppressive, as pie-in-the-sky. He has an amazing resilience. To many young black people now, Farrakhan is tops. There was a poll last summer in *Black Enterprise*, a magazine aimed at upper-income blacks. He came in second.

There is a serious class division in the black community that we must attend to. The middle class is doing better now than it ever had. People who are bicultural, who understand how to operate in mainstream society, have doors opened that they never, ever imagined would be open to black people. At the same time, the underclass is growing and growing.

The clash at this point is whether the underclass is culturally deprived or situationally deprived. Dr. Carl Bell, a psychiatrist, a former gang member, has come up with some terrifying statistics. A black man is eleven times more likely to be killed in a black community than a white man. Black servicemen do not kill each other in nearly the same kind of numbers as they do in civilian society. His contention is it's situational. It has little to do with culture. It's true that we've lost the kind of family cohesion we had in the South. Urban life has rendered that asunder. But is that the result of culture or the situation?

Conservatives like Charles Murray blame the welfare programs, Lyndon Johnson's War on Poverty among them, as the cause of further poverty and a falling apart.* Professor Wilson points out that poverty increased because industrial plants, where so many older blacks had worked, were leaving the cities. If it weren't for Johnson's programs, it would have been worse.†

I do think black people overemphasize the "victimization" theory. If you are accomplished, can cope, and operate with success in the main-stream community, you are acting white. That's the perception in certain parts of the black community. A kind of anti-intellectualism. There's a reluctance to engage in competition because some black people fear that those rumors of inferiority may be true. So rather than expose the myth, they hang back. I don't want to let society off the hook, but that "internal nigger" has to be confronted by black people.

It's easy to understand why people think that, because generally those who cooperated with white authority were doing that to keep black people in their place. Historically, there has been this tradition.

I suggest that middle-class people, those who have benefited from the civil rights revolution, especially the baby boomers, have to develop some sort of mechanism to connect with the underclasses, who are drifting, falling off the edge into the abyss. Mentoring programs are happening all around the country. They're amorphous right now because nobody really knows what works. We just know the situation is desperate.

We cannot simply lay all the guilt at the feet of white people and just absolve ourselves of responsibility. The black middle class has a serious job to do. We have to get on the ball and so something ourselves. At the same time, we can demand society act in a more concerted manner to address the ills of America.

The only way we can really address the deep problems of the black community is through a massive effort directed by the federal government. Not unlike the New Deal approach, with the WPA, the PWA, of the thirties Depression. There is no other way.

It's difficult for white society to stop denying its racism. Denial is rooted in our culture. Our country, founded on the principles of enlighten-ment, was practicing slavery. It required an enormous amount of denial to have these two things going on simultaneously. Racism and its denial are a bone-deep parts of American culture. We have to keep pointing this out. It's never easy to admit.

---

* *Losing Ground* by Charles Murray.

† *The Truly Disadvantaged* by William Julius Wilson. Professor Douglas Massey, in these pages, makes it his major argument.

An Italian clothing company, Benetton, has these interracial ads. One showed a black child at the breast of a white woman. It went over well in Europe, but in this country, no. It's funny, because a white child at the breast of a black woman is what the South was all about. The American version of racism is peculiar and complicated by the whole denial aspect.

Martin Luther King spoke of a color-blind society. So Reagan said, "How dare you advocate affirmative action? That's not color-blind." It's as if we're on an even playing field at this moment. It's simply that black people are finally beginning to gain some sort of feeling of legitimacy in who they are.

One of the reasons I changed my name is because, while in the service, I was stationed not far from Macon. My maternal family was there, so I made quite a few visits. They told me lots of stories. One was about an ancestor called Guinea Sultan. He came as a slave and was part of my family's history. It was the only connection I could find between myself and the land of my origin. So I feel a soft spot at least for Islam.

When this campaign to call ourselves African-American began, I was astonished by the hostility of so many white people to the idea. Why should they be? Africa is our homeland and we're American. We were always taught there was something wrong with who we were. If we openly accept our African-ness, is that subversive of American values? It's curious that white people want us to abandon our African heritage, which we've never been able to embrace.

When we first came here, it was against the law to practice our rituals, to recognize our heritage. Even the drum was forbidden. So now, when black people are just beginning to embrace their ethnic identity, whites look at it as some sort of threat to their hegemony. It's simply that black people are just beginning to realize how much they've been deprived of knowledge of their own selves.

I think we must begin to realize that we are Americans of African descent. And to be comfortable with that identity. I've been to Africa several times, and to other countries. I know that I am peculiarly American. There is no getting around that.*

---

* Horace Cayton, a black sociologist, coauthor (with St. Clair Drake) of *Black Metropolis*, moved to Sweden in the late forties. After several years of a comfortable life, free of racism, he returned to the United States. He was homesick for everything American: ham and eggs, Camel cigarettes, even the tensions. He was palpably, indubitably, hopelessly an American. Until the time of his death, he was working on a biography of Richard Wright, who, himself an exile, was an American lost in Paris.

I'm pessimistic in many ways, but I'm also optimistic. I first believed that when Reagan got in, it would wake black people up. What happened is that so many blacks fell behind. We can say we should have gotten on the ball, but what about all those children born of black women who didn't have the right nutrition and grew up with deficient brain power? We're going to reap the legacy of Reagan's years for a long, long time.

We don't have the luxury of allowing white people to put us on trial by fire. If we're left to sink or swim, we'll sink. The further deterioration of the quality of life will be in the cards. I think white America has to be jolted into reality: if we do not devote the resources necessary to avert the tragedy, we'll become a police state. Crime will acquire more and more racial overtones. Will there have to be some sort of explosion, some sort of civil disorder, before we realize the gravity of the situation?

Think of the money we instantly manufactured for Desert Storm. The crisis in this country is much more grave than that. But we don't have the same kind of will to tackle it. We have to. We simply have no choice.

■ ■ ■ ■ ■

Awakenings

CHARLISE LYLES

She is a columnist on the staff of the Norfolk Pilot, *Norfolk, Virginia. She is thirty-one.*

For some reason black culture is rejected in American society. It is looked upon with scorn by the majority. Our music, though it's emulated, is at the same time scorned. Nappy hair is scorned. That's always been a big issue with me. I straighten my hair but I do it reluctantly. When I was younger I used to joke with my friends that one day when I had my own business I would never straighten my hair again.

It's a pain in the butt to have to coat your scalp pretty much with lye every two or three months. It's a painful process and at times I feel slightly degraded that I cannot wear my hair the way it naturally is. Other people of other cultures can, but I can't and that hurts. It's saying that if you're truly yourself you're ugly. That isn't true. If we went to Africa with straight hair, they would think of us as ugly.

There is a certain theft going on. In order for a culture to be accepted or co-opted, it's diluted. We're going to make it more acceptable by diluting it the way the majority thinks. Your hair is such a part of you. I think you ought to be able to walk into a law firm with a sculpted Afro and get a job if you're qualified.

Dreadlocks are difficult because many people think they're filthy. In reality, dreadlocks are probably cleaner than straight hair because you can wash it more frequently. Sure, dreadlocks, too, should not disqualify you.

It gives a sense of camaraderie when you encounter a black friend on the street and you're able to shake hands in a certain way or use a vernacular that other people don't understand. It creates, however fragile, a sense of unity that is somewhat gratifying, if just for a moment. Just as when an Hispanic person approaches another. They greet one another in Spanish. It's the same, fundamentally.

I must have been eight, nine years old before it really hit me, the distinction people were making between me and whites. I began to realize it by watching television. Even though the Black Power movement and the Student Nonviolent Coordinating Committee were coming to the fore, '66, '67, I was a little kid. It didn't mean beans to me. I was lost in *Bewitched* and *Petticoat Junction*.

I liked them. They were funny. It never occurred to me that there were no people like me on this show. I didn't really think of myself as different. I wasn't thinking of skin color. I liked the magic.

It's ironic that I was watching *Bewitched* the night that Dr. Martin Luther King was killed. They interrupted the show to say that he had been shot in Memphis. I was nine. I was totally confused. My mother was crying, my big sister was crying. All I wanted was for *Bewitched* to come back on. I think that was the beginning of an awakening.

Shortly after Dr. King was killed, my family—my mother, my two brothers, and my two sisters; my parents were divorced—moved from the little house to a public housing project. The Kennedy-King Project in Cleveland. When we moved to this reservation [*Laughs.*] I began to realize that we were poor. Even though we had hard times before, what being poor in the larger society meant hadn't really hit me. Until then.

Before, we lived on a nice street with working-class people. Remember, Cleveland was a big steel town in those days. It was all-black, blue-collar. Nice homes with well-manicured gardens and lawns.

My mother worked as a cleaning woman in the well-off suburbs. She was running an elevator, too. Two jobs. She was always working. It was rough economically.

We were really excited about the move. We thought, oh, this is a big opportunity. The rent will be lower and it was a nicer place—in the beginning. It was spanking new. The federal government had just thrown it up—1968.

Lots of other people moved there. They were from Hough, which was burned down during the riots of the sixties. So there we were, all piled up on top of each other.

They weren't high-rises. Some were three stories, some four, but the density was incredible. We were all jammed together. Say the average apartment had seven kids. That made 28 people on one floor. Then another tier had 28. You had all these kids running around, playing.

The kids on the street we left were nice. These kids were mean. I was getting beat up all the time. They were always looking for a victim. I turned out to be the victim. They'd beat me up and run through the hallways shouting my nickname [*Chants like a child*]: "Shorty got beat up. Shorty got beat up." This would bring me to tears and I would beg my mother to move. "We gotta move, Mom. Please let's move." My mother was a very hardworking, serious person. Four years later, we did move to a nicer project. It was a different kind, row houses. My family still lives there: my mother and my two brothers.

I was in junior high school then, sort of tuned out. I was very busy pursuing a scholarship to a private school. Actually, I was not an attentive student. My parents were having problems and I didn't do any homework or anything. I had flunked fifth grade, and when I went to junior high, I was in the slow section.

My existence is a miracle. One day I wrote something in my English-composition class. My teacher called me up to her desk and gave me the third degree. "Did you write this?" I said yes. "Are you sure you didn't copy it from someplace?" I said yes. "You sure?" "Yes." She was a young white teacher, and as I look back, she was gentle and optimistic. A couple of weeks later, I was moved to a higher class, where the kids took a language and biology and algebra. In that section I read a lot. I went to the library and read constantly.

I think I was trying to escape, because at home—we were still in the old project—it was starting to get ugly. People were getting shot. The killings weren't as rampant as they are today in the midst of the drug wars. But life was cheap and you knew it. Filth was accumulating in the incinerators, broken bottles, people getting meaner. I needed another world to go to, and I found it in these books.

The students at Kinnard Junior High School were all black. The teachers were white and black. Most of our white teachers were young, sympathetic. You felt they must have asked to come to this school because nobody else would. It was right smack in the middle of the projects. It's closed now.

I learned that I was good in French. I really excelled but I was uncomfortable because the other kids were critical of me. I just loved the idea that if you can make different sounds with your mouth, somebody else would understand. There were a couple of other girls in class who were really good. We'd get a conversation going—just a little bit, nothing fluent—but it was impressive.

But I was uncomfortable. At least once a week I would act up terribly. I would just totally disrupt the class and the teacher would send me to the corner to hold up two books over my head for the entire period of the class. I probably acted up because I wanted to fit in with the other kids and let them know, just because I liked French that I wasn't a nerd or a square. A nerd was tantamount to being white. You had to do something to set the record straight.

I always did well in my tests, and eventually received "A Better Chance" (ABC) scholarship to a private day school. It was about twenty miles outside Cleveland. It was called Hawkins Upper School in Gates Mills, Ohio. The people there were very, very wealthy.

There were many Jewish people there. I had never really encountered Jews before and didn't really understand for a long time who they were. They just had not been part of my world. I had never really understood that there was some distinction between white people in general. It took me awhile to piece all that together. I was really naïve about the world. I started to observe the difference in the way Jews looked from other white students.

Generally the hue of their skin was slightly darker and they had curly hair and longer noses and thicker features. They were very nice. A couple of them became very close friends. They invited me to their homes and we did things together. I found the Jewish kids very enjoyable. I do think of them as different, because of their attitude.

It seemed I had more Jewish friends than WASP friends. They were more open and accepting and very curious about my life. I didn't need to be pretentious around them. I didn't need to lie about what my parents did. It was just a feeling.

I really struggled academically my first year. I lost my confidence because the classes were much harder than in public school. These people were asking you to think. I'd never really been asked to think. I'd just been asked to memorize and regurgitate.

It was wonderful.

The teachers were straight out of Yale and Princeton and their education was very fresh in their minds. We had some who were post-hippie types. We often wondered whether they went out in the woods and smoked pot. They were open to my ideas, although I wasn't exactly graceful in presenting them. I would blurt things out in class or struggle to articulate because I didn't have the vocabulary of my classmates. But they would wait. They were interested in my revelations.

I received a lot of awards when I graduated. It was a very happy time. At the same time it was painful because I was very lonely. I felt estranged from my home. Even though it was a day school, I didn't really go home, because I lived with a teacher. I felt distant from my family because I was changing.

I became very critical of them sometimes: the way they talked, the way they did things, the way they looked at the world. Going to this school gave me an opportunity to really get to know a white person. When that happens, you abandon some of your prejudices and begin to see that fundamentally these people are just like you. My family was pretty much dealing with them from a distance, judging them from a distance.

Maybe they'd say, "If you work for a white person, they're going to work you to death." I would say everybody wants their money's worth or something smart like that. I would go home and try to use some of the big words I learned at school, like "perspicacious"—pretty much useless words. I was condescending.

I realize now how much I hurt their feelings, especially my mother's. She had been behind me all the way, really wanted me to go to this school because she knew it was a passport to a better life.

Sometimes to fit in with the white kids, I would lie about what my mother or father did. It was funny. My mother had worked for the family of one of my classmates. We never said anything about it. It was more than shame; I had the fear of being rejected. By my senior year, I decided I'm not gonna do that any more. I am who I am.

I went to Boston University for one year.

Boston was the first time I really encountered overt racism. As I was walking toward the campus one day, a carload of white guys drove by and threw a bottle at my leg. It just missed me and slammed against a brick wall. It didn't cut me, but it cut something inside me. When I graduated from Hawkins, I felt that the days of racism were behind us. In spite of all the busing battles, I entertained the naïve notion that those days were over. This was 1977. When those kids threw that bottle at me, it shattered my illusions. I was never comfortable in Boston after that and I left.

I applied to Smith College and was accepted. At Northampton, there was a lot of campus tension—'78, '79.

I'm increasingly frustrated because things have gotten worse for black people. I feel that I, in my small way, must be active in my community. I don't want to move out to the suburbs. I want to stay here, in this mostly black neighborhood, and be where young kids can see me just going about my daily life.

In 1981, she moved to Washington and became interested in journalism. She worked as a copy aide at the Washington Post—*"You Xerox things." She was a clerk at the* New York Times *Washington bureau and eventually came to Norfolk to work on the* Pilot. *"I covered everything from City Hall to police." She was awarded an Alicia Patterson Fellowship and spent a year in research. "I do hard news. I hate soft, fluffy features."*

What I'm most worried about is the dying of black men. They're disappearing. Many of my friends are married, but not to black men. There aren't any around in their world. I have nothing against interracial marriages, but it worries me that there's such a severe shortage of black men.

I met my boyfriend seven years ago in Washington. He was in the Navy and was very frustrated because he had a good mind and they weren't using it. He applied to go to high-tech school in the Navy and was rejected. I convinced him to leave the Navy and go back to school.

It was a hard decision because he had six years of security in the military. He had to change his life-style, he wasn't going to have any money anymore. But he did it.

He went down to Jackson State University in Mississippi. His home state. He studied chemistry. He started out getting all F's, his family was falling apart, but he kept on and finally made the dean's list. I could have said, "Forget it. Why wait around for this guy? I'm in my prime. I'll go find someone else with a BMW or a law degree or who looks better." But I waited.

He was recruited last year by Upjohn Pharmaceuticals and he's got a great job working in one of their labs. He has just bought a house and is doing well. We're living in two different states, but he has aspirations and I do, too. You've got to believe in the man instead of putting him down. It takes a special patience and endurance. If we don't, these men are going to die out.

Reagan has done a great deal of damage. I came of age in the Great Society, where there were lots of programs. My two sisters and I are products of these programs. My older sister was in Upward Bound and my baby sister was in Head Start. All three of us have gone to college, all three of us are doing well. My brothers haven't had the same opportunity and are really struggling.

My mom? She's a reticent person, but she's been more talkative with me in the past ten years than she ever was before. She was so busy working like a dog all the time. Always working, always cleaning the house, always cooking something great for us. There's nothing that tastes better than my mom's apple-cookie pie on a Sunday. But she was always, always working on our cultural development. She had a vision that our lives wouldn't be the way hers had been.

She moved up north from Mississippi with my father. He was an alcoholic and never worked much. He wandered in and out of my life a lot. He had a tenth-grade education, yet I knew he was an intellect. When I won that scholarship, I went to find my father to tell him about it. He was always uptown at some bar. I found him in an old apartment, where he was staying with some woman. I went up the rickety stairs. There was a chair or two, a little TV. He was just sitting there, watching a baseball game. He had these old black glasses on and looked like Ray Charles. I was excited, telling him about the scholarship and the books I was reading. I didn't know how he'd react.

He took me to a back room and on the floor were rows and rows and rows of books. I said, "Whose books are these?" "They're mine." I saw biographies of scientists and histories. He'd open a page or two, point out a passage and he'd say, "Take this one. It'll help you understand all about World War II."

The last time I saw him, he was quoting from *The Merchant of Venice*. He could quote Shakespeare just like that. He'd walk in the house and quote from *Othello*. "Reputation, reputation, I've lost my reputation." He had a tremendous sense of humor. If you saw him on the street, he was just a crumpled old black drunk in a tattered coat.

Yeah, he was very proud of me and he died much too young. All his years of drinking had finally caught up with him. What was once a strong physique had shrunk to ninety pounds, if that. They're still dying, these black men.

Is white racism on the increase?

There was a silly incident. I'm almost ashamed of it. I was covering an accident on the freeway. The police officer told me to move my car, so I moved it. He told me I hadn't moved it far enough and ordered me off the interstate. It was way the hell out of the way of the scene. I didn't think he had any right to do that. They just picked me up, dragged me through the grass and put me in the back of the police car. I had all sorts of burns. To this day, I don't think they would have done that to a white woman reporter. I felt at that moment the fear that black people must have felt thirty, forty years ago, when they were traveling the roads in the deep South. I felt that at that moment my life didn't mean anything to these guys. I felt very alone.

When I read the newspaper or watch TV, I don't see black people like myself, the normal black people who get up and work like dogs every day. Instead I see criminals. Where are the everyday people that work hard and make this democracy move?

POSTSCRIPT: Shortly after the verdicts were handed down in the cases of Washington's Mayor Barry and the Central Park jogger, Charlise Lyles telephoned me from Norfolk.

"I was deeply disturbed, not by the verdicts, but by the insistence in the black community that the accused were innocent and the victims of racism. I think this sends a warped message to our young people that it's okay to do something wrong and you can get off on a racism rap. It's not okay.

"Because justice has so often been blind in the United States, black Americans have to be ever vigilant in squeezing justice out of the courtroom. But, at the same time, wrong is wrong. We'll become a corrupt people if we allow ourselves to be lawless and claim that racism is responsible.

"In the jogger trial, I was a little disturbed at all the courtroom carryings-on. These teen-agers were referred to as though they were Malcolm X, Martin Luther King, and Nelson Mandela. At the same time, I was a little uncomfortable with the verdict because there was no physical evidence and there have been so many cases where young black men have been convicted of rape and later found innocent.

"I think the energy of the black community in rallying around the youths could have been better spent nurturing these children when they were young, instead of coming to bat for them when it's too late, after they've been neglected and abused and misparented. Instead of histrionics, we need to do a better job of raising our children."

■ ■ ■ ■ ■

School Days

QUINN BRISBEN

Until his recent retirement as a Chicago public-high-school teacher, he had worked, most of those years, in the black community.* "I haven't had a white student in about fifteen years." He has lived in the neighborhood, as one of the few whites, for twenty-three years.

"I've always felt pretty much at home here. I often take the CTA. You've got to pay a mint for parking. Most times I'm the only white person in the car. Occasionally you'll run into a hostile person, but you run into hostile people everywhere. Race is a kind of convenient thing to hang it on when it's there. Hostility doesn't have much to do with that. Class does.

"Our school used to be half working-class black and half underclass. Lately, the scale has tipped. We had postal workers, firemen, people who had small businesses, and some professionals. They no longer send their children to our school. We have what's left. Some of our best students have come from what's left.

"What gets you is these kids have so much potential. Except for the fact that white kids have more pimples, there's not a hell of a lot of difference. Most of the difference is in what's happened to you. These kids, of course, do have a rich oral tradition. The sermons, the songs, the speeches. Most talk better than they write. They're used to it."†

You've got a bunch of black people who have made it and are out of there. Like other people, in similar circumstances throughout history, they're not looking back. Most are trapped where they can't see much for themselves or much for their children.

There used to be a ladder. You could sell newspapers on the street or shine shoes, get a little capital together, and you'd get along. You notice it in the new immigrants. One of my students made an interesting remark. He said most of the Jews he met are Muslims. You know what he meant? Most

---

* He is now teaching at an upper-middle-class private school of high scholastic standards.
† This matter is discussed in much further detail in *The Great Divide* (1988).

of the small-time grocery store owners—laundry and so on—who used to be Eastern European Jews are now from the Middle East—Lebanese, Iranians. When I pressed him on this, he mentioned West Indians as some of the Jews he knew. He wasn't talking about race. He was referring to people who lived over the store in poor neighborhoods and worked eighteen hours a day. And these people made it out.

I grew up in a furniture store in Enid, Oklahoma. When I was in third grade, the teacher asked how do people celebrate New Year's. I held up my hand: "We take inventory." I guess my student would have called my strict Methodist folk Jews.

The rural blacks who came from the South—sharecroppers, a great many—didn't grow up with these certain ways. Where you get a kid a library card as soon as he can sign his name. Where you give a kid his own little savings account and presents from uncles and grandparents go into it. Where you know a little about contracts before you sign one. Where you know something about rates of interest and where to put your money, and what's a good deal, T-bills versus mutual funds or something. Schools don't teach this, not with as much success as some homes try. I'm referring to some welfare homes, as well, where the obstacles are overwhelming.

I knew one girl who was on ADC. In our neighborhood it stands for After Daddy Cut Out. Her mother, I'm afraid, was a welfare cheat. She did not report her income. She made clothes and sold dresses and did wedding gowns in the neighborhood. So she had a little over and above the welfare check. She raised Antonia to watch every penny. Antonia went to college and got all the way through. It isn't the amount of money; it's the fact that she got it together.

Actually, it's a good sign in our neighborhood when a student becomes a religious fanatic. Especially the kind that says the world is coming to an end. If the world is coming to an end, you get your act together. You cut out the booze, you cut out the dope, you cut out the messing around, you show yourself up as a clean, upright person and you spend a lot of time in church. After a while, the world doesn't come to an end and you're in the middle class. This has happened again and again and again, one group after another. In our neighborhood, the Muslims used to be very big. Now they're not much of anything.

Back when they had Malcolm, reaching people with a political program that nobody else offered, they were turning people on. You would see them becoming Muslims and changing their names. They would stay off the white man's liquor, the white man's port. The women would dress modestly and patronize only Muslim enterprises. You would put all your money into a common pot and invest this. This changed. The racism became an embarrassment to the older Muslims.

Old Elijah Mohammed was getting a little Middle Eastern money to finance their real estate. They began to tone down. If you're doing fairly well, you no longer need the emotional release of shouting. So they sit there with their suits and ties in which they're pretty comfortable now. After a while, they notice that having a Muslim name keeps you out of the mainstream. So they quietly drop it for job purposes. A lot of their dreams did not come true. There is no possibility of having a separate black economy in the United States to any great extent. They'd start doing a little better and the women would get tired of the long dresses, and people would gradually drop out.

Louis Farrakhan is trying to work both ends of the street. He'd like to shake hands with Jesse Jackson, to fit in with the coalition. On the other hand, if you want to turn on somebody who is really down in the miserable depths, you can't have too many connections with the relatively powerful.

What makes you popular is your ability to scare people. Farrakhan had it for a while. Of course, he tapped into something. You got very deep frustration and with it, hate. It can hardly be otherwise. Harriet Beecher Stowe could say that beatings made Uncle Tom into a perfect Christian. You don't meet her Uncle Toms in real life. They're mean so-and-so's when they're treated that way. Farrakhan tapped into that.

With someone like Farrakhan, you pick on somebody who can't pick back. Who among the white establishment has the least support? Who are they most willing to sacrifice if they got to? The answer very often comes out: Jews.

In the poor black community, feelings haven't much to do with anti-Semitism. Some of the most popular victims are middle class blacks.

The underclass is getting harder and harder and harder to get out of. Most of the lower rungs of the ladder have been kicked out. It used to be you could enter the labor force with an eighth-grade education. Then you had to have a high-school diploma. Now it's getting tough for people with college degrees. That's no longer a way up and out.

There was a way then in the black community itself, organizations, certain people on the block. The preacher, the numbers man. It was called helping you get over. It didn't matter as long as you got up and out. Boy, has it changed.

I knew a neighbor kid who thought he was going to make out as a pimp. He'd always had these wonderful sharp suits and flashed a roll of bills. Then one day I saw him; somebody had busted a couple of his front teeth. They looked awful. He needed a lot of expensive dental work. You got to commit yourself to some fair-sized payments over a period of time. Your income can't be here today and gone tomorrow, as his was. He was unable to say he'd have any big money next week. He had these beautiful suits but couldn't get his teeth fixed. I told him, "If you want your teeth fixed, you'll have to give up this kind of life. You need a steady income." I saw him a couple of years later; he smiled and his teeth were fixed. He was carrying a brown paper bag and was waiting for the bus.

Today, how can you make it from flipping hamburgers at $4 an hour to the $150,000 it will take you to buy into a McDonald's franchise? How do you do it when the grocery store chain hires MBA's from Ivy League schools instead of promoting the stockboy in the back to store manager? How do you work it when the very name on your high-school diploma will bar you from a lot of colleges?

How do you do it if you go to a school that doesn't train the kids like racehorses to make those SAT and ACT scores? They're horrible frauds anyway. All they do is test how middle-class you are.

Anybody who judges intelligence on a single number is a class enemy. The human mind is so great and diverse. My students know all kinds of wonderful things that they've had to learn in order to survive. But those things aren't on the tests. It's good to know Mozart, but they're never asked about B.B. King. You're supposed to know only a certain kind of grammar, a certain kind of vocabulary.

They tell you the way your parents spoke is bad and wrong. They say these are bad people who say "I be" or "I aks your mama." This simply isn't so. There is such a thing as standard English. It can be taught with the good motives of Henry Higgins. This is the way it ought to be taught. This is your ticket up and out. But what do you do when you go back to your mother and father and speak to them? I know all kinds of parents and grandparents who are uncomfortable among their educated children.

I think we should forge a bridge. You'll need standard English to communicate in the establishment. But no, your parents are not wrong. What your parents know is good to know, too. Matter of fact, the blues ought to be part of the curriculum. You ought to tape all the wonderful sermons in the South Side churches before they disappear. Get all the eloquence that is there and listen to it in class. Robert Burns tapped into a dialect and made it a lasting thing. Blacks have a strong oral tradition and somehow that should be included in the SAT and ACT tests.

As for discipline, class disruption, I learned something about thirty years ago when I was teaching in a different neighborhood entirely. I said to the troublesome student, "One more time and I'll send you down to the discipline office." He said, "Never threaten a civilian. We got nothing to lose." This was an Italian kid. It happens across the board.

It's dangerous to have a bunch of people in a society who've got nothing to lose. I do not think we can afford an underclass. If you can't feel big without making somebody else feel small, you're never going to feel big anyhow. We've got a lot of unattractive history here. We've got to face it and overcome it.

I learned a lot in the civil-rights movement from guys who were old at the time. They'd been through the CIO organizing drives in the thirties. There seems to be a big push about every thirty years. One in the thirties, one in the sixties. Maybe there will be a big one in the nineties. It's going to have interesting consequences.

I think a large portion of the black middle class is going to become white. The remaining barriers will go down. They're going to have it made and they're going to be co-opted. This time we'll be getting down to the nitty-gritty: the plight—and *size*—of the underclass.

I am very conscious in my class when I'm trying to keep order that I am, in fact, threatening people with nothing to lose. This is a dangerous situation anywhere. These "honky-tubes" from building to building in the Loop, where you walk in air-conditioned comfort and never meet a pan-handler, will not protect you. I've never believed a wall can make you secure. Anywhere.

The fascinating thing about *Native Son* is not that Richard Wright makes us afraid of Bigger Thomas even as we grow to know him, but how scared Richard Wright is of Bigger. Of course, Richard Wright had no choice. He had to live with Bigger Thomas. Now there are quite a few blacks who don't have to live with Bigger Thomas anymore. But Bigger's still there.

I think we will really come to grips with poverty in the United States. I hope we make some long strides in getting rid of it. Poverty is too expensive. We can't afford it anymore. If we don't . . . [*He spreads his hands as though blessing the dead.*]

CHESTER KASKO

He is sixty. He teaches history at a public high school in the city.

"All my three brothers went to Catholic school. I was the only one who went to public school. And I'm the only one going to church. I was never contaminated by Catholic education.

"I kind of believe in country. I believe in God, and I believe your first responsibility is to your children. After that, life comes."

He remembers the Great Depression: his father losing the grocery store, a job with the WPA, and surviving a tough childhood.

In my twenty-two years at that school as a history teacher, I had one white student.

We had a tremendous faculty: sixty-percent black, forty percent white. We got along famously. There was never a hint of animosity. The first principal I had was white. When he left, the new guy was a black fellow. He didn't bother anybody. "You've taught here long enough. I don't expect to tell you how to teach." Laissez-faire. When he left about five years ago, the new principal was a black woman from a grammar school. Mrs. R.

She said nobody was any good. She could tell by the bulletin boards. "You don't have any of the students' work up there. In the first and second grades, every kid loves to pin their paper up on the board." Can you picture an eighteen-year-old walking up and pinning his paper on the board?

We said, "You're not in grammar school any longer. We put up what is current, we move it, change it." She never realized she was in high school. We all tried to work with her. But if you didn't follow her rules, she'd replace you. To her request for new teachers, she got very few responses.

To fill the new positions that came up, she brought in people to do her bidding. Each one was cut from the same mold. They were tall, they were dark-skinned, and they were ladies. I think she had a distrust of light-skinned blacks. If you saw them, you would know them instantaneously. They all wore dark skirts with white blouses. That was the uniform of the day. There were a couple of white women, too. We used to joke about it looking like a nun's costume.

The chairman of the social-studies department, a black woman, resigned to go to the district office. Who was going to be the new chairperson? We sat there. And since no name was put forward, I suggested myself. A vote was taken and I was elected. Blacks and whites voted for me.

All of a sudden, there's a meeting of all the departments. I'm not informed. I'm excluded from every meeting. I said to Mrs. R., "In the last twenty years, we've always elected the department chairperson." She says, "This is my school." In a sense, I was fired. I still had my classes, so I didn't care that much. What the heck.

Every time she wanted a microphone set up, she had to come to me. She didn't like that. So she had this one fellow, a bus driver, who subbed about three days, to do it. Ten minutes after the meeting starts, it doesn't work. She comes up to me: "Fix it." I said, "You gave the job to somebody else." She says, "We need it." I says, "Are you asking me or telling me?" She gives me a long look and says, "Would you please fix it?" I says fine. I walked over, threw the switch, and it went on.

Every time I went into the program department to get some material, her assistant, Mrs. D., was in a tizzy about it. "You don't have to come in here. I'll send it to you." A couple of weeks pass, no material. So I go in again. "I didn't get it." I saw my stuff laying on a table and picked it up. She comes running over, hollering, "You dumb Polack! You dumb Polack!" I could have said, "How can you say that to me? You don't even know your own job. You're screwing up, you dumb bitch!" But I just laughed. I kicked the chair out of my way and walked out.

About fifteen minutes later, into the class comes a student with a note. "Come down to the office. Mrs. R." I went down and she hands me another letter. It was in hand print because her clerks are really slow. It said, "See Mr. B." He was the district superintendent. I was B.'s precinct captain when he ran for State Rep. He says, "There's a problem, Bill." I said, "She called me a dumb Polack." He says, "Let me put it this way. Would you like a transfer? You have a choice of any school in the city of Chicago. I got a spot for you right now." He starts naming the schools. Every one is a school people are fighting to get into. The best. "Let me know. I got a meeting to go to." He's always got a meeting to go to.

So I went over to a local pub. I had a nice lunch that a teacher normally doesn't have. A three-cocktail lunch, and I hate martinis. Went back to the district office. He was at another meeting, so I went home.

The next day, the teachers, mostly black guys, some women, too, are saying, "Fight her, fight her, fight her." Mike, the cop, and the bus driver are saying, "You got a dirty deal." They were all pleading with me. They knew what was happening, the animosity was so thick. She was patting this one on the back, bawling out another. Divide and conquer. Before she came, we got together beautifully. Parties, kidding. Oh, there were certain groups, you find that everywhere. Now it was totally by race.

I go to the union and the guy says, "Bill, you got a good deal going. There's a big line waiting to get in those schools." I says, "Yeah, but all my colleagues are saying to stick with it, and we all gotta get her."

So I went home to think it over with a case of Old Style. I killed most of it. I came up with a rational solution. I was fifty-six at the time. Had a little heart condition, one girl in college, another in high school, and a son in grammar school. I'm divorced, a single parent. I'm thinking, "What in the world are you doing, gettin' on a crusade? If you win, you're right back on the spot." If I win, I lose. The school I can choose is two blocks from my house. People are dying to get in there. A good integrated school. Where I live, there's everybody, black, Mexican, working-class white, the whole kit and kaboodle.

I've been at the new school for two years now. I've stopped taking Valium. I still have my Old Style, of course. I feel so much better. It's beautiful at this school. I was so bitter about it then. But I've mellowed a lot.

I don't feel any animosity towards a person because they're black. I hate to use that expression "I got black friends," but you know what I mean. But one thing used to infuriate me and still does. I'd bring it up at school and some of the blacks would take offense. I hate stupid people. But if you're black and stupid, that compounds the problem because you've got two strikes against you. They'd get mad when I'd say, a stupid person has one strike against him if he's white, but for a black, it's even worse. Racism is still there.

I have some racism. I admit it. If I see a black fighter and a white fighter in a ring, I will kind of cheer for the white guy. If it was a Polish-American against an Irish, I'd cheer for the Pole. If it's an American team against any foreign team, I'd cheer for the American. I cheer for the Chicago team. We all have some kind of preju—I don't like to use the word racism. I'd rather say prejudice. To pre-judge.

When Joe Louis fought Max Schmeling in 1937—

I was seven. I was for Joe Louis because the other guy was a Kraut, one of those lousy Germans. My father has seven battle stars from World War I. Black people always say, "I'm not prejudiced." I say, "Wouldn't you root for the black guy in the ring against the white?" He'll say, "That's not prejudice, that's pride."

It's in everything, prejudice. Take a nice-looking woman walks in here. Both of us would look at her. Now a handsome guy walks in and we both kind of, Oh, well, We'd be more friendly to the lady than towards the guy. Unless we might be of another persuasion. [*Laughs.*]

I've had a couple of arguments with different faculty members about affirmative action. Why should your son or daughter get a full scholarship and not mine? You're a teacher and I'm a teacher. I agree some kind of action must be taken, but we can't pull down the top people to bring up the bottom, because we'll destroy our country. We've gotta keep the top people moving regardless of the coloration of their skin.

I think there's been a tremendous improvement in race relations. But there's a long way to go. I don't want the government to step into things. We've got detention centers called public housing projects, holding pens. I'm against scattered sites, too. I just don't want to see the government being the landlord. During the summer, I've been there. I worked at the Robert Taylor Homes doing construction work, demolition.

I belong to the American Legion. Mostly, it's a black post. I go there, park my car, they always got somebody watching. It's like any poor area you go into. If it's poor, your car's in danger. On the North Side, too. The whites.

I grew up in an area that was Italian, Irish, Polish. All the time, the Italian kids would stand on top of the viaduct and throw rocks at us. So I was always leery. To this day, when I park a car under a viaduct, I look around all over. I don't care who it is, I'm leery all the time. I never want to get pinned down against a building. I always want an escape route.

Segregation is part of our lives. When I'm with a bunch of guys sitting in a bar, drinking beer and watching the Bears game, that's segregation. Because all the bars I go into, there are very few women.

Before we have an understanding of the other person, we have to understand ourselves more. Knowing what it is in ourselves. Look at Jimmy the Greek, who got kicked off the television because he said many blacks are better athletes because they have longer thigh bones. On ESPN, four black guys were saying blacks are better athletes. Why didn't *they* get kicked off? Why was it just Jimmy the Greek?

We've got to understand. Some of these people are saying blacks are better physically because they were picked as slaves to come to America because they were muscular. They had good bones but they were kind of dumb. They were bred for strength and the working ability. They weren't bred for the brain. Maybe blacks are dumber than whites. Maybe Shockley was right.*

I personally don't believe it. But what if it might be true? If in the next fifty years, it comes out that you may be a better athlete, but I got more brains? There's a great fear within me that this will be cemented into people's thinking. As crazy as you think an idea is, there's a lot of people who believe that. [*Laughs.*]

I've seen a lot of educated blacks and a lot of educated whites. I've seen a lot of dumb whites. I'm not so naïve as to believe that when people

---

*William Shockley. American physicist, winner of the Nobel Prize in 1956. What had been at the time the exclusive theory of flat-worlders was suddenly given credence by Shockley's pronounced belief that blacks were indeed genetically inferior to whites.

talk, they're being honest. They will say whatever you want to hear. I don't know all the answers. I'm getting old, I'm getting old.

I'll tell you what happened to me. I did a crazy thing. I got on the bus. I'm the only white. All of a sudden, I hear whack, whack, whack. Here are two black kids beating up on another kid. I know him. I got up and said: Stop it! I saw the bus driver looking in his mirror. We had eye contact, his head went down and he looked straight out the window. I grabbed one kid, who shoved me and I went forward. The other kid pulled the emergency on the back door. The bus stopped. They grabbed the kid's bookbag, ripped it off his arm, and ran away.

I took a step toward the door and I said, "Wait, you dummy! They'll be on your case two seconds outside the door." I turn around and there are two guys sitting here and a guy sitting there, and I says, "You sonsofbitches. Here's one of your own getting his ass kicked and you sit there. You're a bunch of cowards. You're a bunch of niggers!" And I *hate* that word. You know, on that bus there wasn't even a word. Everybody sat with their heads down. The busdriver, too. There must have been forty people. It was pretty full. I was screaming.

When I get off the bus, I'm still mad. It's near the end of the line. Most were gone. As I got to the front door, I berated the driver for five minutes. I said, "If you had any balls—" He just wouldn't say a word, looking straight ahead.

The next day, I told it to the kids in my first class. This one kid said, "We heard it already, Mr. Kasko." Some of these kids had been on the bus. This one little kid came up to thank me. The others were laughing: "Oh, you're crazy, Mr. Kasko. You're gonna get yourself shot." But you know somethin'? They were very, very happy I did it. Because I was protecting one of them. By the same token, they were angry because old Whitey, this old white guy, did it and not one of their own.

That's the problem the black kid has, because his parents are one of the people who had his head down on the bus. You understand what I mean? His uncles, his brethren weren't helping, and this crazy white guy did. Those kids could have whipped my tail, but I saved the other kid.

Another incident. Here I am on the same bus. I'm looking out the window. A kid is standing there with his briefcase waiting for the bus. I know him. Here are two guys, grab him, rip his jacket down. One of the guys grabs his watch. I say, "Look!" We're all looking out the window, watching this. So I says, "Sonsofbitches, look at them standing here, not helping that poor kid!" I'm ranting. I'm right out loud, livid. The people on the bus are looking down. And I said to myself, "Why should I be so upset?"

Do you think this would happen in a white community?

Of course. Probably the same thing, probably the same way. I'm willing to bet. I remember, it was some years ago. This white kid comes by, spit on my car. I see this big glob. I come along the gangway and say, "You spit on my car." He says, "So what? You can't do anything to me." I grab him and rub his nose into it. "That's what we do with dogs when they make nasty."

I was working a part-time evening job then. About seven o'clock, I get a phone call. My wife says, "The police are here. They say you beat up on some kid." I said, "Put the officer on." I said, "What are you doing in my house? You better get out right now. You forced your way in. When did this alleged brutality take place?" He's hemming and hawing. The kid's mother is standing next to him. I said, "Would you mind smelling her breath? Because I want to file charges of child neglect on the part of that woman. The kid spit on my car eleven o'clock in the morning and she didn't report it till six P.M. She leaves him on the streets all this time. Child neglect."

In all lower social-economic classes, you get this. But then it could happen in Lake Forest, too. Ahhh, it isn't just race. It's everything.

PETER SODERSTROM

He is a high school teacher in a suburb bordering a large Midwestern city. It had been, for decades, an all-white, predominantly WASP, middle-class enclave. Since World War II, it has undergone gradual, though considerable, changes. Today, it has an extensive black community, working-class as well as middle-class. It is fairly well integrated.

I'm a teacher, trying to do the right thing. It's becoming more and more difficult.

I was a student here in the late sixties. I even eat lunch with some of my former teachers. It's interesting to see the same place and walk the same halls, and see it in a wholly different way.

My dad was very active in civil rights, and I remember marching with him through the streets of this town for an open-housing ordinance. We carried signs, and people were throwing little round cherry bombs at us.

One of the reasons I liked working at this school rather than at an all-white suburb was the mix of races. I wanted that for my own children, too. As I look back over these five years, I think I came in with a very idealistic idea.

As a beginning teacher, I was given low-level classes. Kids that need remedial help. They were predominantly black. As I gained years there, I started getting honors classes. They were overwhelmingly white. Right now I have one black child in my honors class, out of twenty-seven.

This was startling to me. I realized these honors classes get a lot of attention because these are things the school can boast about. It took me a while to catch on: Why, as a beginning teacher, did I get remedial classes? It was a stunning realization. It's like giving doctors the emergency room to train on. Here's where it really requires the specialist, the veteran. With the years, you work your way out of these remedial classes. You gain the clout to say no.

I found that unfair to the kids and unfair to me as a teacher. There isn't a focused curriculum for these kids. The problem's so perplexing that nobody really knows where to go with it. These kids need a person who knows what he's doing. I work with remedial kids now by choice, but I still don't know quite how to do it.

My honors classes are easy. You come up with one question and they fly with it. You don't have problems with writing and reading skills.

The school is very responsive to the community. Parents who can and do make a big fuss get things to happen. These kids in the low-level classes don't have a voice; their parents don't make their voices heard. When I have a parents'-conference night, almost every honors parent will show up. All you have to do is say, "Fred's doing great. He's a splendid student." The low-level kids, I get one or two parents. Those are the ones you really need to talk to.

As the son of a father who took lots of heat for his stand on civil rights, I am now being considered a racist. This word is coming at me now, and it's very startling. I've been fairly active in the halls. If a kid's in the wrong place at the wrong time, I'll go up and talk to him. Frequently I'm hit with a confrontation. The kid will just yell at me, degrade me; or it's just a complete dismissal: "You have no right asking me this stuff."

When the bell rings, you're supposed to be in your class. That has become quite lax. There are kids coming in from other schools, and we don't know which are ours and which are outside students. We have problems with graffiti, with drug stuff, with weapons brought in.

I just had a bad one. I wrote a kid up, a behavioral referral: this kid was doing this, such-and-such. It calls for disciplinary action. I heard this loud yelling and a running halt outside my door. I came out. "Where are you supposed to be? Do you have a pass?" They didn't. So I wrote it up, which is my job.

Two nights ago, while I was at home, I got a call about six o'clock. It was this boy's father. He said, "I want to know the details, I want to straighten this out. I just got this in the mail, a Saturday detention." The kid's supposed to come to school on Saturday and serve some time. He was furious with me. I said another teacher was there who saw it. He said, "What's that teacher's name? I'll find him."

At ten that night, he calls me at home again. "I just talked to that teacher and he doesn't know a damn thing about it. Whatever is happening at that school is bullshit." Finally, after going round and round, I said, "I'm a professional and I'll be happy to deal with you during those professional hours." He said, "I understand now. I'm the lowly black man and you are the professional and I have to come up to your professional level. Is that all the help I'm going to get from you?" And I said, "For tonight." He hung up.

The next morning, I walked into the office and the phone was ringing. The dean was on the phone. This boy's mother is furious and his father was on his way. The first thing he said to me when he got there was, "I don't like your attitude, I don't like anything about you. I like shit more than I like your attitude." That's how the conversation started.

He was concerned that I had said it was a man who witnessed it and it turned out to be a woman. He said, "Tell me, do you know the difference between a man and a woman?" It was crazy. At the end of the conversation, we found that the boy had lied. He sort of came down, but said, "I want you to know there are lots of kids who think you're a racist." Then he stood up and shook my hand. By way of apology, he said, "I hope you understand, one, I thought my son was telling the truth, and, two, everybody thinks you're a racist."

An administrator called me in. She's had reports from teachers as well as other kids that I'm confrontational and go after black kids more than white kids. I had to do a lot of soul-searching. You get called racist over and over again, you start thinking, "Am I looking for black kids? When I see a black kid coming, what am I thinking? Is it different than if I see a little girl with blond hair coming toward me?" I don't know, I don't know. It's hard to say I'm not a racist, and to prove it I have to say that most of the problems are black.

There's this idea that I don't stop white kids. Not true. But— [*Pause.*]—I just thought of something. The white kids and I banter, not a confrontation. I'm more like their parent figure. I just realized that I approach white kids in a way similar to black teachers approaching black kids. I think we exude signals we may not have control over.

As I picture myself going up to a black kid, I just wonder if it's a readying. Getting ready for something.

For a battle?

Whatever it is I'm preparing for. I've worked hard to approach them, maybe stick my hands in my pockets to appear more casual. It doesn't work.

Putting your hands in your pockets. Do you think they might fear you have a weapon?

Wait a minute! [*Pause.*] Even though that's so outside the realm of possibilities for me, even have a pocket knife in my pocket—what does it mean in that kid's world? To me, hands in your pocket is my dad jingling his change. A very warm sound to me. What does it mean in that kid's world, so different from mine?

I just remembered something. One of my students was expelled; he had a gun. A couple of kids got into an argument. One kid ran home, got his father's gun, and brought it to school. Another kid took the gun away from him and he handed it to my student, who didn't know what to do with it. He passed it on to an older kid, who took the first kid aside, calmed him down, gave him back the gun, which he took back home.

The school expelled everybody involved—my student, who held it for one second, the older boy who calmed things down, everybody. The authorities felt the gun should have been given to the administrators or the correct personnel. A parent stood up at a board meeting, someone not involved, and said, "How unfeeling of you. Shame on you, not to understand that in his world, if he had turned that gun in to the authorities, the other kid, excited, would have done him in. You're imposing your world on this kid. Don't you understand?"

I have friends among the black teachers. Some of them are as concerned about the kids as I am. They say we're not going to get anywhere unless we make the difficult truth known and admit it. Other teachers move in a pocket and say: What's the problem? You'll find they are teaching the honors classes. They walk through the hall and don't try to stop trouble when they see it. You can choose not to see anything; it's easy.

The problem is not really in the classroom, where the kids know you and you know them. It's when they become anonymous in the halls. A lot of people are pushing for ID badges. I think it would be really good. To identify the kid who belongs in the school, you cut down on his anonymity.

We're doing *Raisin in the Sun* in all three levels of my classes. Reading the text. The remedial kids are thrilled by the fact that I'm doing the same book with them as with the honors and the two-levels. "Are we caught up with them?" "Are we ahead of them?" We're talking about racism and experiences with it. I was surprised at some of the things they told me openly. One girl said, "We know you. You're not a racist." When I'm accused, I say, "Come talk to my kids. The ninety kids who would bear the brunt if I were a racist."

When I sat in the same room with that angry father, we really saw each other and he came to know I was not really a threat. I looked in the mirror before I came there. I was real nervous about this meeting. It was just to be he and I and the dean, who was black. I looked so white, so middle-class white in the mirror. I was dressed casually, but it bothered me that I looked so white. [*Laughs.*] I don't know what I mean by that.

I walked in and there he is, wearing a kind of working vest and a flannel shirt and boots caked with clay. A construction worker. I saw this disparity between us and it bothered me. I saw him only once since then, although he lives only two blocks from me. I saw him standing on his stoop. I don't think we're on great terms. I still think he hates my attitude.

The dean backs me very much. The school's been embroiled in a lot of trouble recently and he's been pushing for change. He really feels the problem is largely black and the black community needs to deal with it. He took me aside and said, "You know in your heart you're not a racist. You just have to let it go." It's an easy accusation to make and extremely difficult to disprove.

I'm glad to see the year end, and I feel I'm really going to do some soul-searching on this. What am I doing when I walk up to these kids that incites them so much? I have been told I set these kids off. There's something.

If there are kids yelling to each other across the hall and disturbing my class, I'm going to say something. I'll just say, "Keep it down." Immediately they'll say, "What the fuck's bothering you? I know all about you, I've heard about you." It's immediate, real quick.

Another teacher, a gentle, gracious person, told me that whenever the kids get mad at her they call her a racist. Whenever they feel good about her, they say, "We know you're not a racist, we were just kidding." Then all of a sudden they'll get mad at her again and call her a racist. It's almost a game.

Do black teachers come out and discipline the kids?

Yeah, but they have a whole other way, makes us all envious. It's a different vernacular. I've seen black teachers walk up to some kid who's being feisty and angry, put his arm around him, and say, "Come on, what is all this?" The kid just changes, is transformed. Suddenly he's a kid. I couldn't possibly. I'd look like an idiot!

It's not the arm so much as the way they can banter. Words, phrases that have nothing to do with my experience. The idiom and a rhythm. I can't touch, I can't get near it. A whole different style. We're all products of the way we were brought up. What does an adult do when a kid says, "Fuck off"? I don't have anything to fall back on. I don't know what to do next, I'm frustrated. Many of them in their experience don't have a treatment of respect, a sense of what authority is. So there the two of us are: I not knowing what to say next, he not knowing what to say next. It gets all bungled up.

I have a black friend at school. She's a secretary in the office. She came up to me on several occasions and said, "You just have to learn to talk to black kids, and I'm going to teach you." There's never been a time when we can get together. I think it would be really interesting.

I get mad, but the Swede in me tries to control it and lets me know it's not constructive. Yet we end up yelling at each other. I'm an adult, I'm a teacher: "You can't talk to me that way." It's funny as I say it, because I've said it so many times. I just feel so appalled. And humiliated, too. Really humiliated. I need to deal with that in myself. I've been told to back off because I'm going to have trouble. I know some kids have threatened me. I know I've caused trouble because I'm being confrontational. My last period of the day is free, so I leave before three though I'm supposed to stay till four. I leave because I know I'm not going to deal well with it. A friend said, "It's like watching somebody burn out."

We have a whole new type of kid. There are those who say, "You should have been here in the sixties." In the sixties, there was a cause, there was a feeling of hope. Now there's no cause. There's just incredible meanness. I'm not talking about just black kids. I'm talking about an egocentric society, from the top down. They say every new generation has conflict with the older generation. But there's something very different here.

This year has really made me look at myself and see what is going on. What word am I looking for? To reevaluate. Am I becoming a racist? Of my new batch of kids, two-thirds will be black. I know exactly what I'm going to get. Am I prejudging? Prejudiced? What's happening to me?

The school's always saying call the parents, call the parents. You call, the line is dead, it's been disconnected, they've never heard of the person. I realize at this moment, that kid probably just has no family life. And I don't even bother to try and search it out. To me, that's prejudicial. Why am I becoming that? This survival thing. You're dealing with so many kids, trying to get through so much.

We've had several board meetings that have been absolutely packed. Usually nobody comes, but when we talk about discipline, everybody shows up. There are black parents who say, "We have to stop turning to the school and should start cleaning up our own homes here." There are other parents who say, "You have teachers who look at black kids in a different way and have different expectations."

I'll be teaching two remedial classes this summer. I have one girl who's in desperate need of special education. In the community there's a stigma attached to it. Her parent is refusing to have her tested, necessary to get in. The girl can barely put a sentence together, can barely comprehend what we're doing. Yet she stays in my classroom, which is not doing her or anybody any good. Things move so slowly that there she stays.

Odd thing, though, with this girl. We did *Romeo and Juliet*. We'd listen to a recording, chunks at a time. She was the first that would go up and be able to interpret what she had just heard. She just had this innate way. I can't understand it.

I'd keep trying to get them to keep their eyes on the book because I think it would be good for them. They do so little reading. They'd not look at the book, but they'd *hear* everything. And they understood it.

Yet, there's a bravado about doing poorly. I used to put on the board grades of people who did well on a test. They'd get so much heat and ribbing from the other kids, I stopped doing it. It's almost as damaging as putting up poor grades. The bright kids are called nerds. Mostly they say, "You're acting white."

One kid had typed his paper. It was a harsh essay, thoughtful. I held it up for everybody to see that he typed it. They all thought he was a jackass for going to all that trouble. He never did it again.

I feel like a white missionary down in an area where I don't belong. I'm saying here's my religion, education. It worked great for me, it's going to work great for you, too. They don't buy it. That's what you believe in. You're one of the ministers of it. But these kids do have to find a way to live in a world where they're going to have bosses, authority figures all over the place.

Do I ever compliment the slower kids? Constantly. It's something they're extremely responsive to. At first I had to force myself to do so. It sounded phony. I'd say, "That's not quite right, but it's a good thought."

But I now I say, "You've done a good job," and it doesn't sound phony at all.

TIMUEL BLACK

A retired Chicago public-school teacher. He taught for thirty-seven years in the city's high schools and colleges.

I taught students who were mostly black, but I've been at predominantly white schools, too. Students are the same. If they have a good teacher and a good school atmosphere, they will strive to learn.

The perception they have today is that their teachers don't believe they can learn. They feel angry about that because they know there's a lot they need to know that they don't know, and there's nowhere else to get it. They get it almost all in the neighborhood.

At the city colleges where I was teaching, many of these young people had been out in the world a bit. They'd experienced some defeats. They looked at reality and realized they should go back to school. I'm now voluntarily teaching a course at Roosevelt: African-American history. They're very interested. These are younger students, eighteen, nineteen. I've talked about the March on Washington, when they weren't even born. We talk about Vietnam, when they weren't even born. I have to feel my way with them.

Most of my former students in the public junior colleges came from poor families. The girls, particularly, beginning families of their own, looked at life in a different way. The people I now teach emerged from blue-collar and white-collar families, aspiring to the middle class. They are heading definitely toward careers in law, business, engineering, or the arts. They intend to go on to professional school.

There are far more black girls than black boys in class. They outnumbered the boys in the community colleges I taught almost three to one. The last semester at Roosevelt, I had twenty-three students: one white girl, five young black men, and the rest, black girls.

What it means for the future of the black family is terrifying. The children will not have enough of a chance to see a strong black male. Whether in or out of wedlock, the children of the next generation will be living in homes with one parent from the beginning of their lives. Estrangement will impinge on them even deeper, because there are no real models for them to follow.

Last night I attended a local school council. All but seven people were black women. There is only one black male teacher in a school of 360. This is elementary school, the beginning. I said to them, "You have older men in the community—grandfathers, like myself. With all their wisdom and nothing to do, they may be willing to come and play with the children for a little while." I was told that when a male teacher shows up, the kids just gravitate to him. The absence of a black male presence leaves a void in these children's lives. Girls don't have a chance to see a man like the one who will, hopefully, be her husband. If she has a brother, his life is dominated by the mother, the assumption being that men are weak. It's devastating.

The male may still live in the ghetto community in spirit but not in body. If he cannot assert what is the classic idea of masculinity—a man able to take care of his family—the chances are he may walk. Historically, he was encouraged to walk. During the beginnings of ADC, if the man was in the house, the family couldn't get welfare. He was out of work: the steel mills were closing, the stockyards gone. Out of sympathy for his family, he would simply walk away. He'd sometimes come back in the evening, but the welfare department had the creepers, sleuths, the night-watchers. They'd come and look under people's beds.* Gradually, his absence from the family became acceptable and he just stayed away.

The law itself played an important role, in addition to the disappearance of industrial jobs. He was ashamed to stay at home because he was not a man.†

My family came to Chicago in the first black migration from the South right after World War I. My father had few skills, but he had a strong back and a willing mind. Many of them came for the same reason people

---

* Ex-officio methods were employed as well, by other than welfare department agents, in the late thirties. "Honey, Wilkins [the landlord] had him a paid-off bunch of police officers. They were detectives and plainclothesmen. He had a list of every widow woman living in the building and on relief. He gave these names to the police officers, and around eleven-thirty or twelve o'clock, they'd come in and knock on your door to see if you had a man in there. See? Everywhere they found a man, they had those people on relief cut off."

Mrs. Willye Jeffries in *Hard Times* (1970)

† "During the Great Depression, I observed unemployed Pennsylvania miners hanging around street corners. They gave each other solace. They were loath to go home because they were indicted, as if it were their fault for being unemployed. A jobless man was a lazy good-for-nothing. The women punished the men for not bringing home the bacon by withholding themselves sexually. The men were belittled and emasculated. They suffered from depression. They felt despised and were ashamed of themselves. They avoided home.

"Today, they live out their emotions in conflict. They create social tensions, they act out: drinking, drug taking, stealing, promiscuity. In place of complaining, they explode."

Dr. Nathan Ackerman in *Hard Times* (1970)

left Europe, a better life. The blacks, like the European immigrants, were met at the station—in this case, the old Illinois Central—by friends and relatives. They were told where to live, what kind of jobs to look for, whom to see. "I'll take you to my boss. He needs people." They would double up for a while until they saved enough for a place of their own. It's the story of immigrants who just had color to them. This kind of buddy system was operating even through the Depression.

We came in 1919, right after the race riot. We lived in a white neighborhood and my father, who was working in the stockyards, didn't come home for a week. My mother was worried but one of our neighbors said, "Bring the kids over here, nobody will bother you."

After World War II, farming in the South was becoming mechanized; less hands were needed. Add to that, the government policy of letting land lay fallow, paying big planters not to raise cotton. The impoverished rural people ran straight to the big cities up north. Chicago was the big one. But there were no forerunners this time. There was no one to help them get over. Unlike my father, they had no skills other than working on the plantation.

The black South Side was absolutely overflowing with people, because of the nature of the ghetto. So they spread out to the West Side. For a time, there was a distinction between the two communities, the settled urban blacks and the new rural migrants. Much like German Jews and Eastern European Jews. In some instances, it applied to shade of color as well, caste: lighter-skinned versus dark. My mother, who obviously had white ancestry, as most of us did, was very light, but she never played that game. The civil-rights movement—black is beautiful—ended that distinction.

Many of the lighter-skinned blacks may have been privileged, but not by choice. Whites assumed that if they were light, they had white blood and were, therefore, superior to the darker black folks. I remember a white high-school principal asking me, "Are light Negroes smarter than dark Negroes?" I deliberately picked out a dark kid's grades and compared them to the scores of a dumb white kid. He was furious. I proved the point beyond what he had asked. I really wanted to cap things by saying, "And I'm smarter than you." I didn't, but he got the idea.

There were no really strong feelings about Jews. The oppression of blacks makes almost any other group a target. On the West Side today, it's the Arab storekeeper. On the South Side, it's the Korean. The WASP banker, the big dealer, is too far away.

I'm part of a group engaged in Black-Jewish dialogue to reduce misunderstanding. The Israel situation has bothered a lot of blacks. Sometimes it gets confused with Jewishness. I mentioned Jewish friends of mine who do not like what's going on in Israel any more than I do. No more than I did at what was going on in Uganda.

There is a tremendous awareness among black people of Israel's relationship with South Africa—shipping arms, for example. There are no black people I know of who are not conscious of South Africa happenings. Many of them transfer that to all Jews. I tell them of a guerrilla fighter with the African National Congress whom I met in Tanzania. He is a Jew. This deeply affects them.

The urban black may be unlettered, but he's not unwise. If people lump the two together, they're making a terrible mistake. Whites don't quite understand the depth of their despair. "It doesn't matter what we do, it gets taken away from us. There's no use. Let's withdraw. Let's do whatever we feel like doing. If we feel like being disorderly, let's be disorderly. It makes no difference." The Reagan victories cinched it.

We'll find few blacks under the age of thirty who were not born in an urban community. I sometimes test my students. How many were born in a city of 500,000 or more? Almost all those under thirty raise their hands. Almost none of the older ones raise their hands. How many of your grandparents were born in those cities? Almost every younger one will raise his hand. You have three generations who've never had the opportunities of those of us who came before.

Most of the children and grandchildren of my generation, of those who came from the rural South after World War I, are doing fairly well. The others, who came after the Second War, are in bad shape. They are characterized as the underclass. They see no better life available to them. But they're very sophisticated, some ruthless. They feel denied, left out. They have to live.

There's been a break in continuity. They have no tradition. Whom do they communicate with? Not with my generation. We live in different neighborhoods, different worlds. Chatham* has nothing to do with Robert Taylor Homes. In fact, we may give the appearance of being part of the enemy.

If my children had had any kids, they'd be eight, nine years old. They wouldn't associate with the other kids. I know my own children feel a sense of discomfort, guilt. They don't know how to get over it.

Often, the fortunate and the less fortunate are in the same family. I

---

* A middle-class neighborhood in Chicago, mostly black homeowners.

have cousins who live in housing projects. Does my daughter ever get to go there? Why should she? How do you walk up in a Robert Taylor home when the *police* won't even go up there? My cousin called me: her son is in narcotics. He takes her television or radio. What can I do? I'm helpless. A few bucks perhaps, but that doesn't do it.

These kids don't really live in a childhood. They skip it. From age twelve or so, they go straight to adulthood. They go straight to the guys on the corner and feel at home. Every other place is alien.

Timuel Black and I were on the train, heading for the 1963 March on Washington. He was accompanied by his sixteen-year-old daughter and ten-year-old son.

I've been in only one other such event in my life. I was in Paris one day after its liberation. The Resistance was driving the Germans out of the city. The exhilaration and discipline of the crowd was as encouraging as the courage of the people. I was a member of the First Army in the quartermaster corps. This march reminded me so much of that moment.

The Monument, the reflecting pool, all those people, black, white, King's speech, so pure, so touching. We thought America would be moved by this event. Such a feeling of joy and relief. But reality hit us very quickly, didn't it?

Twenty-five years later, a permanent underclass has come into being. A disproportionate number of black youth are part of it. Numerically, this underclass is more white than black, but our leadership imposes the idea that this is really a black, useless, lazy underclass.*

I feel not so much an anger as a disappointment, a sadness. It didn't have to be this way. I don't think these children are the cause of it. I think they're the victims. When I think of my cousin's son, he's not a bad kid. He's caught in a shocking environment, where the norms pull him in. It's symptomatic of what's happening to young America, white and black. He's good when he can be good. He's sorry for what he does. He's been offered help, but he believes he can somehow beat this game without help. A change in circumstance is almost impossible for him. Where can he go where his mother can pay the rent?

As for W. E. B. Du Bois's idea of the talented tenth, who should take the lead, we find all kinds of examples in the entertainment and sports world, don't we? I don't mean to be ironic. Arsenio Hall, a guy from

---

* *The Great Divide* (1988).

Chicago's West Side and Cleveland, is a sudden millionaire. It shows where our values are. We pay millions of dollars for this sort of talent, while kids living in Cabrini-Green, Brewster, and places across the country are throwaways. We don't know what their talents are.

We know some of them are entrepreneurs. They do very well in the cocaine business. What do you say to a mother whose son is in dope and brings her five hundred, six hundred dollars a week? How can you convince this kid not to bring this money home to his mother that he loves and would like to see do better? [*Laughs.*] We're talking about waste.

When we look at the black experience, we're looking, in exotic terms, at the American experience. For good or bad. When we see a world in which to be successful, you must become conservative, there's no reason why there should not be a growing number of black conservatives, among the more fortunate, as there is a growing number of white conservatives. Clarence Thomas, a black judge, appointed to the Appellate Court, may be groomed to succeed Thurgood Marshall. He'll make Rehnquist look like a flaming liberal.*

For the bottom end, there will be less empathy. The white community in America is saying: We have done all we can for the blacks during the civil-rights movement. They haven't measured up. Now we have to move on to other agendas.

So Farrakhan enters the picture. He's not a danger because he has no power, economic or political. What makes him enticing to the black community is his audacity, his ability to talk bad to white people. I think that makes us feel good. We know full well that it's just talk, and he talks well; but it frightens some of the white people. The more the media embraces and castigates him, the more he will last.

This has been so through history. Aside from his ability to fight, Mohammed Ali was telling white people off. The media gave Malcolm X a forum while he was telling white people off. The blacks, middle-class and all, would just chuckle at it. It had nothing to do with whether they were allied to him or not.

I went to a Farrakhan meeting, but didn't get in. At the door, they were going through body searches. Regardless of what I think about the ideology of anyone, I just don't go for that. I told them no and turned around.

Farrakhan's audiences tend to be relatively young people. They're part of the group that feels left out of the mainstream of American life, and

---

* The conversation took place in the fall of 1989.

they're angry about it. They're not unintelligent. You had that kind of worship during the Garvey days. There were people like my father who believed that Garvey's idea about back-to-Africa was a good one. My mother was fortunately more persuasive. [*Laughs.*]

There have always been two strains in black America. Those like A. Philip Randolph and W. E. B. Du Bois, who had a devotion to the buried democratic spirit of the country and a devotion to their own people. And those who said it's never going to work. They are not necessarily bad people. They see themselves as prophets. Young people come along, looking for a better world and a better way. They're caught in the stream and looking for a way out.

■ ■ ■ ■ ■

Campus Life

DAWN KELLY

She is twenty-one, in her third year at the University of Illinois, Chicago. Aside from being a student member of the university's board of trustees, she was elected president of the student government. "I had white, Asian, Palestinian, and Hispanic students campaigning for me, as well as black."

She had attended a parochial high school, "a good one. I didn't have any black teachers, but my mother compensated for that. She always kept us in tune with our history and ourselves. I cried when they didn't acknowledge Dr. King's birthday. My mother said, 'Why cry? Fight back.' We had chapel which all the students attended. I did one of Dr. King's speeches as a tribute to him. They were forced to recognize him one way or another, even if we didn't have school out. That was my mother's idea. The majority of the students complimented me."

Her sixteen-year-old sister attends the same parochial school and her thirteen-year-old brother won a scholarship in a prep school out West. She plans to earn her Ph.D. and teach African-American literature.

Right now I'm a bit perplexed about things going on in my life. I'm affected quite emotionally. A lot of young African-Americans sit around and don't realize that our parents fought for us to be in universities and restaurants. We've become quite comfortable. Some think I'm overreacting. They say, "Dawn, you're too emotional."

In the last two years, I've seen racism and hate, and it disturbs me. I would say that the majority of the people in the world are good—white and black, of all colors. Even here at the university. I think it's always a few bad apples.

The problem started when a female black student was walking through the dormitory early in the evening. She was grabbed by a group of white males who said all kinds of derogatory things to her. When she screamed, they ran away. She can identify one of the men, but she won't testify because she's afraid the university will not back her and the guys may come back. So she's moved home, off the dormitories. I said I'd go to the police with her, but she always stands me up. She's afraid and she has every right to be.

There was a black female resident advisor in the dormitory. A black penis from a cadaver was hung on her door, with a note: "Next time it might be one of your body parts." It was signed by the KKK. She moved home, terrified. I would have felt terribly guilty if something had happened to her, without standing up and saying something. Anyone who would do something so morbid is not joking. Right now, the tensions are so thick you can cut it with a knife.

There's a second student paper on the campus. It's run by the more progressive ones, most of them white. They've printed articles exposing much of the racism and have received hate letters from the Klan.

I think it stems from the country itself. These crimes aren't prosecuted as harshly as they can be. Therefore it gives students as well as other people the impression that they can do whatever they want to do and they'll get away with it.

I eat with white kids at the cafeteria, but most black students don't. You can see Asian kids in one corner, Hispanics in another, whites, blacks, all pretty well segregated. You have individual intermingling, but not groups.

The feeling has always been there, and I blame myself as well as others for not taking a stand before. My mother has totally come down on me. She's a very strong woman. She raised my brother, my sister, and me by herself. She felt I was too passive.

It's one thing to go to school together, but to live right next to each other, sleep in the same room, that's another story. Most white students come from the suburbs and have been isolated, have not encountered various cultures. I think they've lost out on a lot. And that leads to racism, too. That's why we're pushing for multicultural courses on campus. If you would study accounts where blacks and Asians and Latinos have contributed to society, your respect level would be a lot higher. They just don't know.

We've had different accounts of the tensions. Some of my friends had problems with white roommates who don't want to listen to their music or have their friends over. There's a cultural gap. I had a friend who listens to Louis Farrakhan. She has tapes of his sermons. When she listens, not loud, it would disturb her roommate. I guess it's because of his black-nationalistic overtones. I pretty much agree with him, but I guess it would probably frighten the average white person. Our music is different, our culture is different. One person might want to listen to Prince, another to Led Zeppelin, and you'd have a clash.

I appreciate Farrakhan because he's not afraid to tell the truth. People think he's a racist, but he's not. He has an endearment toward his people and wants to see them with empowerment, with a decent standard of living. I think the average white person is afraid to hear the truth.

We may have alienated a lot of white kids, not intentionally. Any time you stand up for something, most people thinks it threatens them. I don't think most of them are racists, but they feel alienated. When you look at them as you might look at anybody, they think you're seeing them as white racists. It's not that way at all. You're just trying to stand up for what's right. In our coalition, we have some white students and Jewish students, as well.

Jewish people in this country even today are discriminated against. Many people don't consider them Anglo or white. They're considered different.

A lot of people think Farrakhan is anti-Semitic. I disagree. He's just calling what he sees. That happens so much in this society, where people have this thing. Many black people feel that Jewish people think they're better and that blacks are on a different level. This feeling exists; we have to be honest.

I think Jewish history and black history parallel one another. I had a black professor who said if you want to know success, read Jewish history. They've been through degrading things, starting all the way back from Egypt and up into the forties and Hitler's Germany. The one thing I can respect about people of Jewish descent is that another Holocaust will never happen because they won't let people forget it.

African-Americans have a problem with celebrating slavery. I think if you celebrate what has been, you can move to higher ground. If you can celebrate your ancestors for dying so that you can move ahead, society won't forget it. Nobody is going to try that with Jews anymore, because they're not going to let it. People won't mess with them because they stood their ground. If we take that stance, it won't happen to us again either. If we said, "We're not going to let you pull at our sisters in the dorm," it wouldn't happen.

I feel that by nature blacks are a forgiving people. They're not racist. I hate it when people throw around the terms reverse racism. I can be prejudiced but not racist. To be a racist, you have to be able to oppress another race. To do that, you have to have economic and political power. Blacks don't have that; whites do. Being prejudiced is something else. You have to prejudge. Many black may prejudge whites, because of all their past experiences.

For my grandmother or my great-aunts to have any love for the white race, considering what they've done to us, means they have a true forgiving quality within them. We think about those terrible things and they're not too long ago. They're in my mother's history.

Her family left the South because her brother, who worked in a gas station, beat up the white boy who tried to take his money. He was a great mechanic and got all his money in tips. He helped take care of the family. How was he gonna let this guy come in and take his money and not have a penny to bring home?

That day he told my great-grandmother what happened. She didn't waste any time. They left antique furniture, they left most of their belongings. Whatever they could carry, they threw in a bag, got on a train, and came North. He couldn't tell a white jury or a white judge, "I hit him because he tried to steal from me." He wouldn't have been believed. So for my mother, my uncle, or my great-grandmother, who is now passed, to have any love or respect for the white race, it's a quality in us.

The white kids on campus can't quite comprehend this because it's never happened to them. I've had people ask, "Why do you make such a big deal?" They truly don't understand, not that they're racist.

For one thing, we don't have an African-American cultural center. We've been waiting for one for twenty years. It's a pity for a school that claims to have an urban mission not to have a center that celebrates African history and African art. We wanted to bridge the gap between the black community and the university. What was happening to black and Latino women on the campus was simply a sign of total disregard for us. They disrespect us because they feel we're nothing, we're not intellectual, we're barbaric. So we black women like these type of things, like to be grabbed.

I think this is what a lot of whites believe. I think a lot of blacks believe it, too. We've been degraded so much that we have imbedded in our minds that maybe we're not that good. Maybe that's why so many black students don't excel in school. They feel, "I can't do it. I'm not as intelligent as Susie, the blonde sitting next to me. I lack something." If you grow up in the Chicago public-school system and this is taught you, it's eventually going to affect you. It's conditioning.

I think society has set it up this way. We don't want to see the true quality of life for everybody. We will let a few people of color—I don't like the word minorities, we're over eighty percent of the world—get to the top. They'll let a couple of us get Ph.D.s, become doctors, lawyers. After that, you have people laying by the wayside, people starving, homeless, without education.

You sit in a class and people tell you if you have full lips, darker skin, look a certain way, you're not pretty. This must affect children. I've seen numerous cases where darker students have been shunned and I've been accepted because I'm fair-skinned. Do we have to look European to be beautiful? That's what TV shows us. It's all over.

I see a country and I see a world that's going to have to change. I truly believe it's too late. We have no spirituality anymore. We have no belief in anything anymore but what we can make, what we can synthesize. We're even trying to make babies different ways but the natural way. We're coming up with all these things that are destroying the earth.

The white man has destroyed the earth. He raped Africa, he raped America. Now we say our ozone layer is ruined. You look outside and it's sixty degrees in December. What are we gonna do, patch it up with Band-Aids? I think the world is going and it's just a matter of time before we all just self-destruct. I think it's over. Maybe that's why so many people are not afraid to stand up—because I truly don't think there's anything to fear in the end.

I believe there's a higher power that I'm going to have to face for my wrongs. Everyone else will, too. It's going to be a final judgment. A lot of my friends feel it, too.

Yet, African-Americans have a will to live and to fight.

FRED WERNER

He is editor of the student newspaper at the University of Illinois, Chicago.
He comes from a town in central Illinois. Both his parents are professors in the college there.
He is twenty-one.

When I came to UIC, I never saw any racial problems. During my freshman year, my roommate was a black Haitian. Being with the newspaper, I was able to follow closely what goes on on campus. I never really saw much in the way of racial tension, even living in Chicago.

This fall there were these incidents in the dorms. Apparently there were some racist things written on the doors of some black students. There were a couple of times when some blacks were harassed in the halls by white guys. It didn't surprise me. That thing can happen when many white kids in school come from suburbs where they've always been around white people.

There were a couple of cases where some black women were pushed around in the hall. No one was hurt, but that's just intolerable. They're understandably upset. It's very hard to combat. I mean, when a nineteen-year-old gets to college, he's kind of set in his ways, a little bit. It's hard to say, "You shouldn't do that." We do photo opinions in our newspaper. When we asked one guy about these racial incidents, he said it's like someone giving you the finger on the highway. You get real upset but there's not a whole lot you can do about it. To some extent, that's true.

At the end of the quarter, there were security guards placed in the dorms. Uniformed people strolling around creates an unpleasant atmosphere.

There's an active black organization here. Dawn Kelly, president of the student government, is one of its leaders. Once these incidents occurred, there was a lot of heated discussion and anger at the administration. They marched on the chancellor's office and occupied it.

They had a valid point in criticizing the university's loss of its urban mission. It was to be a place where commuter students would mostly come, those who couldn't afford to go to Champaign. That has slowly been lost. People like me and from the suburbs are mostly here. After all, the city's population has shifted to the suburbs, a lot of them blue-collar. Tuition has gone up and financial aid has not kept up with it. The number of black students, especially male, has actually declined.

Kids coming out of the Chicago school system have a lot of trouble on standardized tests—ACT and SAT—and their scores tend to be a lot lower. That's played a part in shifting the emphasis from urban to suburban and white.

What the black activists have done has been valuable in raising awareness of the problems, though some don't present themselves as well as they should. In one of the meetings, the chancellor walked out because every time he tried to respond, they would interrupt and start yelling at him. On the other hand, I can understand that for them it's a very emotional issue. It's hard to discuss something rationally if you feel threatened.

There was one white guy who asked me if the newspaper was going to present the other side. He told me about a group of students who were attacked by black guys from the neighborhood. I didn't think it really had any relation to what was going on at school. I guess you could view it as a little bit of latent racism.

The dorm's resident adviser, who was a leading black activist, got into an argument with a white guy, who'd said, "You black students think you can run the campus now, don't you?" This guy has a black roommate who defended him, saying he was not a racist. He'd been drinking, which does a lot of strange things to people. I think it was just an expression of frustration by a white student. UIC is being portrayed as somehow having problems of race relations. It's not fair. There have just been a handful of incidents.

They have been asking for a black cultural center. There's already a Hispanic cultural center and a move toward a women's center. I've heard some say: If we had a white cultural center, it would be considered racist, so why should there be one for blacks? I can understand that feeling. On the other hand, I can understand the logic of the blacks, considering their three-hundred-year history of oppression. It's hard to say who's right. There are some whites who could say they're oppressed. Some are the first in their family to go to college. In some ways, everybody is oppressed in this society.

The *Dartmouth Review* was unfairly labeled as racist. They had a tradition of printing names of who they considered the ten worst professors on campus. They were very antagonistic toward a black music professor and had repeated run-ins with him. I believe a couple of the editors were thrown out of school. It's an example of how criticism of black leaders can label you a racist, no matter what the criticism is. This attitude does great damage to the civil-rights movement and turns off whites who might otherwise be sympathetic to it. It polarizes things.

For example, calling Reagan, or for that matter, Bush, a racist is unfair. They may have acted counter to the interests of black people; that may be true, but that's just being insensitive to the needs of poor people, especially blacks. From what I've read of Reagan's past and from people who know him, there isn't a racist bone in his body. Insensitive, yes, racist, no. My parents admire Reagan, although he has shown himself as not very well educated. Nobody's perfect.

I think I myself am not too sensitive at times to black concerns. A lot of white people aren't as aware as they should be. But that's different from being hateful to a group for no specific reason.

Things going on at this campus can have a positive effect. I, for example, have given a lot of thought to these things recently. Six months ago, I wouldn't have been as conscious of the urban mission as I am now, because of the black students who have been protesting. On the other hand, some of them are more vocal than they need be. I can't think of anything that would bring me to shout at the chancellor. I have a kind of semi-religious awe of the man. He's a man of considerable authority, so why should they yell at him? On the other hand, unless they create a fuss, no one will pay any attention to them.

The majority of our white students are indifferent to all this. Apathy is the word. There may be individuals who are stridently racist, but quietly. Many are not really racist but have negative feelings to what is happening. I think the students reflect what has happened to the nation in the last fifteen years. They've become more conservative. There are some leftist students on the campus. I'm not using the word in a derogatory way. "Progressive" may be the better word. They're a minority.

There's been a campaign for multicultural courses as requirements in the curriculum. I'm split-minded on it. I can safely say the majority of white students, who aren't embittered racists, may be forced to sit in a class which they may not be interested in. They will say, "I have to sit here because these black students shouted loud enough to make the university institute this." You can't force someone not to be a racist.

I question whether forcing people to desegregate does any good. When people are forced to do something, they resent it even more. The solution may be a long way off, but I think there is more understanding between white kids and black kids than there was thirty years ago. The hope is that, slowly, America, the melting pot that accepted immigrants like my family, can do the same thing for the people who were already here.

JENNIFER KASKO

Chester Kasko's daughter. She is twenty-three, a graduate of an Illinois university, where she majored in education.

"I have a very hard time finding a job. Right now my pocketbook is depleted."

She describes the neighborhood in which she lives as predominantly white, no black people. "It's secluded, a white island. Blue-collar. They've closed the steel mills down and men who have worked there for thirty, forty years have lost everything. They've lost their pride."

When the time came for desegregation of the schools, we had black children bused in. The neighborhood didn't fight it, but they didn't like it. There wasn't any problem with the little children. They didn't know any better. At first, the older children resented it. They felt they were being invaded and losing what their parents had worked so hard for. I was in sixth grade at the time. There weren't any out-and-out blows. What I remember was everyone would give the bus the finger.

I didn't do it myself, but my friends did. My dad had always taught at a school where there were black people, and I was always around. I was always taught not to be prejudiced, not to hate. We'd go to all the school functions. I'd ride the bus to his school through all the rough neighborhoods. Some of his students would say, "Are you crazy taking the bus? We don't even like to take the bus." They were scared, telling me about getting purses stolen, intimidation. My sister and I just sat there and were left alone. We were the only whites on the bus and weren't scared at all. It was almost an adventure.

They would say to us, "Are you Kasko's daughters?" They were thrilled to see us, always nice and receptive. We used to play with the black boys on the days teachers made out the grades. There was no problem until one day the school secretary, a black female, told my father it was wrong for us to play together. Until then, we had a great time and couldn't wait till records day. The next year, we weren't allowed to come anymore.

At my school, even though the black kids were there now, we were actually separate in the same classroom. They'd hang around with their group and we'd hang around with ours. It seemed like the white kids were scared of the others. I'm sure it had something to do with the way they were brought up. They never had exposure.

A lot of my friends' parents would refer to them as niggers. One of my friend's dad worked in Republic Steel. He was laid off and a black man was hired in his place. So he had a real vendetta against him: "The niggers are going to take over everything." I always took it with a grain of salt. I thought he was just angry.

At high school, parochial, it was sixty, twenty, twenty—sixty-percent white, twenty percent black, twenty percent Hispanic. Surprisingly, we got along with everyone. When it was our year for Homecoming Queen, the runner-up was black.

We began to notice the problem with the younger students. The freshmen. This was about 1983. It's when Mayor Byrne and Harold Washington were going at it. The girls would wear their Washington buttons on uniform skirts. In obscene places. They were vulgar and would scream down the hall. The girls in our year were quieter, more docile.

The younger girls would tend to carry these heavy bags and would be inconsiderate to others on the stairs. It almost made us not like them. Because of this, the white kids were getting more angry and less tolerant.

At college, our dorm had sixty girls on a floor. Probably two-thirds white and one-third black. Our racial problems started when somebody reported that a couple of black girls had men in their room past hours. They accused our group as the ones who called. It wasn't true, because we had guys after hours, too. So it would have hurt us to call. But they wouldn't listen. We did it, that's all there was to it.

Now they started to leave their doors open and play their music really loud. They'd just keep the same beat for hours. They'd do it purposely, while we tried to study. They joined a black sorority, and things started missing from our rooms. A black girl who was ousted by the others told us that was one of the things they had to do: steal something from white girls.

Did you believe her?

She said it. I heard her. I had a white Swatch watch that I got for my graduation from my brother and sister. Everyone knew I left my room unlocked. I was brought up to be not so protective of everything. I really never had that much. I was a little too open. I know that theft happens in every college and all that.

After that, I locked my room all the time. I was angry because I don't have a lot of nice things. Now I'm a lot less trusting. College really hardened me.

The only reason I got financial aid was that my parents got divorced. It made me angry that several friends couldn't go away to school. Their parents—one a fireman, another a policeman—worked hard all their life to put food on the table. And they couldn't get financial aid. Our parents work hard and don't make that much, just enough to get by, and they get nothing.

Just because a person's a minority, they get financial aid. Some of the kids on my floor laugh about it. "You white people are so stupid. You're supposed to lie to get financial aid." It just bothers me that there's all the people, welfare. It should be even. Everybody should get it, no matter what.

I've been taught not to be prejudiced all my life, but it's hard when you see people getting something for nothing and expecting it. I am tired of people telling me that I owe them for something I haven't even done. I haven't gotten anything free in my life. I've worked hard for everything that I have.

I did my first year of teaching with the Chicago Archdiocese at an all-black school in Harvey. We did have a few Mexican children. I had parents tell me I was picking on their children because I was prejudiced. One parent wanted me to spend extra time with her son. I would have loved to do so, but I had thirty other children in the class and this child was actually learning-disabled and needed special help. She said I owe her. I don't know what she meant. I guess I owe her from years past.

I got along with most parents, and if I had a problem, they were receptive. A lot of parents worked all day and the baby-sitter was a TV set. They worked very hard, the parents, mostly single. The older sister of one of my students was shot dead at a drug dealer's house. I didn't know it, so I was yelling at the kid to sit down and get to work. I had no idea what this poor child had gone through. One day he exploded and I found out. I should be empathetic to what my students have to go through. But I've never been exposed to anything like this before.

I don't have any real close black friends any more. Last year I worked with a girl and she was something else. She was very open and had the system down pat. She said, "You pay your utility bill? Why don't you just move? You pay your Visa bill? Why don't you just change your name?" She'd use her daughter's social-security number and this and that. We spent every day together. I was just fascinated by her. I was wondering if this was characteristic of young black people.

I believe they feel they should get something for nothing. Not most, no. Most those I come in contact with are self-sufficient. What I tried to instill in my students was that God helps those who help themselves. I could use the word "God" because I was in a Catholic school. [*Laughs.*]

Do you think your friend might have been putting you on?

No, she had it down pat. And I used to be so idealistic, thinking everybody in the world could get along. I admired Martin Luther King very much. I loved him. I believe that no person should sit in back of the bus, should have to use a different washroom. A person's a person, no matter what.

But people like Louis Farrakhan and Jesse Jackson are hurting the black culture, because they're telling them it's the white people's fault. You should have pride in your heritage, but not pride in your race over another race.

I went to an Operation Push rally when I was in grammar school. We performed there as baton twirlers. I was about ten. I remember his actual words. To give yourself pride. That was good. But when he said you have to surpass the white race, it just turned sour in my stomach.

They say that most of the people in the projects are black female heads of families. What happened to all the black males that are fathers of these children? This is probably a very racist statement on my part, but I feel the black males should take responsibility for their families.

I still have that bit of adventure in me, but I don't ride the El anymore, like I used to. I'm scared on that. Blacks as well as whites are scared. I used to take that as a way to the Cubs game, to the Sox game. Not anymore.

I don't like some of my thoughts and feelings. I used to feel so different. Welfare has created a subculture, and I don't like that I feel angry about it. It's not a Christian feeling. It's not a helpful, understanding feeling. It's more of a bitter feeling. Even though I was brought up not to be prejudiced, I've almost been conditioned over the years towards being prejudiced. I hate to admit that I am.

I long for the time that I was able to play with Kenneth and Fitzgerald in the school yard and not give a second thought to it. I don't like the hatred that's happening in our society. I just feel there's gotta be some other answer out there. But I don't know what. My eyes have been opened to a lot of things I don't like that much.

CHARLES JOHNSON

He teaches American literature at the University of Washington. His novel, Middle Passage, *won the 1990 National Book Award.*

Things look grim. During the civil-rights years, there was at least a sense of movement toward brotherhood. There was the ideal that once we got rid of Jim Crow, things would be better. It's twenty years later and they haven't gotten better.

There is a new generation of young white Americans who missed the civil-rights movement. They know nothing about that major event in American history. They grew up under two Reagan administrations. They don't feel particularly guilty.

Black children know about the movement through television and what their parents tell them. It's something they didn't go through. There's a resurgence of interest in Malcolm X, but they don't take the whole man. They take only what is appealing to them and use that. They do the same thing with Martin Luther King. On the other side is the problem with young black males. There is the hyperconsciousness of black nationalism.

There are reports across the country of increased racial incidents on college campuses. They concern mainly insensitivity of whites toward people of color—blacks or Asians. I think it's based on lack of knowledge.

On my campus, the president of the student body dressed up for an event as Michael Jackson. He blackened his face and did his moon walk dance. He received a great deal of criticism—that it was a minstrel black-face show. He apologized to the student body. He simply didn't realize that this would be insulting to people of color. He thought he was just having fun. That's why there is this emphasis on courses in ethnic studies that might make people aware of what is psychologically harmful to people of color.

Twenty-five years ago, a white American was acutely aware of seg-regation because it was still in effect in the early sixties. You could see it in the South, WHITES ONLY and BLACKS ONLY signs. Also, the civil-rights movement was integrated.

These many years later, it's quite possible for a white student to have virtually no knowledge of African-American history. It's a great lack of knowledge about himself, too. A student-body president who is criticized for his Michael Jackson imitation responds, "Eddie Murphy is not crit-icized when he imitates white people." It's not quite the same thing. Because of their social and economic superiority, whites are not going to feel put down in the way a black person would. There's a different historical background. As a result, the white male often feels he's being picked on by blacks, by Asiatics, by women, by everyone.

Blacks are no longer invisible. Now people look at one another face-to-face and wonder why someone does something a little different. Why should that person be given special privileges? Every white person doesn't feel he should be perceived as affluent. Maybe he's working his way through school. There's a great deal of competitiveness in terms of race these days. It has a lot to do with the shrinking job market.

Affirmative action is probably the most sensitive racial issue today. On one hand, it's justifiable. You need a structural solution to a problem that's centuries old. On the other hand, it may be necessary but it's humiliating.

A black person, otherwise deserving, may be perceived as special, having gotten a degree of help he didn't need. It sets a bad tone for him and for those who so perceive it. But without affirmative action, the first step toward hiring blacks would never have been taken.

I suspect when I was hired at this university, it was an affirmative-action decision. I was one of the two faculty members hired. It was in 1976 and there was only one other black in the English department. One out of fifty. Now there are two. So it's not that big a change.

At the time, I certainly felt qualified for the job. There was no question in my mind. I worked very hard. I taught twice as hard as many people there. When my classes were overfilled, rather than turn the students away, I split the class in half and taught the second class for free. I never felt I was given special treatment, nor did my colleagues.

My white neighbor is a factory worker. He feels he lost his job because of affirmative action. At first, he was angry and I understood his feelings. Now he says he understands the reasoning behind it. When you make an adjustment, it will be disruptive to some people. Of course, black people have had disrupted lives for two hundred years. He's a wonderful neighbor.

Like many black people, I have been a student of white writers. I learned about them from elementary school forward. But I find that most white students have almost no knowledge of African-American history, which is again American history.

When I attended junior high school in Evanston, Illinois, we read little of the slaves and their presence in the Civil War. You had no idea they had anything other than a passive role. This was 1959. There was nothing at all about their incredible participation in their own liberation.

Native Americans were written out of history, too. In our future books on our history and literature, we should know about more than the westward movement of whites. America has been multicultural for a long time, and we need a more balanced account. Correcting the problem will not rule out the great tradition of Western literature, going back to the Greeks. I feel a lot of affection for these works. I was a philosophy major and care about Plato and Aristotle and Augustine and Aquinas. But I think it's a tremendous oversight not to realize the importance of writers of other cultures. We must be less parochial.

We need to understand the Middle East, for example. It was from the Islamic countries that we got the translations of Aristotle, who had been lost to Europe in the Middle Ages. The Middle East was in its glory when Europe was in its dark ages. If our curriculum opened up, it wouldn't mean losing anything. It would merely add to our knowledge. All a school can do is make students curious about our world and how complex and interrelated all our lives are.

Within the African-American community, there is talk of integration as an idea whose time has come and gone. Many feel integration has failed because it opened up possibilities only for those blacks ready to move—educated, prepared—and left behind the great many without skills. They feel it weakened the black community and made it more than ever dependent on the white world. Black nationalists speak of self-sufficiency, our own separate institutions. The same line is followed by the more conservative blacks.

It's important to recognize that the black community does not reflect one point of view. It's a complex world, from Baptist to Catholic to the Nation of Islam. There are as many voices as in the white world.

If we didn't have Malcolm X, some people say King's job would have been harder. The media portrayed him as the Apostle of Hate in contrast to King as the Apostle of Love. Like the good cop and the bad cop. These guys once met and realized they weren't as far apart as they thought they were. They both wanted to help black people. Jesse Jackson, for example, is much easier to deal with after you've encountered Farrakhan. It's the counterbalance of nationalism and integration.

I have problems with black nationalism. I grew up with an integrationist position. At the same time, I realize that a Malcolm or a Farrakhan strike right to the core of black pride, right to the core of pain black people felt, coming out of the slave experience, of having their culture stolen, of speaking a language not of their own land, of a lost past. It's a sore spot in every black person. Black people who have matured know they are dual people, of a dual heritage. It is African *hyphen* American. In many ways, I believe it is the best of both cultures.

I don't believe separatism can work. The people of the world are so interdependent that no group, not even white American, can separate itself and survive. It's a bad idea.

Thirty million black people have a long history here, going back to 1619. Our contributions to almost every level of society have been marked. I don't mean just doing grunt work. Consider our music, our military presence, since almost the beginning of the Republic. We are intertwined with every event in American history.

I grew up in a suburb of Chicago. It was an integrated school system. We never felt ourselves inferior to anyone. If we ran into bigots, we felt they were merely ignorant. If I encountered someone like that, the whole purpose was to step over him as you do a puddle in your path.

My father had a second-rate education. He had blue-collar jobs all his life. When he retired, he was a night watchman. My mother got through high school. We always had books in the house. My parents wanted me to read. Ours was a working-class family of which I was very proud. You work for what you get. Otherwise you don't get it. Hard work was never alien to me. I see black kids now with a different attitude. They actually believe all the propaganda of racism.

In my generation, a certain group of black people saw racism as an obstacle that you got around or through. This has been lost among the black kids today: the sense that we are a proud people, of major achievements in this country, a resilient people who have survived all this garbage. That means almost nothing can stop us. The kids today: "Oh, God, you put this stuff in front of me, I can't get through it." I think we have a stronger center than that.

There's a sense of despair, of futility. The black underclass, left behind in the ghetto, feels things are rigid and inescapable. It might require more black people helping other black people. Maybe that's why you have a Farrakhan.

Booker T. Washington had a program for black people not unlike that of the Nation of Islam. Morally strict, upright. It was the philosophy of the toothbrush: personal hygiene, keeping yourself well-dressed, clean, hard-working. Those are basically middle-class values. It is also an optimistic vision. It is a vision black people had all through the civil-rights years. Many young people have lost that optimism. Maybe it's because of the Reagan years. Maybe it's because America's not the prosperous nation of the fifties. I think we can regain that optimism.

I think more personal responsibility might be needed: black people taking care of their own families, black males taking care of their wives and children. The family unit is the key. I think it has to start on that most simple of levels.

There are things the government cannot do for black people. The government cannot make a man stay at home with his kids. The government cannot make a man love his wife and stay with her for forty years. The government cannot make a man help his son and daughter go to college. There are things the government can do to redress national problems that have been around for two hundred years. But it's in the strength of the black family that you will find the center. If black kids are performing less well than Asians and whites, we have to look at that.

Shelby Steele loves a quote of Martin Luther King: If you're behind in a foot race, how do you catch up? You run faster. If you're a black college student and your white roommate goes to bed, you stay up and burn the midnight oil. The bootstrap theory.

I see the 1990s as the most intensely race-conscious decade we've had in the century. It will get worse before it gets better, but I think it will get better. I have great faith in the American people, and I think most of them are for integration.

I think the media has played up the anger blacks feel toward whites. It was black anger that helped get things moving in the sixties. Most black people feel that there are white people who will treat you as a human and others who will respond differently. They understand that all people who are white are not bad.

I believe in my bones that the things that separate us make up one percent of who we are, that ninety-nine percent of our lives are similar. The same planet supports us. We have the same environment. You have two arms and legs and I have the same. We have given so much over the years to that one percent, complexion, it's a travesty. I think it's one of the great tragedies of our species.

■ ■ ■ ■ ■

Buddies

RICHIE DAVIS

He was raised in a working-class neighborhood, with a smattering of lower middle class, built shortly after World War II. "A bunch of little rowhouses—brick, front yard, back yard. Probably the least expensive private housing at the time." The families were young, many of the fathers having served in the war. The GI Bill of Rights had enabled them to buy the homes. South Chicago's steel mills were nearby. A Mexican community was adjacent.

He is thirty-two, the youngest of three children.

When I was in sixth grade, blacks started to move into the neighborhood. I was the only kid left at home. My brother and sister were grown up and had left. Many of our neighbors were fleeing. My parents, who had a liberal mindset, out of principle and probably for my sake, made a conscious decision to stay. They didn't want to feel like they were running.

I began hearing "nigger this" and "nigger that" from all the kids in the neighborhood. It was just around the time that Martin Luther King died. I remember a kid telling me that it's good we get a day off from school "because they killed the nigger." I didn't know from Adam. I'd had no relationship with blacks, except I was always told by my parents to never, never say that word.

For the blacks, if you lived in the ghetto and got your resources together to make it out, this was the neighborhood to go to. Like in *Raisin in the Sun*. The real-estate companies took advantage. They'd scare all the homeowners, who already had closet or open racist feelings, and exploited their fears: "Your property will be worth nothing, so sell now." In a matter of two, three years, the neighborhood went from one-hundred-percent white to ninety percent black. I became the only white kid on the block. I lived in that neighborhood until I graduated from high school.

Who I am today, for better or worse, I think is a result of this. I'm wise beyond my years and in some ways I'm immature, because my whole adolescence was profoundly affected.

When the neighborhood was white, I used to catch flak for being Jewish. My brother, who is eleven years older than me, caught even more. We used to get harassed and beaten up regularly. When the blacks started to move in, I had immediate allies. The guys who didn't like me for being Jewish definitely didn't like the blacks for being black. So I found instant black friends.

It was interesting to see these kids from racist backgrounds become fearful. I've learned that people get scared of someone who is different from themselves. You would see their parents encountering blacks for the first time, as I did. It was still new to me just to look at someone's hair, their eyes, their lips—the fascination with something different. I'm sure they did it with us. I think the greatest fear was of the white parents who had daughters.

The amazing thing is that children hadn't learned yet to hate. In terms of sports and music and just friendships that were developed, it was really a beautiful thing to see what could be. Some of the white kids who were the last to go became best of buddies with black kids. Some were too far gone to change.

I'm ten, eleven, twelve years old and started assimilating into the black culture. In my mind, I was black.

Oh, I talked black. I had a whole affectation. I understood all the jargon. I wore the right gym shoes, laced the right way, with the right socks and the right pants. I played basketball and I was good. I was a musician, sort of. That helped.

I couldn't go to another black neighborhood and feel comfortable, because there I would be just another lone white face. But in this neighborhood, everyone knew me. I was sort of a mascot. What was difficult was that I wasn't allowed to be a normal obnoxious juvenile that I probably would have been, should have been. As long as I was quiet and cool, I had protection, because it allowed the bigger black guys to be my

Robin Hood or Don Quixote. There were plenty of black kids who resented me, but I had enough who were willing to go to bat for me. I think they got a kick out of a little white kid who thought that their lifestyle was hip.

Just as the neighborhood was turning, my mother enrolled me in a magnet school. It was interracial-oriented. When I graduated, the magnet school was all-black. So I might as well just have stayed in the neighborhood school. It probably would have been a lot more interesting. But this was a lot safer, I suppose.

I went to a high school, downtown, that took kids from every part of the city, regardless of academic achievement or financial or race. A school without walls—the city was your classroom. It was a real melting pot. Because I came into that school being this white-black kid, I immediately gravitated toward black friends. That's not to say I didn't have white friends. As I got older, I started to mature out of this whole little world I built for myself. I was afraid to take these white kids home with me, because it might jeopardize my position in the neighborhood. It was silly.

I probably still carry a lot of extra baggage. When I lived in the old neighborhood, it took me an hour on the train to get to the high school downtown. I saw nothing but black faces. I don't know how that affected me. After a while, the people on the trains and buses knew me. I remember coming home from school on a cold, dark winter night. I got ambushed by a group of black kids, who when they discovered it was me said, "Oh, it's just him." They laughed and that was the end of it. I'd be sent on my way. It happened all the time. In the ten years I lived there, I never had a finger laid on me by blacks.

I had fears all the time. I had to force myself to walk to the basketball court, because I was always afraid there'd be some new kid who didn't know who I was, and would want to single me out. I couldn't be a coward, because I wouldn't be worth defending by the other black kids. So I always had to stand up and someone always intervened. I was challenged all the time.

Today when I go into a black neighborhood, I watch my back. I put on some of my survival tools from the old neighborhood. I know not to show too much fear or not to be too patronizing. Not to be too obviously hip. Just "How are you?" and look people in the eye. In some cases, drugs drive people so crazy, the money they need, there's nothing you can do.

I've been in Robert Taylor many times. When the blacks were moving into my neighborhood, the real-estate company would buy them flowers to close the deal. I got hired to deliver the flowers because none of the white florists would dream of going into the ghetto. So I got the job of delivering flowers to all the housing projects on the South Side. I never got bothered. It always seemed like I had some guardian angel.

People were good to me. It's not like I'm coming to evict somebody or I'm a bill collector. I'm just a kid, so how much of a threat can I be? One image is still in my mind. It was in Robert Taylor. There's no directory. You ask where someone lives. Everyone seems to know where a certain family lives. I took the elevator to the fifteenth floor. I gave them the flowers and I'm waiting to take the elevator down. You know how notoriously bad the elevators are in the CHA. This elevator ain't coming. While I'm standing up there, the sun is setting on this warm summer day and children are playing and yelling. Little girls are jumping rope and a couple of little girls come up to me and stare, fascinated. A little one holds my hand, touches my hair, wants to see what it feels like. After a while they told me the elevator might not come: "Take the stairs." I flew down those fifteen flights of stairs so fast, I think I was invisible.

Since my high school was downtown, there was no real territoriality. It was the DMZ, no-man's-land. No one could stake a claim to it. So the relationships that developed between people from different neighborhoods were interracial. They seemed to fall into a class thing. Black kids from Hyde Park and from the Highlands, an upper-class black neighborhood, immediately gravitated to the white kids from Lincoln Park and the Gold Coast. The white kids from the blue-collar areas became great friends with the black kids from Cabrini-Green and the West Side.

The white kid who was on welfare and lived with his alcoholic uncle, who used to beat him up, could talk to the black kid, who was probably in the same situation. They could relate to each other. All the bullshit about nigger and honky that had been ingrained in them, they could see as bullshit. That really showed me what could be.

I was screwed up because I was a reverse racist. Blacks could do no harm. One summer, when I was thirteen, I worked as a dishwasher in a camp for Jewish kids. I was so obnoxious and so black and so extroverted, though I'm by nature an introvert and cool—it was something I had to get out of my system. I thought I was tough and hip.

I'm mature enough now to see the whole story. There are black people who are good and caring people and there are black people who are assholes. There are white people who are good and caring and there are white people who are assholes. Unfortunately, the problem lies in the way these two cultures were brought together. Slavery or what. People aren't given an opportunity to drop all that bullshit and treat each other as people. There's bullshit in any culture, and I'm able to blow it up instantly.

I used to be afraid to hate a black person. Now I have no problem hating a black person. There's a lot of bullshit that blacks will throw at you. If I get together with black people who have no idea of my background, I sound like your typical Joe White-Guy. I've dropped my affectations in speech. There are certain games they'll play with you, thinking you're on the outside, and I'll know exactly what's going on.

My best friend from high school, Joe Boone, is now in the upper echelon of the Louis Farrakhan operation. He comes to see me every now and then. We're not as close as we used to be, but we're still friendly. We still know what we have in the past. But I have a hard time understanding what he's into.

I play guitar with a rhythm-and-blues band, R&B, which plays mostly the black dance music that we liked when we were in high school. A seven-piece band, five blacks and two whites. We play at a lot of private parties, colleges, fraternities. It's the kind of music the baby-boomers liked when they were in school: James Brown, Wilson Pickett, Otis Redding. These are the yuppies. They love it.

When I was twenty-two, twenty-three, I was the only white guy in the band. We'd play all over the city. We were young and single and on the prowl, looking for girls. The pretty white girls were fascinated with the black guys in the band and got together with them. I couldn't make any progress with them. I found the black girls wanted to date me, not because I was handsome or sexy or a great musician. It became a little status symbol for them, as it was for the white girls going out with black guys. And because of my background, they could talk easily to me. Here was a white guy they could relate to.

The stereotype is that white guys are incensed that their women are screwing these black guys. That's true. But it's just as true on the other end. When I would be with a pretty black girl, black guys had a very hard time with that. Even the guys in my band. It works both ways. Believe me, most bullshit is cross-cultural. I'm here to testify to that.

My wife is Puerto Rican. It's good for me, because Puerto Ricans are a little mixed up. The whole Hispanic thing. She's halfway between white and black. She was born in Puerto Rico, raised here, got a scholarship to Iowa, where the black girls wanted her to be black and the white girls wanted her to be white. She's dark-complected with straight hair, some black features, some white features. She relates to people as people, and that's probably why we get along so good. She's like me, I suppose.

JOSEPH BOONE

He is a housepainter and decorator. In his spare time, he works with a
video-camera crew. He is thirty-three. He has five children—the oldest,
fourteen, the youngest, one.

"I was raised Baptist. My mom is an evangelist right now. She
accepted Christ as her personal savior and Lord of her life. I was about
twelve when she so decided. We children accepted it, too. Christ to me is a
savior of mankind."

But I follow the teachings of Farad Muhammed and Minister Louis
Farrakhan. I believe that, hey, Christians are my brothers and Jews are my
brothers, and that's just the truth."

I met Richie Davis in Metro High School. People from all over the city. I
enjoyed that. It really opened my mind as a black child. I was alone when I
first came there. Then I met Richie. We spent a lot of time together. We
graduated together.

I'm a very peaceful man, but at the same time, I fight with those who
fight with me. I have engaged in a few, but not to the seriousness of
harming, breaking their arm or, you know. If I feel something coming
negative, I either deal with it or just leave it alone and don't respond. See
what I'm saying? If they being offensive, usually I give people warning. I
taught myself well how not to be a troublemaker.

What attracted me to the Muslims was the brotherhood, clean men
striving to be upright, not fags, not pimps, not chumps, not weaklings. I
ain't saying they perfect. One thing I like about the Brother Minister, since
I've been sitting under him: He has been honest and straight up.

When I had just got through with Metro High School, I felt I needed
some more education. They had an adult-education program at the University of Islam. That's when I was a different type of person. I was more a
hippie or mod type. I used to like tuxedo tail jackets with a Paul Revere hat.
Army jacket I embroidered a flower on it with a peace sign in the middle.
That type of thing.

I have always looked for a fatherly figure and for a community of
people I could belong to. The more I listened to him, a little voice in my
mind said, This is the one. So I chose to join this community.

My mother had ten children by four different fathers, okay. I met my
father when I was twenty-eight. At the time I was working in the laundry
room at the Department of Corrections. My mom called me. "I want you to

come to my house when you're through working." When I got there, she said, "I hope you don't get mad at me, but your father is still alive." I wasn't angry. I was surprised. The man I was named after was one of the other men, whom I didn't really like. Me and my mom drove down to Arkansas and met my father. It was great. He's an older fellow, in his seventies. We look very similar. He's bald up here just like me.

Mom kept our family together all these years. The last man, whose name she carries, Mr. Lashley, fathered the last three children. He changed our whole life because he moved us to the South Side. We were like the third black family in that community. I was about three years old.

Lester Lashley—I will always love that man until the day I'm gone. He's passed away. This man was a very industrious brother. He was a carpenter, a plumber, could fix anything.

Mr. Lashley moved us from a bad scene to a better scene and he provided for us. On all the holidays, he had something special for us. He even cooked some himself. And he whipped us. So I appreciated his example. He was a true fatherly figure, but I didn't have a *spiritual* fatherly figure. That's where the minister comes in. And Muhammed.

My oldest son, fourteen going on fifteen, believes in a lot of things I believe in. My wife, she doesn't. She doesn't profess to be a Muslim, but believe me, she's got a lot of Muslim ways in her. We believe everybody's a Muslim by nature.

When I was a young hippie type, a lot of lusting going on, that's for sure. Messing up a lot of girls. Not in the sense of getting them pregnant and going away and leaving babies behind, but just not being serious and disciplined. A lot of sex with young girls, a free spirit. Loving to hitchhike. Me and Richie went hitchhiking together. At the end of our graduation, we decided to go on a month's hitchhike across the country. We even jumped on a couple of trains.

With what I know, I couldn't just take the chance of going out and actually hitchhiking today. It's too risky. I figure I would end up someplace where nobody would ever see me again.

See, back then, I wasn't aware of all the murders that were being committed because of people's skin color, you know what I mean? When I think on it, it's just as much then as it is now, but it's that I wasn't aware of it. I just came into the knowledge of what time it is.

There was a moment when things were getting better. Dr. King was a very good man, he gave his life for mankind. It *seemed* better, but then again not. I was in that march as a young boy when King marched over to Marquette Park. I was like five feet behind him, me and my mother. We was just marching straight, and when we turned that corner, 71st and California, all hell broke loose. The police couldn't even handle it, 'cause they started throwing bottles and bricks. I definitely remember a rock hitting King in the head. This is as clear as day. I remember holding my mama's hand. We were marching and singing and, man, all hell broke out. Mama and me talked about it once or twice, but not for a long time.

Personally, I think blacks are not racist. I believe black people, or if you want to call them Afro-American, try hard. They're mild and humble people. The black racism I see coming from blacks is against their own self. We do more harm to ourself, because we think in the wrong way. Thinking to beat our own selves down. But as far as just straight black racism against whites, I must admit there is some people that think like that. I don't harbor such thoughts.

The same type of love that King had for all mankind, that's the same type of love that blacks need for themselves. In the same amount. See what I'm saying? And that's the truth.

Integration? Since I come into knowledge and truth and the teachings of Muhammed, it's not a good thing. It doesn't help to keep our family and history and culture together. As simple as that. I'm talking about an Afro-American man. Since the last four-hundred-some years, we have been done a great job. We've been vamped on, as being other than a righteous person. We've been made into something else. Lose your history, lose everything.

You attended Metro High, which was integrated and where you met Richie.

But Richie, see, he wasn't much reflecting his own culture. Richie was a different type. He's somewhat black. Integrated schools can be good from a cultural point of view. It was to me. But I've been a follower of the Minister since '82, going on seven years.

You've heard allegations about his anti-Semitic comments?

I've heard. But I know the man. I've had a long time to sit under him and watch him very closely. He's not a pimp. He's a married man, has problems just like other married men. He has nine children. He's a hardworking man, just like the next man. What was the question?

Jews.

Just like the Minister says, he's a very peaceful man. I'm going to try to give you a little history, how the whole thing started with the Jews. Clear as

I can. I remember the Minister telling us he would never said anything, or even entertain negative thoughts toward Jews. The Minister's not talking about all Jews, I want you to understand that. He's talking about certain people who give him problems. All Jews don't give him problems. Certain types.

They made a statement about him calling Hitler some type of man. Ever since then he began to do research on Jews. He found out a whole lot of negative things. They've got to be held accountable. Just like if you do wrong, you're going to be held accountable for the wrong you do.

Oh, history is something, man. He found out that there's documents in terms of slave trade. Certain Jews actually owned slave ships. These documents in the Congress Library. As far as being very manipulative in terms of natural resources, we're talking about food, hair products, anything you want to know, I'm sure you know that Jews got a lot of control of natural resources and products, okay. In terms of television and the media, I'm sure you know also. Jews have more control than other nationalities.

When the Minister has done lectures, they'll only put certain things into the media, instead of putting the whole truth. Just take excerpts and blow them up. Minister Farrakhan calls Hitler a great man, right. Not in the sense of his being a *good* man. He even says on tape, a wicked, evil great man. We do a lot of studying, brothers and sisters in our community. Muslims. Things are revealed.

We start our own products. Remember some time ago that we had a big loan from Khadaffi, something like five million dollars. He gave a loan to his brothers in the faith. So we can start our own businesses, instead of going out on the street and killing. We'd rather do it economically. Nonphysical. That's how you can get control of your life.

You can say ninety-five to ninety-nine percent of the things the Minister says is based on facts and truth. Without a doubt. I'm not saying the Minister is perfect. I've seen him apologize at least two or three times for things he was guilty of. He's able to admit that he was wrong when he was wrong. But ninety-nine percent of the time the man's right.

Are things getting better or worse?

It's hard to tell, man. Everybody's different. You get some brothers who are very aggressive and some who are very passive. I consider myself one of the passive ones. Easygoing. I would say I'm a normal person in my community.

■ ■ ■ ■ ■

Passing the Corner

KEVIN ROBINSON

Joseph Robinson's son.
The receptionist at the radio station where I work announces the
arrival of "a darling young man who is so charming." He is a bantam-
weight facsimile of Spike Lee. He is nineteen.

He has a summer job in a factory as a pipewelder. "My father got me
in. He's a union president; he's made it."

He attends a city college and majors in criminal law. "I would like to
be a police officer. I like the military-type role that he has. When I went to
Mt. Carmel High, all boys, it was like a military-type thing. Mostly white,
no problems at all. I like the authoritative role, the respect that is given
police officers. I like the money, too." [Laughs.]

I used to belong to a gang when I was younger, the El Rukns.* It was wild to
me, the things I saw. We used to pray a lot. Every Friday and Sunday, we'd
have a service. We'd all face east, hold out our hands, and pray. We were
Muslims and would call God Allah. They'd give praises and thanks for
being here. It was nice, they were good prayers. Then it was back to
fighting. [*Laughs.*]

I saw mostly violence. Getting killed, beat up all the time, for stupid
reasons. It really didn't make sense. The El Rukns had buildings all around
the neighborhood. I grew up around this stuff. That's how I got involved. I
joined because all my friends were in it. Why not?

There was one special guy, Gabriel. He's twenty-two now. He was
known as my big brother. I was with him all the time. He was a leader-type
person. He used to fight all the time, carry guns and stuff. He would take
part in the shootings. He was called Prince Akim, a prince in the El Rukn
nation. You know what I'm saying?

Every time I went out with him, they get into a fight, he wouldn't let

---

* Chicago's most notorious and feared black gang. Some of its leaders, including its
celebrated chieftain, Jeff Fort, are serving time. "El Rukns is still active, but not like it used to be.
It's, like, low-profile active."

me fight. I'd say, "Why can't I help you?" He'd say, "You stand back, I don't want you involved in this, 'cause you're not the type of person. I want you to stay in school."

Every time I see him: "Did you go to school today? Doin' good grades? You gettin A's for me? If you don't graduate from high school, you can't hang with me. 'Cause the way this society's changin', you're gonna need an education, that piece of paper." So I stayed in school.

He always told us we were all together in this, the bad ones, the good ones. If I ever had any problems, somebody beat me up, I would tell him. [Snaps fingers.] He would be there [snaps fingers], beat them up for me, whatever.

He treated me like I was a nice person. His mother liked me, his family liked me. If he went out with some girls, he'd call me before he'd call one of the thuggy guys. If he had a problem, he'd ask me, "How do I do this?" I would show him, and he would teach me how to do this, do that.

He graduated from high school two years before I did. It wasn't that he was dumb; he was on the honor roll. In a way, he was given good grades because the teachers knew he was in a gang. So they were kind of scared. You know what I'm saying? Don't get me wrong, he was smart.

All of us have been arrested before. I was picked up for drinking beer under age. I was put in the paddy wagon and went to the lockup for one hour. Gabriel was never arrested, except for minor stuff. He might have stayed in jail for one night, gang fighting. But he was a leader figure; no one tricks on a leader. Man, if I trick on him, I'll get beat up. If someone commits a crime, someone will say, "He didn't do it, I did it." They'll step up, so he wouldn't get in trouble.

When I got involved, I was about twelve. Gabriel was fifteen. I was with them through four years. I was just there, one of the people who followed. They'd say, "Just watch what we do." When I get older, I'm supposed to do it. I watched them fight, sell drugs, shoot people, various things. I really didn't get involved with that. My personality is not that way. But I watched a lot. I was an apprentice.

I drifted out about the end of my junior year in high school. I didn't stop like that. [Snaps fingers.] I just grew out of it. I'm still friends with everybody.

They had a lot of everything—money, guns, cocaine. Whatever you wanted, they could get it for you easily. If you wanted a car, hey, they'd go steal a car. No problem. Or you can just hang out with your friends, do nothing, and have fun. But when you get to your junior year of high school, there's stuff you want to experience for yourself. I wanted to graduate, get a bank account, my own apartment, cars.

I would tell them, "Why do we have to fight all the time? Why do we have to steal?" They'd say, "We can't get a job." I'd say, "Did you try?" They'd say, "It's easy for you. You got your mom and dad, they're workin' hard." My mother has a big staff job in the hospital. She can get me jobs. Most of their parents are either strung out or just don't care. It was like, "Get out of my house." Or they beat them. I guess that's why they went that way.

When they first met me, they used to come to my house, sit in the living room, and stuff was missing. Money, sometimes video games. They would spend the night, you go to bed. The next day, hey, they're gone; stuff would be missing. My mother would say, "Don't bring them in the house anymore," so I had to stop.

I did fine in grammar school. I was on the honor roll, a nerd. I started changing at fifth, sixth grade, when I was about eleven. I started going out to parties, staying out late, throwing rocks. I felt great about it. It's like, "Wow, I'm accepted as one of the guys. I'm not a nerd anymore. They don't tease me anymore." My mother'd go, "What's wrong with you? Why are you staying out all the time?" That's when you'd get into arguments with your parents, talking back to them, different things. But I felt okay about it.

I was still scared, because my size affected every thing I did. Everybody was bigger than me. Girls were bigger than me. Everybody says, "Do this." I'm so small, I had to do it. If I tried to fight, they'd smack me around.

I was raised with my mother and my sister, my auntie and my cousins, and they're all girls. So I had feminine ways. I did certain things that only girls would do. My mother taught me how to cook, how to comb my nieces' hair, paint their nails, do girly stuff. She would polish my nails and tell me, "That's a nice quality in a man." When you get around guys with your fingernails polished, they'd say, "Man, you wanna be a sissy? Take it off."

I always had to go the extra distance because of my size. That's why I stayed with the girls. I could be a man around them. I always had to prove myself.

I got to reading lots of books, looking through magazines, watching the news, seeing what role the police play. People look up to police officers as maybe a savior figure.

I'm safe around a police officer. I figured if I became someone to look up to, it would kind of knock down my size. If I keep going the way I am, everybody's gonna keep pickin' with me.

Suppose you were a police officer and had to arrest some El Rukns?

I would do it. For the plain and simple fact I know what kind of people they are. They're violent. They're okay, but they want to live in the world the way *they* want the world to be.

I have a bunch of white friends. My girlfriend's white. She's three years older than me. She works in a restaurant in a shopping center. I met her at a party. I go to parties, sometimes all-white, sometimes all-black, sometimes mixed. I like white people. A person is a person. If there's a white person, he's prejudiced, that doesn't even bother me. If he's, like, "Stay away from me, nigger," I'll just look at him like it's a shame and go on about my business. I wouldn't argue with him. You let stuff like that get you, it'll eat you inside.

I've gotten into maybe three fights in my whole life. I was out at Midway Airport with Gabriel. He used to work there as a janitor. On our way home, some white guys tried to hit us with their car. He told me this happened before but I didn't believe him. This time these guys jumped out of the car, swinging a bat. It was like four of 'em, okay? One of them swung on me; I fell. I look up, Gabriel snatched the bat from the guy and beat all four of 'em up, just like that. [*Snaps fingers.*] They lay there; we left. He knows karate real good. Never lost a fight.

Me and my girlfriend, people look at us all the time. But I'm the type of person, I don't care what people think about me.

They just stare, like we're animals or something. You can feel it, sense it. They don't say anything, they just look. Like, "What are you doing with her?" The same as in the white male.

It's different in her neighborhood. It's: "We don't want any black people around here, they're thuggish, ready to fight, steal." Me, I feel safe there, 'cause of my attitude. It doesn't bother me. Never met her father, never met her mother. She tells me they don't like black people. Her father says, "If you date black guys, you're gonna be banned from the family." I'd love to meet her father. I'd love to meet her mother.

I'm not afraid to go anywhere. I'm a nice person. I speak to every-body everywhere I go: "How're you doing?" White, black, Hispanic, poor, rich—I'm nice to everybody.

Well, in certain neighborhoods I'm afraid. I'm terrified of the pro-jects. I wouldn't walk there. I'm skeptical even about going there in a car. People in the projects can't relate to me.

These gangbangers, I know them all because I've been around: where they're from, what colors they wear, which way to wear what. The Disci-ples, their colors are black, blue, and white. Brothers, their colors are black and green. If you go in a certain neighborhood where most of them have blue hats, you wear a red hat, better take it off. Brothers wear their hats to the left. If you're a Disciple, you wear it to the right. They never wear them straight. I know a few white gangs, they'll wear their hats the same way, to the left and to the right. The Latino gangs are mostly into tattoos.

I'm not gonna be a hard police. If I catch somebody robbing a bank, I'll try my best not to use a gun at all, 'cause I'd hate to kill someone. But if they pull out guns, I'm gonna shoot. If someone ran a red light that just turned from yellow, I'd say, "Watch out. Next time somebody might zip out in a real fast car and hit you." I'd be just a nice police officer.

It's the respect. Say you're walking in a bad neighborhood; you're scared, man. You see a police officer, you feel relieved. [*Sighs.*] I would try to use my position to change things. If I saw some kid doing bad, I'd say, hey, don't do that. Why don't you go to the park, play some baseball? I'd go buy a ball and a bat and give it to 'em.

I do that now. This summer I'm organizing a kids' basketball team and I'm paying for the little uniforms and everything. I don't care if they win or lose. I can change a bad kid.

When I was with the gang, we were shooting baskets one time, all having fun, tripping out. A lot of little kids were around. We go home. These guys came around and beat up our little sisters and brothers. They knew that'd make us come around. We say, "Next time we see 'em, we're gonna fight 'em."

We were in the park one day, drinking beer, playing music, talking. It was real dark. They tried to sneak up on us. It was two vanloads of them. They all jumped out. All had bats, a couple had guns. We told them plain as day, "We don't want to fight. Why don't you all go your way, we'll go our way. You can tell everybody you won." They say, "No, man, we gotta fight. We want to show we bad." We told them three times. Our motto is: Strike three, you're out. Everybody pulls out their guns. We got to shooting people, running on, falling down. Three people got shot, of the other guys. One in the leg, one in the arm, one in the rib section. They all lived, didn't no one die. The police came. Everybody scattered. They didn't catch any of us. They did catch the guys that were on the ground.

I think things are getting worse. 'Cause it's harder to live nowadays at a young age. I've made it to be nineteen now, okay? I'm older, mature. I go to work, come home, go shopping, go to sleep. I go maybe to a restaurant or a club. When you're younger, it's totally different. Young guys want to be like older guys, gangbangers.

I have a friend, he's been through high school with me. He's real smart, goes to Loyola on an academic scholarship. He has a little brother, Devon, eleven years old. He's real small, just this high, a peanut. Smokes cigarettes all the time. He's smart as day, gets good grades, A's and B's in school. No problem. Just like that. [*Snaps fingers.*] I say, "What do you want to be when you grow up?" Little Devon says, "I want to be a gangbanger. I want to be a drug dealer. I can make some money. Hey, all the girls like the drug dealers."

I'm afraid to even have kids, 'cause what they're gonna go through. Who wants to bring up a kid in something like that? I want my kids to grow up in an environment that's different. If you grow up in an environment where there's people shooting people, you're gonna go that way. I used to suggest, "Hey, arrest all the bad people," but you can't do that. I'm completely puzzled. I don't know what to suggest now.

A lot of white people think, hey, you're black, you're a criminal. Most black people see a white person, hey, all white people are rich. I know that's not true. How can you make a suggestion like that if you don't know the person, white or black? That's what it is, the stereotype of each other. Eliminate the stereotype and you don't have that problem.

It's the *person*. You gotta get to know a person. I'd love to have a family. I want a little girl and a little boy. If my family was mixed, a white wife, I'd have no problem with it.

I'd like to live in a world where there wasn't even any money. Money is the root of all evil. Yeah. The man who has the most is the one that's in control. If everybody's the same, you couldn't say he has more money than me, so he's a better person than me. Just because he has a BMW and you drive a Hyundai, you couldn't say he's better. If money is eliminated, communication would be the root of happiness. Education is the key. You know what I'm saying?

CHRIS DANIELS

I first met him five years ago: "He has the appearance of a scruffy teen-age Clint Eastwood. Though he's a city boy, there's a palpable country touch here—something Appalachian. Not accidentally, his mother is a Tennessee emigré.

"He has had encounters with Chicago police. 'They seen me in the wrong place at the wrong time. Cops always wanted to whup on me. My mother was always at the police station. When she'd leave, they'd slap me up. They just disrespected me, they'd talk crazy to me. Like, "I hope we catch you climbin' out a window, bam, bam." ' "*

---

* *The Great Divide* (1988).

Ever since he attended an alternative school in Uptown, he has undergone a change in outlook.

I wanted to be a police officer so I could *help* people. But now it's getting too violent. I don't want to be too close, the way kids are shootin' at each other and gangs going crazy nowadays. So I'm taking training right now to become a paramedic. I'm taking classes to become an emergency medical technician, just driving a medi-car. Then I'll start riding in an ambulance. It's a private company.

In the medi-car, I just pick people up, take 'em from like nursing homes. We go from the suburbs where it's all white and upper-class to the South Side where it's black and some of the worst neighborhoods around. There's an anger out there. Me, personally, they don't bother 'cause I'm there helping somebody and they know it. But another white person drives through, they might yell something at them: "Hey, snowball, what are you doin' in my neighborhood?"

Paramedics that work for the Chicago Fire Department see a lot more violent things. Just in my neighborhood alone, a guy got beat to death by a bunch of gangbangers. Around the corner from my house. He was just coming home from his friend's house. They started fighting with some other people. He came walking out of the gangway and they thought he was with them. So they pulled out a bat. They just kept hitting him and he died.

It's so easy. A lot of kids are poor. And drugs. You could get a job at McDonald's and you're only going to make $3.75, $4.00 an hour. You go selling drugs, you're going to make $300, $400 a day. That's money, no taxes out of it, so, hey, it's worth it. And jails—they're overcrowded. I know a lot of 'em, watched them grow up. When they go to jail, it's like some kind of rank they get, honor, and the longer they stay, the tougher they are. They come out on the streets big and bad. So jails ain't scarin' 'em.

A kid's got a friend, he was a good kid but he got hooked into it. Somebody comes up and says, "Check this out" and hands him some for free. No problem. He does it up, sells it to somebody, sees how easy it is. Who buys it? Regular people, politicians, doctors, lawyers. I see a lot of 'em in my neighborhood.

People drive by in their cars real slow, and if they're staring at you, they'll sniff or rub their nose or something. Upper-class people.

You've got Puerto Rican gangs, you've got black gangs and some white gangs, and they don't like each other. You've got them fighting for territory. Three blocks down here, there's a Mexican gang. A black gang came down and beat a guy to death. Now every black guy that would come down the street would get jumped on. *Any* black guy, it didn't matter. He'd get jumped. The Hispanic kids, they just don't like blacks. I don't really hear them talking much about white people. My whole family's white and they don't bother us or nothin'. All the gangbangers know who we are.

There's three homosexual bars down the street, but they're white and don't really get bothered. But they see all black people as part of the other gang. I guess it's the same with blacks.

I seen a change, yeah. Before, everybody sort of got along, but the gangs started in with guns, and they got little kids killing little kids.

White people, as soon as they see a black guy, they're scared, 'cause he's gonna rob me, rape me, steal my purse. I don't see it myself. I look at 'em like people. I ain't gonna bother you, you don't bother me.

You can't be a racist in Uptown; it's too mixed. They had some racists in Uptown, the Rebels, but they didn't last very long.

It's bad all over the city. A black guy I graduated with from Prologue* just got shot to death right downstairs on the corner. I used to hang with the guy that seen it, standin' right there next to him.

Where I live now, they don't like blacks and they don't hide the fact. They don't go out of their way to disrespect anybody, but it's just their opinion. They don't want to live in the same building with them, but they live in the same world with them.

I don't feel that way. When I see three black guys comin' down the street, I don't feel no different from three white guys comin' down the street. Some white people that I know I wouldn't trust. I wouldn't turn my back on 'em. They're worse than a lot of black people I know, a lot worse.

I'm not really a scared type of person. If somebody is going to do something to me, I'm ready for it. I can fight as good as the next man. I might get beat up, but you're gonna have to do that, because I'm not gonna back down. People know that, so they don't bother me.

I was goin' with this hillbilly girl at a party. I took my black friend with me and they was gonna cut him up. I said, "Hey, you're gonna bother him, you're gonna have to bother me." They respected me so they left him alone. They went and apologized to him. Said, "Hey, man, I'm sorry."

If you know somebody, you know them things ain't true. You ain't scared of him because you got an idea of what he's about. It's that guy who's standin' over on the corner looking at you that you don't know at all, that you don't know what's going through his head, so you don't know what's goin' to happen.

---

* The alternative school in Uptown.

I'm not prowhite or antiblack, but I think the city of Chicago is run for the blacks right now. I tried to get a city job and it's practically impossible unless I know somebody. Most of the city workers are black. I know they went through slavery and all that, but I don't think we should have to pay.

Another thing. If a black person gets on TV and talks about white people and how they're scared and makes fun of them, he's a comedian. If a white person gets on TV and does the same thing about black people, he's a racist. I don't think that's right. A lot of people feel the same way I do.

I can live in the same area with black people, I don't care. I don't have no problem. But when they start pushing and hurting . . . Because there are a lot of poor white people. Not all of us are sitting up there in condominiums, driving Porsches. Some of us are out there tryin' to work hard, and when you can't get a job—I've put in applications and they don't call me or nothin'. I just don't think it's fair.

A majority of police officers are black.

A majority?

I see more black officers than white.*

Is it because a black police officer makes a deeper impression on you than a white police officer?

That could be. It's an interesting thought.

When you were a kid, four, five years ago, and you had all those run-ins with cops, what color were they?

All the cops I seen were white. Every once in a great while you'd see a black cop drive by and give out parking tickets. Now everywhere you see black police officers. Maybe it looks that way to me 'cause I notice them more. I do see white policemen, but they're usually sergeants or lieutenants wearing the white shirts. Most of the detectives I see are white.

I know only two black detectives. In my neighborhood, when they come out, all the little gangbangers get off the street, go home. They're scared. But when the white detectives come out, they'll just stay there and just walk around.

You know, I don't think the racial tension is getting worse, I think people are gettin' fed up with the way things are divided. Yeah, the poor black is gettin' it in the neck, but what about the poor white?

---

* The Chicago Police Department is 20 percent black.

It's kind of hard when you're a poor white person to see a rich black guy driving by. Or a rich anybody. But more for a rich black guy, 'cause he's a different color. Same with a black person when they see a rich white person driving by. You know they gotta feel bad.

If they're rich, I put them all together. I mean snotty rich. Not just somebody who's worked hard for his money, but somebody who just throws it in your face that they got more than you and you ain't never gonna even come close to what they got.

ANDREA COLLINS

She lives in her grandfather's three-story house "in an old neighborhood," with her mother, her two aunts, her uncle, Chad, and her three cousins. Her grandfather recently retired after twenty-two years at International Harvester. Her mother works in a bank.

She is in her third year at a large public high school in Chicago, "with all nationalities: whites, Hispanics, Orientals, blacks." She is sixteen.

There are racial problems at school. It's not the students, just a few teachers. I'm in the school chorus, and my drafting teacher said he wanted to be a music teacher because he thought it would be funny if he got a whole lot of black students singing *I'm Dreaming of a White Christmas.* I just felt like crying. I had no respect for him after that. Grown man, college degree, teaching at a high school with some of the best students in the city. I'm proud of being black, but I have friends of every color. I felt bad because he was saying that black people is only to be laughed at.

We have some headbangers and skinheads in school. Some are satanic worshippers and punk-rockers with spiked-up hair. They're prejudiced toward everybody who is not with them. They get into fights among each other. They're a minority, but they cause a lot of trouble.

This school is too technical. We have all this shop and drafting. I'm gonna transfer to another school, because I need more English classes, and business. I want to be a lawyer. The neighborhood is sort of balanced off. We have the basic drug dealers, gangbangers, and everything. But most of us who hang at the club don't even do that.* It's a lot of students.

You have young students trying, doing something recreational, how

---

* The Chicago Boys (and Girls) Club, an old social center for the young people on the West Side.

to express themselves, Project Free, computer classes. I'm president of the Keystone group at the club. They pick me because I know how to deal with people. We go to the old folks' home, nursing. Most of them can't get around because they have arthritis and everything. We just let them know that somebody still care. Most of them, their family put them there 'cause they didn't want to take responsibility for them. So we just go, talk to them, help clean them up, make their spirits feel good.

So our neighborhood got a good part and a bad part. A lot of kids gangbang, sell drugs, and get high. If you look at most of the houses and their families, you will see why. Half of them, their parents not at home, they don't care, they run the streets at all times of the night, don't go to school, either flunked out, just go to school to sell their drugs. We got young prostitutes on the street. We have it all.

I know two young people that just got in jail on a murder charge. They graduated with me from grammar school. Seventeen-year-old and a fifteen-year-old. It was a drug deal going down. They didn't do the actual shooting, but they was there. Throwing their life away. It's ridiculous.

My mother don't let me walk out the house by night. If I need something from the store, an adult has to go. She see stuff happening, it's real bad there. I know most of the people 'cause I lived there all my life, so they won't try to bother me. I wouldn't advise you walk down the street by yourself. Coming out of the store, my mother got her chain snatched off her neck. A four-hundred-dollar chain. I'm getting on the bus, my chain got snatched right off my neck. Back down by them projects.

I had experience with people coming to me, trying to give me drugs. I'm not even gonna say I never used it 'cause I did. I did it a couple of times, smoked cigarettes and got drunk just because they was doing it. Half the time you be so stoned, they don't know whether they're coming or going. They are at the mercy of everybody on the streets. Who to say that they haven't done things that is wrong, but they were so high that they do it anyway? Young kids. I saw how it was affecting my grades at school and I just walked away from it.

I just started thinking about it: "This is not you, this is not cool." Cool to me is going to school, is gonna make something out of your life. You gonna have the things that you want to have. Nice car, nice home, college education, nice job. Not getting high, dropping out of school, having babies. There's a lot of teen-agers around our block that had an abortion or they got two kids, three kids already. Half the class I graduated with, the girls have babies. It's ridiculous. Right out of grammar school.

A freshman at high school, I was scared. Didn't know anyone. Came into class, just sat there, didn't do the work. My biology teacher, Mr.

Dixon, really touched me, he got to me. I came out of his class with a B from an F. He's the one who really got me to thinking.

I was gonna sit there and let the whole year run past without doing anything. He was always hounding me, getting on my back, calling me another little stupid black girl. I would always holler back, "I'm not dumb! I'm not stupid!" He'd say, "You don't do anything. *Show* me that you're not stupid." I felt bad because a lot of people in the community look up to me 'cause there's only two students in our immediate neighborhood that go to my high school. I had to do better, not only because of them, but because of me, too—just to do better, do above the average. I had to show that Mr. Dixon.

I started taking tutoring class from a senior who majored in biology. It showed up in my other classes, too. Algebra and biology is two of the classes that most freshmen mess up in. I came out of both those classes with B's. At the end of the year, we had become more than teacher and student. He was my friend. He told me congratulations and he was proud of me.

In the neighborhood, my friends, they got their little remarks, say we're conceited and think we're too much. They always teasing me. They just be playing. To me that's a compliment.

Sometimes you just can't talk to your parents about this stuff. My mother, she expects a lot out of me. She want me to be better than she is. My aunties, they all proud of me. They brag on me, look up to me.

My mother had me when she was young. She still went to school, graduated on time, everything. She went a year and half to college and then cosmetology school. She has a license for hair and makeup, so if she couldn't find anything better else to do, that would be there. She was always working so she really didn't have enough time for me when I was small. My grandmother raised me. She died when I was eight.

My father's not really even a father. He call on the average three or four times a year. Not a good percentage. Come by with a big gift and expect everything to be fine and good. That's not a father. We got nothing to really talk about. If I was to die right now, he wouldn't know it till he come back around to my house.

My grandfather, he steps in for the father place. He take care of me whenever I need it. Actually he's my father, that's how I look at it. According to him, I'm not his grandbaby, I'm his baby. When young men come to my house looking for me, he always asking them a lot of questions, like a father should do.

When grades roll around, he always has to see them. Just because you're in the ghetto and a bad neighborhood don't mean that it has to be *in* you.

That's why I want to be a lawyer. When I was smaller I used to watch a lot of TV. I'd see these lawyers looking all nice, talking all intelligent. Ever since I can remember back, that's always what I wanted to be. It seems challenging, because somebody's gonna pay you their earned money in order to let you represent them, to decide what is best for them.

I'm not gonna forget where I came from. Being a lawyer, with my insight and what I know, working with the justice system, I can help them out. The people that come after me, that's gonna be in the same neighborhood. It's not like I'm gonna get up and move and leave all the memories behind. I lived in that house from the day I was born into this world.

I've never been in need for anything, I've never been going to bed hungry. I just want the kids behind that's gonna move in that house after we move, to have the good things I had. With all this crime going on around here, lawyers, working with the justice system, can help these other kids.

We live in a pretty good neighborhood, but it's bad in some ways. You go to the El station, you take a chance of getting pushed over into the train. I just want to help out our little neighborhood, and I'm not gonna never stop, if it take me until the day I die.

Church? You don't have to be in church to learn religion. I don't play with God, that's something I value a lot. I don't fool around with nothing like that. Yeah, I go to the Samaritan Bible Baptist Church. I'm the only one in my family that goes there. Yeah, I believe in God. I believe in His world after this world, Heaven. But actually you don't have to be in church to learn that. I go to church because I *like* it.

I'm the independent type. I don't let anybody lead me to do anything. If I don't want to do, then I'm not gonna do it, as simple as that. Whether you like it or not. Whether it's for the good or the bad or the worse. That's just me.

DAVID HILL

You're living each day, wondering like you're comatose,
Someone yells crack and you freeze like a popsicle.
When is the time you're going to wake up?
Because this is the nightmare we all make up.

He is an aspiring rap artist who works as a busboy. He is one of five brothers; his parents are separated. He lives with his mother and little brother in Uptown. His is the only family income. He is seventeen.

"I dropped out of high school two years ago. I'm formally getting ready for my GED. I'm going to Truman Junior College in September. Computer programming."

The life I'm living is on the easy side. I go through different gang territories, so sometimes it's kind of rough. There's the Disciples and the Vice Lords. I'm not in none of them, so I'm like right in the middle of all their confusion and fights. Passing through like an easy target.

They do put pressure on you. You walk down, they say, "What's up, Brother Almighty?" Start talking slang. "You ain't nothin' but that Vice Lord thing." They want me to be part of their group. When I get home from work, I end up right in the middle of it all. Basically, I say, "Yeah, what's up, brother?" and go about my business.

I'm riding on the bus, I wear my hat perfectly straight. This baseball cap. I see them throwing up gang signs, looking at me all hard, just staring, like they want to kill, and I get off the bus.

They'll just look at you hard and wonder what you be about. If they're holding a meeting on the corner, I just walk around it and get home. They know me by face. They don't know my name. Some of them know me as a performer, but some of them just look at me as an average person. Sometimes they leave me alone.

One time I was playing a video game and six gangbangers come in there, trying to hassle me, to jump me. They couldn't do nothing so they went about their business. I know a little martial arts my uncle taught me. Right now he's unemployed.

In high school, I was a rapper. I was doing good, then suddenly somebody framed me. Another rapper threw a milk on a gangbanger and they thought I threw it. They tried to take revenge out on me.

I liked entering plays and talent shows, that I love. I love writing, too. I used to write poems instead of a regular essay and I used to get A's in that. [*Laughs.*] I was about eight years old when I first started rapping. I used to listen to Iced Tea and Curtis Blow. I liked the style they was using, plus it was break-dancing.

It's another way that a street person could express themself without being totally negative or fighting. In your rap music, you can say what you want to say and are feeling, because it's a song. If you just *say* it, everybody might come out against you because you're saying it. Sometimes it's negative, sometimes it's positive. But rapping, you can express that. [*He breaks into rap.*]

> Don't point at the youth because they're just living it
> How could youth sneak drugs past the government?
> They're all mixed up, their minds are brainwashed.
> Whoever sells drugs in this country's on top
> And then on papers we're on the front page.
> It's like we're enslaved.

It's more than just the kids out there; it's the people higher up. You know, looking at the news, seeing people around me, of what they go through. How they avoid being theirselves by using a drug. They're always using it as an escape. They can't deal with their true feelings. Instead of using drugs, I'd rather write a rhyme, so that way I can express myself without being high.

When you're rapping, they can understand it. If you said it directly, the youth cannot understand it, 'cause there are people out there illiterate. They can't read or write but what they can hear has got to be so easy and so smooth. Maybe they can't read, but they can listen well and feel.

That's why rap is so beautiful to me. Just being able to speak to people. It's like the blind can't see, but they can hear. And they can hear clear, clearer than the average man. So if you can at least talk to some of them that's twelve and up, or younger than that, that can understand what you're saying, that makes me feel good because I'm at least reaching somebody.

> They say words hit harder than fists.
> Music soothes the savage beast.
> If a man can hear and feel what you say,
> Then your songs he will steadily play.

To me, it's like a song. Rap is beautiful.

That's why right now I'm trying to come out with a record to deliver another message. They're talking about just their people. I can understand helping your people, but think about what the Lord put you on earth to do. He put you on earth as a family. It's not just my black brother, man, my white brother, man, my Spanish brother, man. We're all brothers, period. Up under the skin, we are bones, we are blood cells, etcetera. But we are brothers and sisters underneath.

My mother taught me well, and I've seen enough. She had me at sixteen. She was poor; she couldn't feed us like a regular parent would, so she had to work extra hard to get food in our mouths. I feel I grew up capable of working to repay her.

That's why I don't like rap groups that puts women down. That to me is negative. That's ignorance, because, believe it or not, a woman does a lot. She goes through a lot more than a man does because she creates. She brings out the future to what is now. Without the woman we have no future.

For a young age, my mother's been through a lot, and I've seen a lot for my age. She schooled me, she taught me right from wrong. Family members, friends, were gangbangers. Matter of fact my father used to be a gangbanger. My uncles used to be gangbangers. So I looked at the stuff they went through, in and out of jail, so I didn't want to be part of that life.

[*He raps:*]

> Since people got addicted,
> When the dope man first gave them the crack pipe
> He said don't believe the hype.
> Drugs don't kill. As you can see I'm still alive.
> But he doesn't use it, so then you use it.
> Then he gives it to you until you lose it.
> Then the story states how people act carelessly
> To form up their history.

■ ■ ■ ■ ■

Lost and Found

ROBERT BROWN

"Use my real name. I want the kids to know." (I didn't.)

He faces me, yet doesn't see me. His eyes are veiled by God-knows-what thoughts. He mumbles, almost inaudibly; yet he is feverish, and the words tumble out.

He is twenty-nine, yet appears much closer to forty-nine. His small, scrawny body seems too small for the chair.

At the moment, I'm a hustler. I steal. Sometimes I'll break into a truck. On the back of it, it have phrases; you can tell what be in the truck. It lets you know it have frozen food. And then again, it have clothes that is transported. TV, house suppliances. Refrigerator, too, we carry it. Not too long ago, we took a case of corned beef. Sometimes we sell a whole slab of beef for ten dollars or less than that. When you become a good hustler, there's nothin' you can't sell. Just about anything.

There is a seal on the truck. You can use just about anything to break it, 'cause it's real thin. It's nothin' more than a clamp. You can use pliers, just about anything and twist it off. You unlock the door, you jump up and you throw things off. Everybody around. It's sort of a Robin Hood, so everybody can get it. We always makes sure we have somethin' for ourselves.

We sell it to everybody in the neighborhood. A couple of years back, we hit a train. VCRs. It stops right by here. We just throws it out to people—kids, ladies. Even the police was puttin' 'em in their car. They supposed to be takin' it from us and reportin'. We know they keeps it, 'cause when we come to court, none of the stuff shows up.

We got fences. They owns a business. Weldin' shops. Car washes. Even local stores. We got A-rab fences. White fences. Two more guys be with me. Together, there ain't nothin' we can't do. Speakin' for myself, not braggin'—I just brushed my shoulder—I'm just good. All three of us got a lot of things that we know how. But I'm not well off. Not at the moment.

See, we all had jobs and we been searchin' for jobs and it got harder and harder. So we have to go back to the life that we left. Day-to-day hustlin' is hard now. It don't always work out. I want to lead an honest life, but how you gonna do it when there ain't no jobs?

Some time ago, me an' the other two pass by a truck by a factory. We see HELP WANTED, so we goes in an' make application, but they says there's no openin' now. So we goes outside and breaks into the truck. Times is hard.

I have a good mind and knowledge of a few trades. I know how to lay carpets. I know how to do plumbin'. Roofin'. I can still lay a good carpet, but I still have to get my papers together. An' you have to have the proper tools and they cost you a lot of money which I don't have.

Mainly, I worked. Cleanin' up in restaurants, moppin' floors. Walkin' from mall to mall, store to store. This guy said would I like to learn to lay carpet? It's not easy like people think. It took me five years before I became a professional.

I learned plumbin'. I had a friend, his father had his own business. He asked would I come and help him. We startin' workin' condominiums. We gutted it out, we replaced everything.

I like layin' carpet the best. I had caught a hernia. By me havin' a lot of pride, I never let 'em know what was wrong with me. They replaced me. I been tryin' to get back, but it's hard.

My mother died when I was just turnin' eleven. My father died five years ago. My auntie practically raised me. I left home when I was fourteen. I just learned how to take care of myself and I been doin' it ever since.

I sold drugs a lot. Just recently I was sellin'. Sometimes you gotta fall down before you can get up. I taken them myself. Even cough medicine, they say it's safe. But you can get a high off of it. These pills, 591-J. You drop 'em into somethin', you shake it up real well. Then there's cocaine and blow, which is heroin. You snort it. Today you can buy it from a kid that is no more than ten or eleven. I have a uncle who is real big in drugs. I can buy an eight-ball, which is cocaine, and make me five hundred, six hundred dollars. People take drugs because they be down or flustrated or even angry to overcome their sorrows. I don't sell no more and am tryin' to get off it.

I used to be a chief with the Vice Lords. People say it's a gang, but we call it a organization. When you get up to a certain age, you stop gang-bangin' and start hustlin'. Some of the Lords, they'll probably sell drugs. Tryin' to make money. Everybody tryin' to find some quick way that they can feed their family.

I got kicked out in my last year high school. Gangbangin' in the lunchroom. A couple of guys and me had a few words. The guy had a knife and tried to cut me. I used to carry a gun in my briefcase. As I was backin' up, the other one grabbed me from behind so the guy could cut me. I reached in my bookbag and started shootin'. I shot the guy but he didn't press charges.

I was in jail but not for that. Another shootin'. The penitentiary is the same like in the street. Once you know what you're doin', you can get anything. But it ain't no good.

I'd rather be doin' somethin' else than what I'm doin' now. Right now, I have a girlfriend and I'd like to marry her. She just got out of prison. They caught her with a quality of illegal drugs. She has a daughter and I have a daughter. I'd like to just sit back and have a decent job and live with my family. More than anything, I'd like to lay carpet. I *love* it. [*He smiles for the first time.*] The type of life I'm leadin' now, I don't want her and the child to live that way.

My day? I get up in the mornin', I eat, I bath, put my clothes out. And I come out and look for somethin' to steal. We find an old house with a lot of old curtains. We wash 'em and sell 'em. Antique tables. Today I helped my friend wash his car. And waited for you to come.

TYRONE MITCHELL

He has the build of a professional football player. His resemblance to Bo Jackson is startling. "The kids all call me Bo. A lotta people do." He laughs easily.

He is twenty-five.

A long-time resident of the project who works as a tenants' advocate has known him ever since he was eighteen. "He was ruthless, uncaring, and unloved. His self-esteem was nil. He was disrespectful of his elders and did things in a violent way. He used to stand on the corner with a neck full of heavy gold chains and a baseball bat in his hands. He was a bully, who scared people. Something seems to be happening to him now. Let's cross our fingers."

We hung out on the streets all night, gettin' high, startin' trouble. Rowdy. I was about eighteen, runnin' wild—guns, gangbangin'.

I've been arrested, in and out of county jail. They put me in Division 5, Tier 2B. There I was with robbers, a couple of guys had murder cases, a couple, rape cases. I was supposed to learn from them. I was in for possession. A UUW, unlawful use of a weapon. I been outa jail just two weeks. I was in three and a half months. Aggravated assault, this time.

I should've known better. Not to come back again. But me bein' young, wild, my mind slipped off my work. I done fell off when I come to the projects. The guys said, "Oh, man, come with us." I thought it was the thing to do, bein' cool.

Before we come here, I was goin' through a man's stage with a youth body and a youth mind. I had a lot of pressure to take care of my family, to help my mother. My father left a long time ago. To put food in the refrigerator, I dropped out of school in my sophomore year. I was sixteen. By me bein' the intelligent one, I helped my two brothers and a sister with homework. Math and reading. I could figure out things real fast. Even after I dropped out of school.

I met this old guy who had buildings to fix up. He hired me as a helper, doin' carpenter work, hangin' drywall, doin' electrician work. I was learnin' while I was helpin'. I stuck with it.

But when we moved down here, I fell. I was strung out on cocaine. Oh, I had really went a long way with drugs. Now people that is on drugs can come and talk to me, because I reformed myself. I'm not on drugs anymore, and I'm not a Vice Lord anymore. It feels damn good to be back.

I see kids now, the same thing I was doin'. Breakin' in trucks, breakin' in cars. I see myself. Before they get to go into jail, I talk to 'em now, grab 'em. A lotta little kids 'round here know I been in and out of jail. "You wanna end up in and outa jail like I did?" And throwin' rocks. Somebody could put somebody's eyes out.

Most of 'em listen. Then you get some that cuss me out, but I grab 'em, hit 'em a couple of times on their butt. They about six, seven, eight. The older ones, ten, eleven, and twelve, really listen. I can't really get to all of 'em. If I gets this buildin' right here and make it into a center—man! Where they can see, hey, he really tryin' to do somethin'!

I feel like an older man at twenty-five. I started young, so right now I feel mature and wiser. I have three kids, two boys and a girl. My daughter is at my aunt's house and one of my sons is out there playin' with his mother. [*He indicates the lot outside.*] I would like to watch 'em grow up, if nothin' happens to me.

I get up in the mornin' about eight o'clock. I stare out the window about an hour and a half. Just watch. It be quiet in the mornin'. Until the kids come out, about ten and eleven, I be thinkin'. You got a vacant lot here, you got a vacant lot over there. It's been around for a long time. I'd like to put somethin' there, redo the ground. If I could get out there and put somethin' on that ground, the other guys in the gang, seein' me workin' this field, hooked up—I think I can really touch, reach these guys. For one, I'd like to put a laundromat right here. [*He indicates a nearby plot.*] That'd be nice for 'em. Everybody in these buildin's gotta go a long way to the laundromat. To Henry Horner. People from Henry Horner don't like people from another project comin' there. That brings on things.

After hour and a half daydreamin', I come outside. I volunteer for the Salvation Army now. They have free meals at 11 o'clock. Two days ago, a guy wanted to beat up a lady that serve the food. They told him to stand in a line to get a plate and would you take your hat off? He wanted to jump in front of everybody. He gone to cussin' out, callin' out all kind of bad names. He just carried on somethin' terrible.

So I come along and talked to him. "Now hold up, you makin' it bad for everybody they tryin' to feed. Her boss will come here and see that and shut the place down and there be hundreds of people been tryin' to eat here every day. If I let you carry on like this, I be wrong. A lot of these people come a long ways to get this meal." I asked him to apologize to her. I be big, but he was bigger than me. He went to her and apologized.

The guys are still on the corner. They go into bad habits 'cause they don't have nobody to talk to. If I could show 'em what I can do—oh, I just wanna get out there and *do* it.

How come I changed? One day I was puttin' on my clothes, ready to come outside. I had my hat turned to the left, the Vice Lords' way. To be honest, I come out of the bathroom, playin' with one of my sons. He took my hat and straightened it up. I go back to the mirror and turned it back to the left. But then I thought about it. Why did he turn it straight? It was like a sign to me. One of my kids turned my hat straight. He was four then. [*With a touch of awe.*] Had to be a sign, had to be. I look at myself in the mirror, it dawned. That had to be a sign from God. So I straightened my hat out and I come outside.

The gang tried to move my hat to the left. I grabbed their hand, no. They ast me, "What's wrong? You dropped your flag?" I say I'm reformin' myself and I advise you to do the same. Because these guys been gangbangin' for years and they got nowheres yet. It's time to stand up and be counted for, 'cause nobody ain't countin' no gangbanger unless you dead.

They just hang out, kickin' it, talkin', doin' nothin'. *Nothin'*. Just wastin' time, wastin' their life. Most of 'em is eighteen, nineteen, twenty. They get older, most of my friends is turnin' to drugs, sellin'. That's the road I don't want to go down. They sell it to the neighborhood an' Puerto Ricans, whites.

When they be standin' on the corner, they come out about twelve in the afternoon till four or five the next mornin'. Just hangin' out, drinkin', smokin' reefers. A lot of 'em had dreams. They talk about what they'd like to do, but they don't have that extra get-up-and-go. They have it built up in them, gangbangin', project life, sleepin' with different-type women, the whole nine yards. They tired, just too tired to get out.

I was a good carpenter's helper. If I ever needed anything, short of money, advice, I could always go to this old guy. When I dropped outa school, before I come here, I hung around older guys, fifty-five, sixty years old. I thought I could learn from 'em, because they bein' old, they would not be tellin' me wrong. I learned a lot.

I heard about Martin Luther King from one of the older guys I was workin' for. He showed me the movie of King and the civil-rights movement. Was Martin Luther King's birthday. I got a good idea of what he was really marchin' for. He wanted blacks and whites to come together. Be proud of our brothers and sisters, without fightin' with each other. I really like that. I listened to him tell about Malcolm X. I watched this movie about Medgar Evers about seven, eight times. He was talkin' about peace and freedom. Now we went all the way back, all over again.

I gets along with white people real good. It's now blacks is fightin' blacks, blacks is killin' blacks. Let's see, how can I put this? [*He pauses, closes his eyes.*] If we can really get together—once upon a time we did get together, downhill. Our gang got together with a rival gang and we had a peace treaty. No more gangbangin'. But somebody come out of another neighborhood and the peace treaty broke. There be gang warfare.

It's gotta be more than me, but I think I can start it. It would have to be more than jobs. A lot of 'em need more schoolin', more education. A lotta them dropped out when their friends got killed around here, and go on drugs.

I'm goin' back to school, startin' on the eighteenth of this month. Workin' for my GED at Malcolm X. When I get my GED, I'm goin' for carpentry to get me a certificate. I know a lot about it, but I gotta go back for more. From there, I can see where I'm goin'.

My mother really likes the way I turned myself around. Just this mornin' she told me I look nice. She asked me how long I'm gonna be like this. I say I'm gonna fulfill my dreams. I'm going forward. As a matter of fact, I'm goin' to Brenda Stevenson's mother's house* tomorrow mornin'. I put her kitchen ceiling up already. I'm doin' a new drywall tomorrow. I'm gonna plaster the cracks and paint it. I'll do the roofin' and plumbin'.

When I was young, helpin' in carpentry, I always thought I'm gonna one day get me a pickup truck with my name on it. My name with my *business card*. Pass out my cards, my phone number on it. Call any time. Everybody'll wanna know: How did you get your own business? That would be my office for now. Business pickup, maybe I'd have me a storefront with *my name* on it. It'll be nice. My kids will be there. As they grown older, I will be teachin' 'em. It feels good: Tyrone's back.

■ ■ ■ ■ ■

911

SGT. DENNIS HINKSON

He is thirty-five. He has been a Chicago police officer for thirteen years. When he was promoted in 1981, he became the youngest sergeant in the department.

---

* A tenants' advocate at the project.

His father, a retired Brooklyn fireman, had come from the West Indies, "with the immigrant desire to get an education for their children, a better life than they had for themselves."

He has a baccalaureate from the University of Chicago. He quit its law school because "law enforcement was more on the cutting edge of society than corporate law.

"When I first entered the Academy, there was some resentment on the part of the many who had served in Vietnam toward the few of us college boys, who hadn't. It passed. I didn't sense much racial tension in this case."

I was first assigned to the police district that covered the housing projects on the South Side. There were no CHA police then.* We had to do it all. They were bad, but not as bad as they are now. Better than the dilapidated houses around. Electricity, running water, buildings that wouldn't fall down on you. I recall many times carrying down a dead body, inevitably on the top floor, wondering if the stairs would hold up.

The people wanted the help of the police but they had been kicked around by authority all their lives and were suspicious of uniforms. They've been rebuffed so many times, a lot of them didn't really know how to ask for help. Most of the police officers come from working-class backgrounds. When you're dealing with a person who doesn't have a job, never really had a job, doesn't know anyone who has a job, communication sometimes breaks down. With a stressful life, they're sometimes rough in manner or abrasive in tone. If you're asking for help, that's the wrong tone to use.

At the time, there was a big drive to integrate the police force. They tried to put as many black officers with white officers as possible. I worked with them all. I remember one time working with another young black guy. There was a disturbance and the man who called us wanted us to take off our stars, our hats, all our symbols of authority. He wanted to just talk to us, man to man. Maybe we could work this out on a personal level. I never had that happen when I was with a white officer.

Curiously enough, I've been on calls when people have said, "We don't want you, we want white officers." They want somebody to just say, "I want this person locked up." That's it, no talk. The white officers were seen as the *real* police. On several occasions, I've been in an all-black area and they've said, "We want some white cops." That was about ten years ago. I haven't heard anything like that in years.

There's always been a great fear of gangs. Today it's worse. They

---

* Chicago Housing Authority.

didn't have the Uzis and automatic weapons they now have. The biggest problem is illegal drugs. When you have such little income and you're hooked, stealing is inevitable. The family, the neighborhood, everybody suffers.

When I was growing up, heroin was the most-abused drug. You hardly hear any mention of it today. Everything now is cocaine and its different forms—crack, ice. It seems everybody's taking drugs. You see people in the stock exchange, yuppies, people in the projects, and everybody in between. It's one of the few items that white people will buy from black people. In some of the poorest parts of the city, you'll see white suburbanites. You can tell by the sticker on the vehicle. You see a late-model luxury car, a Volvo or a BMW. You usually see two white middle-class-looking males. They're youngish, early thirties, college-looking. They drive up to some black kid on the corner and they'll ask where they can get whatever it is they want. Almost like a corner drugstore.

In the middle of the night, an upper-middle-class white person comes into an all-black neighborhood, approaching some poor black kid. They don't know who they're buying the commodity from. They don't know what they're getting. You can't take it back to the store if it's defective. They're essentially putting their lives at risk and think nothing of it. I've seen these scenes. It's mind-boggling.

It's usually cocaine. They're at a tremendous risk. They could be robbed, but how could they really report why they were in the area? There's really no incentive to stick them up, because if you do, they won't come back again. But if you sell them what they want in a good quality, they'll come back and you'll have a regular customer.

There's no question drugs are prevalent throughout our society. Didn't that play a part in the Iran-contra scandal? Wasn't the CIA dealing with drug dealers in Southeast Asia? Panama?

Unfortunately, I know many soldiers who've been killed in this war. I equate police officers with soldiers because this is a war. I know a female officer who was killed during a drug raid. This war isn't making any progress at all and lots of people are dying. It's equivalent to the Vietnam War. I just don't want us twenty years from now to decide we shouldn't have fought this war in the first place. Are we going to put up another wall with names of all the slain police officers?

I'd like to see this war fought differently before we get to that point.

The profit motive is too indigenous in our society for this kind of war to be effectively fought. There's just too much money and corruption at every level, from the White House to the poorest parts of our community.

Every time you arrest one drug pusher, you have twenty others appearing. I wouldn't even call them drug pushers; they don't have to push, there are so many willing buyers.

The only solution I see is to deal with it as a medical problem. A drug is something people take to feel better. Drug addicts are sick people just trying to acquire their medicine as best they can. If we interdict ourselves as we have so far, their desire to acquire some medicine to make them feel better is far greater than our desire to just fulfill a job.

Drug users are suffering from what? Feelings of anxiety, feelings of loneliness, feelings of hopelessness, like black kids facing a blank wall, feelings of not accomplishing—or maybe as a reward for accomplishing, a guy making $100,000 on the stock market that day. It's a temporary high. That's why they call it a high. That's why they call it mind-altering. To escape from that day-to-day bleakness.

We have to ask ourselves why the desire is so high when everybody knows the end result is death.

It has a lot to do with the makeup of our society. The need for instant gratification. A drug is something you take and in a few minutes you feel better than you felt before. A college degree takes four years. With a drug it's four minutes.

The way to handle it should be no different than the way we handle other strong drugs. We have drugstores that are run by pharmacists. You have to go to a doctor to get a prescription.

Most drugs are reasonably priced. People usually don't have to stick up other people to finance the prescription drugs they need. Why can't these now-illegal drugs, only illegal by statute, be made legal? Why can't they be sold at drugstores? Wouldn't it be better if all drugs were sold at Walgreen's or Osco or your corner druggist's than on a streetcorner by some teen-ager?

The big thing is to take the profit out of drugs. That's what it's really all about. It is by far the most profitable activity of organized crime. Much more than gambling or prostitution. And far, far more killings.

Most police officers agree that the so-called war on drugs has been terribly glamorized by the media. A lot of people on both sides of the drug war, the sellers and the narcs, are Vietnam combat veterans. Many of them were in some of the elite fighting units in Vietnam. Since there's been no shooting war for many years, a lot of them went into the drug business. It's very similar.

In Vietnam, there was a significant use of helicopters and airplanes to fight a war. In this war, a lot of drugs are brought in by plane and helicopter.

In Vietnam, tanks were used to transport the fighters. In the drug war, police ride around in what they call smart squad cars, computer-equipped. They have the war wagons, with explosives and shotguns.

Even the strategic-hamlet concept has been brought over from Vietnam. The Americans would go into a village, take all the people out, destroy the village, relocate the villagers to a brand-new United States–built village, and the people would have to live there.

Here, people have been moved out of certain public-housing units, the places rehabbed, made more secure, and the residents allowed back in. There's a problem. The villagers in Vietnam had been a cohesive unit: farming, trade. Once they were relocated the links were broken. The sense of community was lost.

Some of the veterans who fought in the first war which was lost are out to make sure we win this second war. How? To liberate the community from drugs, we'll have special enforcement. The police will be everywhere. If you have a joint or anything in your possession, you'll be arrested. Your car, your vehicle, your boat will be confiscated. In a zero-tolerance environment, some basic rights are lost. If you happen to have a friend in your car and he has one joint, you're subject to losing your car.

So many of our rights have been lost. The right to privacy in your own home. If there's any kind of suspicion that you're selling drugs, the police can come in, get a search warrant, and tear your house apart. I've seen cases where the wrong address has been broken into. We've gone really crazy with this drug-testing thing. For many jobs you have to take a urine test. A lot of people say, "What's the big deal? If you really want the job, why not?" These are people who've never had to take a urine test. For this test to be conducted properly, a grown human being has to watch another grown human being urinate. If there's a greater invasion of privacy than that, I'd like to know what it is. I've had the experience of going through one. Humiliating. If you don't want to submit to a test, obviously you have something to hide. The burden is on you.

If we decriminalized drugs, you wouldn't have so much corruption of public officials. Bribing is endemic to the drug business. And the waste of so much energy. I've made drug arrests. You have to get an arrest slip, take him to the station, the drugs have to be inventoried, then charges, a state's attorney has to be contacted, charges have to be approved, then he goes to the lockup, he has to be fed, then transferred to the county jail, someone else has to watch him there, then he's assigned a public defender, then he comes to the judge. This one simple five-dollar joint has cost the American system thousands of dollars. Is it worth it? This war cannot turn out any differently than the one in Southeast Asia. It cannot be won.

The crusade for drug legalization is right now at the equivalent stage of what Vietnam was in '63. It's just a few people shaking their heads. They're being ignored by the masses, but as the deaths mount up, more and more people will realize this war is too costly.

The little children growing up in our inner cities have experienced more violence than many of our veterans of wars. Working in the projects, I can recall the children as somebody was shot on a playing field. By the time the ambulance arrived, there are all these children looking at a dying person. It's a hot day, everybody's out playing. You see these little kids just looking. Most Americans never experience this. I didn't until I was an adult. It's just so ordinary, so everyday with them, seeing death.

I remember in the projects someone getting shot on the sixteenth floor and bringing him down on the elevator. Women are riding down on the same elevator with their laundry. They don't see the need to get off. Only one of the elevators is working. It'll be a long, long time before it comes again. Just because this person is dying and throwing up blood is no reason to wait for the next elevator. Violent death is simply accepted as a way of life. They still got to get on with their laundry and their groceries.

You end up stopping at every floor. Every time the door opens, you see these little kids exposed to this person on the stretcher, who is dying terribly. These kids have seen a lot of people die. It hardens them. A kid, four, five years old, is playing one minute, shots ring out, a person dies. Of course it has an impact on this child.

There's a tremendous gap between what this kid experiences and what a middle-income kid does. Okay, this kid has just witnessed a violent death. There's no follow-up, there's no psychiatric care. But for any kind of trauma, the kid on the other side of town will get all sorts of help. Remember the situation where some kids were killed in Wilmette a couple of years ago by a lady who became very disturbed?* There was all kinds of psychiatric follow-up for those kids who had seen classmates dying. Whereas the kids in the projects, who've had the same experiences many times, get absolutely no care. Nobody interviews them. They have to just deal with it the best way they can. It happens in their lives and nothing is made of it.

They see the blood splattered there until somebody comes to clean it up. They might see a bullet hole in the elevator. They see it all as the case is conducted, reporters, the publicity. It stigmatizes a child.

---

* It was a celebrated case in which several schoolchildren, of an upper-middle-class community, were shot and killed by a demented young woman.

They become very jaded by life and death at an early age. I've seen teen-agers who've committed heinous crimes. They're questioned: How can you do such a thing? What made you do it? They're just so casual. It's no big thing to kill another person, because they've been around so much killing. It just doesn't have the terribleness that it would have to a middle-class person. Life goes on.

Education has always been the only way out. But it's difficult to study if you're in a two-bedroom apartment and there are seven brothers and sisters and you hear the noise. It's summertime, no air-conditioning, you hear all the sounds outside. If you go to the library, and it closes late at night, you're afraid to come home. It isn't shocking that so few make it out—but that the few who do can actually escape it.

CLAIRE HELLSTERN

For ten years, she had been director of nursing at a medical clinic on Chicago's Near North Side. It is in the neighborhood of Cabrini-Green, one of the city's largest public housing projects.

1979

It was predominantly black when I came here. It's becoming more Spanish.

If you're working with people who are depressed and they have a low income, or you're working with teen-agers who are gang members, you have to be flexible. You can't lack tact. Otherwise, you're gonna get knocked when you go out the door. People from the ghetto, I think, are more sensitive. They can tell if you like 'em or if you have an attitude. I'm probably more cautious than I used to be because I've had my purse taken a few times.

I got into Cabrini-Green because I wanted an unusual job. I must have called every clinic. It's rewarding. I function as an ombudsman. A lot of people are bored with their job. I love to go to work. I don't think I'm a do-gooder. It's just my job, my responsibility.

Our greatest problem is unemployment. Forty percent around here. People on welfare lose their self-respect. I've seen it happen. I think everybody on public aid has to work if they're physically able. It's impor-tant to develop discipline, to getting up on time, reporting, having some self-respect. People don't really want to have a handout. It isn't so great to be on public aid.

1991

It was probably the poorest area in Chicago. The highest crime rate. We had no security guards, so the young people on the front desk were supposed to ask, "Where are you going? Why are you here?" These kids were black and Spanish and lived in the community, and they didn't want any problems with gang members. So while we're teaching a session with pregnant mothers, these individuals would wander in trying to sell hot stuff. So I was always asked to handle these characters.

The best way to handle someone is to use humor and be extremely polite. One time, these fellows were selling something. I said, "Gentlemen, we cannot shop indoors. Please see us after work." So they called me up on the phone. It makes you nervous when they know your name. They said, "Claire bitch, we're gonna get you and beat you up." I said, "Gentlemen, did you have your breakfast this morning? What did you have, Jell-O? Obviously, you have low blood sugar, because you're kind of crabby and you must not have watched your soap opera. Why don't you have a wholesome meal?" They were speechless and hung up. I said, "Good day," and called the police. They called me and threatened me again. They said, "Claire, we know you called the fuzz." I said, "Really, gentlemen. What is your name? I'd love to put a gold star on your eye chart. You have fabulous vision." Again they were speechless. Before they could hang up, I said, "Now listen. You're wasting my time. Unless you're very ill and you call for an appointment, do not enter the building. And I am now saying good day." I hung up and they never bothered me again.

Another time, I was visiting an elderly patient with a pacemaker. My used car went up in smoke. I needed oil. So I parked in front of this nine-story project. As I entered, there were three fellows. I said, "Hi, how's everybody today? By the way, I'm seeing a lady with a pacemaker. It's like a miniature battery that would fit in your watch. It operates her heart. Where's 209?" It's always good to make sure that they don't think you're an insurance man or a detective or a bill collector. Also it's good to look people straight in the eye.

I took care of the patient. I come out, there's thirteen guys. I say, "What a great day for a game. Maybe you could take on Michael Jordan." I'm walking down the sidewalk and a guy drops a lead pipe off the top of the building. Aimed at me.

It landed in front of me. I think it was more of a test. He was trying to frighten me than actually aim it. Possibly they would have picked up my purse. So what I did is put my hand on my hip and I tapped my heel and I stood my ground. I knew I couldn't outrun them, not thirteen.

I grew up in a small town and you learn from instinct it's better not to panic. They may have thought I had a weapon or whatever. Again this was the element of surprise. I surprised them more than they surprised me. Nobody came near me. They didn't say anything. So after a few minutes, I walked over to the car, which I was praying would start going, because I had just put in two gallons of oil. I drove off.

I will relate another story. I went to a Hispanic neighborhood. There were signs on the wall: Insane Unknowns. It's a popular Spanish gang. The front of the building was barricaded so I had to enter the back. A semi-intoxicated person gave me assistance. I gave him some literature in Spanish on cancer prevention, asked him to hand it out. The gentleman went to all the grocery stores and handed them out. I gave him a couple hundred pieces. Any time you make someone feel they're important, they're useful, and you're not condescending, regardless of race, sex, age, culture, or creed, nine times out of ten, you're going to be safe.

Frequently people talk to me. One time that did cause me a little trouble. I was going to work at Cabrini and I said hello to this guy. He pulled a switchblade out of his sleeve and said, "I want your purse, ma'am." I gave him my wallet with ninety cents. He got ticked off. "How come you don't have more money?" I told him that I don't make that much and had my purse taken a couple of times. He got angrier. "I want your purse." I said, "Excuse me, buster, but I hope you don't use my type of comb. I hope you don't wear lipstick. And I hate to have neighbors talking about you walking around with a lady's purse. So for the above reasons, I don't think I should give it to you." He was surprised. Had he a gun to my head or a knife to my throat, I would have acted different.

So he bowed! "After you," he said. I said, "No, no. After you." So we're bowing as ready to duel with swords, but we didn't turn our back. He turned and went away. So I went around the corner and yelled, "Help!" The winos were there, and a big help they were!

I am not frightened. I'm sometimes angry when it happens, because I don't have a mean bone in my body. I also have a survival instinct. No one has ever tried to touch me or cut me or anything like that.

I'm still an idealist. I remember those kids who worked at Cabrini-Green. They had very low income. They learned to do filing, how to answer the phone, help patients fill out their history. Ninety percent of them went on to college, but it was a struggle. They first used to come in late, snapping their gum, wearing halter tops, dragging their feet. After a week or so, something happened. Something interesting they found about the work. A kind of responsibility, I guess. They began to act much more professional. Maybe feeling good about themselves. It's hard for families in projects, on small income, to feel good about themselves.

My own life has been enriched. I ran across a fellow I used to date. He said I was too much. "You're too colorful." He couldn't take it. That was about eighteen years ago. Since then, he's joined the board of an inner-city center. So I hope I've had some positive influence on white friends. Oh, I've had flak from black friends.

Where I work now, at a big hospital, administering a health plan, most of my associates are middle-class blacks. A lady came to see me. She was homeless and frostbitten and had been on a bus for a month. I took her to some shelters, gave her some food and clothes. But what she needed immediately was a shower. I had her take one in the corporate office. Class does not have a color boundary. They don't mind giving clothes, but having someone sit next to them—I did have flak. But the next day, they brought a whole bunch of clothes for her. They wanted to help her. Was it because I didn't snap back at them the night before?

I feel a change in the white attitude, though some of my acquaintances are concerned about reverse discrimination in the job market. When they go for a job interview, there are quotas. There are only so many jobs and they're diminishing. I don't think they're upset about blacks getting ahead, going to college. But when it affects their pocketbook, they may be angry.

I feel affirmative action is essential. There is no way we're going to break this generation-after-generation on public aid unless there are jobs. Unless you're able to bring home a paycheck, how can you set an example for your children and give them hope for their future? It's up to businesses not just to make profits and more profits, but to make sure there are enough jobs to go around.

I'm drawn toward friends who think along similar lines. I'm not on the same wave length with those who are totally out for themselves. I made a mistake once. It was a party I shouldn't have gone to. A beautiful apartment, about a hundred guests. A friend of the host saw me and drew a circle with his arms, a fence to keep me away. He pushed all the other people to the side of the room: "She loves blacks. Don't talk to her." I told the host, "I don't want to ruin your party." So I left.

I think the people there were shocked. When you're at a party and there is drinking and dancing, they don't even pay attention to what is actually being said. They discussed it after I left and took up a collection for a record player for the youth center I was working with.

I've been asked: Do I live at Cabrini-Green? Do I date black men? I've said no. I do not love one group over another. They've said: "Are you a nigger-lover?" The police have asked me that. I used to call them on occasion when something was stolen or someone walked in with a gun. Or if a patient had been raped. I had patients who observed gang murders and were testifying.

When the cops first saw me here, they were shocked. I'm the only Caucasian, obviously a blonde. "What are you doing here?" I explained that this is my work and offered to check their blood pressure. "You're entitled to good health care, too." They'd be so surprised, just like the young men who threatened me on the phone and the guy who wanted my purse. Now I'm seeing a lot of these same cops as patients. It's a riot.

Some of the police do have an attitude about nurses working in the inner city. I think they're more concerned about safety. Some wonder, "Have they got everything together? Are they flakes?"

I have been helped by black people many times. Gang members, too. When I made home visits to the elderly, I was pushed out of every snowbank. They've helped me change tires. At Cabrini, tough-looking guys and girls helped me conduct blood-pressure testing. They helped me distribute toys. They helped carry elderly people up three flights of stairs where there was no elevator.

I remember a dark winter evening in a tough black neighborhood. I came out of this building and was stuck in this six-foot snowbank. These three young guys came along. They gave me directions, they helped shovel, threw papers under the tires, gave the car a shove, and off I went, waving at them and they waved back. No, they didn't do these things for cash. They did it because they want to feel they're necessary. Everybody wants to feel when they get up in the morning there is a reason for them living. They want to be recognized. If you appeal in a certain way to people that you need a little help, most people will help you. Because they're basically decent and want to feel good about themselves.

Do you think some of those same guys who had tried to mug you might have been among those who helped you out?

Could be some of the same guys. You bet. I don't prejudge.

MIKE WROBLESKI

A police officer in a large midwestern city. He has recently retired, having served thirty-seven years in the department.

"My dad was a policeman, too. I was always in awe of him. For as long as I can remember, I wanted to follow in his footsteps. He was always

sensitive about people's feelings. Even though we were raised in a completely white neighborhood, we were taught to treat people the way we find them, not by the color of their skin, not by their class.

"While my dad was still a patrolman, I rose in the ranks to lieutenant." In the span of three years, Mike became a captain, as a consequence of high scores in the examinations. At thirty-three, he was the third-youngest captain in the history of the force.

I was watch commander in the heart of the city. I made assignments as to who's working where. I assigned two black officers to work downtown, where the business people were. The next day, a black officer is waiting for me. He said, "Captain, you're new here. I don't want you to get in trouble. You can't assign a black in that district."

"Do you want to work there?"

"Sure."

"Okay, you and your partner will be there tonight." [*Laughs.*]

Here's a veteran black patrolman, about fifty, and I'm thirty-three, a brand-new sparkling captain, think I'm gonna conquer the world. He was so concerned about this young white guy, trying to do the right thing, he worried about me. I said, "If I get in trouble, so be it."

I was called in by the district commander. "We're not supposed to have blacks working there."

I said, "That's what I hear. You're not tellin' me I can't assign them on my watch, are you?"

"I ain't tellin' you a thing. I just want to make sure you understand that's not the policy here."

I said, "I'll tell you right now, if you don't want 'em workin' there, you better get rid of me. Because I'm not going along with that policy."

I'm no great civil-libertarian, but I said he's got to deal with it as best he can. That's how it was resolved.

To this day, black officers, all retired now, tell me about it. They laugh. "You had us workin' north. You were upsettin' the applecart." All the blacks out of that district wanted to work with me. They'd request to come on my watch. I had a long waiting list. This was 1963.

There was resentment by white veterans that here was I, comin' in, a kid, brand-new captain, defying the old ways: "We all work north, and blacks work south. I don't want to work with blacks." I let everybody know I'm not going along with any racism. "If you won't work with a black partner, get off the watch. You don't have to tell me why, just go. I can't change you, you are what you are. But when you're working for me, you're a professional. You better treat people the right way."

Policemen would react to an individual, first: "Am I dealing with a white or somebody else?" Second, you try to fit that person into some class. If you are upper-class white, you are deferred to. The policeman is as courteous as could be, even though the individual may get a little tough on the officer.

If the black was well-dressed, articulate, you also put him in a different category. But there was this resentment that this black person speaks better than I. And got a big car. Next thing is the judgment: "This black guy got that car illegitimately. From his clothes, he's probably a pimp or running policy. If it's a woman, she's a whore. And they're trying to put me down."

So what would happen is one-upmanship. The black person is explaining, but the white policeman says, "Fine, but you're gonna get a ticket anyway." And here comes the sly little dig. "You can probably take care of this. It shouldn't bother you."

If you were an upper-class white, nobody would tell you to get your ass out of here. Lower-class white, you'd say, "Get your ass out of here." If it was a poor black, you'd automatically say, "Get your fucking ass out of here." God forbid that the lower-class black should challenge. That's head-breaking time. As soon as a policeman felt challenged, he'd take out his sword: "I'm going to make an example of this guy." It's not that you would say it, you'd think it.

When more minorities began to get in the department, whites felt threatened. Most said, "I'd just as soon work with a white." Most blacks said, "I'd just as soon work with a black." The blacks felt the whites didn't really want to work with them. The fact is the whites really *didn't* want to work with blacks. There were no ifs, ands, or buts.

When blacks achieved some political power in town, the white officers who came through the old political system were concerned. Some had nice plush jobs because of clout. Now they were seeing blacks and other minorities using the same clout to get themselves good jobs. When a black mayor was elected and a black superintendent was appointed, the white officers were demoralized.

Things started to happen. When calls of a disturbance came from black neighborhoods, it would take an inordinate amount of time for the white officers to arrive.

"My goodness, I called you forty-five minutes ago."

"If you're not satisfied with our service, why don't you call your black mayor? Maybe he'll come out."

During the mayoralty election, with a black candidate running, pictures appeared on the bulletin board of a district station. It was in a changing neighborhood. There was a gorilla sitting in a tree: "Your next mayor if you don't watch out." There were chicken bones: "If we get a black mayor, this is the new police insignia." Constantly cartoons would appear: "Your star will read Pohhh-lees."

When a notice of an annual black police organization dance appeared on the board, there were words scribbled below: "All black bosses will be required to suck everybody's dicks and bring their mothers. Chitlins will be served."

I was deputy chief by this time. At roll call, I told everybody I'll have no more of this. "If I find out who put this stuff up, I'll fire him immediately." I raised all kinds of hell. "Think blue," I said. "I don't care what you do at home, but when you're working here, think blue." The black cops were pleased that a white guy was taking a stand.

What happened to my life after that is really something. I was getting phone calls late at night. "You nigger-lover." When my wife got on the phone, it was, "I hope you like black cock, you slut." I had to change my number three times, but policemen know how to get unlisted numbers. After a couple of weeks, they'd start again.

I'd get all kinds of magazines and newspapers I didn't order, subscriptions taken out in my name. Food I didn't order. This was their way of harassing me. Anonymous letters.

There were a number of white cops who supported me, who didn't want to be in the same bag with the others. But it's the others who were making the noise.

In the span of a few weeks, we had two police officers killed in the line of duty. One, a black male, the other, a black female. At the same time, I'm getting calls from the black district commander about racial problems at his station. They are writing on the walls, "Nigger, beware." There are complaints from citizens in the district being called nigger by white police.

Up on the bulletin board, behind the desk where the sergeant sits, the police dog has the head of our black mayor. This was just a small sample. A huge painting appeared at the midnight watch in front of the desk sergeant's desk. It was a black man, entwined with a snake, with three women kneeling. An arrow pointed to the white woman's vagina. Some black police officers asked the desk sergeant, "What's this picture doing here?"

"I don't know."

"It doesn't belong here."

"Why not?"

A black officer took it down. A white officer put it back up: "Leave it alone. We want it here." The black knocked it to the floor. "Anybody who puts that up will deal with me." Remember, they were all armed.

The same night, a black officer, going out to eat, had his gun in his hand, to put in his car. The sergeant, who knew him, hollered, "Be careful! There's a nigger in the building with a gun!" Remember, this is an active, working police station. Arrestees, victims all hear this shout. The sergeant pulled out his gun and said, "Every time I see a nigger with a gun, I have my gun out." The black officer said, "What the hell's the matter with you, sergeant? Put that gun away." The sergeant says, "I was in Vietnam. I know how to kill people." The sergeant follows the other guy out into the parking lot. Each guy's got the gun in his hand. It breaks up and that's when I get the complaint.

About one-thirty that morning, I get a call that a police officer had been shot. A black female officer, working undercover narcotics. The second one in a few weeks killed in line of duty. I'm at the hospital and I find family members in a state of grief. Her father had been a policeman. [*His voice is strained; he is crying.*]

I've got these racial incidents. The death of these two black officers. [*He pauses; his sobbing resumes. It's more of an angry sound.*] I have to confront these guys at the station. My wife says not to go, I'm emotionally too upset. I said I gotta go. I called the station not to let the watches go home from the midnight. Keep 'em there.

I brought them all in to the roll-call room. I told them I'd just come from the hospital and we lost an officer, who happened to be black. "Why am I here? Because of these fucking incidents. Here's a black officer who gave her life. A few weeks ago, a male black officer gave his life. I was on both scenes. [*Voice cracks; he sniffles.*] Here, you've got nigger this and nigger that, the mayor an ape, his face on a dog, the black guy and the snake, 'a nigger in the building with a gun.' What if I were to bring her family here? I bet all of you would hold your head down. I'm not gonna put up with this. If I find out who's doing it, I'll stamp their heads into the ground. If you want to take me on, any one of you, come on. Come on, let's get into this goddamn thing."

I said, "If you were down in that alley and somebody had their hands around your neck, choking you to death, and a policeman ran up to help you, would you look to see what color he was? Would you say, if it was a black guy, 'Hey, don't help me, go get a white guy?' Bullshit. You'd say, 'Boy, am I glad you helped me.' " I made this speech at all three roll calls. A few days later, there were markings on the walls of the men's washroom: "Wrobleski takes nigger dick in his ass. Wrobleski sucks."

I received a letter in the police mail. There was the picture of a nude black man reclining on a bed and a white woman with an open mouth. The letter said, "You nigger-lover. This is what my wife is doing when I'm not at home."

He meant to write "your wife," didn't he?

Of course. Isn't that a classic? You don't have to be Freud to interpret that one. This guy can't control his own thinking. His sexual fear is so deep, it's driving him crazy.

You won't believe what happened after. Some of the white officers filed a grievance with the union that I had used derogatory language in the roll-call room. [*He laughs.*] They wanted me to issue a public apology. A couple of their favorite aldermen were contacted. They pulled out all stops to get me. [*He extracts a newspaper clipping from his wallet.*] "Alderman—— accuses Police Deputy Superintendent Wrobleski of making obscene comments denigrating the sexual capacity of police officers. His behavior was outrageous."

The press asked the mayor what he thought should be done with me. He said, "They ought to give Mike Wrobleski a Medal of Honor."

I never found out who did all those things. I imagine they're still in the department. If you don't keep close tabs on complaints involving police and citizens, there may be an increase. Just recently, two white officers picked up two black kids and dumped them out of their police car in an all-white neighborhood that blacks feared to walk through. They were badly beaten.*

In all the years I was in the police department, I never saw black officers display any racism toward white civilians. I saw it the other way a lot.

We live in isolation, not just segregation. If you're in isolation, you don't get a chance to find out who the other people are. They have the same concerns we have about education, about a job, about worshipping. The black ghetto and the middle-class suburb are equally isolated.

Yet, this may sound funny after all I've said: I feel very optimistic. You no longer find those things on the bulletin boards. More blacks have been speaking out. I think the present administration, white, is trying to do the best they can, because it is not in their best interests to have racial strife. I feel, overall, given my experience, things are a lot better than

---

* The officers were brought to trial and acquitted on a technicality.

they were in the past. But unless you stay on top of this—some police officers are again venting their racist feelings—this thing can get away from all of us.

ED REARDON

He is forty-five, a veteran of the Vietnam War.

"I grew up in Chicago, been an Irish Catholic ever since the day I was born. Always wanted to be in the Fire Department. My brother's a fireman. I got on as a paramedic in 1976. It was the best decision I ever made. It satisfied everything I wanted to do in life."

He had recently had a heart attack, and the conversation took place six days before his retirement. "You can't have heart attacks and be in the Fire Department." [Laughs.]

It's funny, this racial thing. I had been in that big strike in 1980, during Mayor Byrne's administration. I walked the picket line; most of my friends did. I lost a few friends. It still runs deep. Here's the funny part. You had a lot of hard-line guys who would never give a black guy a break. They found themselves standing out in Daley Plaza, with Jesse Jackson, singing *We Shall Overcome*, and holding hands. I remember a few of them saying, "My father would roll over in his grave if he could see me now." At the same time, an awful lot of guys who crossed the picket line were black. If a guy is a scab and a black, the animosity is heavier.

We came up with our first contract. It was a good one. It truly got us off our knees. It gave us a lot of things we never had before. Prior to that, they could transfer us, they could promote anybody they pleased, there was no seniority, we didn't have any rights at all. The strike made us a union.

Before that, we were a white social club. Right after the strike, we had a black guy who was an ordained minister and very astute. We gave him the title Affirmative Action Officer. It was written in our contract: Affirmative Action. A lot of white guys really resented it. "Well, that's it for me. I'm never going to be promoted." To tell you the truth, I felt a lot of resentment, too. I felt they were getting preferential treatment over me. That may or may not be valid, but that's how I felt back then. But even a lot of hard-line guys would have to admit today that we got a lot of good black firemen.

In '76, the first black firemen who came in were really outsiders. The busier the company, the more exclusively white it was. Those were the most desirable places to be. In a slow house, the day went by like you were in prison. The busier the company, the higher the morale, the closer the guys were. Nobody wanted any outsider there. This was a family.

After '76, '77, a lot of black firemen started getting assignments in the busy companies. Like or not, the guys had to live with them. They found they could actually work with them, get along with them, like them. When you put the same bunch of guys in a slow house, where they got on each other's nerves because there was no work to do, you had a whole different situation. The harder they worked, the better they got along. Before you know it, you're at parties. I was at a party Saturday night. It was about as racially mixed as you can imagine. Guys and their families. If this isn't an indication how far we've come, I don't know what is.

A black chief might have it in for a company officer, who happens to be white. The black firemen will defend him against the chief, because they have this sense of family.

An old black fireman told me that he was once detailed to a company in Bridgeport.* At a fire, he had to do his work on the front porch. The white firemen would not let him in the house, plus the residents wouldn't let him in. You just didn't do that in Bridgeport. Times have changed a lot.

There's reverse racism, too. A five-man company, mixed, got a mannikin out of the store window that burned. A couple of the firemen, one white and one black, got a hold of a white hat and dressed the mannikin up as a chief and put him in the firehouse window. The mannikin was nondescript. It wasn't black, but it was smoke-damaged, which meant it was darkened. The firemen put it in the window as a joke, just to stand there as a dummy chief. Actually they did it to harass the white chief. This black officer came driving by; he spotted the mannikin in the window and he took it as a racial insult. He ordered the firemen to take it out and made a big deal out of it. He accused the guys of racism. They said, "Race has nothing to do with it; it's a firehouse joke." This guy was supersensitive to everything he sees. He's seeing shadows that aren't there, ghosts under the table.

Since I've come to the job, half our officer corps is black. No matter how you cut it, attitudes bleed down from the top. When the guy before was commissioner, it was a racist fire department.

There was a black fireman in our company, a great guy named Smith. He's now a captain. We called him Blacksmith. [*Laughs.*] As opposed to a

---

* A blue-collar neighborhood, where many white city employees live. Blacks are not welcome.

white fireman in the house who was also named Smith. We never called him Whitesmith.

A lot of old-line firemen will resent a black guy if he comes in with a Muslim name. Right away, they'll brand him a radical, a black activist. Yet a black activist on this job can be a real strong union guy and win everybody over. He might be president of the Afro-American Firefighters Association and at the same time be a real strong union steward. He will have won the respect of the guys. Or if he's a good fireman. It's an individual type of thing. A man-to-man thing. My job isn't to fight fires. It's to run out there in the ambulance and pick them up when they fall down. We work hand in hand with the firemen. A lot of times our jobs cross over.

Affirmative action has never hurt me on this job. I think it might have hurt me coming onto the job. I wanted to be a fireman. But in the long run it did me a favor. It gave me a job I was more suited for. Being a paramedic was far better for me than fighting fires.

There were a lot of affirmative-action promotions, no question about it. A lot were promoted out of order. Almost every case, it was promoting black guys. Most of the Hispanic guys stood up on their own. We got some real good officers out of the deal and we got some duds. If it was a white guy, you'd say, "How did that moron get promoted?" If it was a black, you'd shrug your shoulders and go, "Yeah, well, what do you expect? It's affirmative action."

I think the time of affirmative action has come and gone. I've seen some really good people passed over because of it. Unfairly. People behind them got promoted. The people that got promoted were qualified, but didn't land as high on the list as the two people that were passed over. I think affirmative action is going to perpetuate the kind of bigotry that says, "I told you so." It's doing more harm than good.

I know black guys who are really terrific. At the same time, I've worked in the ghettos of this town and I've seen the so-called underclass. It makes me wonder. I think it's more of a cultural thing than racial.

In Uptown, you're dealing with another underclass that happens to be white. I don't see the difference in them. They're in the same kind of poverty cycle as the poor blacks in Lawndale.*

I've never been uncomfortable with a guy because he's black. I didn't really have the pre— [*Pause.*] Let's face it, we all have prejudices. I grew up in the forties and early fifties, and there were attitudes, given me

---

* A community of poor blacks on the city's West Side.

through the news media and everything else, of preconceived notions about blacks. Prejudice is one of the easiest things to slip into.

It's there between Hispanics and blacks in the department. There's no oneness of kinship between them, as you might expect. Between Hispanics and whites, there is less animosity.

The old-line firemen, the rockheads whose minds are not going to change, have gone off the job. We've got a much younger generation of firemen now. We have a whole bunch of Vietnam veterans, who served next to the black guys in the bush, lived in close quarters with them. Plus we've got a lot of children here of the sixties, that witnessed the civil-rights movement, the stuff on the streets. That's changed people. We call the old-timers dinosaurs.

How did I get this way? My father was pretty much of a lover of literature and culture. And stories, he would tell stories from work. He was a linotype operator, wound up as a proofreader. He also worked in the slaughterhouses. He liked blacks as much as any guy of his generation could. I don't think my dad ever had a bad experience with blacks. It was his attitude that carried me more than anybody else: "Hey, give a guy an even break, I don't care who he is."

I had a couple of racial experiences. I dropped out of high school and wound up in a drop-out school, a tough place. Not too many choir brats. I went down the basement to smoke. It was all black guys down there. One guy was entertaining them with stories. I sat on the bench. He walked over and said, "Get out of here." Nobody was going to throw me out. So we wound up hauling off. I ran out because I was outnumbered. Came back with a bunch of white guys. We had a race riot on our hands. But it never went beyond that room. It ended right there. A standoff.

We used to ride the El like it was our private limousine. You get off into different neighborhoods. There'd be three of us and three of them. If there were three Italian kids, we'd get into it with them. We'd antagonize each other because we were different. I was never burnt that deeply by it.

Is the gap getting any wider? I wonder. I see a lot of reverse racism. Naturally I'm going to be more sensitive to a black guy who's a racist, because I'm going to be the target of his racism. I've seen it in subtle ways. It's not something you can put your finger on. You feel it. You know it right away.

In a black neighborhood, I'm an outsider. A young gangster was shot over at Cabrini-Green. Somebody ran out of the projects, put a .45 to his head, killed him, and kept on running. Here we are: police, paramedics, reporters. We're gathered around where the kid is laying in the middle of the area with lights on him from the building. Here's a guy, dead, in all his accoutrements: eighty-dollar Reeboks, his jacket, all the stuff he wears for status. There's no question we feel like the outsider. Here's a semicircle of all white faces. I said to myself, "Doesn't this look like an occupying army?"

When you tell a person you can't take him to the hospital, he'll say, "If I was white, you could." Which isn't true. It's hard not to take hate personally. You feel it all the time. That's why I can sympathize with a guy if he's black. He's always felt that animosity toward him. I can see how he can become pretty darn sensitive to it, oversensitive in some cases, when it's not even there.

It's understandable. I'm driving with my nine-year-old boy. Here's a black guy crossing the street. A street-looking guy. He breaks into a fast run to make the traffic, and my nine-year-old says, "Looks like he's running from the police." I hit the ceiling. I said, "Where the hell did you get a racist comment like that? What made you say that?" He said, "Oh, I don't know." I said, "Well, you better rearrange your attitude." Maybe it was me that was oversensitive. Maybe the kid would have said it if it was a street-looking-type *white* guy. Maybe I came down on the kid too hard. If the guy was dressed in a business suit, were he white or black, would the kid have said he was running from the police?

When I worked in Uptown, there were different pockets of poverty. One building was all-black, another was all-white, and next to it were nothing but North American Indians. You know how poverty breeds a terrible savagery. It eliminates so many of the conscious things that control your behavior. Let's face it, there's a lot more black poverty in this city than there is white. I don't want to come off too much as a bleeding-heart liberal type. I can be pretty damn reactionary about a lot of things. But I got to blame a lot of this stuff, when I see brutal murders and things like that, on the resentment of poverty. Lashing out. It's a violent culture.

You walk up a flight of stairs and here's a guy stabbed to death. Looks like a slaughtered animal. In the front hall. There's a party going on full blast behind the half-opened door. Never broke its stride. You knock on the door and say, "Anybody know what happened?" "Yeah. He was stabbed." "Anybody see it?" "Nah. I don't know who stabbed him." It boggles your mind.

I once walked into an apartment in Uptown and found an old black man chained to a radiator by his niece. The old guy's arm is blistered. He's helpless. She handcuffed him there. I think to myself, "Wow, this is an atrocity. Would I ever see this in a white's house?" That's my automatic reaction.

I saw a black guy eviscerated by his nephew for the same reason. He wanted the old man's money. What kind of savagery is this? That's the word I used. You think of the savage in Africa, someone nonwhite. You don't think of white people as savages. If these were white faces, you'd take it more personally. Black faces are easier to keep alien. Have I seen this savagery among my people? Certainly. Can it happen there? Are you kidding? It can and it does.

It's easy to fight a war in Asia, but, geez, it's tough to fight one where the enemy is white, where they look like your brothers and sisters. It's easy to napalm an Asian village, but think about it if were those white babies getting burned up.

At the same time, I've delivered black babies and felt as much joy as I did in delivering white babies. A lot of time, you'll use race to get in the way of your feelings. You allow it to become a buffer to your feeling, so you don't identify with what's happening in front of you. This is not happening in your world, it's in *their* world. I've seen the same thing among Appalachians in Uptown. But again, these aren't my people. They're fourth-class.

There's hostility against any white authority figure in the projects. It's not necessarily racial. Sometimes a black in uniform will get an even worse attitude, because he's being a white-man's nigger. It's not a question of everybody in those buildings having a chip on their shoulder. Most people there are struggling to make it, good people.

Younger guys are more apt to have a chip on their shoulders. It's strange, because the older guys have borne the brunt of bigotry and prejudice. They were the guys who were really in the forefront of the battle, not these younger kids. They've got every right to bear a grudge. I'm not saying that they don't. Then, too, older men and women are more dependent on medical care. A young guy feels he's never goin' to die.

It's not easy.

I was shot once with a pellet gun, just for no reason. I was standing in the doorway of the ambulance, we had a patient in the back. Wasn't enough power to hurt me. I heard it coming. Sssping! I've been shot at a lot of times going in the projects. We're an occupying army. Almost every face they see out there is white. We've got a lot of black paramedics but they don't want to work in the ghetto, either.

It's dangerous, you feel the hate, the resentment. I'm going to be angry if somebody assaults me. When it happens, I want to punch back. I'm going to be angry if they make me afraid. It's fear and loathing. They go together.

Is it racially directed anger? Do I get angry at everybody who's black?

Nah. I'll get angry at that individual. It's hard to describe my racial feelings. After a while, in dealing with all kinds of different people in this city, even the most reactionary racist mellows out. They begin to see the good and bad in everybody. If they don't, they're not going to last long. They're going to get pretty crazy after a while.

Hatred is more of a burden than it is a luxury. It hurts the hater more than the other. They can't bend, they can't give. Sometimes I think it's more directed at themselves than it is outside. They can't see it. I know a lot of guys like that.

I know another guy, who was a racist. To hear him talk, you would think he was God. West Side Irish. He wound up with a black partner, working a tough black ghetto. After he worked with this guy for a couple of months, they turned out to be the best of friends. You go over to his house and you see these three little kids, who look like Belfast warriors. They're climbing all over this big black guy. I laugh when I call him on this. He says, "Oh, Chuck is different. He's not like the rest of the blacks out there." "How's he different?" "He's Chuck." His attitudes are challenged and are changing.

Not just in the fire department, but all over the place, attitudes are getting chipped away. Guys who were hard-line find themselves pretty much confused. We still have a long way to go, but I think we've come a real long way. I'm optimistic. I have to be. I have two little kids growing up, and two grown.

My oldest son travels around town a lot, and he's been attacked by black kids on the subway. He's not worried about a racial attack. He's afraid of the crazed junkie who needs to make his bones for that day. He's worried about a crazed, violent type of thing that's going to hurt him. He knows where to go and where not to go. I tell him you have to survive in this town, but if you do it with hate, you're going to be in pretty bad shape.

We can't help but make progress. We can't go back. I don't think Reagan or Bush—who is more concerned whether the American flag gets burned than if some guy can pay his kid's tuition—I don't think they're going to have any impact in the long run. We're not that dumb. The ball's gonna continue to roll. I've seen it rolling in the firehouse.

PART III

Occurrence in Durham

C. P. ELLIS

The year is 1978.

We're in his office in Durham, North Carolina. He is business manager of the International Union of Operating Engineers. On the wall is a plaque: "Certificate of Service, in recognition to C. P. Ellis for your faithful service to the city in having served as a member of the Human Relations Council, February, 1977."

At one time, he had been Exalted Cyclops of the Durham chapter of the Ku Klux Klan.

He is fifty-three years old.

My father worked in a textile mill in Durham. He died at forty-eight years old. It was probably from cotton dust. Back then, we never heard of brown lung. I was seventeen years old and had a mother and sister depending on somebody to make a livin'. It was just barely enough insurance to cover his burial. I had to quit school and go to work. I was about eighth grade when I quit.

He recounts his daily humiliations at school because of his raggedy clothes; his sense of shame; his love for his father, who took him to ballgames and "fishin'," who deprived himself of the barest of amenities for his boy's sake, who "got plastered on weekends because he worked so hard and he'd done the best he could the entire week and there seemed to be no hope."

He remembers his early workdays, pumping gas, running a bread route, raising four children, one blind and retarded, "I hug his neck, tell him I love him, I don't know whether he knows me or not, but I know he's well taken care of."

I worked my butt off and never seemed to break even. They say to abide by the law, do right and live for the Lord, and everything'll work out. It just kept getting worse and worse.

I will never forget: outside our house—rent, forty-eight dollars a month, way more than half my weekly wages—there was a 265-gallon oil drum. What I would do every night, I would run up to the store and buy five gallons of oil and climb up the ladder and pour it in that 265-gallon drum. I could hear that five gallons when it hit the bottom of that oil drum, splatters, and it sounds like it's nothin' in there. But it would keep the house warm for the night. Next day you'd have to do the same thing.

I began to say there's somethin' wrong with this country. I really began to get bitter. I tried to find somebody. I began to blame it on black people. I had to hate somebody. Hatin' America is hard to do because you can't see it to hate it. You gotta have somethin' to look at to hate. [*Laughs.*] The natural person for me to hate would be black people, because my father before me was a member of the Klan. As far as he was concerned, it was the savior of the white people. It was the only organization that would take care of the white people. So I began to admire the Klan.

The first night I went with the fellas, they knocked on the door and gave the signal. They sent some robed Klansmen to talk to me and give me some instructions. I was led into a large meeting room and this was the time of my life! It was thrilling. Here's a guy who's worked hard all his life and struggled all his life to be something, and here's the moment to be something. I will never forget it. Four robed Klansmen led me into the hall. The light were dim and all you could see was an illuminated cross. I knelt before the cross. I had to make certain vows and promises. We promised to uphold the purity of the white race, fight communism, and protect white womanhood.

After I had taken my oath, there was loud applause goin' through the buildin', musta been at least four hundred people. It was a thrilling moment for C. P. Ellis.

The majority of 'em are low-income whites, people who don't really have a part in something. They have been shut out as well as the blacks. Some are not very well-educated either. Just like myself. We had a lot of support from doctors and lawyers and police officers.

I can understand why people join extreme right-wing or left-wing groups. They're in the same boat I was in. Shut out. Deep down inside, we want to be part of this great society. Nobody listens, so we join these groups.

He tells of recruiting young people, "teachin' the principles of the Klan. When they came in the door, we had 'Dixie' playin' and they were just thrilled to death.

"I had a call one night from one of our kids. He was about twelve. He said, 'I just been robbed downtown by two niggers.' I'd had a couple of drinks and that really teed me off. I go downtown and I saw two young black people. I said, 'Nigger, you seen a little white boy up here? I just got a call from him and was told some niggers robbed him of fifteen cents.' I pulled my .32 out and put it right at his head. I said, 'I always wanted to kill a nigger and I think I will make you the first one.' I nearly scared the kid to death and he struck off."

This was the time when the civil-rights movement was really beginnin' to peak. The blacks were beginnin' to demonstrate and picket downtown stores. I will never forget some black lady I hated with a purple passion. Ann Atwater. Every time I'd go downtown, she'd be leading a boycott. How I hated—pardon the expression, I don't use it now—how I just hated that black nigger. Big, fat heavy woman. She'd pull about eight demonstrations, and first thing you know they had two, three blacks at the checkout counter. Her and I had some pretty close confrontations.

We'd go to the city-council meetings, and the blacks would be there and we'd be there. It was a confrontation every time. I didn't hold back anything. The councilmen and county commissioners began to call us at night on the telephone. "C. P., glad you came to that meeting last night." We visited the city leaders in their homes and talked to 'em privately. It wasn't long before they would call me up. "The blacks are comin' up tonight and makin' outrageous demands. How about some of you people showin' up?"

We'd load up our cars and we'd fill up half the council chambers, and the blacks the other half. During these times, I carried weapons, outside my belt. We would wind up just hollerin' and fussin' at each other. As a result of our fightin' one another, the city council still had their way. They didn't want to give up control to the blacks *nor* the Klan. They were usin' us.

I began to realize this later down the road. One day I was walkin' downtown and a certain city-council member saw me comin'. I expected him to shake my hand, because he was talking to me at night on the telephone. I had been in his home and visited him. He crossed the street. Oh shit, I began to think, somethin's wrong here. Most of 'em are merchants, maybe an attorney, an insurance agent, people like that. As long as they kept low-income whites and low-income blacks fightin', they're gonna maintain control.

I began to get that feeling after I was ignored in public. I thought: Bullshit, you're not gonna use me anymore. That's when I began to do some really serious thinkin'.

I spent a lot of sleepless nights. I still didn't like blacks. I didn't want to associate with 'em. I didn't, until I met a black person and talked to him eyeball to eyeball. Or a Jewish person. I found out they're people just like me. They cried, they cussed, they prayed, they had desires. Just like myself. Thank God, I got to the point where I can look past labels. But at that time, my mind was closed.

, I remember one Monday-night Klan meeting. I said something was wrong. Our city fathers were using us. And I didn't like to be used. The reactions of the others were not too pleasant: "Let's just keep fightin' them niggers."

I'd go home at night and I'd have to wrestle with myself. I'd look at a black person walkin' down the street, and the guy'd have ragged shoes or his clothes would be worn. That began to do somethin' to me inside. I went through this for about six months. I felt I just had to get out of the Klan. But I wouldn't get out.

He recounts a turning-point: an HEW grant of $78,000 to the state AFL-CIO, to help solve racial problems in the schools. A meeting was called of blacks, whites, liberals, conservatives, Klansmen, NAACP people. "I said, 'No way am I comin' with all those niggers.' A White Citizens Council guy says, 'Let's go, it's tax money bein' spent.' I walk in the door and I knew most of 'em by face, 'cause I seen 'em demonstratin' around town. Ann Atwater was there. [Laughs.] I just forced myself to go in and sit down."

The meeting was moderated by a great big black guy, but he was very nice. He said, "I want you all to feel free to say anything you want to say." Some of the blacks stand up and say it's white racism. I took all I could take. I asked for the floor and cut loose. I said, "No, sir, it's black racism. If we didn't have niggers in the schools, we wouldn't have the problems we got today."

I will never forget. Howard Clement, a black guy, stood up. He said,

"I'm certainly glad C. P. Ellis come, because he's the most honest man here tonight." I thought, "What's that nigger tryin' to do?" [*Laughs*.] At the end of that meeting, some blacks tried to come up and shake my hand, but I wouldn't do it. I walked off.

He continues: On the second night, it was easier; things were off his chest. On the third night, he is astonished that a black man suggests Ellis and Ann Atwater as cochairs of the key committee. "I thought to myself, 'Hey, there ain't no way I can work with that gal.' Finally, I agreed to accept it, 'cause at this point I was tired of fightin'."

How could I work with Ann Atwater? It was impossible. But it was in our hands. We had to make it a success. This gave me another sense of belongin', a sense of pride. Here's a chance for a low-income white man to be somethin'. Her and I began to reluctantly work together. [*Laughs*.] She had as many problems workin' with me as I had workin' with her.

One night I called her: "Ann, you and I should have a lot of differences and we got 'em now. But there's somethin' laid out here before us, and if it's gonna be a success, you and I are gonna have to make it one. Can we lay aside some of these feelin's?" She said, "I'm willing if you are." I said, "Let's do it."

My old friends would call me at night: "C. P., what the hell is wrong with you? You're sellin' out the white race." This began to make me have guilty feelin's. Here I am all of a sudden makin' an about-face and tryin' to deal with my feelin's, my heart. My mind was beginnin' to open up. I was beginnin' to see what was right and what was wrong. I don't want the kids to fight forever.

During this time, he had been doing maintenance work at Duke University. The president, Terry Sanford, gave him ten days off with pay, recognizing the importance of this venture. There were days and nights of knocking on doors, with little positive response. He was rebuffed by whites; she, by blacks. This odd coupling was too much for most others to take.

One day, Ann and I just sat down and began to reflect. Ann said, "My daughter came home cryin' every day. She said her teacher was makin' fun of her in front of the other kids." I said, "Boy, same thing happened to my kid. White liberal teacher was makin' fun of Tim Ellis's father, the Klansman, in front of other peoples. He came home cryin'." At this point—[*He pauses, swallows hard, stifles a sob.*]—I begin to see, here we are, two people from the far ends of the fence, havin' identical problems, except her bein' black and me bein' white. From that moment on, I tell ya, that gal and I worked together good. I begin to love the girl, really. [*He weeps.*]

The amazing thing about it, her and I, up to that point, had cussed each other, bawled at each other, hated each other. Up to that point, we didn't know each other. We didn't know we had things in common.

We worked at it with the people who came to these meetings. They talked about racism, sex education, about teachers not bein' qualified. After seven, eight nights of real intense discussion, these people who had never talked to each other before, all of a sudden came up with resolutions. It was really somethin', you had to be there to get the tone and feelin' of it.

I still didn't like integration, but the law says you gotta do this and I've gotta do what the law says, okay? The most disheartening thing was the school system refused to implement our resolutions. So I decided to run for school board.

I spent eighty-five dollars on the campaign. The guy runnin' against me spent several thousand. I really had nobody on my side. The Klan turned against me. The low-income whites turned against me. The liberals didn't particularly like me. The blacks were suspicious of me. The blacks wanted to support me, but they couldn't muster up enough to support a Klansman on the school board. [*Laughs.*] But I made up my mind that what I was doin' was right, and I was gonna do it regardless what anybody said.

I was invited to the Democratic women's social hour as a candidate. Didn't have but one suit to my name. Had it six, seven, eight years. I had it cleaned, put on the best shirt I had and a tie. Here were all these high-class wealthy candidates shakin' hands. I walked up to the mayor and stuck out my hand. He gave me that handshake with that rag type of hand. He said, "C. P., I'm glad to see you." But I could tell by his handshake he was lyin' to me. This was botherin' me. I know I'm a low-income person. I know they were sayin', "What's this little dude runnin' for the school board?" Yet they had to smile and make like they were glad to see me. I begin to spot some black people in that room. I automatically went to 'em and that was a firm handshake. They said, "I'm glad to see you, C. P." I knew they meant it— you can tell about a handshake.

I got 4,640 votes. The guy beat me by 2,000. Not bad for eighty-five bucks and no constituency.

The whole world was openin' up. I was learnin' new truths that I had never learned before. I was beginnin' to look at a black person, shake hands with him, and see him as a human bein'. I hadn't got rid of all this stuff.

I've still got a little bit of it. But somethin' was happenin' to me. It was almost like bein' born again. It was a new life. I didn't have these sleepless nights I used to have when I was active in the Klan and slippin' around at night. I could sleep at night and feel good about it. I'd rather live now than at any time in history. It's a challenge.

He worked mornings at Duke and attended high school in the afternoon. "I was the only white in class and the oldest by far." He studied biology, "took the books home at night, and sure enough I graduated. I got the diploma at home."

A union was being organized at work. "I wasn't pro-union. My daddy was antilabor, too. But we were workin' seven days in a row, starvin' to death." In recruiting for the union, he discovered "I knew how to organize, how to stir people up." [Laughs.] The result was an overwhelming union victory. He was elected chief steward and appointed business agent.

When I began to organize, I began to see far deeper. I began to see people again bein' used. Blacks against whites. I say this without hesitancy: management is vicious. There's two things they want to keep: all the money and all the say-so. They don't want these poor workin' folks to have any of that. I begin to see management fightin' me with everything they had. Hire anti-union law firms, bad-mouth unions. I worked as business rep for five years and was seein' all this.

Last year I ran for business manager of the union. He's elected by the workers. The guy who ran against me was black and the membership was seventy percent black. I thought: Claiborne, there's no way you can beat that black guy. People know your background. Even though you've made tremendous strides, those black people are not gonna vote for you.

The company used my past against me. They put out pictures with a robe and a cap: Would you vote for a Klansman? They wouldn't deal with the issues. I immediately called for a mass meeting. I said, "Okay, this is Claiborne Ellis. This is where I come from. I want you to know, you black ladies here. I was at one time a member of the Klan. I want you to know because they'll tell you about it."

I invited some of my old black friends. Howard Clement kidded me a little bit. "I don't know what I'm doin' here, supporting an ex-Klansman." [*Laughs.*] He said, "I know where C. P. Ellis come from. I knew as he grew and growed with him. I'm tellin' you now, Follow, follow this Klansman." [*He pauses, swallows hard.*] "Any questions?" "No," the black ladies said. "Let's get on with the meeting, we need

Ellis." [*He laughs and weeps.*] Boy, black people sayin' that about me. I won, 134 to 41. Four to one.

It makes you feel good to go into a plant and butt heads with professional union-busters. You see black people and white people join hands to defeat the racist issues they use against people. Can you imagine a guy who's got an adult-high-school diploma runnin' into professional college graduates who are union-busters? I work seven days a week, nights and on Saturday and Sunday. The salary's not great, but I can't quit. I got a taste of it. [*Laughs.*]

I tell people there's a tremendous possibility to stop wars, the battles, the struggles, the fights between people. People say, "That's an impossible dream. You sound like Martin Luther King." An ex-Klansman who sounds like Martin Luther King! [*Laughs.*] I don't think it's an impossible dream. It's happened in my life. It's happened in other people's lives in America.

When the news came over the radio that Martin Luther King was assassinated, I got on the telephone and began to call other Klansmen. We just had a real party at the service station. Really rejoicin' 'cause that sonofabitch was dead. Our troubles are over with. They say the older you get, the harder it is for you to change. That's not necessarily true. Since I changed, I've set down and listened to tapes of Martin Luther King. I listen to it and tears come to my eyes, 'cause I know what he's sayin' now. I know what's happenin'.

The phone rings. A conversation. "This was a black guy who's director of Operation Breakthrough in Durham. I had called his office. I'm interested in employin' some young black person, who's interested in learnin' the labor movement. I want someone who's never had an opportunity, like myself. Just so he can read and write, that's all."

1989
What worries me is that racism is getting worse. In the last ten years, the White House has been promoting it. It has become more open. There was a time when it was getting better, but these last two administrations have set it back. With Reagan and Bush, it's like a nod to say okay, try it again. And it's being tried.

I don't think anybody is born full of hate, born a racist. At the Democratic Convention, the cameras zoomed in on one Klansman. He was saying, "I hope Jesse Jackson gets AIDS and dies." I felt sympathy for him. That's the way my old friends used to think. Me, too. And my father.

After I left the Klan, I felt guilt, isolation, rejection. I wound up getting counseling. I was getting calls from former Klan friends, "You betrayed us." I began to question myself. But now at sixty-three, with this new light, I feel good about myself.

Sometimes I see my old Klan friends. Sometimes they speak to me, sometimes they don't. I don't worry about it. I wish them well; they're human beings. I think some of them changed a little bit.

But they're not willing to come out with it. They're afraid to change their own life because they're afraid of life. It would have been easier for me if I had gone on being a member of the Klan. It's been a struggle. Any change is.

My children have all changed along with me. They were with me when I was in the Klan and they painfully left with me. Now they feel the way I do. We used to say the word "nigger." Not anymore. When my oldest son came home with a black girl, I was shocked at first. It wasn't serious; he married somebody else. But when I met her, I felt like I was a great liberal. I don't like the word "liberal." I like the word "progressive."

Most of my friends in Durham are progressive, but there's an economic barrier. Their station is higher than mine. I don't feel comfortable in their homes. Sometimes I find myself standing in the corner in a social gathering and that ought not to be. But the black people in my union are progressive, too. I feel comfortable with them.

Companies fighting our union still bring up my Klan past. It thrills me when they do it, because it backfires on 'em every time. Cargill Grain tried it recently. My picture was put up on the company bulletin board: C. P. Ellis is not the kind of man you want as a leader. The workers just tore the picture off the wall and went back to work.

Our union, seventy-percent black and thirty-percent white, have negotiated one of the best contracts we ever had. One of the greatest satisfactions in my life was to see forty low-income black women negotiate and win. It's the first contract in Durham that had Martin Luther King's birthday as a paid holiday. The company at first said no, but we insisted. At the very last moment, they said okay. I wish you could have seen the faces of the black people light up. Some of the whites said, "We're not going to take Martin Luther King's birthday off." We said, "Okay, idiots, work." Of course, they didn't work. Of course, they took the day off with pay.

Some of my old friends are cautious around me and say "black" instead of the other word. They almost say it, but catch themselves and stop. I respect it and I'm glad they respect me that much. Maybe I expect something that's impossible. Maybe it'll never get settled, unless we sit down and listen to each other as individuals. Skinheads and blacks will find they have much in common. Jews and Arabs, too.

I have the same fundamental beliefs I've had for a long time. But it's hard to find a church out here that preaches the social gospel. I'm visiting churches now trying to find one. I believed Christ cared about poor people. That's something I learned after I left the Klan. I do a lot of riding, and I do most of my thinking on the road, when I'm on to my next meeting.

I think Christ was a god in the flesh. He cares about individuals, he cares about how we're treated. It's got to bother Him to see people hungry, to see people under the bridges, homeless, starving. I think if He came back today, he'd be extremely disappointed.

ANN ATWATER

Today she works for the Durham Housing Authority. "There are fourteen developments. I'm responsible for five. I organize them so people can come together and voice their opinions. Okay, if somebody needs furniture, I go out and get furniture. If somebody needs monies for rent, I go out and get that money. Clothing, food, whatever the problem is. Sometimes they have family squabbles. I just go in and counsel them. I'm like a social worker.

"My children are grown. They are of ages thirty-seven and thirty-three. And my grandchildren are comin' along. I worry about them, about their minds. I try to instill in them what education means. If you got education, you can get most any place you wanna get. Maybe not any place, but get that education. It's hard to pull them over here when their peers is pullin' 'em another way."

When I first met C. P. Ellis, he didn't want anything to do with niggers. I would always say, "Well, I don't want anything to do with crackers." We kept it up and kept it up going all through some of the nights. Cussing each other back, we couldn't get anything done. Just table it to a later date. The other black folks, middle-class, would sit there squirming, not really wantin' to cuss.

When a paper called and said I was named cochairman with C. P., I said, No, no. I laid in bed all that night, not sleepin'. The next mornin', I called back and told them yes, I would serve. I couldn't lay down and think the paper would print a headline: Blacks were scared of whites.

We decided to go out to dinner. Me and C. P. and Bill Rigg, the moderator. He was black. At the cafeteria, C. P. kept pacing up and down the floor. He didn't want to be seen sitting at the same table with two blacks.

With other white folks in the restaurant. They were scared to death. Two blacks and one white comin' in, and C. P. pacin' the floor, back and forth. He didn't want to sit down until we come to an agreement to order dinner.

After that, we started meetings. He brought his machine gun, showed he had it in the trunk of his car. He was afraid the blacks would jump him or beat up his children or somethin'. I had my weapon. I didn't leave it in the trunk of my car; I carried it in my hand. My little white Bible. I told him we would see which one was the strongest, God or the devil.

As the meetings started, attendance got low. We had to go out and recruit people. He was run away from the doors of white people, and black folks told me that I had sold out. We had teachers that I knew didn't want to have anything to do with me.

Several evenings we would have choirs come and sing to the meeting. And we would sing. C. P. heard an old hymn that was familiar to him. He would start pattin' his foot and then start clappin' his hands. and I said, "Oh-oh, we got 'im." We were singin' all the songs we knew. C. P. had his old song book and he wanted us to sing something he could sing along with us. He was meltin' down and meddlin' in, and I thought to myself, "He's comin' on over." At the end, old C. P. was in it as much as we was.

The thing that really got him turned around—On the wall, he had his display of Klan material. There were about fifteen or twenty black youth who wanted to rip it apart. I told them what they should do is read it so they could understand what the Klan was about. They could peep at the Klan's hole card. By saving his material, he found out that I didn't hate him at all.

I had laid my Bible on the table and white youth had wanted to strip my Bible apart. If C. P. was there, I believe he would have stopped them, because that was my wealth. I felt that was his Bible, too. At that time, the Klan material was what he believed in. And I didn't want that torn apart.

Saving his material, singing the Christian songs, this sorta mowed him back. He wanted to know more about the Lord. And a bunch of white guys, friends, started carrying him every Wednesday to prayer service and the ball started rollin'.

One evening I got home from work, there were Klansmen marching up and down, right upon the ditch bank where I live. I said, "If you step down by my house, you see my childrens there, I would blow your head off." But they never bothered, just that one time. I was just frightened to go out, didn't want anybody know I was working with a Klansman who hated blacks. I guess these Klansmen was tryin' to stop me, they musta knowed somethin'.

My oldest daughter was having problems in school. My child couldn't come into school late, they would always send her home. But the doctor's daughter could come late, they would send her right into class. Me being low-income, I would attend PTA meetings and they wouldn't pay me no never-mind. They counted me as a nobody, the same way they did C. P. and his family. I did day work, domestic work.

My baby girl at the school, she would defend herself. They would fight and carry on. Not too many children would play with her, because their parents would tell them that I was out there with a Klansman. That I was no good and had sold out. I had to go there and reset the stage for them and tell them if it wasn't for me leadin' the picket line all that time, fighting for 'em, they couldn't get jobs. I pointed out to them that education is the most important thing they should have and this is why I was out there with somebody like C. P. He wanted the same thing for his children.

He was tellin' me about what happened to his kid in school and I said that's the same thing happenin' to my child. We started off from there and just kept workin' together. His wife has grown turnip salad and brought baskets of food by the house because we didn't have any green vegetables. They had a garden and would bring me stuff so they called him a nigger-lover. And the blacks called me a sell-out.

It's been over ten years, and I'm somewhat regarded in the community. But I'm still low man on the totem pole. They only call me when there's an issue and they need someone to go out there and speak. I've got a lot of medical problems and I pay most of my money to the doctors.

In these ten years, we've come an inch. We still have a long ways to go. Once they got a job, they forgot to reach back and pick up the other low-income people. Some of them got off in their ivory towers and stayed there. I feel we need to shake their minds up, to let them know where we come from, and where we have to go. I'm talking about the black community.

As for white and black, sometimes they work a little closer but you will still find some talk one way and act another. I think I accept white people more now than they accept me. Oh, there's been a change in me like the change in C. P. I used not to talk to any white people, now I talk to any of them. I would pass them on the street, they would speak at me and I wouldn't say a word. I don't know if I was afraid 'cause I was taught that white was superior. But after I learned, the change was there.

Now I speak and ask them if I need information. I go in the store and if the clerk's slow, I call it to their attention. I used to walk in the store and walk out, 'cause I felt they didn't wanna wait on me. Now if I go somewhere, if I'm right and they're wrong, I argue the point. I don't find nobody else, I do it myself.

There was a time I stayed in my community, teachin' black folks how to get things done, problems solved. I very seldom went to the whites. The only time I would go before whites was the city council.

Where before, if a white person would tell me today is Tuesday, I'd say no, it's not. I didn't believe 'em. I'd look on the calendar to make sure this is Tuesday. Now I can call 'em up and talk. I have several white friends I can call on right now. That's the same thing with C. P. He trusts blacks.

Once in a while, when we get together, we talk about other things. We don't go back and rehash. But then, neither one of us had nothing no more than what we had to work hard to get. He was cleanin' commodes and I was cleanin' babies, baby-sittin'. We was cleanin' the same thing. I was living in a house that was leanin' toward the street. The boards were broken in the floor and the water would shoot up in the bathroom. My kids would call it Niagara Falls. The commode would face the street. The door would come open and people would see you on the john. It wasn't until later I learned through this school experience that I could go to the landlord and demand that my house be fixed. I would always tell everyone that was the only house that was welcome and open to the people on the street. You could stomp the floor and the lights would come on. It was just that ragged a house. Now I'm tryin' to buy my own home. I say we come a long ways.

When I first met C. P., he told me he wasn't educated. I wasn't either. I had tenth-grade education and I went back and got my GED. When you don't have education, they call it the motherwit. I think that was what did it. If C. P. could step over on the side of the Lord, we two could win the battle. I think he was realizin' what he was for would only destroy him. Even though I was told I had sold out, I had the Lord to look forward to in this battle.

I had to go back and pray and read Scripture to keep my mental stability. That was the only thing that held me together. There were some nights of cryin', scared to death, worried about my children. But I held it in. At the end, C. P. and I could lock hands and say we won.

I don't know of anything that could change us from being friends. The other thing is—C. P. would never shake my hand. Now we don't shake hands. We hug and embrace.

HOWARD CLEMENT

He is fifty-six, one of Durham's most prominent black citizens; a top executive of the North Carolina Mutual Life Insurance Company, "the largest black financial institution in the world. My family has been with it since 1906.

"My grandfather, on his deathbed, made me promise never to leave this company, which he had served for almost fifty years. I have been here since 1961."

He has been married thirty years and has three daughters.

I grew up in Charleston, South Carolina. Though it was a thoroughly segregated society, I never suffered as a consequence. My parents had so sheltered us that we knew where we were supposed to go and didn't think of going anyplace else.

My brother and I had to daily pass the white high school. We took the fights for granted, boys being boys. There was no communication between the two schools. I knew my place and never transgressed, nor had any inclination to. I took ROTC and went into the Army and all that . . .

I really didn't know what it was to be poor. My father sent my brother and me to college. The finest schools, we think. He sent me through law school and my brother through architectural school. He is now chief engineer for the state of South Carolina.

I went to an all-black high school and to Howard University that was at the time ninety-nine-percent black. I attended Harvard Law School.

My activity in protest movements had been limited. During my senior year in law school, the spring of 1960, I took part in a sit-in in Washington. It was more of a symbolic gesture, in sympathy with the Greensboro sit-ins. This was just six years after *Brown versus Board of Education*. I went down to the Supreme Court and saw Thurgood Marshall argue the Little Rock case. We had to stand outside almost six hours to get in.

I was arrested in the downtown demonstration. My parents were very upset, my mother in particular. Why did I need to get involved? My father didn't think I was using good judgment. "You've just jeopardized your standing before the South Carolina bar. If you think they're going to admit you, you're a fool."

I appeared before the Committee on Character and Fitness. It was thirty years ago but I remember it as though it were yesterday. The chairman was an old southern aristocrat. He questioned me about my involvement. He said, "Boy"—of course I saw red but kept my mouth shut—"if you hadn't done that, you wouldn't be fit to practice law in South Carolina." I was shocked. I was sure I'd be disqualified. I was the second black in the history of South Carolina to pass the bar on his first try.

It wasn't until 1963 that something told me to join the March on Washington. It was August 28, I think. We boarded a bus four o'clock in the morning. I was the only employee of my company to go. The management frowned on its people becoming involved in controversial activities. My wife was frightened. She didn't know what to expect, but I was determined to go.

I was about two arm's lengths away from Martin Luther King. Mahalia Jackson stood in front of me. Though my father was very critical, it opened my eyes to a lot of things going on in Durham. The poverty, the employment discrimination, the poor housing, the many wrongs. I got involved. The papers described me as a militant black activist.

My father threatened to disinherit me if I didn't cease and desist from my foolish activity. He had wanted me to stay in Charleston, practice law, and look after our considerable property. I made a lot of white people angry, too, one of whom was C. P. Ellis.

In the sixties, Durham was evolving into a more open community. Black people were being elected to public office for the first time. In '74, I became chairman of the local Democratic Party. My father, who himself had run for Congress against Mendel Rivers, had switched to the Republican Party. He suggested that I switch, too.

The fact is I was becoming more conservative myself on some issues. I began to question: Why was I a Democrat? I don't see how they helped the black community improve its conditions. We were actually retrogressing. The Democrats talked a good game but they seldom delivered. They had us in a bag. In 1984, I switched to the Republicans.

That created quite a stir because at the time I was a member of the Durham City Council. Everybody figured my career had come to an end. It was a city of twenty-five Democrats to one Republican. I've run for election three times and have been successful each time.

In 1989, we elected our first black mayor, Chester Jenkins. I backed the conservative white, Strawbridge. Our slate was thrashed, except for me. The truth is, Jenkins didn't ask for my support. He did all he could to disavow any association with me. One newspaper put me to the right of Jesse Helms. Of course I openly supported Harvey Gantt against Helms.

I perceive myself as a moderate Republican. I favor affirmative action, though I have never supported it vocally. There's a bit of unfairness in it that Helms used to his advantage. I will never openly oppose affirmative action. I see it as a way to level the playing field, but there must be some other way. What it is, I don't know.

It's funny, isn't it? C. P. Ellis has become more liberal and I've become more conservative. I'll never forget that 1970 parents' meeting. When he got up and bitterly complained about his son's lack of educational opportunity, of bad housing, and no jobs for people like him, I remembered black people saying the exact same things.

I had sat down with them, in those neighborhoods, teaching these mothers how to express themselves when they went before the school board or the city council. I thought they should learn to speak for themselves. At first, they were too embarrassed because they didn't have the words. Three or four nights a week, I'd go down and meet with these mothers and their children. It was a real education for me.

I'll never forget one night at a housing project. A six-year-old boy, muddy and grimy, was pulling at my tie. His mother said, "Get away from Mr. Clement, you're messing up his tie." That night she called me up to apologize. "You're the first black man my son has ever seen with a shirt and tie on."

When C. P. Ellis, a poor white Klansman, got up with his litany of complaints, I was hearing all these black mothers. During his appearance at the city council, he was trying to get the black picketers off the streets. He called us scalawags. There he was in his overalls and dirty shoes and there I was in my three-piece suit, button-down shirt, and he was calling me trash. I had a negative opinion of him then. That was before I began to understand how things worked.

The white bankers, the power structure, never seen openly with C. P. Ellis, would be calling him at night, giving him money, telling him what to do. After we became friends, he confided in me. He started turning when the same people who called him at night would avoid him on the street. I would walk down the same street and shake hands with him. It confused him.

At that meeting, I said, "C. P., we're brothers." That statement hit the news like a fire hitting dry straw. My father read about it in the *Washington Post*. I had called a Klansman my brother! When he ran for Congress in '48, the Klan had done everything to frighten him. I'll never forget, I was fourteen at the time. They'd follow our cars, throw bricks through our window. My father had to sleep with a shotgun by his bed. Now I was calling a Kleagle of the Klan brother. A lot of my black friends thought I'd gone cuckoo, too. [*Chuckles.*] I feel now that was one of the best things I've ever done.

I'll never forget the expression on C. P.'s face. He was stunned. "What that nigger callin' me brother for?" [*A prolonged laugh.*] That episode drew us and Ann Atwater together. Ann has slowed down considerably. She has not been well. At that time, she was big, black, and bad. [*Laughs.*] She frightened everybody. C. P., too.

He was afraid to come to my house because he thought he wasn't good enough. "Man, Howard, I'm not dressed." He was going through this transformation. He had lost a lot of his white friends. He was being ostracized and feeling lonesome. They were calling him nigger-lover.

He invited me to speak on his behalf when he was running for business manager of the union. The members were mostly black. I happen to be anti-union in my sympathies, but I appeared on behalf of my friend, C. P. Ellis.

In my last campaign, he passed out my literature in outlying areas I had never been and helped me get elected. I'm afraid he's a little unhappy that I'm now a Republican.

I don't look on "conservatism" as a dirty word. I don't associate Jesse Helms with true conservatism. He's a reactionary, there's a difference. Those of us who've achieved a modicum of success have adopted the attitude of our white counterparts. We want to maintain and build on what we have achieved. At the same time, there's a class cleavage that's taken place. The not-so-fortunate are growing in numbers by leaps and bounds. Their economic situation is almost hopeless, especially among young black males.

For the past two years, I've been working in the black community, serving as a role model, I hope. The older black male may be the best role model for the younger ones.

I have not and will not divorce myself from the have-nots. I live within walking distance from a low-income housing project and refer to it as my neighborhood.

I do believe that self-help is going to be the order of the day. If we're going to save ourselves, we're going to have to help ourselves more. My company is a living demonstration of self-help. We shouldn't go with our hands out, depending on the white society to help us.

The black people need to invest more in our corporations and businesses. Not to establish a segregated thing, but as a matter of growth. The Jewish people did it. When I was in college, my father would always talk about what the Jewish community was doing. We need to invest in ourselves; it's a matter of survival. We'll have to deal with our own problems and emphasize discipline and self-respect. People say that's blaming the victim. I say it's reality.

I don't see the government in Washington as part of this. They've got problems of their own. I think it's going to take a public-private partnership. Of course I've been called an Uncle Tom, because I don't go along with the idea that the white man is wholly responsible for our ills.

I think George Bush is basically a good man. His veto of the Civil Rights Act of 1990 was ill-advised. He should have signed it. I don't condone his use of the Willie Horton case in the campaign. It was reprehensible, but I understand why he did it. This was his way of winning.

I think racism is more pervasive and rampant today than it was ten, fifteen years ago. It's much more subtle. Since Martin Luther King was killed, there hasn't been another leader who can articulate the sin of racism as well as he.

Look what's happening on the college campuses. My two oldest daughters graduated from the University of North Carolina. But my youngest doesn't want to go to a white campus. She ended up going to Hampton University in Virginia. It's a small private black school that my wife and grandfather attended. Better here than having to face the subtle hostilities of a white school.

Each of us is afflicted with a lot of contradictions. I don't apologize for mine. I think we really have to look at ourselves from a soulful posture and come to grips with where we are. We have to take a hard look at our community, and it starts with me as an individual. My colleagues of the black middle class have to come to some consensus. Where do we go from here? We cannot depend on the white community to do it for us.

■ ■ ■ ■ ■

Lawyer

GILBERT GORDON

He is an eighty-year-old lawyer. "I've been associated with blackness my entire professional career. I wrote the brief that outlawed racial covenants in the United States. I consider myself a liberal, probably radical. I've always, I thought, had an enlightened view of race. I've considered myself as being without prejudice. It's not true."

It is the most obsessive feature of American life. Every American, whether white or black, carries with him the consciousness of race, always, always. Everywhere you go, even where there are no blacks.

When the black riots took place in Chicago,* the whites as far away as Lincolnwood and Glencoe bought guns, though they had no contact with blacks.

It obsesses everybody, even those who think they are not obsessed by it. My wife was driving on a street in a black neighborhood. The people at the corners are all gesticulating at her. She was very frightened, quickly turned up the window and drove determinedly. She discovered, after several blocks, she was going the wrong way on a one-way street and they were trying to help her. Her assumption was that they were blacks and they were out to get her. Mind you, she's a very enlightened woman. You'd never associate her with racism, yet her first reaction was that they're dangerous.

There was a very black young man on the train, who was reading some copy. I looked over his shoulder and saw the phrase, "My father had eleven wives and loved each of them dearly." One word led to another. He was from Nigeria. We became friends. I realized that even though he was as dark as any American black I'd ever met, I was talking to him in a different way and he was talking to me in a different way than any of my black peers had ever talked to me.

I never thought of an American black as not being equal. I know too much about genetics and race and sociology. I'm too educated to believe that nonsense. But I've always had the *feeling* that he believed I was addressing him as a nonequal. I don't believe I was, but I'm convinced he thought I was.

A very dear friend, a black school teacher, in talking to us one day made a language slip. It was one of those common errors that American blacks make, the use of some words. The minute she said it, she quick corrected herself and looked at us just as though her slip was showing. I don't believe she would have reacted that way if we all were black.

My first knowledge of race came with a black family that lived across the street. They were the only ones in the neighborhood. Our next-door neighbor said if I play with "that nigger," I'm gonna turn black. I was about six or seven. I believed him. For several months I examined myself every day to see if I was really black. When I discovered I wasn't, I was very relieved.

Since the sixties, with the beginning of the black-consciousness movement, there has been a definite change. I have felt myself discriminated against by black clerks. In a line of many people, she will serve a black person before a white. I have felt more dislike from blacks than I

---

* The summer of 1968, following the assassination of Martin Luther King.

thought would have existed. An increase in hostility, without any question. I sense it in buses. In crowds, I'm more likely to be pushed by a black female than a white female.*

I got off at a wrong subway stop in New York. I was in Harlem, walking down the street, scared to death because it was one-hundred-percent black. A well-dressed black man, with a briefcase under his arm, came over to me and said, "Do you mind if we walk together? I think it will be safer for both of us." So arm in arm, we walked together. At my destination, we said goodbye. He felt he could be the subject of an attack, too. So we gained strength from each other. It was really a question of a class danger.

I'm not scared in Chatham or South Shore,† but I wouldn't advise anybody to walk the streets of Chicago at night alone. There's too much haphazard crime. I'm afraid that a lot of crime that middle-class blacks thought they were escaping accompanied them.

I represented black people who were being dispossessed by developers. A lot of them went further south and found conditions bad again. Wherever they went, the things that plagued them followed. For more than half a century, many of my clients have been working-class blacks, and some with a bit of property, not much by white standards. Some were middle-class as well as poor.

Some years ago, in the late fifties, the village I lived in, on the outskirts of Chicago, was experiencing its first black family. The house was bought under a pretext. They had a white friend buy it. No blacks were allowed to buy houses.

When the black family moved in, the mob came. A group of citizens, including my wife and me, provided coffee and sandwiches and cots and blankets for those who would stay the night with the beleaguered family. The mother was a graduate chemist and the father was a physicist, but it made no difference to the mob. The village manager was a real stand-up guy. He challenged the mob. The family stayed, the mob dispersed. (It so happens I was a candidate for one of the village offices in the forthcoming election. Needless to say, I was roundly defeated.)

It's the covenants and restrictions that caused these things. The idea that you can put together all the most unsuccessful people in our society

---

* In the twenties and thirties, the phrase "Push Day" was making the the rounds. It was the day, Thursday, as I remember, that "colored people" were reputed to have organized a campaign to jostle whites. I had assumed it was the theory of flat-worlders exclusively until I had heard it expressed in surprising quarters.

† Two middle-class black neighborhoods.

and expect anything but shit and corruption to come out of it is ridiculous. These people ought to live in scattered sites over the entire city. It works if given a decent trial. You don't *move* a black ghetto. You *eliminate* a black ghetto.

That was one of the terrible deals made years ago by quote liberals unquote. It was decided that public housing projects be concentrated in the black areas, and the wide open spaces of the North Side be left pure white. It was a devil's deal. The result is Robert Taylor Homes and all those other monstrosities that house human beings in warehouses. We abolished slums and created ghettos. We ought to get rid of all the high-rise projects, demolish every one. They are inhuman.

I don't believe more prisons is the answer. There's no reason why a person convicted of a nonviolent crime should be incarcerated. He could be given house arrest, with devices to restrict his liberty. The sole role of prisons should be to keep someone in check so he won't kill. The son-ofabitch, if allowed out, might kill you and me. There's no other way, but that's not punishment.

Once I attended a black church in Chicago. The minister, in his remarks, mentioned an absent parishioner. "Sister Carrie isn't here because she is taking care of a Jew lady who is very sick. I don't wish that Jew lady any bad luck, but if she does die, I hope she takes care of Sister Carrie." I sat there fuming. The only white in the church. Another minister came over to me and invited me to say something. I got up and said, "Racial prejudice of a black against a white is just as bad as a white against a black. You shouldn't have any truck with it." The amazing thing is I got an enthusiastic response. I heard, "Yes, sir. Yes, sir. Speak. Speak." Lots of applause. I think black anti-Semitism is exaggerated. There is black antiwhitism, and since Jews are the whites blacks have been most in contact with, it seems only natural that they be the most singled out. It was the Jewish merchant on the street and the Jewish housewife. I realize there's a Farrakhan around, but I think black anti-Semitism is a phony issue.

There is a big difference between the Jewish hirer of daily help and the non-Jewish hirer. The Jewish household hires black women and the non-Jew hires Polish or Swedish or Irish. Down South it's probably different, but it's the general case up here. Often the non-Jew will say, "I have a Polish lady working for me." The Jew will say, "I have a black lady working for me."

There's a tremendous debt that many white families owe to the black women, who came and did for them, took care of their children. My wife could never have held down the job she did were it not for the black woman who worked for us. I know among black women, there's a feeling: "My children were neglected because I was taking care of someone else's children." It is ground for resentment.

I think black people gain more respect when they assert themselves, much as I dislike some of the manifestations of what you might call the black intifada. It has caused a recognition by whites of the rights of blacks, a grudging respect.

The role model of the pimp has caused the greatest harm to black kids. I'm always happy when I hear a black on TV talk about serious matters in an educated and intelligent way. Very happy that he's not blundering and is making a good impression. It makes me feel good and I worry if he doesn't.

When I hear of a crime being committed, I'm relieved if it's a white and not a black. Talk about obsession! Why the hell should I worry if I were not obsessed by it?

Do you think you're being patronizing?

Yes, I do. Nevertheless, I'm relieved. I called up my brother in New York and told him to vote for Dinkins in the mayor's election. I said, "Vote for the guy, he sounds like a literate and intelligent man."

Would you have said that to a black acquaintance?

No, he'd a chopped my head off. He'da a said, "You're a patronizing sonofabitch." And he'd be right.

I just don't think they're taking any shit from Whitey any more. I think this goes for the rudeness on the bus and the black woman who told me off unfairly. She knew I wasn't going to mug her. She could tell I was too old. She knew she wasn't in danger. But she wasn't gonna take any crap. This is good and bad.

I like to pretend that I have a scientific, intelligent attitude. I don't like to admit that I'm subject to being swayed by stupid things like racism. But in my mind, I'm worried. Maybe I am a racist.

I remember being resentful when so many of my middle-class black clients were afraid to see me anymore because they felt they had to go to black lawyers. There was a radical change in my practice. They would conceal the fact that they were coming to visit me. It affected my life, financially for the better. Unless a lawyer exploits poor people, he will not make any money from poor people.

But it was hurtful to my ego. That might have affected my attitude.

That hurt. [*Voice rises*.] I was pissed off, if you want to know the truth. I thought: "For chrissake, goddamn it, these guys!" I mean, I give 'em good service, I don't exploit them, I break my ass. And they're ashamed to come to me. They're going to black lawyers, and because black lawyers have such a tremendous press of business, because there are so few of them, they're not able to perform adequate service. I knew I was performing better service than they could get elsewhere, black or white. White lawyers wouldn't touch them. I thought, "Holy Mackerel, here I am breaking my ass and what appreciation do I get?" That hurt a little. A passing phase.

I still have a few black clients from the old days. They come all the way to this suburb to see me, friends of mine from years back. Some of their children and some of their grandchildren. They still come.

At one time I had a romantic vision of myself as a savior of people, a righter of wrongs, and the blacks were the people being wronged. I think I've become more realistic and maybe more prejudiced, too.

I think every white person in our society carries a bias with respect to blacks. I think every black person raised in our society in a black environment, until the Martin Luther King movement, carried a sense of inferiority and oppression. I think it has deeply stained the character of every single individual in our society. It has stained every black. It has stained every white.

I get pulled back and forth on this damn thing. I see too many faults in blacks because I have seen too many virtues. In either case, I feel prejudiced and it bothers me. All my pretentions. I wonder if they're not phony.

But I haven't changed my conviction that the black people in America got a goddamn fuckin' raw deal. And are still getting it. And I want to do all I can. I hate to be conked on the head and called a honky, but I understand it.

I think black people, even at the cost of abusing guys like me, have to show themselves, be militant. I think it's gonna show, now and then, in ways that are unpleasant to guys like me. I don't think the black community is by nature a violent community. I don't think they're defying Martin Luther King. He gave them ideals and hopes and dreams, and they still have them.

ALEX BERTEAU

He is a partner at a black law firm. His ex-wife is a lawyer, too. "She was in a Fortune 500 corporation." He has three children. He is forty-four years old.

*Three months ago, he had quit as the member of the law department of
one of the city's largest banks. He had been there sixteen years.*
This conversation took place on Martin Luther King's birthday.

The other day I was talking to a young associate, a lawyer. He was born in
1962. There are things that influenced me that he can't possibly relate to.
He's black, too. I explained to him that this date personifies a lot of things
for me. Here I am, born 44 years ago in a little Louisiana town where
everything was segregated. I only went to kindergarten because my parents
and other black parents sponsored the school in a Baptist church. Under the
state law at the time, only white children were allowed to go to kindergarten
schools at public expense.

As I spoke to this guy, it dawned on me that he never saw a bathroom
that said WHITE and BLACK. When I came out of law school in 1973, this kid
was ten years old. I don't think of myself as an old person, yet he was saying
to me, "I can't feel what you're saying, except that I've heard about it." He
was five when King died.

I remember distinctly when we used to come to Chicago to visit
relatives. Black families always packed big luncheon bags, fried chicken,
because there were no places to stop between Louisiana and Chicago.
There were no restaurants you could really go into. There were no hotels. I
remember them cooking chicken for days. Blacks could not use the bathrooms at service stations. I remember all this too well.

I have mixed feelings about a lot of what's happening today. Black lawyers
who came along at a particular time had access to only certain schools.
There's a measure of resentment that black lawyers in their fifties and
sixties have, because, after the sixties, blacks were getting into Harvard
and Yale and Northwestern. An old black lawyer would tell you he never
had a retainer. He never had somebody say, "Here's $50,000 a year for you
to represent me in the upcoming year." It was unheard of. It's going to be
criminal or divorce work or maybe a real-estate closing. There were hardly
any sophisticated black businesses that you had as clients.

Now, there's a new frustration. These people, going to better schools,
are still finding it difficult to punch into the power structure, to get the good
jobs these schools have prepared them for. You may be in the mainstream
emotionally, but in the corporate law department, you're a minority, alien.
They're not prepared for you. First of all, whites didn't know what to do
with these people. Partners didn't come up to them saying, "Welcome,

aboard. We hope you spend your career with us. We want you to be a partner someday." They're there; that's it.

I can tell you about black MBAs coming from the same high-quality schools, thinking, "I paid my dues educationally and I'm getting my ticket punched." It just doesn't happen. I feel it was beginning to happen in the seventies. After Reagan, it stopped happening.

As you went through the process, got close to where you'd be considered for partner status, you were told, "We weren't quite as happy this year with what you did." You'd spend another few years at it, whatever time they demanded, and you'd hear, "We saw some improvement, but not a lot." You give them another year and then comes the comment, "This isn't working. You ought to consider looking around for something else." You had fulfilled their needs. You dressed up the place with your black face. Sometimes they say, "You can remain here as an associate." This can be a very humiliating experience, because everybody then knows you didn't make it. You can be a hanger-on.

Look at it from the firm's side. What value is this guy to us? Has he brought us worthwhile clients? He's probably first-generation college-educated. His father and mother are people of no importance. They can't bring any big accounts in. It's not like there are forty-five thousand big black corporations and this kid is wired to them. Why then should we keep this person around?

This firm has existed for several decades. Why would the people there be sympathetic for somebody not making it? They're indifferent. Would you go out on the limb for somebody who didn't fit the traditional mold, who wasn't bringing in clients? He may have had pure legal talent, but he's never going to be a rainmaker—a guy who goes out, gets the business, and brings in the client. Rainmakers are the ones who call the shots.

There seemed to be a positive change in the seventies. Whatever momentum was there went bang, after Reagan became president. I'm not about the business of tearing down Ronnie. He's just somebody who came along. He happened to be in the place for eight years. What I'll never understand was how we could take a man, born in almost the first decade of the century, and get him to preside over the next to last decade, to do everything in his power to throw us back into the first decade of the century. What a rip-off.

I work with many of those we call yuppies. The people who have the cappuccino machines. They're well educated, they're MBA types or lawyers from the best schools. They're ready to reap the rewards. "I've gotta go skiiing this winter. I'm a member of Club Med. I want to rehab my basement. I'm restoring a little Fiat." They appear not to have any sensitivity. It's as if they expect you to say they are fair-minded, don't discriminate, and are better than any generation that went before them. They are intelligent enough to know things are wrong. Yet they want a pass.

On the other side, you'll find minority young who can't use the proper verb tenses, who can't speak a proper sentence, whose syntax is execrable. In my generation, if you couldn't speak well, you were conscious of it. You'd recognize the need to improve, to do better. I find it fascinating that their attitude is: I may be speaking this way and that, but I ain't takin' no stuff off no honky. I'm not takin' any shit. Maybe I speak with dems and dats, but I have a right to go into Marshall Field's and buy this and that. I can go to the 95th at the Hancock for dinner and they better let me in. In my day, those are places people didn't go to, unless they were conscious of all the appropriate things you should do or not do. I find it interesting that these younger people will not take any crap.

If I listen to them talk, and to their objectives, if they have any, it disappoints me. But I'm very much pleased in their recognition of their ability to have their own lives and be free to express themselves, and that they're every bit as good as somebody else.

When Martin Luther King went out and did what he did, he found a particular kind of black fellow out there, who had not been given the kind of recognition he'd hoped for. I was in some of King's marches and people pretty much behaved. They were disciplined. King was a religious man, who always prayed before he marched, and he asked the people to conduct themselves well. Today, I don't think they'll be that disciplined. You can't expect them to be that understanding. The attitude of the younger people I see is: "Either we get our share or we're gonna tear this thing up." It's that simple. It's a switch. My generation would never have thought that we're going to go and tear something up or rip it down.

He was an ROTC officer at the University of Illinois, Chicago, from which he graduated in 1967. He immediately joined the Army as a second lieutenant. "I had a regular army commission because I was number one in my class."

In the spring of '68, I drove cross-country from Fort Benning, Georgia, to Fort Ord, California. When I was traveling alone in the South, I always made sure I stayed in well-lighted areas. I don't want to be on any side streets.

In Memphis, I drove past the motel where Martin Luther King was assassinated a week later. At Fort Ord, I'm glued to the television set, hearing about the riots out east. They had us on alert for possible riot duty, because there was some looting in the town nearby. They were worried about San Francisco or L.A. Luckily, none of our units was called on.

The guy who greeted me at Ord was the son of an undersecretary of defense. One day, he said, "I've got bad news for you. You're going to Vietnam." Then he says, "If you want, I can make a phone call and I think we can get you off this." There's this rush through my head, a zillion things go through my mind. Here's this guy, a graduate of Princeton, blue-blood elite, his father's best friend secretary of the army, telling me this.

I wasn't raised that way. I was raised that you do what you're supposed to do, you pay your dues, you don't shirk your responsibilities. If it's your turn, you don't pass it on to the next guy. It was a dilemma because I didn't believe in that war and hoped not to have to deal with it.

It made me come to grips with the values I was raised to have. This guy, twenty years from now, is gonna run for political office of something. He's going to say he served honorably in the Army. And I gotta go and get my ass shot off and maybe be dead and gone.

I decided that if I ever got orders to go to Vietnam, I would either, A, go or, B, go to jail. If you have a conviction, you ought to have the strength of your conviction. I have great affection for those who went to jail.

When I elected to go to Vietnam, maybe I rationalized that I was going to be different. I heard stories of how we treated them. They were true. I was going to be the American who was going to treat these people as equals and not as gooks. One of the things that always bothered me was that black Americans were calling these Vietnamese gooks, because white Americans called them that. It was the only time that they were going to be invited by white Americans to call somebody else a derogatory term. Many of them seized it. I forbade them to call these people gooks.

I'm the first black officer in the history of the unit. This is 1968. All the blacks look at me and say, "He must be an Oreo—black on the outside, white on the inside." The whites are sore: "Why would they send a black down here?" I'm saying, "What the hell am I doing here?"

These southern officers told their lieutenants: "If we ever catch you associating with this nigger, we'll have your ass." A number of them came to me quietly and said, "I don't want them sending me on nothing but Cambodian missions." So I spent my year isolated. None of them could afford to associate with me. On the other hand, as an officer I couldn't fraternize with the men. The blacks didn't know what to think of me. It was weird. Vietnam was a disservice in so many ways.

One night I get a call to come quickly to this quonset hut. It was a dispensary. I find a lot of yelling and screaming. A young white soldier is on the operating table, six guys are holding him down. He's bleeding from the head.

What happened was: Here's a redneck from Arkansas, who goes to an enlisted-men's club. It has a jukebox with fifty records. It had like forty-eight country-and-western and only two soul songs. The unit's sixty-percent black. The blacks used to give the Vietnamese woman who worked there these coins to put in the machine, before the club opened. You could program this thing to play all night if you put in enough coins. The only song was Aretha Franklin all night long.

They're drinking and this white guy says, "My daddy always said the only good nigger is a dead nigger." He was able to slip in enough coins to make the jukebox play country-and-western, and he keeps talking about niggers. So this black guy unplugs the machine and he says to the white guy, "You got so much to say about niggers, why don't you say it so everybody can hear it?" So he repeats it and the black guy hits him on the head with an iron rod. That's how he ended up on the table in this medical facility.

The guy's delirious, railing about niggers and not letting them get away with it. Peeking through the windows are all these whites, and they're going crazy: "Let's get the niggers." I'm a black officer in the middle of all this.

The blacks and the whites, each group, break into the arms room and take their weapons. The blacks line up in the battalion area with rifles and the whites line up on the other side with rifles.

We had to call Saigon. The MPs are on the alert. The commander didn't know what the hell to do. They came up to me: "Why don't you go down and talk to them? The blacks." I said, "I'm just a soldier like everybody else. This is *all* our problem."

So I and a white officer walked all along the white side and then the black side, but they wouldn't listen. Finally, after three hours of this Mexican standoff, we convinced them. The men went back to their barracks and put their guns away.

Some war!

When I came back from Vietnam, I was assigned to an induction center downtown. It was our responsibility to process the people who would ultimately be the bodies to go to Vietnam. Every day we had about five hundred people come in. One group would take the physicals while the others took the mental exams. The demeanor of the minorities and the whites was incredibly different.

When we gave the mental exams to the whites, they were attentive to the instructions and generally did well. In the room, it was very businesslike. When you peeked at the blacks in the physical line, it was a lesson. Those who were disqualified usually caused a rumpus. Where they came from in the neighborhood, either it was basketball or football, there was a lot of pride in their physical prowess. They resented doctors telling them they had flat feet or a weak heart. Loss of status. Whereas the whites would be standing there with a fistful of documents trying to explain to the doctor they got allergies, flat feet, amnesia, doctor's letters saying they're not physically fit for the army. When the blacks went to take the mental exams, you couldn't get them to be quiet. They wouldn't be serious. For the white guy, it was fine if he flunked the physical as long as you don't call him stupid. For the blacks, if you tell him he only scored three on the mental test, it was fine as long as you didn't say he wasn't physically fit.

The whites come in knowing the big picture. If you get a high enough mental score, you're not going to be an infantryman carrying a rifle in the boonies. The blacks and the other minorities were the natural cannon fodder. They were the ones who usually ended up being the bodies that got shipped back.

My parents were very religious and raised us to be that way. We went to church every Sunday. My black Baptist perspective is that there is heaven and hell, no in-between. You're either going to one place or the other. There's a right way to do something and a wrong way.

My father worked as a foreman for a chemical company on the South Side. He took us to museums, made sure we read, and put all of us, my three sisters and me, through college.

I went from school to work in the law department of a bank. I was there for sixteen years. I left three months ago. It was not an easy sixteen years. I don't really think I'm one of those black people who has a chip on his shoulder. I wasn't raised that way. But my experience there . . . When I came, there were twenty-eight lawyers in the department. There was one white woman and one black, me. When I left, there were eighty-five lawyers. There were forty white women, one black woman, and two black men. They don't understand why I got upset about it.

I had believed that if you do the best possible job, you will be rewarded for your efforts. I realized my parents had sheltered us from the real world.

Louis Farrakhan understands the real world. I think he does some good. Even when the Panthers were running around years ago, there was a measure of positiveness in what they did. If for no other reason than they made white America aware that all blacks were not docile. All blacks were not of the same mind. All blacks did not go to church and pray.

I marched with Martin Luther King and there were people on that march who were not religious. There was no other way to vent their frustration. When King was saying a prayer, they weren't listening. They were saying, "Let's get the bullshit over and let these people know how we feel." Historically, the black minister was the only guy allowed to quietly vent how we feel about things. It's true that he picked up the mantle of leadership, but who knows how long he'd have been allowed to exist if he had not been a minister?

Farrakhan presents other options. I think he's less violent-prone than white America thinks he is. But if you think he is, he is. A person who's telling off Whitey is venting the feelings of what most blacks feel, but are unwilling to say it for a wealth of reasons.

I have read what he is alleged to have said about Jews. You really can't talk to some Jewish people without everything deteriorating rapidly. You're either for me or agin me. My very best friend in law school was Jewish. We rode to school together five days a week for three years. Was it '67? Gaza? Israel taking it over? I said these people are homeless and are entitled to a home. They're living over there in tents. He became livid. He told me to get out of the car. We have never been what we once were to each other. It's one of the things that hurt me most in life. Israel poisons relationships.

We regard Israel as the bastion of democracy in the Middle East. Yet South Africa's major supplier of weapons is Israel. I don't know if Farrakhan really, quote, hates Jews. If he is saying Jewish people exercise an influence disproportionate to their numbers, it's true. All you got to do is look. Jews are—what?—seven percent of our population? About forty percent of the legal community in Chicago is Jewish. They're a power to be reckoned with.

You remember the Bakke case? That played a role in what antagonism there may be between blacks and Jews. The University of California had this program, setting aside slots for minorities. Bakke was a white, who wasn't allowed in though he had a higher score than the ten who were chosen. He sued. Blacks, Hispanics, and the other minorities were hoping the Court would say it was okay to keep the ten spots because they were trying to bootstrap themselves into the training. If you took a hundred positions as a model, what the minorities were saying is, "We want only ten out of the hundred."

Jewish groups filed all their briefs on behalf of Bakke. People with the highest scores should be chosen. Their history is a great one in this respect.

The black history is somewhat different. That didn't matter. They were against quotas.

The real problem is something else. When I, a black, listened to Reagan in the debates and heard him ramble on about when he was a boy, before he knew we had a problem, I thought of all those scatterbrained movies he was in as a campus hero. I thought about my poor grandmother down in Louisiana. These people who had to tip their hats and step off the sidewalk. All that was happening to my relatives, my ancestors. All those millions of lives that had come into existence and passed. And here's Ronnie Reagan, whom everybody loves so much, smiling, cavalierly saying that it really wasn't a problem.

This man represents something more than just a guy who was in office for eight years. He personifies the total indifference that most of white America feels. I've done everything I was supposed to do and yet he's rained on my parade. If I find it difficult, with my credentials, what in the hell chance does Joe Blow have, coming from an underprivileged area?

In the year 1990, if I hail a cab, particularly after six o'clock, there's a good chance the cabbie's going to be concerned that I want to take him in a black area and he doesn't want to go there. I don't have the duty to explain, "I'm not like those kind of people you're thinking about." I'm a lawyer, I have money. Why should I bare my soul? He's just a guy trying to make a living and I'm just a guy trying to get home, and we ought to have something in common. But he's not going to give me that chance. If he sees somebody white standing on the corner, he'll go to him. Even a black cabdriver will do that. Fear's the big thing.

I do see less of young white Americans asking blacks to make concessions that their fathers asked my father to make. Yet in many ways, it isn't a hell of a lot different.

It's kind of tough when you deal with young whites who have made it. When the subject comes up, affirmative action or any other kind of redress, you hear: "It wasn't me. I didn't have anything to do with what happened in the past. You want me to pay dues for that?"

The truth is, it *wasn't* him, it was his dad. His father had his foot on my father's neck, and paying my father subsistence wages enabled this turkey to go to Harvard. He's got a college degree and I'm standing out here illiterate and barely able to speak English. He says, "Don't lay it on my doorstep," yet he's getting all the fruits of it. To attack affirmative action is to ignore history.

I've chosen to join a minority firm because I wanted to go to a place where I wouldn't have to watch my back any longer. I want to be the best lawyer, help build something, yet not become an isolationist. I intend to do business with the white corporate world. Yet, it's a place where I'll get a slap on the back once in a while. Respect.

■ ■ ■ ■ ■

Reflections of a Bruised Tiger and an Ironic Cat

KID PHARAOH

In his younger days, he had been a professional boxer. He was regarded as an excellent club fighter, middleweight, "who coulda been a contender."

For the past thirty years, off and on, he has picked up a buck or two as a minor syndicate tiger, more often as a freelance: a "collector," a quondam bookie, a man of muscle.

1965
He was standing outside his hot-dog shop, observing the heavens. "I'm looking at them high-rises. Wish they were mine.

"I'm dedicated to one principle: taking money away from unqualified dilettantes, who earn it through nepotism. I work at this and am good at my trade. I don't labor. Outside of being a prizefighter, I took an oath to God I would never again labor. But there's a million people on the street that want to be taken and should be taken, and they're gonna be taken.

"I work on contracts, like in business. It's an oral contract. They come to me with some trouble. If called upon to perform, I perform. If not, I subcontract. Example: They're usually in debt or someone owes them money. Or they're extremely fond of women. There's all kinds of conditions. They're afraid, everybody's scared. I give them security. If their wife is an infidelist, I muscle the guy she's makin' love with. I run him off. If somebody's after him, I chase him away. See? Now this guy's in debt to me. The biggest mistake of his life. He should really paid 'em, because I've got him for the rest of his life. I'll always noodge him for some currency or another. You can't imagine how many insecure people we have in this country. I play the Freudian theory. Long may Freud live.

The American Negro not only has everything, now he's tampering with our white women. Women today seem to prefer pigmentation. I have two nieces, I'm worried about that. That colored guy—and I'm the last guy in the world to be prejudiced—this guy comes to the big city and has a comb job on his head. They bust out in these attractive suits and they seem to have some kind of education about them. Most of the girls who prefer pigmentation are not metropolitanites. They from Ohio, Ioway, Indiana, or some of them buck towns.

Some war veterans who are laying in some basket in a hospital, they'll never go to him to arouse his biological urge or pat him on the back or give him a vote of confidence, a note of thanks—nonsense. He's entitled to nothing, he's a mooch. What about the average layman who has labored hard and long in this country without an education, raised a family, sent boys off to war? He's in his vintage years. All of a sudden his building is worth thirty-five thousand dollars and he goes to bed feeling secure. In the morning, a Negro moves in and his building is worth seventeen thousand. They've destroyed everything they've ever moved in. There's a revolt in the making, let me suggest it to you. When it will come, I don't know. How it will come, I don't know. Who will organize this revolt . . . but it'll come.

The best people for communities are the Japanese. They're never above a whisper. Their homes are immaculate. Show me a Japanese on the street after ten o'clock. Show me one, I'll offer a universal challenge to all. Did you ever see one arrested? Did you ever see one under the influence of an intoxicating beverage? Did you ever see 'em pregnant, Japanese girls who are not married? Of course not; there's love in the home. Say for the Negroes, they're animals. There's no love in the home. Not only wants to move the white man over, he wants to be there with him. They have a long-range plan of dissolving this pigmentation through intermarriage.

1991
These recent years have not been kind to him; he has suffered hard times. There is a touch of world-weariness, yet he is philosophical in his resignation and, at times, even ebullient.

I was driving down the street and I see this man with a flat tire. He's terrified to get out of the car because there's three blacks on the corner. So I pull up and say, "What's the problem?" He says, "I've got a flat." I says, "Why don't you get out?" He says, "I'm afraid of them black kids there." So I says, "Don't worry about 'em." I says to one of them, "Hey, you, come here." He says, "What?" I says, "Change that tire." He says, "Okay." Volunteered instantaneously the minute I chose him to do it. I told the guy, "Give the kid a sawbuck." He did, and on his way he went. He said to me later, "I was absolutely terrified I was going to be killed." He didn't know how to handle blacks. I do.

The moral is they'll obey the proper authority. They'll back up if you intimidate them a little.

Suppose there were three white kids on the corner and you said, "Hey, change that tire."

They'd tell me to go fuck myself. "Do it yourself," they'd say. You gotta give blacks consideration, compensation, tell them what to do. Let them know you're on top. There'll be no problem from them, believe me—none.

Don't cops try that?

[*Voice rises.*] Cops don't know *if they're on foot or horseback!* Why does a man want to be a copper? Ninety-nine percent of coppers are cowards. In school I used to see a guy who was as quiet as a churchmouse. All of a sudden I run into him, haven't seen him in X amount of years, he's a copper. He says to me, "Hey, how ya doin?" All of a sudden he had a voice on him, this weasel. How'd he get so *brave*?

Coppers run out of the car, put fear in the kids right away. The worst thing you can do. You just walk up to them, say in a friendly way, but firm, "What's the problem, boys?" I directed them: "Hey, you, change that tire!" Whatever they had in their mind, I changed it right away. It's fear, sure, but different. Not like when you say, "I'll shoot you to do it." You ain't gonna get no results that way. I put it in such a Godfather way of communication that they understood what I wanted and did it.

You made them an offer they couldn't refuse?

Absolutely. I wasn't mad at them. I was going to compensate them. They were glad to do it for me, not for that old guy.

Let me tell you about black kids at home; they're obedient. They'll show their mothers and fathers respect. The whites will not. Blacks don't call their mothers and fathers names. Whites do. The black kid shows his mother and father and grandmother the highest respect.

Another thing. It's the black guy, not the white guide, who'll sense danger in the jungle. These safaris. They sense something, maybe a leopard in a tree. They see something white guys can't see. They have that natural instinct they've inherited for hundreds of years in the jungle. Natural cunning. They can spot a rattlesnake a mile away. They're clever. They've been blessed with this added dimension of knowing how to protect themselves.

You seldom see a black prizefighter, unless they fought for twenty years, with a broken nose, cauliflower ears, cut eyes. None of them.

Aren't all safeties in pro football black? They can pick up and run backwards where the white guy can't even run forward. They have a natural instinct that the whites just never get.

They're a little behind mentally. I'd say sixty years. Through evolution. They say it's the education we never gave them. There's an argument there. They always got the argument of the two scientists with the beans. Booker T. Washington and the other guy, I'm trying to think of his name.* He was superintelligent. What about Raffish Attatucks, another black genius?† The man who came around in the early 1800s. He helped Washington militarily. He helped Jefferson with his speeches. These are exceptions to the rule.

Let's talk biologically. There's no greater pimp than a black. He supplies the girls with narcotics. He knows how to intimidate them. The most interesting thing is how they'll go out and turn a trick and give *all* their money to the black guy. A good pimp has two or three white whores going for him. Even in the Minnesota strip in New York. These are the girls who came out of Minnesota and hustled around 42nd Street. All the white prostitutes who had nigger pimps were from Minnesota. When the officials from Minnesota went to New York to encourage them to come back— they'd give them jobs and forgive them, their families wanted them back— not one of them left. Isn't that interesting?

It useta make me mad. Not no more. Hell, no. I just changed. Leave them take 'em.

I'm now problack. The blacks in my building will tell you. There must be eleven families here and they pay, so to speak, nothing. I get along with 'em wonderful. They'll say hello to me where they won't to other whites in the building.

I'll drive the blacks to work. In cold weather, I used to take all the black children to school.

A woman, she's an artist, says to me, "What kind of work do you do?" I says, "I'm in the coal business. I deliver a load of coal to school

---

* George Washington Carver?

† Crispus Attucks?

every morning." So she says to me later, "I never could figure it out, and one day as I was laying in the bed, I started to laugh so hysterically that the load of coal you were delivering was a load of black kids that you were taking to school." She still talks about it every time I see her. She says, "I can never get over it."

But you're not a racist?

Hell, no.

Blacks have got a great future in this country. The majority of blacks who live in those projects got absolutely nothing. They better get off their ass. They don't have an incentive. They need guys like Michael Jordan, like Walter Payton, somebody who'll get them going. Some of them we won't be able to help. Some will go off to prison, some will just fade away. Oh God, I forgot the count of blacks in prison. Their college.

My brother was professor emeritus of the University of Terre Haute. A federal pen. He was enjoying his twelfth year, lecturing on what to do and what not to do, and how to figure out another crime so he wouldn't get caught.

The Black Muslims are bosses of the penitentiary. Everybody fears them. He's locked up in a cage like an animal, he's got no future, so if he kills, what are you gonna do to him? They loved my brother. He had a rapport with 'em.

Did I ever tell you how my brother got the black guys to get the warden to take Franco-American spaghetti off the menu? There was a lawyer out of Detroit, who was sentenced fifteen-to-twenty. He'd help inmates, look up their cases and get 'em out on an appeal. The warden got hot at him and took the light bulb out of his cell so he couldn't read anymore. He wanted to get even. So he told my brother to get the Black Muslims and ask 'em for a favor. "Go to the warden and request with force that Franco-American spaghetti gives you ptomaine poisoning and you want it off the menu."

Everybody assembled and they come up those iron stairs and they said, "Tell the warden to come out." He come out, he don't want a riot, don't want to blow his job. "What can I do for you boys?" "Warden, Franco-American spaghetti gives us ptomaine poisoning. We want it off the menu." He says, "I'll honor your request. I'll take it off the menu." The lawyer got his revenge, intimidatin' the warden.

If white guys went up with the same request, the warden would find out how much good time they have, take it off the books and give these guys thirty days in the *hole*.

The blacks will take over, but not by force. Strength is in number not in slumber. One man, one vote was the worst fucking thing the Supreme Court ever ruled on. You tell a thousand profound gibbering idiots, "Here's a five-dollar bill, pull that lever," they'll do it. One man, one vote will be controlled by the ruling powers.

Oh sure, whites'll pull the lever for a five-dollar bill. But the numbers come in big cities and the population is blacks now. The one ethnic group in Chicago now is the Polacks. The blacks are second, but coming up. The Irish were up there, but they're out. Eventually the blacks will get it. It doesn't worry me at all. I get along with them. Maybe somebody else can't, but for me it will be just ducky.

I voted for Harold Washington. During the time of the election, I walked in to make a bet. These mob guys are there and they say, "What do you got on your lapel?" I had Harold Washington on the thing. They says, "You can't come into this fucking joint unless you take that button off." I took it off, made my bet, put it on again, and drove off. That was in Daley's ward. To *hell* with them. They didn't scare me. I wore it everywhere. I liked Harold. He took 'em all on and beat 'em. I like a guy against the odds.

Who creates these race tensions? The white guys. They don't want 'em here, they don't want 'em there. They push 'em around, don't let 'em go nowhere. Actually, I've got along with blacks all my life.

A black can see danger long before a white guy can, not only in the jungle. He can tell right away if the white guy is a good boss or a bum boss. They just have a way about them, and they're ninety-nine-percent correct. I don't know how they do it, but goddammit, they call it every time. It's the most remarkable instinct they have about 'em. If the guy's no fuckin' good, they've pegged him a long time ago. They're good readers. They know a friend and they know an enemy. Some never got a chance actually to *read*. But they can read people, you better believe it.

Garbage has come over to this country, and I don't mean blacks. A guy named Madison Grant wrote a monumental book called, *The Destruction of a Continent*. He said the scum of the world would come over and destroy because they would be prolific in numbers. Why let them in this fucking country? The minute I get in a cab, I say to the driver, "What nationality are you?" A lot of 'em say they're Iranians. I don't say nothin', see? When I make my stop, I say, "Give me some small change." They think I'm gonna tip 'em. I never tipped a fuckin' Iranian. I'd rather do time. I like to tip a black cabdriver. I say, "Put this in your pocket, cousin."

When you see an attractive white woman with a black guy—?

I think it's awfully kind of that black man to give that broad lodgings and nourishment. A slight sarcasm. But I'm not sore at her. In the course of my conversation, I usually ask the broad, "May I inquire, do you deal in coal?" She doesn't understand it.

Doesn't the black guy sock you?

Oh, I don't say it in front of him. The next time I run into her, she's not with the shine. I say to her, "Who's that colored guy you were with?" They all have the same answer: "A friend." A friend! It's biological. I knew a girl once whose father objected to her for going around with a black guy. When he was sleeping, she got an ice pick and stabbed her father in the balls. Isn't that interesting? [*Laughs.*]

Some guys say whites are biologically immature, that shines are far superior to the white man. They say a black guy can shoot and reload, where a white guy can't. They say, "I'm not followin' no shine, I ain't got a chance." In some cases, I'm afraid it's true.

The future looks great to me—God, yes. Example: You go to City Hall today, you'll see an enormous percentage of blacks. You need a favor, you go to a black guy. White guys don't seem to take a chance anymore. I just enjoyed that experience the other day. I know a guy working there. He said, "See that black guy." There was a line a mile long. I was in and out of there in two minutes. A white guy doin' it, *hell, no.* They're scared.

I happened to go to a funeral. It was in a Catholic church. I came out empty. I didn't feel sorry for the guy, it was the most cold-blooded thing. When you go to a black church, they stand up, they singeth, they rejoiceth. Such jubilation. They come out cleansed, they come out free. You see all the shines coming out of a church with love and smiles on their faces. [*Shouts.*] *Show me one guy who comes out of a Catholic church with a smile.* I'll erect a monument to the guy who comes out with a smile.

The blacks have the future. They'll go to church, they'll take care of their business, they'll go home, they'll lay the body down. They will sleep. A shine will lay down in a chair like this, out he goes. The white guy won't sleep. He'll need a tranquilizer, a shot or two to get him down.

It could be guilt that keeps him from sleepin'. He's got no direction, he's a failure. Nobody's tellin' him which way to go. You go buy a newspaper, they'll tell you what show you're supposed to see. You're hungry, they'll tell you what restaurant to go to. You have a mental problem, they'll tell you what this psychiatrist will suggest you do. You cannot function today without a fucking newspaper telling us what to do. They eventually tell us where to go and how to die and who's going to bury us.

The blacks will tell you to go fuck yourself. They'll do what they want to do. They may not have got to the fucking top of that mountain yet, but they're gonna get to it. We're dead, the white guy. We're just about extinct.

What bothers me? Economics bothers me. I'll start again tomorrow. Every day I shoot rockets to the moon. Hopefully.

Rudyard Kipling teaches us that the things we do, two by two, we shall answer for them, one by one. The whites will answer one by one for all the things they did two by two, by fucking the blacks for centuries. They're telling us: move over, dude. It's our turn now. I love it.

FRANK CHIN

A Chinese-American playwright and novelist.
  "When I was a little kid, during World War II, I was raised by white folks: a retired vaudeville acrobat and a retired silent-screen bit player. We lived in a tarpaper shanty, outside Sacramento.
  "A war veteran, with one eye missing and a few drinks, said to them, 'What are you doin' with that Jap kid?' I said, 'I'm no Jap kid. I'm an American of Chinese descent.' I didn't know what it was, but he didn't either. The rest of my life, I've been trying to find out exactly what it is." [Laughs.]
  He later moved in with his grandmother and aunts in Oakland. "All we spoke in the family was Cantonese."

I hung out with blacks. I learned if I could make them laugh, I wouldn't get beat up and I could walk away and maintain my dignity. They actually came to respect me because I could talk my way out of fights in a way that would make them feel good. They would walk me to school.

Some people looked at this as a rejection of things Chinese. On the other hand, the blacks would say, and the whites, too, why was I talking about all this Chinese stuff? "We think of you as a member of the family." That always bothered me.

The Tower of Babel story always bothered me, too.

Oakland is the Tower of Babel. All these languages. And nobody even speaks English like everybody else. I've come to believe that monotheism encourages racism, whoever practices it. There is only one God and everyone else is an infidel, a pagan, or a goy. The Chinese look on all behavior as tactics and strategy. It's like war. You have to know the terrain. You don't destroy the terrain, you deal with it. We get along, not because we share a belief in God or Original Sin or a social contract, but because we make little deals and alliances with each other.

I like whites and blacks. I take them as individuals. I admire white culture: Shakespeare, the great ideas of Western Civilization. I also like black culture. In the sixties, it became a force in Asian-America. It always had a large presence in Oakland. I grew up with rhythm-and-blues, jazz, our original American art forms.

The fifties was still our age of innocence: the Eisenhower era. Everything was looking up: Perry Como. Since I grew up a loner, without any idea of parents, I thought Mommy and Daddy were just nicknames, like Shorty and Skinny. The idea that parents had a propietary right over children was alien to me. A lot of the ideas of Chinese inferiority came late to me, from the outside. The one thing that saved me from being raised in the stereotype was my isolation during World War II, being raised by these white folks.

The sixties and the civil-rights movement came along, and the blacks were asserting themselves and getting our attention with phrases like "Power to the People." These wonderful black-leather jackets and the shades and the black berets were new even to the blacks themselves. It was like a parade, everyone in uniform.

As for the yellows, the civil-rights movement made us aware that we had no presence, no image in American culture as men, as people. We were perceived as being bright but with less physical prowess than the blacks and whites. We were more favored than the blacks, but we lacked their manhood. So a bunch of us began to appropriate "blackness." We'd wear the clothes, we'd affect the walk and we began talking black. We'd call ourselves "Bro" and began talking Southern: "Hey, man."

We started talking about the sisters in the street and the brothers in the joint. I'd been in the joint and I didn't see any yellows there. I didn't see so many of our sisters walking the streets. That wasn't our thing. If it had been, we might have had a better sex life. [*Laughs*.]

[*He imitates the Black Panther rap*.] "Brothers and sisters, we've gotta organize, get together, and fight the *pig*. Brothers and sisters, Power to the People. Right on!" I said, "*What is this?* This isn't Chinese. It's a yellow minstrel show."

At this time, the government was throwing a lot of money at the gangs. The War on Poverty was on. Chinatown gangs, whose main business was being criminals, suddenly had social significance. They were perfectly happy to collect chump change.

I was teaching a class in Asian-American studies. My students were Chinese-Americans and Japanese-Americans. They were from the suburbs, outside Chinatown. My purpose was to break down stereotypes. So I decided to do an agit-prop thing, having them *play* the stereotypes.

We were rehearsing, doing a rock-and-roll version of

> Ching-chong Chinaman,
> sitting on a rail,
> along come a choo-choo train,
> cut off his tail.

Guitars, everything. The Lum gang walks in, walks up to the singer [*Simulates a deep, menacing voice*.]: "Stop singing that song. We don't like it." Lum comes up to me, he's holding his fist down, staring a hole through my chest. A student, a quiet little girl, who'd become a militant, is behind me saying, "Don't take no shit from nobody." I'm saying, "Shhh, shhh!" Porky, who's standing behind Lum, is yelling, "Kill 'im! Kill 'im!"

Lum is growling, "Stop singing that song. It makes fun of Chinese people." I say, in my gentlest voice, "Have you ever heard of satire? We *know* it's a racist song. That's why we're singing it. We're making fun of the people who make fun of Chinese. Do you understand?" I could see I wasn't cutting it. Porky is hollering, "Kill 'im! Kill 'im!" Finally, in frustration, because I wasn't responding to a fight, they walk out.

The gang council decides that we're too controversial. They call me to a meeting. The leader of the Chinatown Red Guard taps me on the shoulder and says, "I want to talk to you." I turn around and just like in the movies, his fist is coming toward me. He knocks me down, my glasses go flying, he punches me in the stomach. Just like in the movies, he hits me in the back of the neck. While I'm on my hands and knees, he stomps on me and starts kicking me. I'm saying [*in a whining voice*], "This is the wrong movie, guys."

He says, "Identify with China!" I say, "Wait a minute. We're in America. This is where we are, where we live and where we're going to die. There's not going to be any revolution. That's crazy." He can't hit me anymore. He's already done that and it's not working. I've interrupted his speech. This had never happened to him before. He curls his lip and says, "You cultural nationalist!" I go, "*What?* What's a cultural nationalist? Don't you know how to swear? Call me motherfucker, call me asshole, call me anything you want, but what's a cultural nationalist?" He doesn't know what to say to that, so they leave.

George Woo, a big guy, who's now teaching Asian-American Studies at San Francisco State, was pretty tight with the gangs then. He runs after the Red Guard and tells them if they ever beat me up again, he'll take it personally, that I'm his friend. All of a sudden, the leader of the gang council comes up to me and says, "I want to shake your hand. No one ever talked back to Alex that way before." We're all buddy-buddy now, because George said he'll take it personally.

The word flashes through Chinatown. Twenty-five minutes later, another gang of kids shows up. Must be fifteen, sixteen years old. One of them has a Tommy gun. "*Where are they?* We heard someone beat up a friend of George's." [*Laughs.*] I said "No, no, that's not my style. Let's do it with words."

The civil-rights movement of the sixties affected the Chinese-American community in a number of ways. In ways that aren't very flattering to us. When I went to interview some Asian-American actors who played Charlie Chan's Number One, Two, Three, and Four sons, they were blaming the blacks for the yellows not getting more parts. "Here we've been good people, keeping our noses clean—" Suddenly they realized what I was up to and they saw *me* as a threat. I was making Chinese-Americans controversial by speaking out against racism.

It's an old story. The good Chinese were the Christian Chinese. The good Chinese were the ones who shucked all Chinese ways. They revere Paerl Buck and the missionaries that worked Chinatown. That's what bothered me, our history in Chinatown, San Francisco.

In Chinatown's twelve blocks, there are forty-two Christian churches. On the walls of Chinatown, there's a plaque honoring Ross Hunter, who produced *The Flower Drum Song*; a plaque honoring the song "Grant Avenue"; a plaque marking the birthplace of the first white child in San Francisco; a monument to the first white school. *Nothing* for the Chinese. There is one exception: a monument to Sun Yat Sen. He was a Christian.

Most in the community saw the civil-rights movement as a threat. They objected to school integration because they didn't want their children to be influenced by blacks. The fact is the mimicking of blacks that I experienced were of a few. White journalists have emphasized that aspect. As though the Chinese don't think of themselves as Chinese-Americans. As though we're an enclave, like Americans working for Aramco in Saudi Arabia.

Chinatown may be a stronghold of Chinese culture, but we're Chinese-Americans. We saw the movement as a threat because we might be indentified as a minority. We were thinking of ourselves as being assimilated. We had worked so hard at being acculturated that we didn't know anything about China anymore.

During the Depression, my uncle was raised in a Chinese Baptist Home for Boys. To raise money, they put on a show. It was the first Chinese-American blackface minstrel show in the history of the world. I came across the autobiography of the founder. I showed my uncle a picture in the book; the boys in blackface. He burst into tears. He was one of the Chung-mai minstrels. He got sad and I got angry. It was humiliating.

At the same time, we thought we were above the blacks. My family owned some property in the black district of Oakland. I once went with my mother to collect the rent. I said, "These places are terrible." She says, "Yeah, but they drive Cadillacs. It's what you call nigger-rich." That struck me so hard. I had never heard my folks put down blacks, denigrate people that way. Yet we were slumlords, taking advantage, exploiting them. It was a moment of moral confusion. I was eight at the time.

We feel because we're more civilized, quote unquote, because we're more middle-class, that we deserve more acceptance than the blacks. We don't riot, we don't make waves, we didn't protest, we're more American. We don't see that we've described ourselves as a race of Helen Kellers, mute, blind and deaf. We're the perfect minority.

We embrace Charlie Chan as an image of racist love. Most of us still think the good Chinaman is the Christian, Charlie Chan. There's a Chinese-American sociologist who said, "The Chinese, much to their credit, have never been overly bitter about racial prejudice. They have gone into jobs that reduced visibility and are moving out of population vortices of New York and San Francisco's Chinatown to outlying areas. Such a movement should be encouraged, because dispersion discourages visibility." The stereotype is embraced as a strategy for white acceptance.

The prejudice against blacks still continues, but we're smart enough to know it isn't quite civilized. We're also smart enough to use it to get our share. It happened to me. It was in the sixties. The railroads were taken to court for failing to integrate. They fell under ICC rules. So they put up a call: they were hiring brakemen. I was encouraged to apply. I was a clerk for a railroad company. It was the lowest of the low. I was fairly assured I'd be hired, implying I'd be more acceptable than a black. By default, I became the first Chinese-American brakeman on the Southern Pacific. I was the lesser of the two evils.

We believed what whites believed about blacks. We adopted all the white prejudice. The blacks adopted the same prejudices about us. David Hilliard of the Black Panthers got up in Portsmouth Square—luckily most

Chinese there didn't understand English—and said, "You Chinese are the Uncle Toms of the colored peoples." It was apt. At the same time, the solution was not for us to become black.

The new immigrants, the Indochinese are a revelation. They still speak all the dialects of Indochina: Lao, Viet, or Cambodian. They pick up English as a matter of necessity, as a language of commerce. It's strategic. It's a white-man's world and you have to get along. Yet, all these languages are being spoken. They're using English as a dialect of Chinese and not following the rules. In Chinese-America, it is the new immigrants threatening our relationship with the whites, not the blacks. They are the unredeemed Chinese Chinese. It's an interesting, exciting time.

■ ■ ■ ■ ■

There Is a Tavern in Our Town

VAN GALLIOS

"I'm probably fifty-six years old, probably middle-aged. I'm a downtown Chicagoan. I was born just a few miles from where we work down here at the restaurant. Middle-class, probably above-average income because I'm in business. College-educated. One of a family of eight children, very close-knit. Our business is the biggest part of our life."

He and his brother run a popular restaurant in Chicago's Loop. For years, it has attracted a "sporting crowd." Photographs of athletes and the city's clout figures, past and present, cover much of the walls. It is one of the few family-run establishments surviving in the city's downtown area. "It is middle-of-the-road. We take care of a cross-section of the public. People that come into our place feel comfortable in jeans or a tuxedo."

It is different than it was. In the earlier years, I'll admit to a lot of preconceptions based on race. They were mostly wrong, but sometimes correct. I don't think it was the color of the skin so much as the socio-economic background of the people. A guy would come in with a certain cavalier strut and I would make a quick judgment and try to turn him around. I see less of that.

Years ago, we'd get a lot of gray-flannel-suit, striped-tie people, white. They would resent being in the same restaurant with blacks. That was our basic business, from these people. In recent years, with the integration of offices, people are working together. They learn to work with each other. They respect each other a lot more. So we have fewer prejudiced customers, and that reflects on us. We are much more liberal than we were back then. I sense it in myself.

I have become much more tolerant of black people, people that I didn't know too much about. It seems that if you don't know somebody, you have a little fear. Rather than saying, "Hey, I'd like to learn about this person," you sort of withdraw. Maybe this is natural. I've always tried to be above that, but I was caught too. Now I more and more look into the person.

Our business is maybe fifteen-, twenty-percent black. The rest is white. Before, we'd get a lot of company parties, all white. Now they're mixed and they get along real well. Quite often, the leaders are black.

When I was young, we lived on the West Side. We had a two-flat. I'll admit that our family was in the white flight. We moved a couple of times because the neighborhood was turning black. And there were corresponding troubles.

I remember one incident. The racial movement was about two blocks from us. People were getting ready to sell their houses. It was 1965, '66. Some real-estate people came in and called a meeting at a neighborhood tavern. I'll never forget that. They brought in this black fellow. He had on a postal uniform. He had already purchased a house on this block. He stood up and introduced himself.

He said, "I'm moving here because I want a better life for my family. I hope that you people stay. I want my kids to be in the same school with your kids. We're not here to bust the neighborhood but to improve our lot in life." He was very articulate and seemed like a nice guy. We listened, all the owners of the homes.

After the meeting broke up, we said, "We're going to show solidarity so that we all stay here along with this fellow and not leave our homes." It was Christmastime. The meeting broke up and we all went to the bar. They wouldn't serve him. The bartender said, "We don't serve niggers." Just like that.

It was crushing. I was representing my family, see? So I went home and told my brother about it. He said they were blockbusters. "They set this up to actually panic you." We checked it out and nobody had ever heard of them. I think they were unscrupulous real-estate people trying to use us.

What happened at the bar?

The fellow just got up and walked out. But he did move in. The neighborhood is all-black now. We stayed there a year or two more. We sold our house to a black couple and they were very nice. My mother was elderly and really didn't want to move. They were our landlords now. They agreed to take the second floor and we could stay as long as we liked. My mother got real friendly with the woman: "Oh, she's so nice and she helps me with the laundry." But there were a lot of children and they were running like wildfire. My mother had her purse snatched a couple of times while sitting on the front porch. And I had my windshield smashed a few times. We felt we had to move for safety reasons. Every month a block would move. We moved to a lily-white suburb. But I'm basically a downtowner.

At the time I wouldn't describe myself as a racist, but I was somewhat prejudiced. Maybe less than a lot of people in my neighborhood, because I worked downtown and I knew more black people. When it comes to people, I'm a liberal. When it comes to morals, ethics, and behavior, I'm conservative.

In '68, when the riots broke out, the political-convention riots, our landlord asked us to close the restaurant. Because they were rushing up and down the streets. I remember some photographers came in with their heads bandaged and bloody and their cameras broken.

We said, "We're not closing. We're staying open." We just watched the front door and didn't let anyone in with clubs or anything. It was a real wild thing going on in the street. They were storming up and down with banners and trying to break windows.

Weren't they mostly white kids?

Whites and blacks. We didn't have any problems with it. We weren't touched.

(He indicates his secretary at her desk in the office; she is busy with ledgers and papers. She is a young black woman.)

I wouldn't have had her twenty years ago. It just wouldn't have been considered. Even the waitresses, they were all white. The word was around: "We don't hire blacks." In all honsesty, we didn't at the time. Not for any thought-out reason. We felt that if we're going to hire black people, maybe we'll make sure their skin is light, so we don't offend some people. Would we lose business? Oh sure, the customers would tell me. Now they don't. I think it's really working.

I remember when they were putting in the Eisenhower Expressway. Have you noticed that if you go out west, all the exits are on the right, except for a couple where the exits are in the middle? They made it harder for people to enter those areas. You had to go off and make another turn. They felt that black people moving out that way would be driving around their streets, and they would make it as hard as possible for them. They thought it would deter them.

Things are better now because people aren't learning to be afraid. Now children of the white-flight people that went west into the suburbs— these young people are coming back into town. There was a void before, and now they're coming back to enjoy the vibrancy of the city. They don't have the fears that maybe we did when we were younger. They're not afraid of each other so much.

I remember when I first moved to the suburbs and I told somebody we're downtown, the response was, "Really? Can you walk around down there?" I'd say, "Sure, it's nice." They'd say, "We would never walk downtown." If they would come to the symphony, they'd park as close as possible. They'd never walk around. Now you're getting more people who are not afraid of people because of their skin.

When I tell people our doors are open till late at night, they say, "Don't you ever get robbed?" I think that's been exaggerated. I don't think downtown was ever *black* black. There was a time when all the downtown movie houses, which are closed now, were having these militaristic exploitation films. A lot of young black people had to come downtown because there were no theaters on the South Side. They had to have some entertainment. So they would get off the El and wander through the streets. They were intimidating to the average white person, because they were from a different culture. They walked different, they looked different, they dressed different, and that created a fear.

Today a young white will walk up to a young black and ask about anything. How do I get there? Twenty years ago, they'd shy away.

The big change I see is in myself, and I think it's good. I think I'm more tolerant now, where I wasn't before. "Understanding" is a better word. I'm not going to look for the wrong in a person. I'm going to look for the right. When I see a black person come in now, I'm no longer on the defense.

There was a time when young black people would come in one door and out the other. They would get toothpicks or the little mints near the cashier at the door. Or else they'd want to use the bathroom. Our space was limited and people would get their purses stolen, okay? We were on the defense all the time. I instructed the cashier that if somebody walked off the street and we were crowded, we would say we just don't have any room. "Try the public one next door in the garage."

This one time I happened to be walking toward the front and a young black man was arguing with the cashier. He'd come in from the outside and asked where the bathroom was. She had instructed him to try next door; ours was for the customers and it was too crowded. I said, yes, that was our policy. He said okay. As I was walking around, watching the food and the customers—it was very busy—he brushed by me and almost knocked me over, heading for the bathroom. I said, "I thought I told you this was for our customers." He said, "I am your customer. I'm over there with my wife; we're dining." I said, "But you came from the outside." He said, "I was in your vestibule using the phone." I said, "Why didn't you say that?" He said, "Why should I? If I were white would you have said what you said?" I said to him, "You're right and I owe you an apology." He said, "I don't want your apology. Just leave me alone."

The man was correct. He sat down with his wife and they had a nice dinner. I tried to send him a drink as a way of apology but he didn't accept it. They finished their dinner and left. He was right and I was wrong. If I were in his position, I'd have done the same thing.

So what do you do? You just behave better the next time, if you're any kind of person. I always think about that. You don't make a rash judgment on a person just because he walked in the door or because he's black or white or Chinese. If you behave a certain way to a black, you'll behave the same way to a white eventually. If you're open to them, you'll be open to people of your own color skin as well.*

I was a racist. Yet life puts you in a situation like that, doesn't it? Here was a case of prejudgment, prejudice. I was guilty. Case closed. I respected that man for not accepting my apology. Why should he?

That was maybe eight years ago. I'll never forget it because I never felt so wrong. It has stayed with me. I think it changed me for the better. We get people coming in and they steal some purses or coats. We've learned to spot these people. But I think one second longer now before I challenge

---

* An elderly white woman, middle-class, petite, soft-spoken, recounts a recent experience: "I find that in my advancing seniority, I must use the bathroom more frequently. When I go out to shop and do errands, more and more places of business are turning me down. They say: 'We have no public bathroom.' Or 'We can't allow the customers, it's just for the employees.' This is infuriating to me, especially when my bladder is demanding.

"One afternoon I was at a health-food store that I regularly patronize. The young man said, 'The washroom is only for employees. There's a place next door.' I went next door and they would not allow me to use it. It was only for employees. By this time, my bladder was insistent. So I stood there very haughtily and I said, 'I insist.' At that point, the manager, standing nearby, gave me the key.

"I don't know what it is. I guess it's fear of damage, fear of crime. If I'm turned down, and I *am* harmless-looking, everybody must be turned down. There's a general fear that is all-pervasive. A fear of strangers. It's very discouraging."

them. It's like street smarts. You sit back and watch rather than jump in and make mistakes. It's better.

I think there's been a resurgence of racism in certain sectors. But I don't think there's that much fear anymore. This is *my* feeling. If we have a solution for this race thing, it will take time. But something can be done now.

The media have to be a little more specific in how they show people's relationships. I believe there's racism both ways. I never believed it was a one-sided thing. I think those of us who are coping with it and learning not to be racists ought to be in the forefront leading the fight against intolerance.

Want to hear a funny story? We had just hired our first black waitress. She was very good. Mr. Smith, let's call him that, walked in with his friends. He was a black banker in the area. We'd talked about racial things from time to time. I said, "Mr. Smith, we have a black waitress now and I'm going to seat you with her." He said, "If I wanted a black lady to wait on me, I'd go home for lunch." I always laugh at that.

There's a black middle class that's growing, but it's pretty bad for a great many blacks down below. This is a very opportune time to do something about it. With less of a threat of World War III, the nuclear thing now is pretty much diminished. We should demilitarize. There's no excuse now for not doing that.

The billions we were putting into the military should now be used for health programs, infant mortality, the AIDS thing. I think it's time for human needs to be met. I mean children are brought into the world with absolutely no chance. I mean it's bad enough that they have to be born in poverty and products of third- and fourth-generation welfare recipients. Uneducated. Do they have to be born into disease, too?

I'm talking about any people that are suffering. Let's get with it.

■ ■ ■ ■ ■

From the Far Side

MARK MATHABANE

He has written two memoirs, Kaffir Boy *and* Kaffir Boy in America. *In 1979, he came to the United States from a South African township. "To me, America was in every way the promised land. For the first time, I could have*

the opportunity to understand what is meant by a human being. My heart
was captivated by the ideal."

    He lives in Kernersville, North Carolina, with his wife. She is white.

My understanding of black life in America was largely based on reading
Ebony and *Essence*. And my encounters with black superstar athletes and
entertainers. These men and women had wealth and power and seemingly
had independence from whites. So I concluded that racism had been
abolished in America. The sacrifices made by Dr. King, Malcolm X, and
all the unsung heroes and heroines had not been in vain. Equality and racial
harmony had been achieved.

    I saw all these people in the movies. It was back in those days when
they were invited to South Africa to perform before integrated audiences,
so the government could use their visits to publicize the lie that apartheid
had ended.

    My Uncle Pietrus loved those magazines. In every way, he copied the
trends in America. He straightened his hair with those creams to make it
less kinky. He bleached his face to make lighter. He dressed very much like
the glamorous blacks in the movies and advertisements. The thing he failed
to copy was their accent. This was a source of great frustration to him. If he
could manage that, the masquerade would be complete. He could then
qualify for the status of honorary white.

    Racial classification was instilled in black people: the idea that you
could escape the indignities and oppression if you became white. Many of
those called "colored" have spent all their lives trying to pass for whites.
There was a time when tests were conducted to determine if you belonged
to one race or the other. In one, they ran a pencil through your hair, and if
the pencil got entangled, you were summarily classified as black. If you
had been white until then, you were promptly declassified as black. Families were torn apart.

    Uncle Cheeks was the more militant because his life had been spent in
jails. He was often arrested for general crimes. When he was denied a way
to earn a living, he turned to robbery. He robbed the suburbs. When he
came out of prison, he was a bitter man. But he was also possessed of a
certain wisdom. I remember after I had shocked the family around the
campfire reading the Declaration of Independence, about men being equal
in the pursuit of happiness, he said, "Let me give you a little wisdom, for
what it's worth."

    He said, "Nephew, I may not know America, but I know the white
man. Wherever blacks and whites have been together, and whites had the

power, the blacks must be their slaves." I countered, "Uncle, what do you say about Arthur Ashe, Sidney Poitier, and Belafonte?" He said, "I still insist. Racism may exist in America."

My first encounter with America led me to conclude there was something terribly wrong. When I arrived in Gaffney, South Carolina, to start at Limestone College, I discovered this town was constituted of two worlds. The whites lived in relative opulence. They had paved streets, clean and decent homes. The black world was steeped in poverty, pain, and suffering. It was the very same poverty, pain, and suffering that I had left in Alexandria and Soweto.

I hadn't been familiar with the North. In fact, I couldn't distinguish between different parts of the United States. I had an offer to go to Princeton but I took the one to Limestone simply because I couldn't tell the difference. I began to hear and read that Freedom Fighters from the North, men and women, black and white, came down to the South to end this oppression and that there was much pain and bloodshed and death involved. Life was said to be better in the North. So I began to move from college to college, eventually ending up at a small one in the North, Dowling College on Long Island.

Many black students, as well as whites, were oblivious to the heroic struggles fought for the mothers and fathers and grandparents to win them the right to vote and to attend decent schools. That shocked me because if you forget that crucial part of your history, where can you get the resolve to protect what has been won by blood and sweat and toil?

When I told them about apartheid, they failed to see the connection to their own struggle here. Racism in America tended to be seamless, yet it was pervasive. They showed the same indifference and apathy of their white counterparts. The irony is that many came from poor families and were on financial aid.

For six, seven years, I was leading a schizophrenic life up North. Not to know what you're fighting against, to be constantly banging your head against invisible walls, it kills your soul. There were times when I longed for the world of apartheid. People would say, "How can you long for that abominable world?" At least in South Africa, I knew what I was fighting against. I knew what the limits were, so I could brace myself. Here I am told I'm free, I'm the equal of everyone, fair play is the name of the game. Yet, try as many of us do we seem to get nowhere.

I spent so much time, so much heartache in search of an apartment in New York. I would call on the phone and they would say, "Oh, we have a lovely front ocean home for you to see." They were deceived by my accent.

They thought I was British. When I appeared a few hours later, well-dressed, suit, tie, and all, I'd be told the place was rented. I didn't drink, I didn't smoke, I did nothing to lead them not to rent me the room. It had taken two hours to reach this place, by train, ferry, and subway. I had a white friend call and he was told the apartment was still available. To me, who had lived in South Africa under the Group Areas Act, there was no difference, really.

So I decided to go back to the South, where you know where you stand. I would at least know who my true friends are. And my enemies. I was surprised to find that because of the civil-rights struggle, the few changes that have taken place toward integration have been more genuine and have had admirable results.

At my first attempt, I was shown a dozen apartments. All had white managers eager to show me the best. This was in Greensboro, North Carolina, where the first sit-ins occurred. It was cosmopolitan, integrated; I never experienced a rebuff.

There were people who didn't like me. The Ku Klux Klan marched, but I knew it was the Klan. I also knew when I gained acceptance, it was genuine. The discovery I made was that virulent racism had been transferred to northern cities, places like Howard Beach, Yonkers, Chicago, Boston. They were torn apart, polarized by emotions which not too long ago were thought to be the exclusive preserve of the South.

I asked myself: Why? The answers I came up with: Despite slavery and Jim Crow, the black and white people lived in close proximity and knew each other. Whereas in the North, before the black migrations, their acceptance was intellectual and theoretical. When they began to move into the cities, into the workplace, into the schools, into the neighborhoods, they had to be dealt with as a real presence. The reaction was a visceral one, full of hate.

When people heard me speak, they suddenly judged me differently. One time I said, "I know American blacks who speak English well. Why are they regarded as different from me?" They went into convoluted explanations: "No, we're not prejudiced at all." What I discovered was that I didn't approach them with the hostility and anger that they perceived black Americans had. I could see a little bit of truth in that. I had gone beyond my anger and hate because of my South African experiences. When I approached a white person, I gave him the benefit of the doubt. There was little confrontation. It's doubly difficult for black Americans to avoid being angry or tense, because they've been through the furnace of racism and have been burned.

The reality is a mixed bag. It depends largely on who you meet first. If you meet a black mugger, your experience will be different from encountering a reasonable, sensitive, and proud black person. Very few whites have ever set foot in Harlem. In South Africa, there's a law that forbids whites from entering a ghetto. In America, there is no such law in effect. So what's to prevent you from using the stereotypes you see on television every night: murder, mugging, crime? It's very easy to say, "I don't go there because look who they are."*

There is a legitimate fear, of course. It arises from the fact that black communities are disintegrating. The family structure has almost been decimated. In South Africa, we were deprived of much of everything through apartheid. But the one thing we refused to let go was our sense of family. It's the one thing that endures. There were midnight raids on the home of my parents for the crime of living together as husband and wife. Yet they stayed together because they knew how important it was psychologically to us children growing up.

I have seen it happen here, with the husband forbidden to be in the house of a welfare mother. I oppose that with every fiber of my being because I know how important a stable family structure is.

The city is oftentimes inhuman. The bond that ties people together is shattered by much of city life. I remember the feeling of community, where, as a child, if I go wrong and my parents are away, the neighbor will look after me, where we go next door for sugar or a piece of bread and get it. That seldom happens today in the city. The spirit of community still lives in small hamlets. That's why I live in Kernersville.

My wife and I had problems with black and white people. Some blacks wondered how I could contemplate marrying a white person when I'd been through the oppression of apartheid. They felt I had to be more angry toward white people. I knew from childhood that anger and hatred can be blinding and lead toward self-destruction. I almost died at one time because those passions were consuming me. I was about fourteen or fifteen and right in the thick of the schoolchildren's marches through Soweto. We

---

* "Chicago television news programs feed racial anxiety and antagonism by giving dramatically different treatment to African-American and white suspects. While white suspects usually appear on the news as individuals, black suspects often appear as the incarnation of a threatening and anonymous underclass, according to a study by a Northwestern University researcher, Professor Robert Entman.

"White suspects were much more likely to have their side of the story told. While only nine percent of all black suspects got their version of the events into the news—via a reporter's interview with the suspects, their friends, relatives or attorneys—nineteen percent of all white suspects were able to offer some sort of explanation."

Ted Cox, *The Chicago Reporter*, January 1991

had to fight for our rights because our parents were so battle-weary. I was saved because my mother told me, "You must learn to look at people's hearts." She did.

White individuals were the ones who kept me from being consumed by the anger I felt because of such injustice. I knew I should resist condemning white people as a group to perdition because the police mowed us down.

The reason I was able to go to school was because a white nun helped me get that paper without which I could not register. The only way I was able to learn to read and write, to break the shackles in my mind, was because a white family gave me those books which were denied in tribal schools. The only way I was able to come to America was because a white American tennis pro, Stan Smith, gave me an opportunity which my country had denied me. How can I deny my senses that there are white people who are different? I couldn't live with myself. A sweeping judgment is very dangerous.

It was painful for me when I was told marrying a white woman was a betrayal of the race, that it was a sign of disrespect for the black woman. I answered: "On the one hand you say segregation is wrong, the Mixed Marriages Act is wrong, the Group Areas Act has to go. I agree with you, because individuals have to be free to do as they please as long as they don't harm others. If you say that is wrong, how can you say a black person cannot befriend or marry a white person in the name of black pride? How can you justify that which you abominate in white people?"

My family was fully and openly and lovingly accepting of my wife. She herself comes from a family with a strong liberal tradition. Her father, a minister, was chased from his church and run out of town in Texas because he rented his house to a black family.

Nevertheless, there are liberals in name only, who support integration—but when it comes *home*, they have a different feeling. My wife stood her ground. Sometimes people focus too much on what I had to go through, but they don't understand what she had to overcome.

Most of the trouble is with the male, black and white. We know that in slavery days the white male violated the black woman with impunity. Among some black men, having sexual relations with a white woman is seen as a conquest. I find this painful because you're dealing with human feelings, and people get hurt. It's treating the relationship of man and woman in a cynical, power-driven way. It's no different from what a white male does. You have acquired the same bestiality he had when your women were his slaves. You have confirmed what he always wanted you to be.

The reasonable black man ought to be wary of playing that power game. In the end, it compromises something very important, something black people have cherished a long time ago. It is despite how they are treated by white people, they will resist fighting back in kind. If we suffer from racism, by fighting back in a racist way, we confirm the prejudice of those who began it.

Oftentimes, the problems that afflict the poor and the powerless are not racial. They're problems between the haves and the have-nots. I have met poor whites. I befriended one who walked to school wearing his sister's panties because his family couldn't afford to buy him underwear. They used a propped-up door as a table. They were exploited by the gentry not because they were black. They were as white as the people who oppressed them.

South Africa is a mirror in which I see a lot of America. There are black yuppies who are very conservative. They work for multinational companies and drive BMWs. They act as a buffer between the privileged few and the aspirations of the many. They say, "Yes, apartheid is wrong, but you don't need to radically change the society." The only thing that distinguishes the two societies is that here there is a rule of law and of institutions that act as checks and balances. These are under siege today because politicians without backbone are abandoning causes to the prevailing wind of public opinion.

Today many people believe there is no longer any need for civil rights. Many believe there is no longer any need for unions. There is no longer any need for holding authority accountable. Reagan was never held accountable for any of the things he did. To blindly follow custom is the danger that faces America.

Tomorrow looks a bit sad because of the nature of the current generation. The older ones have been conservative and their contemporaries who fought them are battle-weary. In the past, the visionary force was in the young. But if the young are more conservative than their elders, we're in for it. Perhaps there will be a change in the nineties. Something seems to be in the wind. I hope.

America, as I learned as a South African high-school boy, was born out of struggle. The Revolution in this country was inspired by the Enlightenment. Yet liberalism today has become a dirty word. Yet what gave birth to our finest hours in America? The American Revolution was not a conservative one. It was a liberal, radical revolution.

RIAN MALAN

He is a member of a powerful Afrikaner family. His great-uncle, Dr. Daniel Malan, as prime minister, established apartheid in South Africa.

In his memoir, A Traitor's Heart, *Rian Malan reflects on his life in his native country. Until his return to South Africa, he lived in the United States for eight years.*

When I came to the United States in 1977, I thought people would ask me about apartheid and my complicity in it. I spent a lot of time rehearsing explanations. I never got a chance to use those lines. It seemed very strange to me.

In all my eight years in the United States, I got only one hostile reaction. At a party in Los Angeles, I was introduced to a black woman poet. "Where are you from? Australia?" "No, South Africa." She turned on her heel and walked away. This was my only rebuff in America. Most often, I've been slapped on the back and told, "Good job." Especially in cities like New York, cabbies would turn around, clasp your hand, and say things like, "You guys know how to deal with them."

The first time I visited the Vietnam Memorial in Washington, a bunch of vets heard that I was South African. A guy started yelling, "Hey, Jimbo, come over here, we've got a South African." They were pumping my hand and saying, "Congratulations. You guys know how to deal with Commies." I remember one guy at a bar saying to me, "South Africa! You got lots of toads down there. Did you get one for me?"

A lot of white Americans confide in me: "At last, you are somebody to whom we can unburden ourselves." You hear it all. "We dislike affirmative action." "They're taking over." "They do crime." They do this and that. You often hear the racist litany, wholly uninvited. People unload some of the poison in their hearts because they figure you, a South African, will be sympathetic.

There is a countervailing reaction from black Americans, equally surprising. Because I was a white South African and surely a racist, I would not bullshit them. Since I had to be a dyed-in-the-wool racist, there would be no ambiguity here. I'd represent a confrontation for which they'd be prepared. They felt I would not patronize them or speak to them with a forked tongue. They've known whites who say politically correct things to their faces and then go home and fulminate about welfare mothers and black crime.

There's a corollary in South Africa. There, you often hear blacks say they prefer to deal with Afrikaners rather than the English because they are unreconstructed racists. The English-speaking South African may say to your face that all men are brothers and then hurry home to his mansion in the suburbs. With the Afrikaner, there is no ambiguity. I hear the same thing from white Southerners in the United States. "Blacks prefer us to Northerners, because they're hypocritical and we say what we think."

When white Americans run into me, they seem enormously relieved to find themselves in the company of someone they assume is a fellow racist. They don't have a chance to foam at the mouth in this way every day. It was perhaps an underground feeling being released, saying things to me they wouldn't say to you.

The people I hung around with were middle-class. Professionals. The others were glancing encounters at a bar, in a cab, at a newsstand. I ran into both extremes: blue-collars and dowagers with purple hair, dripping with pearls and diamonds. I met country-club patricians who were as outspoken as their blue-collar counterparts.

I was at a fund-raiser for General Singlaub, a hero of the far right. You remember his name from the contra-Irangate hearings? There was fine food and drink, and Fawn Hall was delightful to look at. As I was smoking outside in the ornamental garden, two couples were there, elegantly dressed. The guy, who spoke to me, looked like a CEO was supposed to look—silver hair, cleft chin. He unburdened himself of his many grievances. He was gung-ho in favor of white supremacy in South Africa. "You guys have to maintain power. It's ridiculous to consider the alternatives." I said, "To do this, you invite a darkness in your heart." I wanted to talk about what it's like to be a secret policeman in South Africa, involved in assassination squads. This guy looked at me as though I were some kind of nut, almost pityingly. "Machine-gun the bastards," he said.

During the course of the decade I've spent here, I think race relations have worsened. Things that were not spoken about during the civil-rights years are suddenly being discussed. In 1979, I ran into very few individuals who expressed antagonism to black claims for restitution. Now you hear it at dinner parties, without any fear of embarrassment. It has increased in the course of the Reagan years.

It's harder for me to gauge, but I sense a similar shift in attitude among blacks. There appears to be the ascending star of Louis Farrakhan. He reminds me of Eugene Terre'blanche of White Earth. He's an enormously charismatic leader of this paramilitary right-wing sect in South Africa. His henchmen wear uniforms that resemble those of the Nazi storm

troopers. Their literature is full of references to Aryan mysticism. Farrakhan is also a powerful orator. Though I'm white and come from the far
side of the planet, I could feel the pull as he appealed to black pride.
Terre'blanche was a failed actor. I understand Farrakhan was a failed
nightclub entertainer.

The racism is so unashamed now. Being from South Africa, I'm
obsessed with race. Any chance remark about race registers with me, click!
I just sense the whole zeitgeist here has changed. I'd increasingly hear,
"Fuck the blacks. They're responsible for crime. They do nothing but beg
crumbs from the white table. It's about time they stood up for themselves."
I think it's that whites, feeling threatened by crime, see it as something with
a black face. People I've met were victims of street crimes, having their car
boosted or handbag snatched. They saw it as a racial matter.

When Ronald Reagan was first elected, the economy was coming out
of a recession. With the yuppie gold rush on Wall Street, there was this
sudden new confidence in certain sectors of white America. There were the
people who benefited from Reagan—the "Master of the Universe syn-
drome," as Tom Wolfe called it. "We're going to flex our muscles and voice
our opinions now." They wouldn't be saying blacks are animals or missing
links. That's the tenor of what you hear in South Africa. No, here was the
notion, "I'm tired of caring. I don't feel guilty anymore. They can just look
after themselves." It's possible to have these messages in code.

It might be best for these things to actually be put on the table. If this
tumor is to be drawn from the guts of the people, you can look at it and say
this is the nature of it. You can never hope to cure a condition unless you
make the correct diagnosis. You can't make the correct diagnosis if you
pretend it doesn't exist. I think there's been an unhealthy trend in America
for a long time not to discuss race. It was governed by a taboo in which
people had to be very careful what they'd say or how it might appear. I
think airing prejudice could be healthy. A lot of black people may have
their feelings hurt, but at least we'll know what we're dealing with. Then we
can begin to counteract it. Race prejudice is something that thrives in
ignorance.

I keep wondering what kind of message young blacks—teen-agers
and little children—have been getting these past fifteen years from society
at large. Perhaps they've been encouraged to think of themselves as victims
and that the system is stacked against them. The message would be:
"You're bound to fail and it's okay to fail. It's not your fault." That must
surely inculcate fatalism.

What strikes me in America is how few blacks I've met socially. In all my circle of friends, there was one black. When we went out to eat, there was this one black who would occasionally show up. Here, my world was almost exclusively white.

This is not the case in South Africa. True, there are so many blacks to every white. But there is a great deal of interaction these days, social as well as at the workplace, between whites and blacks. In Johannesburg, if you go to a press party for an art show, there are many more black faces there than there would be in the United States. Last New Year's Eve, I went to a trendy party in the northern suburbs of Johannesburg. The woman who threw it was in advertising. Out of a hundred guests, twenty were black.

I remember having a long argument at dinner one night. It was a ferocious discussion of IQ tests conducted by a Canadian academic. The nature of racial intelligence. Several people found this enormously disturbing, Nazi in its thrust. We had this heated argument of nature-versus-nurture and the role of politically induced factors, such as the quality of black education.

When I first came here in 1977, I hardly came across anyone who believed in the link between intelligence and genetics, and would have the boldness to say so in polite society. Back then, it would have been deemed offensive and taboo. You'd have kept those notions to yourself. Perhaps you'd have discussed it with New York cabdrivers, but not uttered it at a table where there were people you didn't know.

In spite of this new frankness about race, we're inclined to look at the problem where it surfaces, among those we associate with, and not at the broad mass of Americans. If you come from a society like mine, where so many people are deformed by racial prejudice and fear, you guys have actually made some progress. The clock may have been turned back a little, but I believe you can actually sort it out, short of violence. The good will to do so actually exists. Yet after eight years of Reaganism, it's not an assumption I can easily make.

■ ■ ■ ■ ■

From the Near Side

MARIA TORRES

She teaches political science at a city college in Chicago.

"I was born in Cuba in 1955. My mom was a university professor and my father, a doctor. They had supported the revolution, but felt its course was too radical. There was a lot of violence in the early sixties because of the intense counterrevolution. The United States had set up the Peter Pan operation. Its object was to disaffect the middle class. They scared them into sending their children to the United States. In 1961, I came to Miami on a plane filled with six-year-olds."

I remember when Kennedy was killed. I was in third grade. This was in Midland, west Texas. The kids at school said Fidel Castro had him killed. When they found out we were Cuban, they really took it out on us. They followed me and my cousins and threw rocks at us.

It took me at least fifteen years to reconcile with Cuba because of the deep emotions I felt. People didn't distinguish between the Cubans here and the Cubans there. I'd say, "That's not me." There are Cubans that are communist and Cubans that are not. We're not.

When I was in fifth grade, my best friend was a black girl. I was the spic in the class and she was the nigger. People threw things at us and that brought us together. She was very talented, a marvelous pianist. I lost contact with her after eighth grade. I ended up lucky and she got pregnant. She became a prostitute and was killed by her pimp.

We had a teacher in this Catholic school who had been in the Peace Corps. She talked about the need for peace in Vietnam. It shocked all of us because it was so strange to hear somebody in Midland speak out against the war. My father decided to join the John Birchers because he felt she was a communist.

The John Birchers were also against us for being Latinos and my friend's family for being black. There were fights. The kid whose mother was the head John Bircher called my friend a nigger and had his teeth knocked out by her brother. My mother threatened to divorce my father. She said, "The Birchers are great on communism, but they're racists and hate us. That's more important." It didn't seem to matter, because they both have become staunch political conservatives. They're middle-class intellectuals who believe in civil liberties. They're full of contradictions.

I've been in Chicago for ten years. I see a confused relationship between blacks and Latinos. In 1982, we had a lot in common. When the Alvin Ailey dancers came here, they performed dances I had learned as a little girl in Cuba. Actually, I felt more African than a lot of African-Americans. Cuba is a country of mulattos: the culture, the dancing, the music.

What brought Latinos and African-Americans together was our powerlessness. We were not part of City Hall. A few poverty pimps were given grants because it's easier to buy off a small percentage of Americans than to really integrate the many. In 1983, the great many grass-roots groups in the city worked together and elected Harold Washington as mayor. The Latino vote played a major role because it was the one community that switched. It was the swing vote.

I was a point person in bringing Latino issues to City Hall. While we gained in respect, we butted heads with technocrats who happened to be black. If it were whites or Latinos, it would have been the same. Everything in this city is cast in terms of race. It became a case of Latinos versus blacks.

It was an uneven kind of relationship. Latino and African-American progressives were saying there was not enough being done in this matter. As Harold's second term got under way, an interesting alliance was being formed. Chicago, at that time, was atypical. As the rest of the country was moving toward the right, we were an oasis, a social-democratic administration. With Harold's sudden death, it all fell apart.

Let's face it, there was a lot of antagonism. We live in a society where race defines almost everything. I was always white growing up until I came to the United States. Then I became nonwhite, a Latino.

I've never tried to pass. My best friends from graduate school are African-Americans. But I've never been allowed, even by them, as someone who has also suffered discrimination. That's always been denied me. There's always this pressure to say the most exploited community is the African-American. I've experienced it, too. This has made unity so difficult to come by.

What we lack is critical thinking. I find African-Americans as racist against undocumented workers as white ethnics. They're viewed as people who are shady, greasy, stinky: the busboy, the maid, the cook. The last immigrants are in fact undocumented workers. In turn, Latinos have a feeling against African-Americans because they're black.

My baby-sitter, who is Mexican, is scared if she sees a black on the bus. She's afraid she'll get mugged. Even her eight-year-old daughter has the feeling. I think that a black woman walking through Pilsen* would have the same feeling about Mexicans. There are these common misconceptions, these stereotypes, that lead to irrational racism.

My daughter, who is four, was not aware of racism until we visited Cuba. People there are not hung up about it. You hear "el negro," "el blanco," "el chino." It's part of daily conversation. You can't struggle against racism by not talking about it.

Job competition is the key. Latinos have always been brought into industries when there is a labor shortage. The history of Latino labor recruitment is one of collusion between government and industry. After '61, even privileged Cubans were brought up to break strikes. We know that blacks were used at certain times in the same way. People come here for jobs, not to be unemployed.

Latinos are interested in affirmative action because of the historical discrimination against themselves. Most accept the fact that you need special programs for inclusion. At the time African-Americans and Latinos are entering what have been exclusively white institutions, there are growing inequalities. The promise of the civil-rights movement has not come to pass, so we're disenchanted.

Latinos feel that not enough attention has been paid to them. Of course attention must be paid to blacks. This country's economy was based on slavery. But it was also built on the backs of Latin American countries.

We have more of a sense of our history than blacks. We have had a continuous flow from Latin America, whereas the African-American community does not have that same connection with Africa. Their ties were truncated in a violent way. While you can't erase skin color, you can erase a people's connection to their homeland.

As the Latin American communities tried to become more American, especially in the fifties, they also understood they were not accepted. To show their loyalty, they'd go off to fight the wars and come back with Medals of Honor. A friend of mine said he never faced discrimination in the army: he was always put on the front line. [*Laughs.*] He came back from World War II and saw that his little brothers and sisters were not allowed to attend the white high school. This was in Texas. Loyalty did not pay off.

The closer you came to the American bone, the more discrimination you felt. As long as you were working in the fields, nobody gave a shit whether you spoke Spanish or English. All they cared about was how many

---

* A predominantly Mexican community.

bushels you picked. When you walked into the university, you were suddenly a threat. The more integration there is into the system, the more racism is felt. That's for blacks, too, of course.

I have friends who were involved in the Cuban counterrevolution, but they departed from American foreign policy when they recognized the racism within that movement. The profiles that CIA had of Cuban-Americans were outrageous; they're loud, boisterous, not to be trusted. They were integrated into the CIA all right—as informers. Batista may have been a dictator, but because his grandmother was partly black, he was not allowed into the American country clubs. It tells you who really ruled Cuba.

I remember having to fight with Harold Washington on the language issue. He wasn't clear about it. I was saying that you don't need to know English to be a mason or a sanitation man. His position was: If you're here, you should be able to speak English. Even he didn't understand that language was part of identity. It's like asking an African-American to straighten his hair because that's the way Americans do it.

African-Americans are much more U.S. than we are. We're a lot more "other." José Martí said it beautifully: there's *nuestra América*, our America, Spanish-speaking, where we touch each other, and the other America, where they don't let you do that or that. African-Americans are much more part of the white world than they are of ours.

In the national consciousness of Americans, the issue of slavery is much more understood than the issue of conquest. Americans have put slavery away as something of the past. Conquest is something that continues to happen. We intervened in Mexico, We intervened in Cuba. We took over Puerto Rico. We have recently intervened in Panama. Need I mention the others? We are still being conquered.

Latinos really don't fit the immigrant model, certainly not that of the Europeans. We're more the exiles. I think most Latinos yearn to return home. They have a homeland. That's another thing that makes them different from African-Americans.

The United States really needs to find its soul. It has to be one that recognizes its strength in diversity. What makes a world power really great is being able to say we're rich because we have different kinds of people. The minute you do that, you relate to other countries differently. As long as you're riding on empty, on military power only, you don't have to learn anything. You can put a gun to somebody's head and you don't have to learn their language, you don't have to understand them or who they are or why they're here. You don't have to respect them. You're in charge, but it certainly doesn't make you loved.

■ ■ ■ ■ ■

Overview III

DR. KENNETH B. CLARK

Psychologist. For several years, president of the American Psychological Association.

His findings were crucial in the Supreme Court's 1954 Brown vs. Board of Education *decision that desegregated American public schools.*

On this late afternoon, he greets me in his office, an hour's train ride from New York City. He speaks softly, as of something lost and long ago. At times, his reflections are offered in so subdued a tone, you strain to hear. There is the play of a faint smile, ironic.

I was full of optimism at the time of the *Brown* decision. Thurgood Marshall* and the other lawyers, and my social science colleagues, whom I involved in working with me, thought this was going to be a turning-point. How naïve I was! I thought the *Brown* decision was going to be very important for whites, too. It would take a burden off their backs.

I felt that segregation was damaging mentally to whites as well as to blacks. At long last America would have some way of getting out of its moral schizophrenia. I thought that within ten years or so, America would be free of it. I'm telling you this as an example of my naïveté. I expected southern states to resist, but I thought that their resistance would decrease and that we were on the road to some sort of functional democracy. I even wrote an article about it. [*Laughs softly.*] That was in 1954. And I felt that through the sixties.

Years before the *Brown* decision, I wrote a paper about the deep feelings of insecurity and inferiority on the part of whites concerning the problem of race in America. The presence of blacks was very difficult for them to handle.

If you look at the history of various immigrant groups, you'll see they were fleeing oppression and really believed that the United States had streets paved with gold. The only thing they really found were blacks,

---

* At the time, Mr. Justice Marshall was chief counsel of the NAACP, representing the complainant.

constantly below everybody else. They had conflict among themselves, ethnic rivalries. But one thing white immigrants could do in America was to believe they were moving upward because the blacks were always there, down below.

The presence of blacks in America was very valuable psychologically for upwardly mobile white ethnic groups. While there could be conflicts among them—each new immigrant group subjugated by the earlier immigrant group—the true test of their Americanization lay in their hostility to blacks: the someone always below them.

The black was visibly different and was kept inferior by institutional ritual.

Look at the American labor movement. With very few exceptions, it was never able to grow strong and effective because it was oppressed by its own racism. There's a curious kind of tragic humor in racism oppressing its perpetrators.

Racism in the South, confrontational, was never as complex as it was in the North after *Brown*. Among white ethnic groups in the North, the insecurities became more conscious. As long as southern laws and racial conflict were discussed, northern whites could go one of three ways. They could be self-righteously liberal in working with blacks against the laws of the South. They could be indifferent. Or in a minority of the cases, they could identify with southern whites. Yet in New York City today, there is a much higher percentage of segregated schools than there was before *Brown*.

What I found fascinating—and I'm disturbed at myself for finding it so—is the tragically humorous condition of northern whites. The civil-rights movement made northern white ethnic groups more democratic. The Poles, Jews, Italians, Irish, could all get together in their hostility to the blacks. It has become another aspect of the democratic creed.

In coming to America, they envisioned social and economic equality. They had actually thought it existed. Though it turned out not to be the case, they were able to mask their racism behind the illusion of classlessness. Being white in America made them feel equal to all other whites as long as the black was around down below. They voted this way. Consider the blue-collar vote for Reagan. He may not have been their friend, but they felt equal to him.

The illusion of classlessness among whites led them to believe that all whites had opportunities to do this, that, and the other until the blacks came along. Every psychologist knows there are individual differences in every group. Every white applicant for, say, a policeman's job, believing he'd get the job or promotion were it not for affirmative action, is engaging in a fascinating sort of idiocy.

To this day, I cannot understand how the masses of whites, of modest or limited means, could trade economic realities for the illusion of racial superiority. In the war on poverty, a substantial number of whites were poor. In actual numbers, there are more poor whites than poor blacks. But they would not join with blacks in antipoverty programs. I'm fascinated. They would deprive their own children of economic opportunities in order to remain distant from blacks.

It is premature to believe that class has subordinated race in this matter. As the relatively small number of middle-class blacks increases, the number of underclass blacks increases geometrically.

I don't think it's accidental that the number of blacks, especially black males, in graduate and professional schools is decreasing. They were permitted an increase during the temporary period of the civil-rights movement. The Bakke case indicated enough was enough. The attack on affirmative action was successful.

It is not accidental that given even the limited number of blacks in professional schools, the majority are females. Maybe it's too simplistic to say that black males are now an endangered species. But the evidence, I'm afraid, is there.

The female isn't perceived as much of a threat. My wife used to say to me when she was appointed to a board, "They have a two-fer, black and female." We'd laugh. The white male, dominant, has always associated his racial views with feelings of insecurity because of the stereotyped notion of greater black sexuality. It's the horror taboo: the black male and the white female. There was no such taboo when it came to the white male and the black female. These insecurities have come more and more to the fore.

In the sixties, on the part of blacks, there was a feeling of certainty of the move upward. A number of us, including myself, thought we were moving that way. What we didn't take into account was there was a point beyond which whites were not going to take this. Look what happened to the Democratic Party. It had various groups: blacks, other minorities, women, who were taking it seriously. That's when the party diluted its own constituency.

There have been advantages to certain blacks from the civil-rights movement, and they're not likely to give up those advantages. Blacks are human and one of the human challenges is how selfless you can be. A number of people have asked me for years, "How can you write the things you write? *You* made it." I was the first black professor at City University to get tenure. I should have safeguarded this. I came out of Harlem schools; why couldn't I say other Harlem students could become professors, too? I knew it was a very small percentage. I try to understand blacks who have made it and say American racism does not constrict. The only answer I can come up with concerns the human perspective. If you're successful, you're not going to identify yourself with failures.

In the 1940s, my wife and I conducted experiments among little black children. They found white dolls more attractive than black dolls. If we had really desegregated the schools and increased the educational opportunities for black and white children, if we had reduced the stereotypes, we educators could have changed those results. But we haven't and we don't intend to.

We educators, fine people, wouldn't bite the bullet: How do we really educate our children? I was on the Board of Regents for twenty-plus years. The feeling is we don't need to. We have come to believe that the social problems in our cities *are* indicative of the inferiority of blacks. A black friend calls this a self-fulfilling prophecy. I, always looking for some humor in tragedy, have thought the competition from the Japanese would get us to sit down and say, now look, damnit, we can't afford to waste ten percent of our population. But . . .

I had always believed that whites needed some way to get out of the prison of racism. Whether they were conscious of it or not, *they* were restricted by it. Obviously I was wrong. I thought that the *Brown* decision and the civil-rights movement would liberate the whites as well. But if they were liberated, you'd have to liberate blacks, too. They didn't want that sort of liberation.

If you oppress someone, if you make it clear to them that there are "opportunities," but they are not going to be permitted, what do you expect them to do? They become catatonic or, if they have energy, they're going to fight back. And they do, in antisocial ways. A very small percentage of them fight back in sports. As Arthur Ashe has pointed out, it's minimal.

Why don't we have full employment? You would have to employ blacks as well as whites. What would you do with the anxiety of whites: working with people toward whom they feel superior?

Bayard Rustin used to ask me, "With your cynicism, your pessimism, as intense as it is, why haven't you committed suicide?" My reply is: "I'm curious. I really want to see this process, this joke, up until I die."

I don't have doubts about integration. I have doubts about the nation, about its ability to be rational in this matter. As a result, I see someone like

Farrakhan being very effective in maintaining media attention. I suspect that white supremacists would love the separatists. My sense of irony might lead me to believe that black-separatist movements were probably anchored by white supremacists. [*Laughs.*]

I am not sanguine about any kind of solid decency and justice in the area of race in America. The best we can settle for is appearance. I'm at the stage of my life where I'm not going around shouting and expressing rage. As a psychologist—I hate to use this word—I'm enjoying watching the irrationalities of my fellow human beings, including myself. I look upon my life as a series of glorious defeats. No, not despair. I am merely looking at what exists.

■ ■ ■ ■ ■

Rise Up, Shepherd, and Follow

REVEREND C. T. VIVIAN

We were in Selma, Alabama. We were trying to get a voting-rights bill. I'm leading about forty people down to register. We come to the door of the courthouse; it's locked. Sheriff Clark walks us down these steps. We walk back up every time. This goes on for an hour. He won't allow us in.

One of these times, he relaxes his shoulders and drops his head. I thought he was about to talk. He suddenly pushes his billy club straight into my solar plexus. He's a well-built, heavy man. It knocks me back down the steps. Instead of falling, I hit every step, running backwards. All my life, I'd been able to run backwards quickly. That childhood thing came back to me.

I found myself on the sidewalk with the billy club in my hand. I'm ready to run back upstairs when it seemed like the sky opened for me. I remembered what a policeman in Mississippi told me: "When you're hit in the solar plexus with a billy club, you automatically grab it. You have it in your hand and that's an excuse for beating you, shooting you." Well, here I am on the sidewalk, ready to run up those stairs with the club in my hand, without thinking about it. Suddenly I remembered: These clubs are not used by nonviolent men. They belong in the gutter. I threw the club away and ran back up the steps. We met halfway. I began to talk. Sheriff Clark turned his back on me.

I said, "You can turn your back on me, Sheriff Clark, but you cannot turn your back on justice." He looked over his shoulder as if to say: "What does one do with a guy like this?" [*Laughs.*] He began to push me back again, so I gave ground, still talking. All of a sudden, out of the corner of my eye, I saw a billy club coming. Again, one of those childhood things came to me. I went up on my toes. I used to be the Ping-Pong champion of Macomb, Illinois. It's a fast game. You don't have time, it's reflex.

That club hit me right below the nose, across the mouth. It tore all the inside of my lower lip, and the blood came gushing down. I was down. I got up and kept on talking: "What do you tell your children at night? What kind of people are you?" It enraged him. "Arrest that man!" Of course, they beat me in jail.

In the jail cell, I fell on my knees and thanked the Lord for the joy of knowing that my life had been fulfilled.

His encounter with Sheriff Jim Clark was captured by photographers and revealed in the celebrated television series Eyes on the Prize.

I can't talk about what made me without thinking about my grandmother. She was deeply religious. It made me so, very early in life. One night, when they wouldn't let me go to church as a punishment, I was tempted to lay down in the road and let a car run over me. That sounds strange for our times, doesn't it?

His family had a couple of farms in western Illinois and lost them in 1929. They moved across the border to Missouri.

My grandmother and mother, having lost their farms and home, had only me. They decided I must have an integrated education, so we moved back to western Illinois. They picked a college town, McComb. They started planning when I was six and saved me when I was eighteen. I went on to college.

With racism, you have to make some good out of things that happen to you. If you're white, the normal route is to go to high school, college, seminary, and to a pulpit. If you're black, you may go to a year or two of college before you give out. You work at a dozen different jobs, and then, with all that experience, you center down on the spiritual, and may receive the call. You may not afford seminary, so you train under your local minister. You begin to read, teach Sunday school, and learn on the job.

I've done all sorts of things, you name it. I've been an assistant chef, owned a newspaper, owned a shining parlor. It helped me through college. During my last two years, I wrote term papers for white kids. I promised them an A or a B or I didn't get paid. Once a kid got a B– and didn't pay me. His father had an auto dealership in town and was very wealthy.

If I'd put my name on the paper, I'd have gotten a C. I often had to argue for a B. I could not say I had written papers for white kids who received A's and B's. It would have been immoral. But they weren't immoral in their racism. I'm not saying that each of these teachers was an outright bigot. They were so racist, they didn't know it. The judge doesn't understand how much racism affects his decisions. On the average, when a young black kid commits a felony, he averages five years, seven months. When a white kid does it, the average is two years, six weeks.

When you're stopped by police, you often don't know why. There's hardly a black American, when he sees a police car coming down the street, who doesn't think, "Uh-oh, they may get out, beat me, shoot me, and nothing would be done about it." Almost any black person, passing by, will stop, want to know.*

We have a sitting President who was partially elected with a racist ploy, the use of Willie Horton.

What really made it worse was his crime: rape of a white woman. It is the sexual fear that is basic: the sexual insecurity of the white male.

Guys have shot it out because white guys couldn't stand to see black guys with white women. What have white soldiers told European girls when they were overseas? "Blacks have tails." Talk about the devil!†

---

* I was riding along Chicago's Outer Drive with an elderly black couple. Two lanes away, the police stopped a black driver. As the others sped along, my companion slowed down, stared across the expressway, and mumbled, almost inaudibly, "I wonder what that's all about."

† Charles A. Gates had been company commander of the 761st Tank Battalion during World War II. It was a wholly black unit. On January 24, 1978, forty-three years after the war's end, it won a Presidential Unit Citation. "At the close of hostilities, strange things started to happen. Army Intelligence started checking out areas where Negro troops were located. They tried to poison the minds of the people. While we were in England, they went so far as to tell the people that Negroes had tails like monkeys and things like that. We just ignored that. We were on the front lines all the time."

Alfred Duckett had been a black war correspondent during the war. "There was a psychotic terror on the part of white commanders that there would be a great deal of association with the white women. In France, we had a chaplain who warned people in the communities that—and I'm not kidding—that we had tails. And that quite often, without provocation, we cut people up. A man of God."

The Good War, 1984

Blacks are beasts, right? We know they're oversexed and thus subhuman. If they ever get to a white woman, then, "Oh goodness, we couldn't win her back because she got a taste of Eden." Do you know the expression "If she goes black, we can't get her back"?

All right. Blacks are capable of anything all other human beings are capable of, all right? But white people deal with the exception and make it the rule. They don't say if one white man thinks a certain way, that's what *all* white people think. But if two percent of blacks think a certain way, they will write scores of magazine articles on the way black people think.

Small as the Black Muslim movement was at the beginning, it got all sorts of play. At the time, black Americans were in the streets by the millions thinking other stuff. White America found the exception and made it the rule.

The growth of the Muslim movement came directly as a result of the media, not because of black people. After something is revealed long enough, and it does some good, no doubt about it, it's going to attract people. It was the product of great PR, thanks to the media.

With rare exceptions, white people are reared to be racist from early on. It's in their gut. With blacks, the anger is there, of course. When the black woman sees most black men being constantly put down, making it difficult for them to have families in the American tradition, she is angry. When she sees some of the guys, who are doing well and can take care of a family, with a white woman, she is angry.

What society has done to her father and husband is being done to her son, and she is angry. She knows it's not a two-way street. She knows there are very few black men who have made it, and since there are ten times as many white women as black, competition is tough. She sees the white woman as having an open situation, while hers is closed, she is angry.

Blacks have a condition, not a problem. Whites have the problem, racism, that creates our condition. All we can do is react. Institutional racism, though not acknowledged, makes it official. It is impersonal. Individual anger is a personal thing.

What did black people ever do to white people, as a race? No reply. What did white people ever do to black people, as a race? You can fill a blackboard. If a white person says, "I'm a racist 'cause a black guy beat up on me," you ask, "Have you ever been beaten up by a white guy?" "Well, yeah." "Are you prejudiced against white people?" "No." "Are you angry at that one white man?" "Yeah." "Well then, why aren't you angry against the one black guy instead of against all black people?"

Every white man knows that if he were black, his life would have

been different. If he were honest, he'd admit he would never have made it if
he were black. He doesn't even have to think about it.

*What about the young white construction worker who says "I'm out of it,
because of affirmative action. They chose the black guy just because he's
black."*

He's not out of it. He's living off the fact that my father and grandfather
didn't work. You can't break a man's leg and blame him for limping. You
have a moral responsibility to fix it. If you've been living off it, you can't
say you're not part of it, that it was something done by somebody else. If
you want to be fair, you can't have a head start and say, "Catch up," without
doing something to make up that difference.

Oh, if there were full employment, whites and blacks all with jobs, it
would change the picture considerably. We could use governmental works,
too, like the WPA in Roosevelt's day. There's a shared destiny, corny though
it sounds, of black and white workers. But outside the union, they don't
necessarily share it or fight for the same things.

The strength of the black community was in men working in steel
mills and packinghouses, steady jobs. They were the real role models.
There were a few doctors and lawyers. They were helpful, of course. But
what really made the neighborhood stable was the fact that men were
working all the time. When those plants shut down, you know what
happened. What happens to a white blue-collar community when their jobs
disappear? Same thing. The neighborhood deteriorates.

That's why the civil-rights movement affected more than just black
people. The women's movement, gays, Hispanics, Native Americans. I call
it shaking "the people tree." Whenever you shake a tree, every leaf trem-
bles. Whether we like it or not, we're all connected in one way or another.

If blacks at the bottom can in fact move for their freedom, everybody
feels they can be free. It's no accident that Frederick Douglass, the black
abolitionist, was the only male speaker at the first women's-emancipation
program in Seneca Falls. The feminist movement went right along with the
fight against slavery. It was natural.

We're dealing with our country, that is going to be more and more
"minority." There is no way out of having an integrated society.

Everybody gets tired, as years and years go by and the dreams you
hold don't get fulfilled. It affects even the songs we sing. There was an old
song of defeat, a blues: "I've been down so long, down don't bother me." But
there's another theme that's always been sung throughout black history. It

was sung at every black meeting of any size. Our national anthem: *"Lift Every Voice and Sing."* [*He sings it.*] We have lived on hope all our lives. We have to keep hope when hope unborn has died. Our whole anthem is a prayer. It's to God we're singing.

There is no way you can separate religion from life. You cannot be a Christian and a racist at the same time. You can't just send missionaries, followed by soldiers or the commercial bit. There can be no redemption until there is acknowledgment of sin. Guilt is heavy in America, and the only way to throw off this burden is by changing the conditions that created it. But first there must be acknowledgment. Since the eighties, acknowledgment has diminished. Black people are told: "We gave you your chance and you failed." The truth is, we did not fail. They never lived up to anything they wrote down. America has never repented for what it's done to our people. Or shall we talk of the Indians and broken treaties? Our society has never lived up to anything they've said to anybody of color. So it's not a matter of "We gave you." They haven't given us nothin'. You cannot rob me and give me anything. If I rob you on the corner and then say, "Here's five dollars," it's absurd. I can't *give* you five dollars, right?

WILL D. CAMPBELL

He has neither a Genevan gown nor a steepled church. He refers to himself as a "bootleg preacher. A sort of Seventh Day Horizontalist." He attended Yale Divinity School and was chaplain of the University of Mississippi during the years 1954 and 1955. He lives in Mt. Juliet, Tennessee, just outside Nashville.

I was born and raised in Mississippi, where, for a number of years, it wasn't safe for me to go home. Now that has changed. Last year, I preached at the funeral of my father. He was ninety-one. I was welcomed with open arms. Twenty-five years ago, I'd have run a great risk.

John Lewis, who had been beaten many times and left for dead, is now a Congressman. Andrew Young has been our UN ambassador and mayor of Atlanta. Many of our largest cities have black mayors. Certainly there have been gains.

American race relations have always worked like a sieve. The mesh will open, expand a little bit whenever there is what white people call a crisis. When people take to the streets. A black friend once told me, "Harmonious race relations is when you've got your foot on my neck and

I'm not asking to get up. A crisis is when I start plucking the hairs on your ankle and say, 'Hey, man, how about letting me up? If you don't do it, I'll try to get you off balance and throw you off.' " The mesh then opens up.

During the civil-rights movement, more black people entered the mainstream. But it was a very limited number. The lives of most are unchanged. There's no gain to open up the Burning Tree Country Club. How many blacks can afford the thousand-a-month, or whatever it is, membership fee? What does it mean to open the finest restaurant in Nashville if these people can't even afford the five-and-dime store? I'm glad they're open, but how many does it touch?

I'm glad we have such a thing as merit employment, but what does it mean if the tests are written by white values? If the questions have to do with pheasant under glass, white and black ghetto people will flunk. They'll score poor and won't get the job. If you ask them about the breeding habits of cockroaches, they'll make a good score. You ask a black ghetto kid why his grandmother had iron beds and he'll know: to keep the rats from crawling up. A kid from Scarsdale will flunk. He'd say, "I don't know. I guess they just liked iron beds."

The white guys who run things are still making the rules and capable of changing them. The Supreme Court is now doing that. "What do *they* want now?" What *they* want is no longer to be *they*. When they started getting in our way, those who make the rules said, "Hell, we'll change the rules."

What about the blue-collar kid who says, "I never stood on the neck of a black. My folks never had slaves. Why am I the fall guy?"

I had to face that with my son, who is in high school. He was afraid to walk the corridors because these black guys would circle him. You don't say, "They don't mean any harm." They do mean him harm. That's where we are today. All you can do is talk about history.

There's an anger on the part of young blacks. It's a mistake for me to say to my son or to this blue-collar kid, "It's not true." We have to acknowledge this kid is getting a rough deal. It does have to do with history. It does have to do with past sins. The fathers have eaten sour grapes so long that the children's teeth are set on edge.

In 1963, at a conference in Chicago—a conference to end all conferences—I said if black people are as good as we are, they're just as bad as we are. I encountered a lot of grief with that one. We're stupid if we think black people are anything but human. But it's the old story: We hate the people we've wronged.

My people are the blue-collar folks of the South. That's why I hate the term redneck. Remember the poem by Edwin Markham: "Bowed by the weight of centuries, he leans upon the hoe and gazes on the ground." As he so leans and so gazes, this searing, parching, midday sun turns his neck red. We've equated that with racism.

We have to distinguish between fascism and bigotry. This is a racist nation. I am a racist and you are a racist because we've had the advantage from the day we were born. We may not be bigots. I'm not a bigot. I've been educated—or converted, for that matter—out of it. But I'm still a racist because my tribe still has the power and seems determined to hang onto it. As I think humans always will.

I'm very pessimistic about what we used to call the nature of man. That's what human beings are about: self-loving and self-preserving. That's all the theologians meant by original sin. We think more highly of our-selves than we do of the other person. Despite Jesus, Isaiah, and the Prophets, we go on doing that. We don't seem able to break out of it.

That's why I've always been reluctant to say to another group, "Here's what you ought to do." As a white, I can't say to a black American, "Here's what you ought to do." All I can say is, "This is the way it's always been throughout history. If you recognize that all people are self-concerned, it becomes obvious that the only way this cycle can be broken is for black people to do it themselves." Now this sounds like one hell of a cop-out, but it isn't.

Just yesterday, I was reading about Joseph Davis, the brother of Jefferson Davis. Ideologically, they were poles apart. They didn't get along. His best friend was his slave, Benjamin Montgomery. Why didn't he free him? He could have. When he was fifteen years old, Montgomery ran away. When Davis later asked him why, he began to chronicle all the evils of the system itself. Davis said, "How would you feel if it wasn't the case here?" He made him his bookkeeper and together they read and discussed philosophy, poetry, history, mathematics. After the Civil War, he sold his land to Montgomery. It became an all-black community. It succeeded. It began as a somewhat Utopian community. It is still success-ful. Why? Because no one was saying, "The whites are going to do something for us."

I know this sounds like the same old white garbage to say to people, "You gotta do this yourself." I'm not telling *them* what to do. I'm just telling them what white people are like and what human nature is like. If something's to be done, they have to do it themselves. I'm not talking separatism. I'm talking economics.

What's to be done? We have to give up some of the power. It's kind of bootleg and kooky, but it's radical Christian. It goes back to the Anabaptists. My anarchist genes are starting to raise their romantic heads. The call of Jesus and the prophets was not to get more power, but to relinquish some of the power they do have. It's not easy.

What may happen in this country is another movement of some *type*. It scares me because I certainly don't see a Gandhi movement on the horizon. I see people on the streets and bleak times ahead. But the power at some point has to be wrestled with and redistributed.

I don't know what's ahead for us. You can't predict the future. I would hope we could learn something from history, but apparently we don't. Yet in my home state of Mississippi, I have seen more changes than any other state in the union. When I was chaplain at Old Miss, my most radical position, after the Supreme Court decision, was it would take us twenty years to work out the sheer logistics. That made me a dangerous left-winger. The word was Never.

I never went around pressing the decadent South. Nor did I say the North was worse than we were. But I remember going through Mississippi when it wasn't safe for me. I was frightened, but not as much as the cabdriver up north, who locks the doors as he crosses a certain neighborhood. I remember thinking, "These people are not ever going to solve their problems, because they don't know one another."

I'm not saying people who know one another won't kill one another. We do that all the time. I'm saying in a volatile clash, we're less apt to kill somebody we know. At least, in the South, we knew one another's names. What has amazed me is that with all the radical changes in the South, there hasn't been more violence. Certainly, there's been too much, but I predicted far, far more.

It's a Persian rug of a tale. Weaving, unweaving, reweaving. I think we've got to unweave it to get the strings of the thread and make another rug. A carpet that will be inclusive. We haven't done that yet.

This country is far more segregated today. Last week, I was at a conference in South Carolina. There was not one black person out of fifty, sixty in attendance. Twenty years ago, that wouldn't have happened. I wouldn't have gone to anything—a social occasion, a wedding, or a political meeting—where there were not blacks and whites.

Today, I may be the only white in a gathering of black people. They jokingly say, "Hey, man, what are you doing here?" I say I'm being pushy. That's what we used to say about blacks. Now it's my time—our time—to be pushy. It's very uncomfortable. I don't like being pushy. I don't like going where I'm not wanted, but by God, I'm an American and I will go to places, just because some things ain't right.

In the marketplace it's different. I see black and white out on the sidewalk, smoking during their break. So I know they're inside working together. But when the day is over, they go back to their segregated homes.

In a college cafeteria, you see blacks sitting on one side, whites on the other. The whites says, "We opened this thing up. We tried to get *them* to come." The question we need to ask is this: Why didn't *they* want to come to meet *us*?

We have not yet diagnosed the problem because we haven't even acknowledged it. Blaming rednecks is the real cop-out. We have never acknowledged the degree of Negrophobia that has plagued this country from the very beginning when we took it away from some dark-skinned people, committed genocide to hold it, fought wars to expand it, bought and sold dark-skinned people to build it. God knows, Abraham Lincoln, the Great Emancipator, was not your basic old-fashioned integrationist by a long sight. We have never acknowledged the disease. Until we do, we're not going to find an antidote for it.

FATHER LEONARD DUBI

He had been one of the city's most renowned activist priests. As a passionate spokesman for his blue-collar parish, he had on numerous occasions challenged the city's most powerful men and institutions.

Today his parish is in Hazel Crest, a southern suburb of the city. It is adjacent to Harvey and Markham, poor and black, as well as to Flossmoor and Olympia Fields, affluent and white. It is a village of 15,000, with its own board of trustees.

It is an ordinary place with ordinary people, but there is an extraordinariness in the ordinary as we're dragging them into the future. That's what's so exciting for me. It's not a big thing. It's like a baby and it's growing, and so is the consciousness of the people.

Our community is in this turmoil of economic and racial change. The white people who have run have gone because of race, though they don't say it. Those who have chosen to remain accept an integrated setting and want to raise their kids here. They want to live on this land in the world of the future.

My parishioners are working-class people. A lot are white-collars, some have gone to college, most are high-school people. They came from families where racism was the accepted thing. A woman here was telling me of this mother, her former schoolmate. With her baby playing at her feet, it was "nigger" this, "nigger" that, all the time. Imagine that little child, hearing that from infancy. People in my parish grew up in such families and are now making a radical shift in thinking.

How come this change? One reason is practical: money. They couldn't afford to leave. So they have to stay and start living with their black neighbors, talk to them, and find they have common interests. The reason blacks move here is they want the same amenities as others: good schools, good parks, good services, safety. It's hard economics that has caused people to see each other as people.

The racial change has been going on here for sixteen years. We see black people moving in not as a problem but as a change. The blacks moving into my parish are probably better educated and make more money than the people they've displaced. Know one of the first things a black parishioner told me when I came here six years ago? "I have no problem when a community becomes black. But it's wrong when the community is poor, with high crime and low education and drug addiction and abandoned homes." Some of these subdivisions will be all-black, but most will remain integrated, because people are coming in for the property values. There are tremendous deals here, thirty, forty percent less than in the same-class all-white suburbs. We've got white families and black competing for the same homes. The price is right.

When I first got here, the parish was in disrepair. The school was losing students. People didn't want to talk about a five-year plan. We had to go to the archdiocese for help. The public school was ninety-percent black. St. Anne's was eighty-percent white, because people don't want to send their children to a school where the test scores are down and the discipline is conceived as being too lax. My fear was that St. Anne's might become a haven of racism.

We started one-on-one interviews, about a couple of hundred. No matter what the issue was when the interview started, it always came down to race. It was on everybody's mind. We did this for six years. We have a very good organization now in the community. It's grown and grown.

The shift in thinking has been amazing. A real education is taking place: who is doing what to whom? They understand that the real-estate industry and the banks and the government have a responsibility. When people start to see through all this, they can move together and reverse these patterns. That gives them hope. It's not just the power of love I stand for as a clergyman, but the power of *knowledge*.

I think the role of a pastor is to be a prophet. We're announcing the future in the way we live. We have a room filled with several hundred people, and it's salt and pepper. It's the way the world should be.

Because we're church-based, our meetings begin with a prayer. It's Catholic and Baptist and Lutheran. Ecumenical. It's like a revival. It's fantastic!

We have problems. The black people wanted to build a Cathedral of Joy out here. I love that name. [*Laughs.*] They wanted to build it in the old Bonanza Steakhouse. They have the money, they have the standing. For some reason, the village trustees and the zoning board didn't see it that way. Permission was denied. The Cathedral of Joy is suing Hazel Crest for $4,000,000. The suit was announced last week.* The community would have benefited to have a major black church, Baptist. We had a meeting at their building in Flossmoor. About a thousand people showed up. Cardinal Bernardin was there.

There is still bewilderment and suspicion and antagonism among us. Who said it was going to be easy? But we're finding out that the black people moving in want the same kind of things white people want. Oh sure, people who didn't like my stand have moved out, but now, almost to a person, I find support. We have black people on all our councils. They're readers at the masses. In our congregation, we pray every week for an end to apartheid in South Africa.

When I first got here we had a series of burglaries at the church. We caught somebody in the act. He happened to be black. My fear was that this would polarize the community. It didn't. People saw it as the act of one person. It was not a black-white issue. We now have a neighborhood watch.

I really see a waking up. I believe it all starts with self-interest. Call it selfishness. You start with that but it just doesn't remain there. It's enlightened self-interest. We're not just individuals. I prize individual freedom, but my freedom is limited by responsibility to a community. There's tension all the time between the individual and the community.

I remember when I was a little kid, five or six. I saw a black person for the first time. My father and this man had been out drinking. They were sitting in our kitchen, laughing and having a good time. I thought that was great. Yet I grew up with prejudice. When I became a priest, my dad and mom moved away because they witnessed a murder. A black person killed a white. My dad still has this hardness of heart when it comes to race. When he's with an individual, he's very loving and warm. But when he thinks about it in general, he's bitter. He has a great deal of fear.

---

* As of this writing, the case is still unresolved.

What I've seen in my twenty-two years as a priest have been the benefits that have come to this country through changes in the laws. At first, it was the political thing to do, then it became the right thing to do. I don't know if these laws have got into people's hearts. Barriers are brought down when there is communion. I've seen it work when I led a coalition of middle-class blacks and whites to stop an expressway that would have destroyed a neighborhood. I've seen it work in factories, in trade unions, where there's a common interest. It's more than a rubbing of shoulders, it's real dialogue. Attitudes don't change until there's a significant connection in their lives between themselves and people of a different race.

It's been a long time since I've served in an all-white community. Back in 1974, as I was looking at the kids in the parking lot outside my church and thinking, "Boy, they're nice-looking," it dawned on me that something was wrong here. I've been away long enough to realize that I never want to go back to an all-white community.

I would hope that everybody has that kind of an experience: to one day realize that it's wrong. People have choices, but being all one or all the other is not the future. Running away is not the answer.

If we can have it happen in the south suburbs, we'll be able to address the issue to racism to Chicago, and beyond that to the country and beyond that to the world. We think globally and act locally.

PART IV

Times Past, Time Present

EILEEN BARTH

She is seventy-eight. In the thirties and forties, she had been a social worker in Chicago. During the fifties and sixties, she worked at a child-care center, where most of her colleagues were black. She has been retired for the past fifteen years.

"I've become somewhat isolated. I don't go out a lot these days, so I don't know from personal experience what's happening now. I get things second-hand, mostly through television, radio, and the press. I think they make problems worse because they sensationalize. They don't analyze."

The Great Depression opened my eyes to a lot of things that were wrong. I learned about poverty firsthand. There were more white than black on relief. One could say the blacks were more accustomed to poverty. But still they said, "I wouldn't come here if I could find work." I worked in the black area. It was bad, but I feel there's a lot more hopelessness today. Then, people felt the Depression would end, that life would be better. The war came and ended the Depression. But the government at the time was trying to help, to provide creative programs. People don't feel that now. Black people, particularly, are in great despair. In the sixties, they fought for their rights, expected that their lives would be better. For many of them, it's worse.

Though I worked with black people most of my life and felt comfortable, I was never absolutely sure that I was accepted. I felt closer to some than to others, just like with all people. Perhaps I might have done things that offended people. I may have pulled boners; I don't know. Racism is such a poisonous thing, because behavior so often is unconscious.

Before the civil-rights movement, there was a very wide separation between blacks and whites. I don't think the separation is as great today. There has been more speaking out. Blacks now let themselves open up and say how they feel in no uncertain terms. I think there are friendships between blacks and whites that didn't exist before. In spite of everything, I think the racial situation is healthier than it was before. Blacks are no longer invisible. People didn't talk as much about the problem as they do now. Now the blacks demand attention. They say, "Get off my back." They're saying it all the time.

I've always felt guilty because I'm white. Whites have repressed blacks, so I feel guilt. Years ago, at the university, a black student lived in our building. A few of us girls decided to be particularly friendly to her *because* she was black. We didn't say it in so many words; no one mentioned it. We simply didn't want her to feel pain over being alone and neglected or possibly being treated badly by other students. I suppose I wanted her to feel that there were white people who could be friendly. I don't think it was patronizing. It may have been guilt that promoted it.

About ten years ago, I had an experience with some neighbor children. Next door lived a couple of white kids. Down the street in a project building lived a couple of boys the same age. The four of them started to build a tree house that branched out onto the sidewalk. They were mischievous kids who in the past dropped bottles on people. They really enjoy tree houses and I felt bad when I told them, "I'll not allow it. The tree house must go." I didn't yell, I just explained why.

Shortly after, I noticed pieces of glass in our house. In the bedrooms, too. Quite a few windows had been broken. Little nails were mixed with the glass. I guessed it was the boys. When I asked the two younger brothers about it, the little white and the little black, they said, "We didn't do it. Our brothers did it." I found out that their older brothers had used slingshots.

When I confronted them, they admitted it. During the confrontation, the black kid said, "You're accusing me just because I'm black." I was floored. My husband, passing by, yelled, "Cut that shit out!" I said, "I'm accusing Lloyd, too, and he's white." I'm sure he was using that excuse because he had heard others use it. They weren't particularly sorry about it. "If this happens again," I said, "I'll call the police, because it's vandalism." That was the end of the mischief.

Our street is middle-class, made up of various racial groups: Koreans, Chinese, a black family. We're all friendly. In the neighborhood, cars and garages have been broken into and there have been several muggings.

There's a lot of poverty in this community and homelessness and desperate people, mostly black.

There was a block meeting just the other day. A resolution was passed that we'd be alert, watch each other's homes, and call the police if we saw anything suspicious. What wasn't said, but the undercurrent was obvious: gentrifying the community, getting developers in, improving the property, making it high-rent. And getting rid of these people. The implication was so thick you could cut it with a knife. I thought it was a terrible meeting.

I hate it. I hate the idea of the isolation and fear that people are beginning to feel. And suspicion. But I am a bit fearful of walking out at night toward the park. I remember going to the mailbox on a Saturday evening about seven. It was a block away. There wasn't a soul on the streets. All I could see were cars speeding by. I felt absolutely alone. The only pedestrian. It was an eerie feeling. I walked home rather quickly. I was just a little unnerved, but very sad that I was the only one out. If this were another time, there would be people out walking on a Saturday night. There would be friendliness and a sense of fun. It was absolutely bare. People using their cars rather than walking. It's fear of the stranger who might harm them. It's the fear of blacks, because they're more desperate.

As I walk two blocks to the grocery or the restaurant, the thought flashes through my head that they might attack me. Young blacks frequent these streets. The feeling doesn't last very long. Any group of poor people might do it, especially if they're young. There are a lot of old, bedraggled people and winos with bent frames. I don't fear them. They seem too weak to do anything.

I was born in a small city in northern Wisconsin. There were no blacks. I hadn't seen people of color until one day, I saw black people on the street. They were servants of rich families that had come up from Chicago to vacation in the Apostle Islands. This was the first time I had seen people who were not white. Yes, I did see a few Indians. Native Americans.

When I was about six, we had a neighbor, a generous, loving woman, who always helped people when they were down and out. One day she talked about helping a "coon" family. They had a little shack in the country and they were suffering. She was very concerned about them. She referred to them all the time as "coons." I found out later they were blacks. She was worried that other people might not help them because they were "coons."

When I came to Chicago in 1931, I became conscious of the feelings against black people. I found out about restrictive covenants. I knew there were laws in the books forbidding restaurants from discriminating, but everybody accepted it. Nobody enforced the statutes. Near our district office, from which we administered relief, there were few places to eat. The white social workers would go to a fairly decent restaurant not too far away. The black social workers had to bring their own lunches.

Some of us decided to test it, this obvious ban. We went in one day, black and white. We sat down and waited and waited and waited. We had only an hour for lunch. We kept calling the waitresses and they kept disregarding us. Almost at the end of the hour, she banged the utensils on the table in a way that was meant to be insulting. We were all very embarrassed. We ordered lunches very quickly and came back to the office late. We decided to go back the next day, and all the tables were marked "Reserved." We talked to our office supervisor about it. She was a black woman. She was very upset with us. [*Laughs.*] She was scared and didn't want to make waves. So we decided not to go back. It was a traumatic experience. I felt put-upon and discriminated against. It made me realize how difficult it is for a black person to live in a society of this kind. They had to watch every move they'd make and be ready for any humiliation. It was a good lesson.

I remember riding to Wisconsin with several black colleagues. The husband of one, a cop, was driving. I was the only white in the car. Just as we were leaving the city, we were stopped by a white cop. I don't know why. Somehow, I doubt this would have happened to white people. The husband got out of the car and had some discussion with the other cop. He came back and said it was all right. I felt very uncomfortable. I didn't know if I should say something about it. I remember saying, "This is ridiculous." Why were we stopped? Nobody in the car said anything about it. We talked about something else. On reflection, I think this has happened to black people so often, they didn't think it was worth discussing.

When you say blacks are prejudiced against whites, it isn't quite the same as whites being prejudiced against blacks. The blacks have a reason. Their history. If black people sometimes go overboard in their feelings about whites, it's to be expected. It's just part of a response to all those years of oppression. It isn't surprising.

About fifteen years ago, a black friend of mine, a social worker, said that the black kids, wounded and alienated, will go crazy and become violent. She used the word "animal." Unfortunately she was a good prophet. She believed they were lost.

The nonviolent movement of Dr. King helped make many of the gains and won the sympathy of many whites, who saw black people behaving so admirably. They responded to taunts, to hoses, to beatings with nonviolence.

It seemed unnatural, but they did it, so it wasn't *that* unnatural.

JOSEPHINE CLEMENT

Howard Clement's aunt.

A quiet street, tree-lined; it is the archetypal avenue of the middle class of middle-sized American cities. Here are the homes of Durham's black professionals and merchants.

In this house is a plenitude of African art: paintings, sculptures, artifacts, books.

She is one of the doyennes of the city's black society.

As to the future, I wouldn't dare predict. Things change so rapidly. There are new alignments; old ones fall apart. I see a change from my childhood in Atlanta, where the lines were drawn very strictly on color. It didn't matter what your situation in life; if you were black, that was it. Now the division is more socioeconomic.

I noticed it when I took my daughter to a Girl Scout camp. We took turns car-pooling. There were two little black girls we didn't know. They had been brought in from a housing project. For the first time I was faced with the dilemma of seeing my child alienated from other black children. I was very uncomfortable, not liking it but not knowing what to do about it. Their behavior was so abominable. They had knives and were terrorizing the other children. The color line was blurred. They sabotaged the camp and it had to be abandoned.

How come? Black people who have made it by dint of hard work and education have been told: You may come in but not the others. When I was on the board of education, dealing with integration, I was told this. I couldn't take it. I said it had to be open for everybody.

We have never really comprehended the true meaning of democracy. Nor for that matter the Scriptures. The truth is we look for ways to exclude people. We're going to have to look for ways to include people.

Right now, in Durham, we're grappling with the school problem. It epitomizes what I'm talking about. We have two districts: one is the city system, the inner city; the other is the county system, of middle-class children, black and white. We're talking merger and people have very strong feelings. There's a difference in the tax base. The city system gets about one-fourth the yield of the county. Yet the inner-city children need it more. The segregation is as much by class as by race.

When black people lived together in communities, you had a whole-some mix. The middle class does carry the virtues of a people. They are hard working, they aspire upward, and so forth. Yet we have become alienated from our own people.

I grew up in a tight little cocoon. Although Atlanta was very much segregated, I didn't know it. I'm not saying I didn't run into racial hostility, but my parents protected me from the more soul-searing experiences that black children often ran into. You had warmth and support in your neigh-borhood. When I went down the street, every lady on her porch knew me. Families knew each other, backgrounds, cousins, uncles, aunts. We felt that kinship you don't have now. This is not just a black phenomenon. It's happening everywhere.

Your occupation didn't matter that much, because everybody had a hard time. We understood this. Children who came out of the alleyways got along with everybody else, if they deported themselves well and aspired to be someone. Today people are afraid to go into projects. We have isolated them psychologically as well as physically. Things have definitely gone down.

We had a good period. Of course, no culture moves smoothly. It just doesn't advance like an army. But with Mr. Reagan, things have regressed. He gave people permission to be their worst selves. We're still dealing with that. What is it he said? He didn't know there was hunger. He didn't know there was racism. He just wrote it off and dismantled a lot of good legislation.

It's the same thing with a family. You have to constantly make sure the children are trained to do things that are in their best interests, and in their development, submerge the id, the other side, psychologically. If you tell them they can beat up on a stray black man who comes into your neighbor-hood, something like that, they will. We have to constantly work at it.

Are we saying this is the best we can be? Somebody said God is not through with us yet. We haven't gotten very far; just scratched the surface. We like to call ourselves higher animals. I think we have a long way to go.

The black male is really at risk in this country. Since the time of slavery, the black male has been feared and everything's been done to pull him down. It's now beginning to tell on us. I have two fourteen-year-old grandsons, twins, and I worry about them because they're so vulnerable. I really feel we're going backwards. I hate to think that my grandchildren are going to have to fight the same battles we had to.

We once had a passion for education. My father's family came to Atlanta in 1897. He worked hard, cleaned up a pharmacist's office, laid his fires, and rode his bicycle across town to Morehouse College.

My mother grew up in Mississippi. She was more middle-class than my father. She finished at a young ladies' academy in Columbus, Mississippi, but never taught school because her father would never allow her to go out to rural Mississippi.

There is such hopelessness in the black community today. The drug situation is paralyzing. Yet white America pays no attention until the problem of the black community spills over into the white. It's like seeing a fire on the next block spreading. You'd be stupid to go into your house and close the door. It won't stop the fire.

Whether we like it or not, we're inextricably bound together. Unlike the Indians, we have stayed and lived with the whites. The bonds are there. We're like the biblical Esau and Jacob. It's a love-hate relationship we're engaged in.

A lot of white people understand our struggle, but most don't. Roosevelt, during the Depression, put white people back on their feet with his hand-out programs. Here, two, three generations later, they're the ones who don't want the government to hand out things. Our people are still down there on the bottom.

I do not understand why we can't provide a job for everybody. When you see the abysmal unemployment rate among young black males, you understand the correlation between drugs and broken families. What happens to self-esteem with not having a job? The energy is still there but it gets diverted. Life will not be denied. Everybody wants to be successful, so the young male does it in one of the few ways open to him.

I see him on the next block, near the high school. He rides around in a BMW or a Mercedes. His values don't include home or family. His mother can't pay the rent. She doesn't have enough money for food in a month. He gives her a thousand dollars and she looks in the other direction. He's probably dealing in drugs, but who's going to ask questions when you're about to be put out on the street? If you're drowning, you don't stop and analyze who is throwing you a rope.

I was unaware of Jewish people when I was growing up, except that they had grocery stores on the corners of the black neighborhood. They were fresh from Europe and they lived over the stores. The mother would have one baby in her arms and another on the way. Pretty soon they'd move away and another family would move in. I never thought of them as Jews. They were white. I didn't think of them as Jewish until my sister and I went to Columbia University. It was the Jewish students who reached out to us when the other whites did not.

You would feel bitter about anyone who has his foot on your back. You wouldn't be human if there weren't bitterness, but you have to try to overcome it. It doesn't get you anywhere. Even if you've been rebuffed, you have to keep knocking on the door. Otherwise, you won't get in.

We're better off than we were in the past. I couldn't vote in the Democratic primary when I lived in Atlanta. It was all-white. Today I *run* in the Democratic primary. We've got a long way to go, but we must continue to fight. Life is not easy. Our young people think you press a button or take a pill and life will be successful. It never has been. There's always been a group to put you down. There was a little doggerel we learned in school: "Every dog has a flea upon his back to bite him/ And that flea another flea, and so ad infinitum."

Everybody has to put somebody down. It's a human failing. If the white man thinks I am less than he is, that's his problem, not mine. I don't care if he thinks that way or not, I'm going to do my best. Your being a full human being doesn't diminish me. I don't have to diminish somebody and make him something less. This is the killing ground of the spirit. I have only this one life that I know anything about. There may be another life that I don't know about. I hope there is, because we've made such a mess of this one.

■ ■ ■ ■ ■

It's a Boy!

CLARENCE PAGE

A columnist of the Chicago Tribune *and member of its editorial board. He won the Pulitzer Prize for Commentary. Frequently, he appears as a television commentator.*

Except for a four-year absence, when he worked for the Chicago CBS station, he has been with the newspaper twenty years. He was the second black reporter ever hired by the Tribune *as a full-time employee.*

When I broke in here as a police reporter, I learned a new phrase, "cheap it out." News out of black neighborhoods were viewed as cheap news. [*Laughs.*] If I got a tip on a double homicide, they'd say, "Oh, South Side. Cheap it out." Some old-timers still use the phrase. It was demeaning to me to see how this double standard worked.

If I was going to survive and make it as a reporter, I had to understand how news judgment was made. I got to be an assistant city editor. But it was so demoralizing to be a lonely voice around a big table of fellows who were largely suburban white male. Trying to sell them on the idea of a South Side homicide being as important as a North Side homicide was as incomprehensible as my speaking Martian. Eventually I decided I didn't want to be management anymore. I'd fight my battles elsewhere.

You could say there's a triple standard in black, white, and Hispanic news; rich, poor, and middle-class. One of my white colleagues said, "News is what happens near the news editor's house." That's why it's so important to have a multicultural newsroom.

The double standard is still there. A fire death in the inner city is not worth a fire death in the outer city. [*Laughs.*] Isn't that an interesting phrase, "inner city"? So is the word "underclass." When I say underclass to a black person, he tends to think of a specific pathological group with a specific set of problems. When I use the word with a white person, chances are better than even that he'll think black. Whites tend to generalize about blacks. We do the same thing, in a lot of ways. I may be doing it at this moment. All of us learn racial generalizations early on and it sticks with us. It frustrates me as a journalist.

I am optimistic. It comes from being around long enough to have seen things worse than they are. Twenty years ago, I was the only black person here. We have quite a few now—not enough, but a lot more than we used to.

I was in high school when the Voting Rights Act was passed. Segregation didn't bend with its passage. When we got a black mayor elected in Chicago, I saw a low-intensity race war break out. The young blacks find white people not nearly as enlightened as they expected. They find out how lonely it is to walk into a predominantly white newsroom. You're dealing with the same questions as a new arrival in town, as well as with some extra ones.

I learned that if it's dark out and I see a white friend, don't approach him too quickly. Don't startle him because the first thing he's going to see is a black man. I have startled people without meaning to. If I'm walking with a group of black males down the street, I'm aware that a white guy passing by might be scared. I imagine those black kids in Central Park were well aware of just how intimidating their presence was. To a large degree, they acted out what was expected of them.

If you expect a kid to be a thug, he's going to be one, nine times out of ten. If you have low expectations, he'll meet them. Today, our society has low expectations of young black males.

When I wake up in the morning and see my pregnant wife beside me, I know from ultrasound we'll probably have a boy. A young black male. How different I think as the father of a young black male than if I were a white father of a white male. There's a certain level of expectations society has of my kid different from the other one. If he's a teen-aged boy walking down the street wearing Adidas basketball shoes, jeans, and a troop jacket, he's regarded differently from a white teen-ager in Adidas basketball shoes, jeans, and a troop jacket. They wear the same outfit, yet are looked upon so differently.

I think of moving to the suburbs because of the schools. But I think: "Where will I be welcome? Where will I be possibly burned out?" In 1990, I think about that. If I were to move into a predominantly white suburb, the first thing that crosses their mind is not the Pulitzer Prize, it's "a black family in our neighborhood." Even among the most liberal white families, the question is: is it bad for my property values?

What else do I think of when I wake up in the morning? Getting to work. I hope the weather's nice, because if it's bad, a taxi will pass me by and pick up a white person halfway down the block. It happens to me all the time. I'm dressed in a suit, tie, carry a briefcase. Just like the white guy who got the cab. I'm a member of the *Tribune* editorial board, right? I dress the role, right? Just getting to work, I think about that.

I'm conscious of how I'm dressed because I want this cabdriver to see that I'm not a welfare recipient. The average white guy may go out there in dirty blue jeans and expect the taxi to stop just like that. And it will. It will stop for him more quickly than for me, three-piece suit and everything.

When I'm on the El, I see people reacting certain ways. I've got prejudices, too, because I've dealt with pickpockets and purse-snatchers. I have formed a profile in my mind of such a potential thief: a young black male. I don't want to project that image to others, but I'm thinking it.

Black people are more afraid of crime than whites. They've got reason to be. We are victims of it more often. I've experienced a mugging, I've had a gun pointed at me, and a knife, and I've given over my wallet. I've had to deal with high-crime neighborhoods a lot. My family has experienced crime.

If you are Bernard Goetz with a gun in your pocket, I don't want you to feel intimidated. He shot four individuals, two of whom were going through the motions of intimidating him. Another was sitting on the bench, not even close to him, the one Goetz shot and paralyzed. He fell on the floor and played dead. Goetz looked at him and said, "You're not hurt so bad, here's another." So he pierced his spine and paralyzed the kid for life. This kid didn't even have a record. Because he was black and with the group, Goetz generalized. He shot them all.

The kid was from a middle-class home. He was eleven when his father died. His mother, now a single mom, low-income, moves back to the Bronx from which they had escaped. His life changed over night. What would happen to my wife and child if I died? What happens to people who are a paycheck away from poverty? This is something white folks don't think about when they see this new class of black folks getting into the mainstream. They don't think how many of us are only a paycheck away from poverty.

I don't worry about it as much as I used to. I'm finally starting to get comfortable with the fact that I'm not going to fall back out of the middle class. It took me years. Often, I wished I had the cavalier attitude of some of my white peers who grew up middle-class.

When my wife told me she was half white, I asked her what she considered herself, She said, "I was raised by my mother to think I was mixed and I still think of myself that way. But society says I'm black, so I go along with it."

Black people are already a rainbow coalition, because even if you're black and Asian, you're black.

I'm always wondering what other people think of me. Even now. What they think of why I am where I am. Am I where I am because I'm black? It used to be: Would I be further advanced if I were white? Nowadays, people wonder: Am I being advanced because I'm black?

Now that I won the Pulitzer Prize, I wonder if people wonder if I won it because I'm nonwhite. [*Laughs.*] My predecessors, who deserved it, who toiled in the vineyards longer than I—did the judges feel obliged to give it to me? I have aspired to a new level of insecurity.

In my younger, single days, I'd go to these Rush Street bars just to spite them. I'd better explain. There are bars on the street that still have a reputation of giving young black people a hard time. We've learned to be sensitive about going where we're welcome and where we're not.

It didn't matter if I was a professional, they'd always give me the once-over and say, "You can't come in wearing jeans." I looked past the door and saw most of the guys in jeans. "You haven't got enough IDs." I always had a bunch of them with me.

Things have improved a lot. Kids who are fresh off the campus are a lot more comfortable with whites than my generation was. But the discomfort level is still there. You don't see any more of a black-white mix than you did twenty years ago.

Know what the problem is? We black folks didn't live up to the expectations of the white folks who helped us out during the civil-rights movement. They didn't live up to our expectations either, because we were expecting more of white folks than this.

We didn't live up to the expectations Jews had of us. They expected blacks, once Jim Crow was beaten, to aspire toward success the way Jews did: education. Blacks decided to aspire the way the Irish did: City Hall. Politics.

Black-Jewish tensions have been considerably overblown by the media. The coverage of Louis Farrakhan says it all. Among the great many black people, he's rated as useful and entertaining. An educated clown. People will fill Madison Square Garden and watch him for his entertainment value. How many have joined his movement? Very few. He can say anything and the media will rush out there.

When I worked for Channel 2, they chartered a plane and flew me and a crew to Indianapolis to cover a routine Farrakhan speech. We had to put it on the air that night. It was his usual stuff, nothing extraordinary. I know why they sent me down there. They were hoping he'd say something outrageous. This is their thing.

Naturally, Farrakhan welcomes all this attention. What respect he has from black people comes to anybody who stands up to white folks and tells it like it is. My wife was thrilled when I took her to see him. She heard so much about him as entertaining. Did she become a follower? No. There is a side of us as black people that resents the way we are ignored as individuals, the way mainstream America insults us. In a way, Farrakhan is feeding off that sentiment.

I wake up in the morning, watch the news, and hear of a heinous crime. "I hope he's not black" is the first thought that crosses my mind. Before I even see the picture on TV. A lot of black folks are the same way. When I was a kid, my uncle used to say, "Please, Lord, don't let it be black."

A white backlash is the last thing that worries us now. We've always had a backlash, but never called it that. Why should we worry about it now? The truth is we don't fear white people anymore. We don't have the kind of fear our fathers and grandfathers had.

Our lives are still controlled by white people, and that's still on our minds. Malcolm X once put the question: Why do the media never refer to all-white neighborhoods as segregated? An all-black neighborhood is always referred to as segregated. Why? Because they know who's doing the segregating. Black people didn't segregate themselves. An all-white neighborhood is never referred to as a ghetto, yet the youngsters who grow up there are socially deprived of the benefits that come from a pluralistic society. Many grow up socially disabled.

So when I wake up in the morning and see my pregnant wife and the odds are overwhelming it's going to be a boy, a young black male . . . [*Trails off.*]*

■ ■ ■ ■ ■

The Birth Certificate

SYLVIA MATTHEWS

For several years, she had been my associate at WFMT, a radio station in Chicago. Her desk was adjacent to mine.

She has olive-colored skin. I had always assumed she was Caucasian: Jewish, perhaps, or Italian.

One day, she brought in her birth certificate. Color: White.

To have a birth certificate that says I'm white is, in certain ways, a passport. After all, I live in the United States.

My mother is from the West Indies and is not much darker than I am. Could she pass? She didn't pass when she came to America. She was considered black. There's racism everywhere. In Jamaica, the darker you are, the more negative the implication. My mother was light and so considered one of the elite.

My mother doesn't feel like a black American. I don't either. All my life, from when I was a kid, people would not know what I was. My father is Welsh and Dutch. His relatives were relieved that I wasn't darker. He had wanted to marry my mother for years. She said no, no, no. When his mother offered her three grand to get lost, my mother immediately said, "Let's get married." [*Laughs.*] My parents were divorced when I was six.

I spent summers in Connecticut with my white cousins. I felt very much nonwhite, because they were all very blond. People would look at me

---

* It was a boy.

and wonder, "Are you Greek?" "Are you Italian?" "Are you Armenian?" No one thinks of me as black.

I think it's because of the atmosphere I grew up in. I went to a private progressive school in New York City. Most of my friends were Jewish. All my friends had more money, but I was accepted completely. Still, I felt like a poor relation.

I remember anxieties. I was eight or nine when my father and I drove through the South. I remember the "White" and "Colored" signs. In one restaurant, they all turned to look at us. I was afraid I was gonna be found out and removed. It was this feeling of passing, like they were gonna catch me and kick me out.

If I had grown up in Harlem, I might have been a different person. When my mother ended up in New York, she had no common ground with American blacks. She was being discriminated against, but it wasn't something she had grown up with. She had grown up in a family with maids. They lost everything when my grandfather died. So she came here.

When I went to college in 1970, the blacks on campus were becoming more active and united. I did a sleazy thing at the time. My grades were not great and I wasn't going to get a scholarship, but I was trying to save my dad money. So I put down "Black" on my application, hoping I could sleaze in. [*Laughs.*] This is the one time I wanted to pass as a black. [*Laughs.*]

The blacks on the campus were looking for me to participate because they knew by grapevine of my application. I was invited to a couple of gatherings and didn't go. It so happens I'm not a joiner, of white or black groups. So they started calling me a honky bitch and disdained me. I was told later that they'd walk by me and laugh. I was oblivious to it at the time. They felt I was trying to pass and deny my heritage.

I've often been made aware that I wasn't the same as everyone else. Parents of friends would ask, "What is your background?" I was accepted everywhere, but I felt different. I don't feel like a white and I don't feel like a black. I consider myself off, slightly off. [*Laughs.*]

It was important to my mother that I grow up as an individual, not identifying with one group or the other. In this country, my mother would want to be white, just because you don't get treated like so much shit. Now, if you're poor and you're white, you get treated just the same as a black person.

Today it seems more acceptable to be racist. Just in the kind of things you hear people say. I live in a mixed area now, but it's getting gentrified. Even though my circle is somewhat enlightened, racism is so deep. It may come out in jokes. Before, there was a certain cachet in being with the civil-rights movement, and people who were truly racist kept their mouths shut. Now there's been a real slipping back. Things like affirmative action are very much resented. When it comes to jobs, it's okay to talk racist: "That black guy got the job I should've gotten." Black people are not going to disappear from this society. There's a job crisis and it applies to all of us.

I hung out in yuppie bars, where they hang ferns all over the place. I don't go to those places much anymore. Since Reagan, whom the country felt good with, it's become fashionable to stop caring about people up against it: "This is what *we* have to live with and this is what they have to live with. O*kay*?"

I was attacked by a black guy once. I saw him crouched behind some bushes as I was entering my building. And started screaming. He hit me on the head with a rock and ran. It was a crazy person, could have been a white guy just as easily. For weeks and weeks, I walked around with stitches in my head, a horrible headache, and completely terrified. If I saw any black man anywhere, I freaked, particularly if he was young.

Before, it was just a matter of being alert. I was upset about this feeling. "Am I turning into a racist myself? I've got to do something to break this mindset." So a couple of friends took me to the Checkerboard Lounge on the South Side to hear some blues. They brought some Valiums in case I got nervous. At first, I was really tense, and then I relaxed. It was a wonderful evening, and it snapped me out of this reactionary feeling that I was walking around with. It was thirteen years ago.

I grew up in New York City and I've been followed and harassed by people of all ethnic backgrounds. [*Laughs.*] I knew there were plenty of evil white men out there, too. It wasn't that. You read the newspapers and you see that so and so was raped and beaten in her car by three young black men. You read the paper every day. Of course it affects you. They play it up too much. After all, newspapers are owned by white men.

I was appalled at the way I felt. I was furious with myself. Walking down the street, seeing any young black man anywhere, and freaking out. Being terrified and wishing I had a gun.

I have a black friend who lives in Birmingham. He's had a lot of painful experiences as a kid—the dogs, the firehose—but he doesn't talk much about them. I'm sure he has a lot of bitterness he doesn't unload on his friends. Yet he makes a lot of racial jokes. It's what behind them that counts.

Would I want to be black in America? No way. [*Laughs.*] The cards are stacked against you from the start. It's a horrible thing to grow up with. The idea of bringing a black boy into the world is different from the idea of bringing a white boy into the world. The white son: bow down, praise the Lord, an heir, and all that shit.

I went to Montana for a summer with a black woman from Bed-Stuy* in Brooklyn. We were on a farm. The little Montana kids, who'd never seen a black person before, would go up, rub her face and look at their hands. It was a mind-blowing experience for her, who dealt with a lot of racial stuff. It was through these children she discovered that she was just different, that's all. She and they were amazed. They hadn't yet been taught to be racist.

When I lived in a small university town in Oregon, one thing drove me nuts. There was this holier-than-thou attitude: "We're not racists here." I'm saying, "What about these little Mexican ghettos here?" There's three blocks where only Mexicans live. There were no blacks, other than the nine guys they imported from L.A. for their basketball team. I said, "You're not racist because there's no massive group of people you have to deal with that are different from you. Don't cop this 'innocent' attitude." All they talked about was weaving. It used to drive me nuts.

I can't regard myself as black because I don't have the cultural background. My mother didn't connect with black culture in America, so there was no chance for me to do so. I think it would have added to me as a person. I'm a mixed bag. Most people think of me as a white person. Which would I prefer? When it comes to functioning in this society, I'd prefer being white. It's easier. But when it comes to feeling—and this may be stereotype—the blacks are more soulful. There's more aliveness in their culture.

I can't regard myself as white, either, despite my birth certificate. I hope I never think like my stereotype of a white: a racist. We all have racist attitudes. I don't think it's the worst crime. What's terrible is if you don't try to confront it. Or you don't acknowledge it. Or you don't let it make you uncomfortable.

EMILY MATTHEWS

She is Sylvia Matthews's mother.

She is light-skinned and might conceivably "pass." She has the delicate air, the elegant manner—though the surroundings are seedy—of a "properly brought up young lady." There is a touch of Blanche Du Bois here.

Emily Matthews is not what she might appear and she will not ascribe this as anything to do with color. Emily Matthews can tell you about the

---

* Bedford-Stuyvesant is a black working-class neighborhood.

problems she had as an island girl of African descent. That's what it said on my student's visa: "African descent." I can tell you about coming to this country and the shock to find out that I was walking within a cape, and that cape was my color. I was enveloped in this, no matter what I did or how I spoke. I was always in this envelope.

Jamaica was still part of the British Empire. We grew up in the pattern of the British middle class. We were a copy-cat society. We identified with whatever Dad did: the schools we went to, where we lived. Dad was in agriculture, employed by an American company on a banana estate. He was the plantation boss. I came to the United States because my dad died when I was a teen-ager. The Caucasian part of me came from my father's side. His father was Scotch. My grandfather on my mother's side was very much the Indian gentleman. On the island, we discriminated against one another according to shades. We were encouraged to move toward the Caucasian. It was thought of very highly if one of us married to somebody lighter than we were.

Mother, who was of a darker shade, encouraged the femininity in me, while father, who sought a companion, taught me to race horses. Later in life, I felt I had become almost a travesty. There was a subtle encouragement to go with the light skin, my father's.

Mother encouraged me to have friends lighter than myself. When we rented our extra room, she wanted a young person about my age. I suggested a school acquaintance, whom I admired very much. She was bright. She was also very black. My mother wouldn't hear of it, because she was too black.

Dad raced horses. He lived on the credit system, on his personality, far beyond our means. We moved from one house to another in Kingston. Sometimes coming home from school, I'd go to the wrong address because we moved three times in one month. Although we had very little money, we lived like the English. We had maids, we had everything done for us. As a result, I'm terribly awkward in the kitchen.

When my father died, everything fell apart. He had lived on sheer charm and no money. He was quite a ladies' man, too. Rather a rogue. When I was in convent school, I discovered that I had a half-sister. It was never discussed at home.

My mother had been a nurse. A very good person, industrious and hardworking. She was very shy and kept to herself, because I think she felt outclassed by my father's charm and wit. He had in a sense married below himself. When he died, mother had to go to work again. She worked very hard for years to put me through school.

When I graduated from high school, there wasn't much opportunity for much of anything on the island. I had to start earning something. The nuns at the convent school I attended gave me a job as a student teacher. I was dejected because I'd love to have attended a university and get a degree, but had no means.

Then came this opportunity in '44, the war years. There was something called the Cadet Corps. A course in nursing was offered at the Boston City Hospital. You'd have a uniform, get an allowance, take special courses at med school. It sounded very glamorous.

Now I'm in the United States, and this is where I first encountered the dilemma of color. I collided with it in Miami. A friend and I were to spend one night there and fly out to Boston the next day. We were sent to a hotel, but if we wanted dinner, we had to walk several blocks to the colored section of town. With my sheltered background, a block was something you chopped. Fortunately, a black attendant helped out, getting us sandwiches and coffee.

We were confused and angry. The next day, we decided to take the train, just to get out of Miami as soon as possible. As I waited in line to change the tickets, the lady said, "You should be in the other line." After I'd been standing there for an hour. I looked across and saw the black line.

At the Boston nursing school, the white girls, many from the Midwest, wondered about the island some of us came from. Did you wear shoes back home? They were amazed that we spoke English with such ease. We were treated as a curiosity. It wasn't painful, just embarrassing.

A nursing instructor, whom I followed around, said to me, "You'll have to work twice as hard to get half the credit." To be honest, instead of working twice as hard, I determined to get as much credit for the least amount of labor. A personality weakness of mine, I think.

Why are you putting yourself down?

It's a problem of image, self-image. If you have a strong self-image, you weather this better. But if in your background, you're not established as a person, if you're viewed in a certain light only because of your color, you're colliding with confusion. Who am I? What do you see when you look in the mirror? What is it you see that is different from what other people see?

I didn't really repress my anger too much. It wasn't so much because of the color. It was the scheduling. Myself and the other colored nurse worked an awful lot of nights. To an excessive degree, because we weren't expected to have any social life. It was always pointed out to us that if there was a party, we had to bring our own escorts. Mixed dancing wasn't allowed.

We did have colored girls coming up from Tuskegee Institute, but interestingly enough they didn't want anything to do with us West Indians. The black Americans seemed to reject us. Perhaps they thought we were something special. I tried to be friendly with them but was pushed aside.

A white girl invited us to her home in Maine. The family, middle-class, was just wonderful. Not very well-to-do. Everybody in town looked at us, because they hadn't seen black people very much. It wasn't a put-down, it's just that we were strange.

Her brother came home unexpectedly and for some reason he had a thing about race. He had been in the army, and I wondered if that had something to do with it. He pulled out a cigarette case and said the skin on it "was from some nigger we lynched overseas." The young woman was very embarrassed. We left the next day. She was one of the very few who invited us.

It was in Boston I met my husband. A black friend introduced him to me as a freethinker. One night there was a party at his place. We got a little noisy and a neighbor called the police. The young officer escorted me out and said nicely, "Watch out who you go with." He meant to protect me. I was a little confused, because I was fond of Charlie right away.

The problem was not being at ease with him in public. We went out very little. Once we went to a dance. Some guards arrived and he took me away immediately. He felt nervous, thought they were looking at us disapprovingly. This was '47, '48.

His mother was very disapproving of us. His sister pleaded with me not to do such a rash thing as marry this young man. He'd be deprived of opportunity because of me. I felt very put-upon, because we cared for each other. I was defiant and we married. It turned out we were not right for one another, but it had nothing to do with color.

His mother worried about Sylvia. What would she look like? She turned out to be a little rose, and his mother and sister, who hurried over, were very relieved. They became very fond of her. But I was never invited to their new house. I feel they sold the old house in case I showed up. They never had anyone else over when I visited.

To tell you the truth, I don't really know my daughter. I have not been as close to her as I might have been. When she attended different colleges, all her friends seemed to be white. I've never really discussed it with her. That's her business. I wanted her to have a stable life so I sent her to this progressive school. It was a struggle. My husband was working as a court reporter and I as a nurse.

I haven't been socially active enough to have an opinion on anything. I have retired myself and am deeply neurotic.

Did Sylvia ever speak of her mother's drinking during all those growing-up years? I do not drink anymore. I cannot ascribe my drinking to racial problems. That would be a cop-out. Sure, the rebuffs I received here were shocking and I did withdraw, but it was something in me, not the outside.

I'm fascinated by my only child. I wonder if she has happiness in her life. She certainly didn't have a model in me. I think she confides more in her father, so I don't pry. I feel as if she never had a mother. We joke on the phone. I said, "You're the only thing I have really accomplished in my life, and I didn't do much there. You brought yourself up." We laugh about that. She has been leading me by the hand since she was eight years old.

It's marvelous how she copes. I'm intrigued by her. She's everything I'm not. It's a marvel to see how she's created herself. I don't know how to approach her. I feel as if I have no genuine emotion, sometimes. I didn't live it when she was small, so there's no way I can be close to her.

I was rather elegant then, when Sylvia was born. As I was growing toward middle age, I was still rather attractive. An old friend of mine said, "You were the prettiest one of our circle." I said, "Why didn't somebody tell me?" She said, "We thought you knew." While I had it, I didn't know I had it.

I was defiant about things, but in doing so I was going against nature. Being defiant will get you into trouble in the end, whether it's against nature or against the social order. I stopped defying long ago. In being defiant, I defeated myself. I felt that my arrogance turned around and struck me.

I *should* have worked twice as hard. Instead, I worked just enough to get by. I studied just hard enough to get a passing grade. I didn't have enough pride in myself. I cannot relate this to race. I can't cop out like that.

When Sylvia was born, they came to my bed with the birth certificate. I decided right away to put down "White." In my mind, I said, "Give her a chance." If she wants to proclaim later in life she's this or that, it's her business. The lady with the paper looked at me strangely. But since I was in a big private room, light-skinned and elegant, she didn't question me. If she questioned me, I would have said, "Ask her father." I wanted to give her an even chance in life.

■ ■ ■ ■ ■

The Adoption

JUNE SCHROEDER

She is forty-six, a school librarian in a small Minnesota town. Years ago, she and her husband, Jim, adopted a black baby. He is now seventeen.

"Why can some people transcend their backgrounds—anti-Semitic, antiblack, homophobic—and others can't?

"My grandfather signed his name with an X and my father had a Ph.D. He was a taxonimist. He wrote a couple of books on fish, reptiles, and amphibians.

"When my father came back from a trip in southern Illinois, he said, 'Pitiful. Tom couldn't eat in the restaurant. He'd just sit in the car and we'd order something for him.' Tom was a black student. I was little. It never occurred to me to say, 'Why didn't you guys sit in the car, too?'"

I was a cute little blonde girl. There was a lot of incest in my family. I am an incest survivor. When I was little, I'd go regularly to my mother and say Uncle Bill did this and daddy did that or the custodian did something. She would always make up excuses. "The janitor did it because his son died in World War II." My uncle did it because of something or other.

Mother would say things like, "Daddy doesn't like to talk about it." Or, "We don't like to talk about it." I would tell her constantly, but, I think, if she helped me, it would take out the underpinnings and everything would fall apart. She would have had to leave my dad.

When I was about nine, it was the time of the McCarthy hearings. You had to sign a paper saying you were not and never had been a member of the Communist Party. A grad student in my dad's department refused to sign it. My dad leered at me and said, "If they made Bob sign that, the next thing he'll have to sign is a paper saying he never played with little girls." I really felt victimized. That is how I kind of identified with the underdog. Oh, my dad was glad to sign the loyalty oath. My mother was one of the first employees of the university to sign it. She had her picture in the papers.

My dad didn't want fluoride in the water. He said it was a communist plot. He was a big NRA man.* You see, he made the leap to the university

---

* National Rifle Association.

level so fast, he was still crude. He didn't know a thing about music or art, and when he was around other people, he felt inadequate. He wouldn't vote for Stevenson: "That goddam egghead probably reads paperbacks." [*Laughs.*] There were few paperbacks at the time.

One time we were in a department store by the yard-goods section. My mother, her mother, and her grandmother. Four generations. My great-grandmother whispered to my grandmother, "Look over there at that black man. He's looking at little June." The idea was he wanted to get in my pants or something. I can remember even at that time thinking, "My God, this is crazy. I go all the time and tell you Uncle Bill or Dad or these other people are molesting me." No black people had ever given me any trouble. Yet, they were so worried about that.

I remember it so well because they were talking about what colors they should get for my cousins' dresses: red for them because they had brown hair and blue for me. My grandmother kept whispering: "Keep an eye on that black man." They won't help me when I ask for it. Instead they do this.

Mother got a job with the phone company giving out directories. I usually went along. We went into a black section and she'd tell people: "This black man was drunk and he came at June." He didn't do anything. I thought, "Oh, my God, once again." She would always tell it to friends when the subject of race came up. I think this is when I began to identify with blacks as the underdogs, maybe.

My dad felt bad for blacks who had to eat in the car, during his collecting trips. But when he listened to the boxing matches on the radio, he'd get real excited and holler, "Kill that nigger! Beat that black son-ofabitch." At the same time, he'd tell a story that would move him to tears. About a black kid on death row in the South. When he went to get executed, he said, "Save me, Joe Louis!" From my dad, I got a mixed message. All this racist talk stopped abruptly when we adopted James. [*Laughs.*]

My parents were really anti-Semitic. They were so busy hating Jews that they didn't know they hated everybody else. My mother learned it from my dad. She remembers the KKK coming for the Catholics in her small town. There were no blacks there. When she went to teachers' college, she was afraid that if she answered some of the test questions right, they'd think she was a Catholic. She knew it was terrible to be a Catholic. My father had never been around minorities, but when he came back from World War II, he really hated Jews. He had always been an outcast. His stepbrothers and sisters and stepfather hated him. He learned how to box to defend himself against his family. And to hate.

When I was in high school, a Jewish woman came to our house to look at some of the birds my father had collected. She talked about being in a concentration camp. I was just horror-struck. My mother said, "They just tell those stories to get sympathy."

When I was in eighth grade I was very lucky. I was in the first class of the first black teacher in town. Mr. Edwards. English. He was wonderful. Very formal. I was an outcast, fat and aggressive. He was kind. The class loved him and when we found out it was his birthday, we got together with another class and gave him a big cake. He was so moved, he was almost in tears. My classmate's mother was worried about this. "This is not appropriate because you're doing it for him and not for any other teacher." We said, "Who the hell cares about any of the other teachers? He's wonderful."

There was a racist joke in our house. My father brought back some iguanas from his collecting trip in Mexico. He always told about George, the black iceman, who didn't know about the iguanas. One day he was so scared, he said, "I ain't gonna deliver no mo' ice here." I started to tell the story in the English class, but when I got to the dialect part, it dawned on me how terrible the story was. I let the story hang. I have a feeling Mr. Edwards knew why.

I had another teacher who was a real jerk. Something came up about blacks and I said they're just like we are. This jerk said, "Would you marry one?" My first reaction was to say yes, but I got scared and said no. He said, "See?" I felt awful. I was twelve. I was still having trouble getting to see blacks as equals. I felt a little patronizing. Yet I felt like an underdog because I was still getting molested regularly. That was my nightmare every night. I began to realize this prejudice was tied into sexuality. "Those black men want to rape you." I was the little kid asking for help and not getting it. It was made into a joke.

I was still a racist then in a lot of ways. When I was a junior in high school, I wrote a paper on the song, "The Boll Weevil." My dad always said that black people are happy and carefree, like children. I never questioned that and put it in my paper. I had this wonderful teacher, who wrote something on my paper: "This is absolutely not true. This is prejudice." It hit me so hard, oh, God.

My worst fantasy was someone breaking in to rape me. I always imagined a black person. It was white men, my family, who bothered me, never a black, yet—I am so racist, in many ways, still.

I was about seven. We are at J. C. Penney's. Remember those brown square drinking fountains? My mother would always say, "Don't put your mouth on the drinking fountain." There was a black man and his little boy in line in front of us. He held him the boy and said, "Don't touch your mouth to it." My mother said to me, "Did you hear that? He cares for his little boy as much as we care about you. Isn't that funny?" My mom was amazed.

When I was about thirteen, a flasher came by and flashed at some kids. It was outside the department store. I felt, "Oh, that fucker. These guys are always doing that to little kids." I told the salesgirl about it and all of a sudden the place was crawling with police. I thought, "How weird. So much worse has happened to me and nobody did anything."

My parents were very unsympathetic to poor people. Because they saw themselves as having pulled themselves up by their bootstraps. That is bullshit. World War II came and my dad got a loan to go through college. I'm sure they worked hard, but they didn't do it all by themselves.

I was really into the Young Republicans. I went to state conventions. I'm real glad, because that's where I met Jim. I was also interested in civil rights and attended CORE meetings, too. They'd say, "What are you in the Young Republicans for? This is weird." It never bothered me. I was for Goldwater. That he inherited a department store didn't bother me. I remember a Feiffer cartoon in which Goldwater said: "If you had any gumption, you'd have inherited a department store." I never saw that as a problem at all.

Jim was always the guy that sat in the car and waited when we were in the peace march. We were now married, had a baby and everything seemed fine. But when Jill was about thirteen months old, she was diagnosed as having a brain tumor. We went to St. Louis, where there was a huge hospital complex. Things were so bad for us, we were sleeping in the car.

We didn't know what to do, feeling our kid was going to die. One day, Dr. Sims, this black woman pediatrician, walked in and said, "I understand you need some help." She realized how bad things were for us, flat broke and not knowing anybody. She got us an apartment.

That was the summer Johnson was president and there was the War on Poverty. Dr. Sims got Jim a job working in the black section of St. Louis. He drove a bus and would take these black kids around. Jim was edging much more to the left, seeing how these kids lived. He was more liberal than I was, because we got into an argument about whether welfare people should have telephones. I said, "Why the hell should they have a telephone? *I* don't have a telephone." He said, "Our situation is going to get better. Their's isn't going to get any better."

About that time, I met this black family whose little boy had pica and was retarded. He got it from eating chips of lead-based paint off the wall. That floored me. I thought, "Jesus, this kid lives in that apartment." I blamed the landlord, and that was a big change in me. Remember, we were poor and our baby dying on us, and we had not inherited a department store. All of a sudden I could see why these people feel the way they do. I think you have to have a personal experience. Your politics come from your personal experience.

There was an army base across the river from St. Louis. Jim was going to take the kids to the swimming pool out there. The army personnel refused to let the black kids in. Jim came back, furious. "We're going back tomorrow and I'm going to call all the newspapers and TV stations and we're going to have signs." That was the first time we ever did anything like that. He said, "We might put some of the S's backwards so it looks like the kids wrote them." [*Laughs.*]

We were still conservative enough that when King started to talk about Vietnam, we said, "Oh Christ, what's he doing messing with Vietnam? Can't he just stick to race?"

I didn't want to go to Mississippi and put my body on the line. I was afraid. I remember those meetings where we'd all hold hands and sing "We Shall Overcome." That used to embarrass me. I thought, "Oh God, it's so emotional." I remember old black men crying and I wanted to get out of there. I bought into it a little, but not enough. Oh God, I wish I could still do it.

Even before we knew Jill was going to die, we talked about adoption. Hardly anybody went across racial lines then. It was 1965. Dr. Sims said, "What about a black kid?" We just looked at each other and said yeah. But when Jill died, I had to have another baby and have it okay. So we had Julie. But we knew we had to have a black child too.

Jim was now working in a hospital and getting his degree in social work. We ran into this older social worker, rough around the edges. She said, "We have your baby. He's short, only eighteen inches long." [*Laughs.*] I loved that. She was so concerned about his fitting in height-wise instead of color.

There was a complication. The mother was from Jim's hometown, where his father was the Republican sheriff. The agency was right across the street from the sheriff's office, and everybody would find out who the mother was and who has it. So on the weekend, the social worker met us at McDonald's and handed James to us across the window. [*Laughs.*] It was always a family story with us: "We got you at McDonald's."

We took him home and my mother bought Julie a little black doll so she would not feel strange. She wasn't too keen about it, but she was passive. It was easier for my dad, even though that week, in a traffic jam, he said about the other driver, "Oh, that black bastard."

From the time we brought James home, everything changed. We never brought him to see my other grandmother, my mother's mother—the one in the department store, remember? At Christmas and Thanksgiving, they'd sit down and tell racist jokes. I just broke with that side of the family. I never saw them again.

When we first thought of adopting James, I said to Jim, "God, I don't want to lose friends." Now I look back and think, "I don't want them as friends." The night before we adopted James, I had a nightmare, absolutely scared: "What are we doing? How much trouble are we going to have?" We haven't had any.

Last year there were a lot of teen suicides in town. They asked the kids to write down the name of the peer they'd go to with a personal problem. His name appeared more than anybody else's.

People sometimes say racist things to me or Jim, not knowing we have a black child. I got a job at a school twenty miles out of the city. At a Christmas party—I had only been there a week—the principal showed me a Brazil nut. "What do you call these?" I thought, "Oh God, here it comes." I said, "I call it a Brazil nut." He said, "I call them niggertoes." It was such a shock to me that I jerked the glass in my hand and accidentally got wine all over his shirt. But I did say, "Don't you ever use that word with me, ever again."

The fraternities on the campus have parties in which they have "Fiji" pictures of blacks with bones in their noses. I was outraged when the university wouldn't do anything about it. That pissed me off. I wrote a letter to every member of the Board of Regents and said my son is afraid to attend the university in his home town because you will not act on this. It's dismaying to see people who give lip service but don't really give a damn. They look like they want blacks but would rather not cross the bigoted alumni. Remember, this is one of more enlightened towns and universities in the country.

I was amazed to see a T-shirt in the major department store that had the most stereotypical Native American you can imagine. Another had a shirt with a beautiful African design. At the checkout counter, I noticed a cute little emblem on it: Made in the Congo at the Happy Hands Plantation. I said to the girl, "I can't buy this, it's racist." The young girl said in all sincerity, "I don't get it." Of course she doesn't get it. So I wrote a letter to the paper: "What are we having next? T-shirts with a 1930s map of Germany, saying, 'Produced at the Jolly Auschwitz Concentration Camp'?" We have a long, long way to go.

JIM SCHROEDER

June's husband. "I'm a social-worker type. A reconciler of differences, trying to placate people. I was that way in my family."

My father had a trucking company that hauled timbers for coal mines. He always had jobs for people. They always borrowed money from him. He bailed them out of jail. My dad would say, "If you don't have the money, you can always pay it off in work." Almost all the people he dealt with were black. This was in southern Illinois, along the Mississippi, deep South. He seemed beloved in that community. They all called him Big Charlie and were in his house all the time.

The happiest times were out in the fields where I worked all day with black men. They took me under their wing, Charlie's son. They were my mentors. They told me stories, showed me how to do things. They were very competent. I am still struck by their skill in just about anything: they fixed trucks, built fences, cut the horns off cows, knew how to hunt. I'd go out to the woods with them.

I remember this lodge where you could drink beer, had fish fries. My dad joined. There was an argument about blacks being inferior. My dad stood up: "I believe they're as good as we are. We're leaving." My mother and dad walked out. He'd take his black assistant to a restaurant and when they wouldn't serve, they'd both eat in the truck.

In his mind, prejudice did not make any sense. But he's still a Republican and he thinks all Democrats are crooks. He likes Reagan. His Republicanism is his religion. Yet he was strong for the Civil Rights Act. He thinks Martin Luther King was very good. He's a bundle of contradictions.

My parents were superpatriotic, which caused a lot of difficulty for me as an adolescent. He was the type: "If English was good enough for Jesus, it was good enough for you." [*Laughs.*] In many ways, my father is very ignorant, but in other ways, wise and courageous. As a sheriff, he was the first one to hire black deputies in southern Illinois.

He later lost the election. It was ironic. The student vote at the college beat him. They were radicalized at the time. He looked like a stereotype and sounded like it. Did you ever see the guy that did the Dodge commercials on TV? My dad was a dead ringer for him. Real gruff, six feet, two-fifty, three hundred pounds. At a political meeting, he called a black person "boy" and this got quoted in the papers. Times were changing more rapidly than he was. He was out of synch.

I was uncomfortable with other kids using the word "nigger." That was common. I'd say "colored." I was always uncomfortable with racial jokes, but I didn't stand up and say, "Hey, I don't want to hear that." I just didn't say anything.

There was a white fellow from Mississippi who came to visit his cousin. I had never encountered anyone so violent and angry. He was scary. He was trying to get a group of us into going in the car. "We'll ride around in the nigger section with a ball bat and we knock people in the head." This was at the time of all the violence in the South on TV.

I was a poor student and having a lot of conflict with my parents. I was doing heavy drinking and some wild things. I became aware of the university four miles away. I was able to save money because I worked. Plus tuition was cheap. I got to know some Cambodian students and couldn't be with them enough. Some friends in town said, "What are you hanging around those Chinks for?" I was a person who was always inclined to cruise down the middle and offend no one. I broke off with the Cambodians. I still feel terrible about it to this day that I didn't have the courage.

It was about this time that I met June at a Young Republicans meeting. I went there for social reasons, too. This was 1963. She was a walking contradiction. The Republican thing and Snick.* At the Student Union, I wanted to sit with the Snick people but I was afraid to. I was really for them and in awe of their courage, but no way would I have done that. They were having campus debates at the time, the Vietnam War. I was starting to question things.

Events started rolling rapidly. We had our first baby. We were twenty; we married so young. I was a maintenance worker at the university. Our baby got sick. We had no insurance, nothing. A black pediatrician orchestrated our salvation. She set us up in a room, got us funding, got me a job in the Johnson poverty program. I drove a bus of black kids, kept them off the street, planned things. Most of the staff was black. To encounter educated blacks was new to me, a revelation. Until now, I had always kept a certain distance.

I was driving a bus one day; we must have had forty black kids in it. There was a military base and a swimming pool. The word was: "No way are you taking those kids there." But we did have the right to take these kids swimming at a federal facility. So we just went. I was the authority driving the bus. I said, "We have a right to do it." And we did.

---

* SNCC, the Student Nonviolent Coordinating Committee, to which June also belonged.

It got a whole lot of coverage in the press. I felt real proud. I got a lot of esteem from the people I was working with.

Jill, our baby, died, and I didn't know what to do. Dr. Sims suggested that I become a social worker, that I was a natural. A professor took me under his wing and got me involved in the black community in St. Louis.

The Schroeders spent two summers with the American Friends Service Committee in antiwar work and lived among the farmworkers in California at La Paz, César Chavez's headquarters.

When James was about three or four, he became aware of Big Grandpa. By this time, the family wounds were healed. My father was so proud of him. He'd put him in his sheriff's car, turn on the siren, and say to his black deputies, "Here is my grandson." One time the state's attorney was visiting us and my father announced proudly, "Here is my half-breed grandson and my hippie son." James and my dad do real well together.

At times, I feel a little uncomfortable about the adoption. We've heard comments: "They'd like a healthy white baby, but there are these hard-to-place kids . . ." I find this offensive, patronizing. Does James think, "My dad and mom took me because they couldn't get a little white kid"? This must be real painful for him.

Other parents view James as everybody's model: "I wish he'd come over and be with my kid." At times I wonder what pressure hex has on him as "the good kid." He's extremely diplomatic. He won't get sucked into a conflict. He will make his statement; take it or leave it. When we visited Jamaica, a guy said to him, "You're half and half, aren't you? Which side do you like better?" James said, "Yeah." [*Laughs.*]

After walking the middle line most of my life, I have with time gotten more courage. In the old days when someone told a racist joke, I listened and said nothing and felt terrible about it. Now I tell them off. They back-paddle. Last year on one occasion, a person went on with a string of offensive racist jokes. He kept on, so I said, "Look, I am personally offended. I have a son who is black and I want you to cut it out." It just knocked him off his feet. He later came to me and apologized profusely. I felt good about that. It's the climate we've helped create by going along. If we had some moral leadership, things could be altogether different.

■ ■ ■ ■ ■

Overview IV

LERONE BENNETT, JR.

He is executive editor of Ebony. *He is the author of* Before the Mayflower, *a history of black people in America.*

There's been this misunderstanding of the sixties. Media people have been bashing them as a matter of course: "People protested when they had nothing else to do." Actually, it was one of the great decades of the century. Everybody thought the promised land was around the next turning. It wasn't. We should learn from that.

Thanks to the sixties, we have a new climate of race relations in the country. Black mayors in our largest cities. Corporate executives. On the other hand, we have Depression levels of unemployment, the collapse of the public school system, and the epidemic of hard drugs. Everything appears to have changed, yet nothing has changed. Black people are still on the bottom.

In a way, we're back to the first Reconstruction period. One hundred years ago, we had these great civil-rights laws. They were stronger than those passed in the 1960s and 1970s. We had a black governor in Louisiana. We had a black majority in the South Carolina legislature. We had Senators from Mississippi. *We had it made a hundred years ago*. The Supreme Court and a conservative movement reversed it as they're trying to do today.

People are disillusioned. They don't think it will ever work. I don't believe that. I'm committed to the historical view that this is a struggle. You win a few, you lose a few. If you can't hold what you won, you go back and organize again. Nobody gave black people anything in this country. Nobody's gonna give them anything, not even the time of day, if we don't organize.

We hear people say, "We tried integration and it failed." That isn't so. Integration has never been tried in this country. It has not even been defined. What is integration? If you put two, three blacks in an all-white institution, it's not integrated. It requires a complete change in the way you think as an institution. Real integration involves a change in values.

When blacks came out of slavery, hundreds of thousands of black soldiers and laborers were the key in the transformation. Those were crucial moments in the summers of 1865, 1866, 1867. Black people roamed all over Georgia and South Carolina with major demands: education and land. Forty acres and a mule. It was inconceivable to them that the federal government would free them and not give them the wherewithal to make their freedom real. It was a betrayal of the Emancipation.

What Martin Luther King realized a hundred years later is that we did not provide the twentieth-century equivalent of forty acres and a mule. We needed the vote, but we also needed the economic foundation. The revolution of the sixties provided us with one, but not the other.

Blaming the victim has become fashionable these days. They are lazy, should get out and work, lift themselves up by their bootstraps. We're not very history-minded in this country. After the first Reconstruction period, after the votes were taken away from us, after we were pushed out of the city halls and legislatures, the same phenomenon emerged in the 1890s. Booker T. Washington was saying what black conservatives are saying today. A period of this kind always produces the black intellectual who says we ought to stop protesting, stop marching, and pick ourselves up by our bootstraps.

Frederick Douglass and all the great black leaders kept the two things together: protest and organize as well as strive for excellence and self-determination. You don't eliminate one part of the equation and expect it to work. King said it. A. Philip Randolph said it. Frederick Douglass said it: "Power concedes nothing without a demand. It never did and it never will."

There's an anger, there's a bitterness, an overwhelming disillusionment. You see idle men standing on streetcorners. You see broken families. You see young people destroyed by dope, an epidemic of which brings murderously high rates of violence. Rap music is the expression of anguish of black America, which faces its greatest crisis since slavery time. So there's a numbness, a dead end.

A whole new environment has been created for young people by the electronic media. You have a never-never land of new gadgetry, of new rhythms, new desires, new dreams, and the sense of "I want it now." All day long on TV, they see people who have three square meals a day, gleaming appliances, and swimming pools. "Here I am cooped up in this one-room place with roaches and rats. Who decided I had to live this way and the people on television can live that way? Who decided that the South Side had to live this way and the North Side that way?"

You get young black kids killing each other over NFL jackets and tennis shoes. For society to create situations where people need these means of expression is a crime.

It's not that we haven't black leadership. It's that we've not had anywhere in America white leadership comparable to that produced in the black community. People are shocked when I say it. Yet what we need now is a white Martin Luther King to tell poor white people there's no way in the world they can save themselves unless we save all poor people, including blacks. This is the moment.

The massive attack on the sixties takes the form of antiaffirmative action. They're against quotas, they say. For three hundred years in this country, there's been a 99.9 percent quota of white males in all the institutions: the church, the university, the corporate world. There is no way you can begin to create a level playing field without affirmative action. In the late sixties, after the death of King, there was a great Puritan confession. Universities, banks, corporations were confessing: "We've done wrong, we must make amends. Find us some blacks and we'll put them in management programs." It lasted two, three years. Then people started dragging their feet, and now we're where we are today.

During that period, I sat on a number of boards with people who said, "We want to do it right. We're for fair employment, but our middle managers won't do it." Everybody was looking for a super-Negro to hire. I've said to them: "People are the same everywhere. You've got some brilliant ones and some dull ones. Don't look for a black Einstein. Put him in the middle where you put all other middle people."

I still have hope. Know why? Given the way blacks are forced to live in this society, the miracle is that so many still stand and love and teach and earn degrees. The miracle is not that so many black families are broken, but that so many are still together. That so many black fathers are still at home. That so many black women are still raising good children.

If you go to the Robert Taylor Homes and see the indescribable conditions, the miracle is that college students come out of these places. What sociologists visiting these dreadful projects miss is that thousands of black boys and girls somehow manage to survive. It is the incredible toughness in people that gives me hope.

My hope is based on the incredible story of African-Americans in this country. We survived the slave trade. We survived slavery. We survived segregation. We survived shacks, blood, cotton, roaches, and rats. History says we can and will survive if we do what our spiritual tells us: Keep your hand on the plow, hold on.

W. E. B. Du Bois died at ninety-six. He'd lived through the first

Reconstruction, its betrayal, World War I and the betrayal of its truce, through the New Deal and World War II. He was tried in court and humiliated. Yet, in his final death statement, he expressed hope.

Do you know what happened the day he died?

They launched the March on Washington. August 26, 1963.

■ ■ ■ ■ ■

Mixed

HANK AND PAMELA DE ZUTTER AND AMANDA

He is white; his wife is black. A former Chicago newspaperman, he's been teaching journalism at Malcolm X College for the past nineteen years. She had been his student.

Occasionally, Amanda, their ten-year-old daughter, enters the conversation.

HANK: If I were to describe myself to a white guy, I would first tell him what I do for a living. If I were talking to a black guy, I'd tell him how I feel. The white guy would ask, "What do you do?" The black guy would ask, "How you feelin'?"

At a white party, the first thing you talk about is your job. It's not "How're you doing?" but "What are you doing?" I've come to respect both ways, but I prefer to be at a party where I can let loose my job. I've come to really respect the art of the party from black people.

PAMELA: At a party, we hardly talked about jobs, because some people didn't have any. You didn't bring up things which everybody couldn't talk about. Everybody could talk about feelings. It was really one way to toss off the hell you've gone through Monday through Friday. It was generally factory work, if you had a job.

When I went to a white party with Hank and I was standing there holding a drink, everybody would come up to me. Before they even asked my name, they'd say, "What do you do?" It was strange. I was used to people making small talk, getting to know me.

At the family reunion in Birmingham, it was mostly "How you feeling? How you doing?" There was a lot of hugging. For the most part, I had changed. I was the one saying, "What kind of work are you doing?" [*Laughs.*] They weren't ready for it.

HANK: At Malcolm X, my students—mostly black, some Hispanics—are of all ages, genders, all backgrounds. I have a hard time speaking of black people as black because there's a terrific sense of individuality. You develop a personal style, you're not just a black person. My students like to think they have thoughts of their own, styles of their own, and want to be respected for that. They want to know what I think as an individual, not just as a white guy. I'm accepted for who I am.

It's a rare student that makes me feel white, in judging me. One dirty look, one dirty comment, ruins my day. I can then understand how black people feel when they're insulted by one crazy white person. I'm always telling them, hey, he doesn't represent all of us. Don't get hung up on a Nazi or a Kluxer; you've got bigger problems. Yet if I encounter someone who gives me that racist look, I'll develop a defensive attitude and turn white. [*Laughs.*] He's trying to put me in a bag. It may be one person, but all of a sudden it becomes *them*. I see my students do it. It's so irrational. If one white person insults them, then *they* are doing it. I start saying the same thing. [*Laughs.*]

I've seen this happen to Pam. If one racist out of a group of nineteen treats her in a racial way, she'll remember that one person. The other eighteen don't exist. They become coconspirators because they let him get away with it.

Seventy percent of the college are women. The black male, who may feel put down, sees the school as a place where, if you do too well, you'll have a hard time in the playground, as a sissy, as not a real man. We've inherited a kind of whirlwind.

PAMELA: There is something different about the college students now. The students in the past believed they could achieve more. Today they feel more locked in. They don't have that fire. I see fewer people really trying to break out of whatever their personal hell is. Right now is probably the most negative time in history for blacks. There is a far larger degree of hopelessness among black youth.

I still feel hopeful. I do crazy things. I'm in my late thirties and I'm in school again. I've always believed I could just do about anything. I decided to become a planner, so I could perhaps play a role in the black neighborhood. When you look at the West Side, you see decay set in as the neighborhood becomes black. You have to question these things.

I feel that as a black professional I have to educate people about home-owning. It's something that was never learned, because if you lived in a slum, the landlord never did anything. If you buy a decent house and never do anything, it becomes the thing you lived in before. Maybe it's some learned behavior that needs to be unlearned. Maybe I'm just a dreamer.

HANK: There's more of a sense of hard realism among my students. Even if they do well in school, they'll have a hard, hard time out there. I have to tell them that without an education, they don't stand a ghost of chance. I can't guarantee they'll get a job, but there's more to education than just getting a job. Unfortunately, for most of my students that's what they're there for. It's economics.

And all the years of Reagan: "Let the money go where it wants to go." It has taken all sorts of jobs away from the city, from the neighborhoods, disinvested entire communities. It has left people bereft of tangible goals: "Will I ever get out of this place, God? The store on the corner is gone. I've gotta catch four buses to get groceries. Are things ever gonna get better?"

My students don't like their neighborhoods anymore. Almost a hundred percent would move if they could. The neighborhoods used to be this, they used to be that. It sounded like Eden before the Fall. "Oh God, my neighborhood." They'd write a beautiful piece about how wonderful it was to sleep in Garfield Park back in the sixties. About the store on the corner, going for malted milks. Everyone in the neighborhood watching out for everyone else. Oh, that doesn't happen anymore. Then they'd talk about the hellholes of today.

PAMELA: Since the riots, the community's been demolished and not rebuilt. The sense of community was based on the fact that the people didn't have a lot of things, So they would share what they had, a sense of camaraderie, that allowed them to survive. The one thing I'm proud of blacks is the degree to which they've survived on so little. As a race, we learned to make do.

HANK: The words you use are different. I've noticed little phrases we use every day. White people turn out the lights, black people cut them off. White people spill their drinks on the floor, black people waste them. "Be careful, you're gonna waste your milk." "Passed" instead of "died."

Then there's the unspeakable business of proper English versus Black English. One of the hardest things to teach is the proper form of third person singular present tense verb. "He doesn't do it" or "He don't do it." That rule makes absolutely no sense. No one questions it in the white community. That's just the way it is. Anyone who doesn't say "doesn't" is uneducated or stupid. It's just a question of what you're exposed to. There's nothing inherently better about "he doesn't" than "he don't." They both communicate the same thing. You no longer have to use race, you can use language to discriminate.

PAMELA: I've encountered white people who have problems with English. I had always thought that white people spoke perfect English. I discovered it was a class thing.

HANK: I try to discourage people from speaking of the underclass because it confines them even more. It's like calling people untouchables. "The underclass," as it's used, includes not just the street criminal, who'll be locked up and killed early. It includes a lot of mothers, children, uncles, and aunts who can break out of it, if the system permitted them to. It becomes another excuse: "You're underclass because you're an unwed mother." It's a dangerous term. It's useful, though, in pointing out that class more than race, these days, dictates decisions affecting people's lives.

PAM: Underclass to me are people who will never be employed, I first encountered the term in *Huckleberry Finn*. Jim talked about Huck as an underclass person. He saw Huck as the poorest of the poor. The kind of person who moved around from place to place, where people would have him. That's the first image I have of it in literature outside of Dickens.

HANK: When I get to Malcolm X, it seems that I come to an area where time and progress don't exist. There seems to be a belief that everyone's gotta make it for himself or herself, that no one's gonna help them. This has created the situation Pam talks about: Where she doesn't feel the drive of students helping each other over the top, rather than trying to pull each other down.

How do your folks feel about your marrying a black woman?

HANK: My mother, a sweet woman, who's still alive, has come to accept it. She's had a difficult time accepting anyone who marries her precious children. She treats Pamela no different than she treated my ex-wife.

PAMELA: The only thing I heard your mother say is that there's good in all races, good in all people. For two years, I had only talked to his mother on the phone. His sisters knew I was black but his mother thought I was white. She came here for the funeral of Hank's uncle and was going to spend one night in our house. His sister immediately had this talk with her to explain that I was black. She was really cool about it. First of all I made sure the house was sparkling clean. At least I'll pass that hurdle. It seemed to work. [*Laughs.*] When we finally got married, my mother and his mother sat side by side. It was really enjoyable to me.

HANK: Mandy goes to a racially integrated school. In the early stages, kids play with each other regardless of race. As they get older, blacks kids tend to group together and white kids band with white kids. I wonder how it's affecting her now that she's in fifth grade. Do you have to choose between whites and blacks?

AMANDA: Half my friends are black. One of them is mixed Cuban and German, which is a pretty weird mix. The other half of my friends are like white. Sometimes it's just classes. But it's just so strange at lunch. Blacks kids sit with black kids and white kids with white. It slightly started in about second grade. The little kindergarten kids, they're just, like, who cares?

HANK: I thought we'd have more trouble than we really had. I don't even see dirty looks given to us. When we go out together, people seem happy to see us. Maybe I'm looking for that, maybe I'm not looking over my shoulder. I feel people see us as a symbol of change and hope, especially when we have our blended family: her child from her previous marriage and my two boys from a former one. In the restaurant we'd get warm smiles. I'm sure it may be different in other places.

At Malcolm X, I don't make a big thing out of the fact that I have a black wife. I let my students discover it. They respond overwhelmingly favorably. It's the rare black male, attracted to Farrakhan, who sees this as a raid on the gene pool. [*Laughter.*]

In my nineteen years at Malcolm X, I have encountered only one student, out of maybe thousands of students there who put down Jews. And I'm tempted to talk about him more than about the nine hundred and ninety-nine other students, who had nothing to say about this.

Maxwell Street has been for all the years known as Jew Town.* It is not meant as an insult. It is meant as a description. A black kid was complimented on his new suit of clothes by his teacher. She was Jewish. He said, "My mama bought these at Jew Town." My students, who remember everything in the past as the good old days, always said, "Jew Town was terrific."

If you go to Maxwell Street today, you'll find that many of the merchants are Korean. When my students write papers about Maxwell Street, they talk about what they miss, how the new merchants, the Koreans, aren't anything like the old Jewish merchants, who understood them, with whom they felt a camaraderie. Frequently they write of how much they miss Jew Town. I see more of that than I see anti-Semitism.

Consider how Farrakhan was laid on people. They tried to get Harold Washington to denounce him. The city had just been through one of the roughest mayoral elections in its history. A black man was elected mayor and the city council treated him as though he were dirt. They did everything they could to screw up his programs.

The poor black man, who's been beaten down all his life, votes for this man because maybe there's something here. Right off the bat, you slap that voter's face. You say to him: "You're still black and your vote doesn't count. Even though you have the right to vote, there are different ways we can screw you." Then you ask Harold Washington, the black man he voted for—of whom you sent out scurrilous literature, racial, personal, "he molested little boys," dirty pool, the whole book—you ask him to denounce Farrakhan. To the poor black who elected him, two black men are being picked on by the white system. He finds it difficult to separate the two. The issue of race has always been in this city. Before race, it was ethnic warfare. As blacks became vocal, it became race. When Harold was elected, blacks felt for the first time they could invest in this city.

I polled my students when Washington announced his candidacy and they didn't know who he was. This was December of '82. We didn't have a show of hands. We had secret ballots. They didn't have to please me. They knew I favored Washington. Thirty-eight percent of the ballots went for

---

* Chicago's celebrated open market. In recent years, it has been greatly diminished in acreage by expressways.

Daley. Thirty-one percent went for Jane Byrne. Thirty-three percent for Washington.

I asked my students to explain it. They said, "Just because he's black, we're supposed to vote for him? Uh-uh. Our vote doesn't come that easy. We've been fooled by people before, white and black. Let him prove himself." He proved himself. He earned their vote the next time around.

PAMELA: We had a friend who was working at the time for Jane Byrne. I was leaning toward her, even though she had literally disenfranchised the people who put her in. I had the same attitude as Hank's students. You don't vote for a person because he's black.

The whole issue of racism, no matter where it comes from, is based on ignorance and lack of exposure. There are some blacks in my family who assume all white people are wealthy. They had been exposed to very few whites.

HANK: A lot of attitudes have to change to make room for the pluralism we want, so my daughter doesn't have to feel she's got to choose between whites and blacks. So people won't feel threatened, so they can laugh at the different images we have of each other. The longer I look at race, the more invisible it becomes. We have to be a lot more light-hearted about these differences. If a black person is encouraged to live in a white community, it isn't the end of the world if the white person next to him doesn't like him.

There has to be an acknowledgment on the part of white people that black people have introduced a whole lot of interesting things into their lives. They've created the music they prefer, even when it's done by white imitators. They've enriched our speech. They have made America a much more interesting place. If black people weren't around, we'd be a much poorer place culturally.

AMANDA: *I* wouldn't be here. [*Prolonged laughter.*]

PAMELA: At the same time, blacks themselves have to really promote education, change their attitudes toward institutions. The Art Institute has free days, you know. We've got to do something to shape our cultural awareness. And keep these good things about the race within the race. We have to do something ourselves to build the community. It's really got to come from within.

In my younger days, when I first started working, I thought that all the whites in the company were better-skilled than I was. I discovered there was a young white girl, hired as a writer, who couldn't write. She had been an editor and couldn't spell. My illusions were busting as I worked in all kinds of places.

I went to my first office job thinking I've got to be careful, be cool, speak perfect English, do the right thing. I needed the experience of seeing white people, in higher positions, who really didn't have good skills. I worked with white people who could barely spell, punctuate, who had gone to midwestern colleges. They looked right, wore the right clothes. There was a black person who looked gross, but could outwrite her. In recognizing this, I became more confident in my own capabilities. Intimidation needs to be put in place.

I went through my militant stage. I remember when I was fifteen, I had an Afro and made myself dashikis. I wore big earrings. It was real exciting. I refused to let any of my family call me Negro. "Black" was the word. I remember when people would get *mad* if you called them black.

In my militant days, when I got on a bus and saw another person with an Afro, we'd start talking about being black. It was like having a religion. I remember the salute and the handshake. There was a sort of camaraderie. That's pretty much gone, because we're so varied. You can see it when you walk downtown. You're on your own.

AMANDA: But it still happens, Mom. Dad was getting into the car one day and he had his jazz T-shirt on. And the guy says, "Hey, man, you like jazz?" And they get into this long conversation. The guy was black.

HANK: When I met Pam, I had hair almost down to the pit of my back. That was the equivalent of wearing an Afro. If you were white and had long hair, you were a brother. There was a lot of hitchhiking going on then. You picked them up and shared whatever it was they had, legal or illegal. [*Laughs.*] You'd let them stay at your house and you at theirs. There aren't these symbols today. I think the whole hippie thing was an attempt, conscious or unconscious, to find the same kind of community that blacks felt they had.

My black male students talk about street crime all the time. Every time they get into a car that looks halfway decent, they're so afraid they're going to be pulled over. They'd be asked if the car was stolen, ask to see the papers. I have white friends whose neighbors resent every black person who drives a car that isn't a clunker. If it isn't, they must be dope dealers or stolen money for it.

The students talk about simply walking out of a store with their groceries and waiting for a bus. A white woman comes out, and because of all the things she's read in our friendly media, is convinced this young black man is about to rip off her purse. She goes the other way even though she doesn't want to go that way. They know it, they catch it. There may be a literacy problem among blacks in terms of the written word. But there is no literacy problem when it comes to reading people.

If I come into class not feeling good, my students will know it immediately. They'll say, "What's wrong?" They'll want to know if I had a fight with my wife. [*Laughs.*] "Why are you this way? You're not the way you usually are." I used to resent it: "No one should have the right to prowl through my real feelings like that." [*Laughs.*] They want to know my feelings first. Then they're ready for teaching.

I think this amazing ability to read people must be able to translate itself into riches in the job world. How many jobs rely on the written word, anyway? The highest-placed executives don't write their own letters. They hire someone to write them. Why aren't my students, who have this unique ability to read people, working where this quality is so important? They're experts and could be marvelous in managing people. They manage their teachers sometimes. [*Laughs.*]

Why can't our society acknowledge the tremendous wealth of human understanding that is here? Why don't they hire these people even if they say, "He don't" instead of "He doesn't"? They can hire writers to change it. They can wire *computers* to change every "he don't" to "he doesn't."

PAMELA: I worry about the illiteracy of the majority of Americans, their intelligence. I had a big fight with the woman I work with over the minimum wage. I told her about people working hard and not having anything at the end of the week. How we're making people go on welfare because it comes out almost the same. She felt Bush was right in fighting even that little boost in the minimum wage. Something about balancing the budget. And right in front of her was a headline about Bush okaying a twenty-five-percent increase for federal government executives. She didn't understand what I was talking about. Can't she put two and two together? She's classified as literate because she says "he doesn't." This scares me more than anything.

She makes it easier for someone like my nephew to evade his own responsibilities. When things get tough, some of my black friends say it's a white man's world and the problems have always been created by him. In some ways it's true, but not always. My nephew, who at the time was not in school and not employed, would try to blame everything on the white man. I said, "You have a couple of children you're not even supporting. Is that the white man's fault, too?" That woman's attitude leads him to his.

HANK: [*He notices that Amanda is sound asleep.*] Our daughter, who is now asleep, represents to me the embodiment of each culture. She has hair that can go either way. It can be straight and long and luxurious. It can be curly and wonderful. She doesn't need a permanent, she just has to put water on her hair. She can be as tan as she wants to be or as white as she wants to be. She can talk black if she wants to or she can talk white and proper and pass the tests. She carries a strength that neither of her parents has, because she's the product of our daring to reach over, because we loved each other.

She's the future, if people realize that the more we cross over, the stronger we are—as a country, as a planet. Those species that have gone on are those that have managed to adapt themselves, that have dared to cross that line.

LEO AND VERA KING

She is white; he is black. They have been married thirty-eight years. They have four children, ages twenty-seven to thirty-seven.

VERA: I am a seventy-year-old doctor who is not retired. Leo and I met because we were involved with civil rights, long before the civil-rights movement began. We've had lots of ups and downs in our life, but it's been pretty good. Living with him enlarged my horizons tremendously.

LEO: I am seventy-eight. I left home when I was fourteen and went to work in a sawmill so I could go to school. My father told me it was the female in the family that needs the education, because the male can get a job any time. I decided to get schooling on my own.

I went to Little Rock, got into Arkansas Baptist College. I was trying to overcome my dislike for whites. Came the Depression and I found my way in to Chicago. I came in the rumble seat of a Model-T Ford the first day of January, 1932. Cold ride, but I made it.

I arrived with five dollars in my pocket. Things looked bleak but I was the kind of fellow that didn't quit. I found various jobs but left to go out on my own. I was on my feet when the war broke out. The draft board suggested I try for Officer Training School, but because of my participation in civil rights, I was rejected. I saw active duty as an enlisted man. When I came out, I was broke again and went into business.

My grandfather had a farm in Sunshine, Arkansas. It was at the bend of the bayou, the land owned by blacks: the Free Nigger Bend. It was so-named by my great-uncle, who was justice of peace there for forty-six years. He also was the minister, who pastored the church and ran the school.

When I was small, I didn't have any feelings about whites, but as I grew older . . . Me and another little boy went fishing. I had the boat out in the lake and a white fellow on shore said he wanted the boat. It wasn't his boat, so I ignored him. When I came to shore, he said, "When a white man tell you to do somethin', you gotta do it. Now I'm gonna make you dance." He had a gun in his hand. I was frightened but I wasn't gonna dance. I gave a shove with my oar and it tipped the guy into the lake. I rowed like hell out of the way. From then on, I was afraid of the white man. I was around ten years old.

What capped it off was Lemuel. He was my father's first cousin. He'd done a little boxing in Illinois. I was twelve. We were walkin' into town and two white guys was working on a car. One of them said, "That nigger's been on a farm somewhere." Which meant a prison farm. Lemuel said, "Hell, no, I haven't been on any goddam prison farm in my life." "What you said, nigger?" Lemuel repeated what he said. The guy picked up half a brick, walked over to Lemuel and says, "Nigger, I'm gonna teach you how to talk to a white man." He slapped him in the face, his brick in the other hand. He left the print of his hand on Lemuel's cheek. Lem had a pencil he kept in his cap. He just stood there quietly and slowly stuck it in his pocket. But that right hand came up so fast, I didn't see it. It exploded in his face. The guy fell into some oil down there and he was my color, man. The other guy got so excited he ran out to fight Lemuel. Lem just grabbed him by the collar, and the guy went through the glass.

I heard the whistle blow and the people hollering, "A nigger's beatin' up a white man!" They shut down the cotton gin and was jumping out of windows. I said, "Lemuel, run, the lynch mob is comin'." I took off. I was afraid to run because that might be suspicious. So I just walked fast. Lemuel ran and they were running after him.

My grandfather worked for Mrs. Rose Deampett, the heir of the Kings, who owned most of the county. She gave my grandfather the land and my great-uncle an education. So Deampett went over there and got Lemuel and rode us out of town.

When I got to Little Rock, I got a broader education. I got a job with a family that worked me very hard for nothing. No consideration for a black person at all. I had that bad feeling. But there was a Jewish family next door that was much more humane. I began to appreciate the difference. I got another job with a Swedish family. They came from Wisconsin. When he passed, she let me have the money to pay for my tuition. She was so considerate, that for the first time I began to appreciate someone that's not black that I really loved.

I attended Lewis Institute in Chicago before I joined the army. I was working in the lab on an experiment in electronics, when this white guy came over to me. He was from Louisiana. "You like it here?" I said, "I like it better than Arkansas." He said, "I don't understand. My father has old Oscar workin' around the place. He works when he wants to, he gets a place to sleep and eat, so he's got nothin' to worry about." I said, "He's goin' to stay that way and be called lazy. I would much rather swing on a streetcar in the morning, go to work, buy my own refrigerator, pay my own rent, buy my own clothes, and be independent." He said, "I never looked at it like that." I said, " 'Bout time you did."

VERA: I graduated from Rush Medical College and did my internship and residency at Cook County Hospital. Black, poor—everybody up against it came here. It was altogether different from my sheltered upbringing in Syracuse. I was already concerned with social problems because of my parents' influence.

I met Leo and we were married in '52. I was living with my mother when he visited us. When he parked the car in front of the building, they put sugar in his gas tank. A neighbor. The landlord was a timid soul and worried about this black person visiting us. My mother stood up, all five feet of her, and said, "Well, I'm not afraid." He backed off.

Leo and I lived in that apartment for three years. We found out later there were several friendly neighbors. They were on our side, without our knowing it. We were working long hours and didn't have time to make friends. But we were in the eye of the hurricane. There was a lot of worry and anxiety around.

Leo educated me a great deal. My mother and some dear friends were afraid this might harm my career. They were particularly afraid that if we had children, it would be hard on them. That was a common attitude among many liberal people at the time. Leo's answer was simple: "They'll have the same problem, no more, no less, of other black children. If you don't want to have any black children, then we better not be together." That was the last time we ever discussed it. We did start our family immediately. I was already thirty-three when my first child was born.

We took our first camping trip to the Rocky Mountains and it was delightful. Leo was the only black everywhere we went. Most people were friendly and invited us to share their campfire. They all thought he was either a minister or a member of the Harlem Globe Trotters. What else could a tall black man out here be? [*Laughter.*]

We built a home and moved to a cooperative community in the suburbs. It was a new development. Middle-class.

LEO: When we first applied for membership in the co-op, we were denied. I had to take a psychological test to prove that I was normal enough to live with. It didn't please me but I was determined to build that house. That's how we got in.

VERA: I had to be closer to the clinic, so we moved to Maywood. It was at a time when the whites were fleeing. The school was eighty-five-percent black because the whites were sending their kids to private schools. The irony is that some of my black patients told their children not to play with our kids. I'm not sure why. Was it because I was a doctor and they thought they weren't in the same class?

The schools in Maywood were so neglected, so bad, that we decided to move to Oak Park.* This was '63, '64. The only way we could be shown a home was if I went alone. We had to find a straw buyer. Leo never did see it until all the papers were signed. We reported our intended move to the Illinois Human Relations Commission. It was reported to the village authorities.

The famous chemist, Percy Julian, was the only black living there. He had been Oak Park's window-dressing Negro for years. We were ordinary folks. It was a little scary. The community rallied around and protected us.

When Martin Luther King planned to march into Cicero, we got swastikas painted on the garage, our tires slashed, windows broken. There was more open anger. It had a message. As long as the movement stayed south, fine. But if this area were to change, there'd be trouble. A stone was thrown through the bedroom window of our youngest son. It missed him by a foot. We reported these things to the police. The usual answer was: boys will be boys. They never did anything about it.

Our kids never told us about other incidents. They were aware we'd be bothered. All of our children graduated from Oak Park High and made their own way.

---

* An old western suburb of Chicago, celebrated as the home of Ernest Hemingway and the site of Frank Lloyd Wright houses. It is now integrated.

I think their father was the big influence in their lives. He worked very hard and they helped him out when they were young. Among his jobs, he managed inner-city apartment buildings. He did the repairs, dealt with vandalism. There were great difficulties. They saw all this. He never shielded them.

LEO: The welfare system is just not working and there's nothing cooking in the pot. "Why work when I can get some money and get by?" The bottom line should be if you don't work, you don't eat.

I was sitting on the sidewalk one day and there were two young girls, thirteen and fourteen. They were tenants of mine. The fourteen-year-old had a baby in her arms. The thirteen-year-old was saying, "I'll be glad when I have my baby." I said, "Are you pregnant?" She said, "No, but I'm gonna get pregnant, so I can get a check." It's like old Oscar, that guy told me about years ago.

VERA: They have to be shown a reason not to get pregnant at fourteen. Maybe it's their way to get some imitation love when they're not getting any real love. When I was an intern at County, I saw the same kind of things. Now it's much worse because of the neglect—not neglect, the *contempt* of those in power. It's not just welfare people, it's working people, it's the old.

LEO: The contempt was once covert, now it's overt. Generations of people who are out of work, don't know how, no sense of responsibility, growing into adulthood. That's the result.

Looking back from the time I first began to realize what was going on in this world, there is a difference. It's more frustrating now, when things opened up a bit over the years. Before it was out in the open, there was a line of demarcation. It's destroying minds: "It's there and I can't reach it. Others can."

VERA: Since the civil-rights movement, when there was some optimism, there's been a slide backwards for the majority of them. It's more than just indifference. It's an unspoken but deliberate attitude on the part of those in power. It's not benign neglect; it's malignant. I'm very depressed. I have certain guilty feelings about having left and moved into the country and have gotten away from the fray.

For the last fourteen years, Leo and Vera King have lived on a farm near Hastings, Michigan.

LEO: I spend most of my time gardening. It's a nostalgic trip for me, the farm. Our relationship with neighbors has been surprisingly good. One recent incident annoyed me. A family up on the hill was shooting this way, at my garden. I could hear the bullets. They were up to mischief, I would say that. I called the sheriff and it stopped.

VERA: We're in a poor rural community. Very few make a living out of farming. Most of them have jobs in town, have little gardens, and live here. They all have trucks and look alike, with their caps and their beards and typical quote redneck attitudes. [*Aside.*] I know that's a prejudiced remark. You see a lot of Confederate flags. These are young people, who don't know blacks, and are growing up with racism.

I don't think the line is racial any more; it's class. But with the underclass growing, racism is erupting. When I think of what the administration has done in polarizing our society—Don't get me started on a soapbox.

LLOYD KING

He is the third child of Leo and Vera King. His is thirty-one.

After he learned that I had met with his parents, he wrote me a letter:

"It seems children are always talked about when the subject of interracial marriage is broached, but we are never addressed directly. Many of us have something to say, not only about how we are perceived in America, but how we ourselves perceive America and the racial tension that exists, that has always existed. I am a child of that tension.

"The real tragedy between blacks and whites in America is not that we hate each other. Hatred by itself is a pretty shallow force and can only cut so deep. The real tragedy is that we love and admire each other. American culture as we know it would not exist if this weren't so.

"The tragedy lies in the complex folds of this love and admiration, which is somehow twisted into intolerance. We're like a married couple that got started on the wrong foot, foolishly believing that the man was superior and subjugating the woman, and like an unhappily married couple, we're sick to death of one another, sick of tension and strife that may be soothed occasionally, but never seems to go away. Rather it builds and builds, making us want a divorce before one of us goes crazy and kills the other. Yet, we love each other. Like a Greek play, there would be no tragedy if it weren't for the love.

"Give me a soapbox and I'll stand on it."

I remember growing up in the household of Leo and Vera. It was really active. There were intense dinner conversations that would go on for hours and hours. The bulk of my education was at dinner with my parents.

Since our father was black and our mother was Jewish, we called ourselves Jewbros. Me and my brothers, the race of the future. Everybody's going to be brown in the future. The pure blacks and the pure whites are going to be bred out of the race. I used to read science fiction as a kid. The good writers had everyone in the future being chocolate-colored.

Being the son of Vera and Leo is from day one having race as an issue. I became conscious that I was black in the sixties. I was pretty young. We moved from an all-black suburb to an all-white suburb and I had to get coaching all the time from my parents about how to behave, who to be, and what to do if someone calls you a nigger. It's something I've been grappling with all my life. At times I was down in the dumps, now I'm much more comfortable with who I am. I figure the world's got a lot of problems; either we straighten them out or we die. I hope we straighten them out.

If you got one drop of black blood in this society, you're considered black. Isn't it called the lethal drop? I went back and forth about that a lot. Sometimes I would put down "Other" in that little box, when you had to put down your race. Sometimes I'd scratch them all out and put down "Human." I studied anthropology in college for a while. If you try to define race or an ethnic group, it's tough. There are so many gradients, so many grays.

I was about ten in the early 1960s when Black Power came out. I used to hang with the Black Panthers. My mother was working in a Black Panther clinic. So I grew up thinking a lot about revolution. I thought black was definitely superior to white. It took me a while to realize that being considered white wasn't that bad. I began to realize that I love white culture. One of my favorite writers is John Cheever, who's the super-WASP. I married a WASP. I may have got it from my father. He started growing up in this all-black town, but at a young age got interested in Tolstoy and stuff like that. He had one of these turnarounds. He kept saying that he hated whites, but he loves them. And the white culture. That's why he married a white woman.

Racial tension has existed from day one in this country. You can't talk about American music, American art, even American dance and literature without understanding the love of the different races that founded this country. A lot of animosity, of course. Like a married couple, we have to live together. Sometimes we don't want to. Sometimes we want to beat each other up. Maybe one of us wants to get out of the marriage, but we can't.

I'm a musician, so I see a lot of things in terms of music. I think about the way white people love black music. They just go nuts over it. First, the white slaveowners outlawed drums. It's just not Christian, you're communicating, it's a way for insurrection. But even though they got rid of the drums, they wanted blacks to come up to the big house and entertain them at parties. They dug the music from day one.

The inverse is true. Blacks love white music and the instruments that Europeans made. I play the flute. Africans had bamboo flutes but the silver flute is something else. It's amazing what you can do with it. It's amazing what Bach did in codifying this twelve-tone system and harmony. It's equally amazing that there's a counterpoint in the rhythms that come out of Africa that you can find nowhere in Europe. When the two meet, it's very exciting.

It's no accident that I got into jazz. It's where black meets white. And that's what happened to me. I'm a child of black meeting white and it's a perfect home for me.

Now, the other side of the coin. Yesterday was the anniversary of Fred Hampton's murder.* When I was a kid, I hung out with somebody who was shot in that raid. Four times in the belly. I was scared. I was eleven or twelve.

Then I was into rock-and-roll. I was heavily into Jimi Hendrix. A lot of people I knew seemed to be dying of overdosing. I was experimenting with drugs myself. I would break into my mother's infirmary and steal drugs. Experimenting. Because that's what we did in the sixties. I thought I was going to die of that. There was a lot of fear. I began to retreat.

For a while, I wanted to be really political. I came from a politically charged past. My white grandfather spent time in a Czarist prison for teaching peasants how to read. I was born into it. I thought I'd continue this strain, so I studied economics. I figured it boils down to money. The Golden Rule: He who's got the gold makes the rule.

In the white suburb, you'd get chased around by the greasers. They'd throw rocks and call you nigger. To me, it was fun in a way. You could run away from them and thought you were part of the struggle. It was different in high school. I got pretty much caught up with an artsy crowd and with hippies.

---

* He was a leader of the Black Panthers in Chicago. In a midnight raid, he and a colleague, Mark Clark, were killed by the State's Attorney's task force, while they were asleep. Several others were wounded. In 1990, the Chicago City Council voted to commemorate Fred Hampton Day. Subsequently, sixteen white aldermen objected, maintaining they had thought it was Dan Hampton, a Chicago Bears lineman, they were honoring.

I went to Marlboro College in Vermont. There was a lot of pressure from my father to get into the hard sciences. He comes out of the Depression and he feels you'll not survive unless you have the hard stuff. Up there, I realized what I really wanted to do, so I switched to music.

It was a period of disillusionment for me. I think I inherited from my mother this vision of the world as a Utopia, where everybody got along and the poor were fed. I was escaping from my parents and a legacy. It was also a denial that I was black.

I was at an all-white school. I was hanging with all white people. I was getting into a more European culture. I was attending to classical music. Bach, Beethoven, and Stravinsky were my new heroes. At the same time, I was still very much into jazz. I did a fifty-page paper on John Coltrane. It was the beginning of an awakening.

I was playing tenor sax in an R&B band. It's a salt-and-pepper group, black and white. This is 1981. We were playing a gig at a blues club in Joliet. We're well paid. There's a big urban-blues renaissance that didn't happen in the sixties. That whole blues thing is like jumping through the hoops for Whitey.

We played two tunes and they owner pays us off for all three nights. He says, "Please leave my club." The Ku Klux Klan was putting heat on him. We'd noticed KKK graffiti on the dressing-room wall. The good ol' boys didn't like the idea of a salt-and-pepper group and threatened to wreck the place. If we were all-black, it would have been okay. I remember racial problems as a little kid in Oak Park, but this was the first time since I'd been a teen-ager. Remember, I'd gotten away. Race wasn't an issue with me, I thought.

These blues clubs depress the hell out of me. It's packed with young white people, mostly from the suburbs. I call them Cub fans. It's more like slumming. Remember the white guy on the plantation calling to the black? "Sing something for us." They were entertainers like these guys hadn't seen before. They were cutting loose in a way the more repressed European culture couldn't. Today these Cub fans feel this old black blues singer is preaching some sort of wisdom they didn't know about. There's a void in their lives, and they think he's gonna fill it. That's debatable. It's also a time when they can jump up, get drunk, and act crazy. It's a big party-time for them.

At a South Side blues club, you might see twelve, fifteen middle-aged black guys. They got off work, come here for a beer and the blues. It's not a place for them to act up. For them, it's more like sustenance. "This is what I need to cool off after a hard day's work." The singer doesn't talk between songs. He just goes from one blues to another. It's like you're in their living room.

At this time, I was personally lost, insecure about my skills as a musician, deeply in debt. I got a job teaching college down in Tennessee in '86.

Teaching at a white college boosted my ego. When I found out I was an affirmative action case, I was devastated. I wasn't their first choice. In fact, I wonder if they'd have interviewed me if I weren't black. I was not the hot spit I thought I was. I understand the historical reasons for it, but I found it tough to take.

I was there to save the school from a lawsuit. I found out that my best friend on the faculty wanted his other friend to get the job. He was a great classical-flute player, much better than I was. They interviewed him, a white male, a white female and myself. I found out they hated the woman but liked Jim and me. They thought he was better, but the administration said they had to hire me. "If he's your second choice, he's it." My friend now thinks that I turned out to be a better teacher than Jim probably would have been. He wasn't upset at all. *I* was upset.

I feel like I infiltrate the white world. I bring some African roots with me. I get co-opted on the way. My mother is white, the first bit of being co-opted. I go to this white school and get a white degree. I get co-opted by the system. At the same time, I change the rules. The more black people you get in there, the more the rules change.

I started getting grants and being hired without affirmative action. When you're black, you cannot help but second-guess everything. Does this person like me because I'm black or because I'm me? Does this person hate me because I'm black or because I'm a jerk? You're always second-guessing, unless it's another black person. Why do you think black people only hang out with other black people? They don't know what's going on half the time. You're working at an incredible disadvantage.

I live on the North Side now and hang out mostly with white musicians. I see a lot of love between the races here because they're nuts about music and it cuts across racial lines. My wife manages my business. She gets the jobs at parties and hotels. She also manages an office downtown. She got her MBA from Kellogg.*

When I started going with her, she got some flak from her family, not much. They're upper-crust suburban Connecticut. It was *Guess Who's Coming to Dinner?* Her mom worried for a while. She didn't want to have brown grandchildren. She's over that now. We plan to have kids.

---

* The Kellogg School of Business Administration, Northwestern University.

I can't get too mad at white people. Half my family is white. But I don't stand in judgement of people who get pissed off. Part of me says, "Yeah, go ahead, good." My father's not like that and he's as black as black can be. He abhors ignorance. He sees ignorance as a cause of a lot of anger. You can't deny the anger people feel and it's got to run its course. Black people have got to get upset. I think they're going to get more upset.

But it's going to get ugly sometimes and there are going to be people like Louis Farrakhan and they have to be there. It's a purging process, like going to a psychiatrist.

It wasn't until three, four years ago, I had the nerve to talk to anybody in a urinal of a white movie theater. Something about it just brought back bad feelings. Though I'm half-white, I know that there's a myth going around about the black man and sexuality.

One of the things a lot of white women have told me is when they look at musicians on stage, they look at the way they move. A lot of black people move pretty loosely. Sometimes they have fantasies about how this person is in bed. It drives the white males nuts.

There are similarities between the black poor and "white trash." A kid like Elvis Presley grew up and had a rhythmic freedom that lot of white upper-crust kids just didn't have. They went nuts for it. "White trash" listened to Grand Old Opry on the radio. Black people tuned into that. Then white people started listening to race records being played on the air. They had similar tastes. They were loose.

Cops hassle me, but I'm too educated now. When I was young, I used to get a lot of grief from the cops. In this white suburb, when I was riding my bike, I'd get stopped by the cops. They thought I stole the bike. I was scared of cops. I don't know one black person who has never had an encounter with cops.

One day, I'm running to catch the El. This is the third time I got stopped by cops that year, okay? Once they searched my laundry because they thought I stuffed a stereo in there. This time I'm running for an appointment with my barber. I realize I don't have any money. So I stop by my bank on the way. I take out sixty dollars. I take a short-cut through the alley, counting my money. A cop car pulls up. They slam me against the wall, throw me in the car, no *Miranda* rights or anything.

I had a book under my arm. I think it was Salinger. I'm well-dressed. He said, "You stole this woman's purse." I said I didn't steal any purse. They take me to this lady's apartment building a few blocks away. They parade me in front of her window. She's three stories up. I look up. "Don't look at her!" I try to explain. "Shut up, you got no rights, kid." They really let me have it the whole time. I happened to look up a second and saw an old woman in her seventies with glasses. The window was dirty. I'm this black kid, three stories down, and she's going to identify me. I can't believe this. They had me walking back and forth. Fortunately, I was wearing glasses, too. She said it wasn't me because the guy that robbed her wasn't wearing glasses. They gave me my book back and said, "Get out of here."

Did they apologize?

[Laughs incredulously.] *What?*

It was '83 or '84. I was sitting there very polite. This is the way I behave around policeman. I didn't want to be late for my haircut. I was yes-sirring and no-sirring my ass off. When he gave me back my book, I said, "Thank you. I understand you're just doing your job." And I was gone.

If that happened to me today, I would give them hell. I feel big and bad. I wish they would pick me up now, because I've got a big mouth on me now.

I look at older people now and I love them. My father is beautiful, though he gets stuck in a few gears now and then. He says things that I think are crazy, and a few years later I find out that it wasn't so crazy. That old guy knew what he was talking about. I always make the analogy between a person and the world at large. If somehow, somewhere, the world could get objectivity. If there were some big universal mirror . . .

I have faith we can mature. Stranger things have happened. Maybe America, maybe the world is in its adolescence. Maybe we're driving home from the prom, drunk, and nobody knows whether we're going to survive or not. Maybe we'll survive and maybe we'll be a pretty smart old person, well-adjusted and mellow.

I am guardedly optimistic—definitely guardedly. If everything is going to hell, it would be hard for me to get up in the morning. But I can't honestly say, "Sure, things will get better." We might not make it home from the prom.